D1521877

Gesher Vakesher
Bridges and Bonds

The Life of Leon Kronish

SOUTH FLORIDA STUDIES IN THE HISTORY OF JUDAISM

Edited by
Jacob Neusner
William Scott Green, James Strange
Darrell J. Fasching, Sara Mandell

GESHER VAKESHER
Bridges and Bonds
The Life of Leon Kronish
by
Henry A. Green

Gesher Vakesher
Bridges and Bonds

The Life of Leon Kronish

by
Henry A. Green

Scholars Press
Atlanta, Georgia

Gesher Vakesher
Bridges and Bonds
The Life of Leon Kronish

by

Henry A. Green

Publication of this book was made possible by grants from the Tisch Family Foundation, New York City and the Miller Family Foundation of Miami Beach. The University of South Florida acknowledges with thanks this important support for its scholarly projects.

Library of Congress Cataloging in Publication Data

Green, Henry A.

Gesher vakesher = Bridges and bonds : the life of Leon Kronish.

p. cm. — (South Florida Studies in the History of Judaism ; v. 130)

Includes bibliographical references and index.

ISBN 0-7885-0151-8 (cloth : alk. paper)

1. Kronish, Leon. 2. Rabbis—Florida—Miami Beach—Biography. 3. Reform Judaism—United States. I. Title. II. Series.

BM755.K74G74 1995

296.8'346'092—dc20

[B] 95-22949

CIP

Printed in the United States of America
on acid-free paper

To My Parents
M. Sidney (Sholom-Moshe) and Sarah Green

TABLE OF CONTENTS

ACKNOWLEDGEMENTS

As a youth in Canada, I grew up in a family active in Jewish life. During the mid-1950s, they too joined in *mitzvah* work–creating a new sanctuary. Synchronistically, the name of their new congregation was also Beth Sholom.

Synagogue was at the center of our family's life. It was there where I became part of the scouting movement, was active in youth groups such as B'nai B'rith and the National Council of Synagogue Youth, and attended cultural events that drew popular speakers from home and abroad. These included not only intellectual giants, political leaders and charismatic rabbis but also Israeli *halutzim*. Of all the memorable events of my pre-bar mitzvah years, my encounter with David Ben-Gurion would have the most profound effect on my adult life.

Over the next several decades I spent extended periods studying and working in Israel. By the time I moved to Miami in the mid-1980s, Israel had become my second home.

Shortly thereafter, I was invited by Laura Hochman and Abraham Gittelson, Jewish educators, and Lydia Golden Jacobs, a community activist, to join them in planning a Jewish community center exhibit in Ft. Lauderdale that would trace Jewish life in America. Naively, I suggested that we focus on the state of Florida.

It was not long before I realized that little research had been collected and interpreted on Florida Jewry. Although Florida currently has the third largest concentration of Jews in the United States and a history of Jewish life that extends back into colonial Spanish and English periods, scholars have preferred to focus on Jews in other locations (especially the Northeast) to draw their generalizations about American Jewish life.

This absence of material led to a re-evaluation of the project and the beginning of MOSAIC: Jewish Life in Florida, a project to retrieve the history of the Jews of Florida. The Judaic Studies Program of the University of Miami, in association with the Soref Jewish Community Center and the Central Agency of Jewish Education, took the lead in establishing the infrastructure of the project, its administration, research and financial development. Countless volunteers assisted in gleaning material from archives, repositories, libraries, and private collections.

Societies and scholars were approached to support the project. Without the ongoing assistance of the Historical Museum of Southern Florida, the Florida Historical Society, the Southern Jewish Historical Society, the American Jewish Historical Society, Hebrew Union College-American Jewish Archives, and the Association for State and Local History, the project would never have come to fruition. Samuel Proctor, Randy Nimnicht, Abraham Peck, Stephen Whitfield, Marshall Sklare, Judith Elkin, Michael Gagnon, Seymour Liebman, Raymond Mohl, Patricia Wickman, Andrew Brian, Howard Kleinberg, Ira Sheskin, and Charlton Tebeau helped immeasurably in directing and identifying leads and sources. In addition, the Government of Florida adopted the project and opened up their files for research. George Percy, Director, Division of Historical Resources, Department of the Secretary of State, and Joan Morris of the Florida State Photographic Archives, were invaluable in beating drums.

This flurry of activity led to several projects: a 2,000 sq. ft. exhibit of Jewish Life in Florida from 1763-1990 that toured first throughout the state of Florida and then nationally; nine individual community modules that were prepared as permanent exhibits for each site in Florida that hosted the exhibit (including Miami); an exhibit book, *MOSAIC: Jewish Life in Florida*; a multicultural curriculum for grades four and seven endorsed by Betty Castor, the Florida Commissioner of Education; Jewish walking tours of Miami and Miami Beach; and a host of scholarly articles and presentations that focused on Florida Jewish life. Among the most recent writings to appear are Deborah Dash Moore's, *To the Golden Cities* and Stephen Whitfield's, "Blood and Sand: The Jewish Community of South Florida," in *American Jewish History*, October 1994.

MOSAIC's initiative also led to the founding of the Sanford L. Ziff Jewish Museum of Florida. Housed in Beth Jacob Congregation's 1936 Art Deco sanctuary in Miami Beach, the Jewish Museum of Florida will open in the spring of 1995. I am deeply grateful for the opportunity to have worked with James Orovitz, Maynard Abrams, Heléne Herskowitz and Sandra Angel Malamud, all past presidents of MOSAIC (1990-1994). Their commitment to innovative forms of Jewish education, and dedication to bring the message to the community, are the reasons that a Jewish Museum of Florida exists today.

This, then, was the broad context in which I was honored to receive an invitation to write a biography of Rabbi Leon Kronish. Although I never had the privilege of meeting him before his stroke, my grandmother and parents, Canadian "snowbirds," often had attended functions at Temple Beth Sholom and brought back first-hand reports.

Rabbi Leon Kronish is a towering figure of American Jewish life. He has been at the forefront of reshaping Reform Judaism and bringing it within the fold of Zionism. As chairman of Israel Bonds in the United States he helped coordinate efforts to bring Israel millions of dollars in investment funds. Rabbi of a congregation of fifteen hundred members, he was able to attract to Miami Beach the most distinguished Jewish personalities of the second half of the twentieth century.

The life of Rabbi Leon Kronish in many ways exemplifies the characteristics of first-generation, New York-born American Jews of the early twentieth century: their migration to the sunbelt; their subsequent establishment of a vibrant Jewish infrastructure; and their commitment to live Jewish lives. But Miami lacked the formidable institutions of a New York. The evolution of community and Jewish identity depended on lighted candles like Rabbi Kronish to emblaze a vision and point the way.

Rabbi Leon Kronish's contribution to Jewry in America and Israel has been acknowledged in a *festschrift* honoring him on the occasion of his seventieth birthday *(Towards the Twenty-First Century: Judaism and the Jewish People in Israel and America*, 1988). And in appreciation of his life-long service to the welfare and cultural life of the community, the City of Miami Beach renamed Chase Avenue, where Temple Beth Sholom stands, Kronish Plaza. This biography is also a testimony of appreciation.

To write a narrative of a life involves scores of helpers. Some record oral histories; others collect documentary data. Heléne Herskowitz, chairperson of the Miami MOSAIC exhibit module, is largely responsible for overseeing and collecting much of the Miami Jewish history (documents, photographs, and oral histories) available to us today. Sol Lichter organized the Leon Kronish collection and patiently shared with me four decades of Temple Beth Sholom activity. Yehuda Shamir prepared a first interpretation of this data.

Temple Beth Sholom members and friends, both in the United States and Israel, gladly opened their homes and hearts when I called requesting an interview. I am sincerely appreciative of their generosity: Jack Chester, Gary Gerson, Yehuda Ben Chorin, Leo Krown, Sol Stein, Morris Sipser, Joel Arnon, Rabbi Richard Hirsch, Rabbi Stanley Ringler, Rabbi Alfred Gottschalk, Rabbi David Polish, Mike Levy, Shlomo Avineri, Dennis Rice, Judy Drucker, Sarah Nelson, Rabbi Harry Jolt, Myron Brodie, Ruhama Hermon, James Knopke, Howard Klein, Norman Lipoff, Susan Miller, Barbara Jaffe, Burnett Roth, Shepard Broad, Ann Broad Bussel, Isabelle (Hecht) and Neal Amdur, Rabbi Irving Lehrman, Rabbi Malcolm Stern, Rabbi Herbert Baumgard, Elie Wiesel, Rabbi Gunther Plaut, Harold Vinik, Myra Farr, Sam Seitlin, Dr. Max Gratz, David and Phyllis Miller, Rabbi Meyer Abramowitz, Bruce Menin, Seymour Gelber, Nancy Liebman, Harry Smith, Yehuda HaLevi, Zev Kronish, Marvin and Betty Cooper, Helen Kotler, Marvin Stonberg, Rabbi Joseph Glaser, Rabbi Alexander Schindler, Shragai Cohen, Shula Ben-David, Emily Bertisch, Avraham Avi-Hai, Arthur Rosichan, Meir Rosenne, Bernard Mandler, Jack Gordon, Rachelle Nelson, Steven Haas, Ephraim Shapira, Rabbi Morris Kipper, Dorothy Jacobson, Leo Osheroff, Sam Rothberg, Ruth Gudis, Jean Soman, Tony Blank, Howard Zwibel, Stanley and Jules Arkin, Solomon

Garazi, Stanley Myers, JoAnn (Weiss) Bass, James Orovitz, Abe Resnick, Miriam Zatinsky, Milton Gaynor and, especially, Zonik Shaham, who embodied the meaning of modern Zionism.

Many friends and colleagues, whether by their conversation, or by their comments on chapters, have pushed me to explore more deeply the voices of memory and the variance of Jewish experience. I am grateful to Frank de Varona, Eli Evans, Marc Lee Raphael, Deborah Dash Moore, Robert Rosen, Evelyn Mayerson, Nancy Green, Haim Beinart, Gregory Bush, Janice Rothchild Blumberg, Marjorie Hornstein, and Ezra Spicehandler. Paul George introduced me to a very unique way of seeing Miami (walking tours) and has acted as my South Florida mentor, frequently correcting my errors. Rachel Heimovics not only served as my editor from time to time but also counseled me regarding my interpretations of Reform Judaism. Special tribute is also due to David Caploe, who, more than he can know, affected the shape and tone of the entire book through his sensitive and detailed comments on matters of substance and style on too many drafts of every chapter.

Other individuals also have helped along the way by providing access to data or the data itself: Ginger Greenspan (Jewish Theological Seminary), Sylvia Posner and Henry Resnick (Hebrew Union College-Jewish Institute of Religion), Bill Brown and Phyllis Robarts (University of Miami), Abe Kagenoff and Bernard Wax (American Jewish Historical Archives), Sam Boldrick (Dade County Public Libraries), Donna Genet and Betsy Kaplan (Dade County Public Schools), George Neary (Miami Design and Preservation League), Wendy Kaplan (the Wolfsonian Museum), Janet Chusmir and Sam Verdeja (*The Miami Herald*), David Abramowitz and Jack Levine (*The Miami Jewish Tribune*), Bonnie Reiter (the Greater Miami Jewish Federation), Fred Shochet (*The Jewish Floridian*), Audrey Finkelstein (Miami's Jewish Women of Achievement, the American Jewish Committee), Rabbi Haskell Bernat (Oral History Program, Temple Israel of Greater Miami) and Becky Smith and Dawn Hughes (Historical Museum of Southern Florida).

Several editors have read various drafts and rescued me from tunnel vision. I am indebted to Gerri Reaves, Joanne Coburn, Michael LaRosa and David Cohen.

Throughout the many years of this project Rabbi Gary Glickstein and Rabbi Ronald Kronish have constantly stood by me, advising, prodding and encouraging. It was through Ronald's initiative that the project was launched. He gave me *carte blanche* access to family archives and memorabilia and arranged for everyone I contacted to receive me. Ronald always made the effort to read the many drafts, offer thoughtful criticisms and answer my many questions. Without this guidance, the rich texture of his father's life would not have been available to me. It is, in part, his drive that has brought this project to conclusion.

Similarly, Rabbi Gary Glickstein has opened up the temple's archives of Rabbi Kronish, (institutional files, minutes of board meetings and personal correspondence). He too has read and commented on earlier versions, often from a comparative perspective (post-1985). His insights and sensitivity to the project are deeply appreciated. This volume appears on his tenth anniversary as rabbi of Temple Beth Sholom. Both he and Ronald have taught me the meaning and legacy of Rabbi Leon Kronish's spark.

Lillian and Rabbi Leon Kronish have graciously taken me into their home and shared with me the family life that so long sustained them both. On many occasions I had the privilege of meeting their son, Ronald, and their daughter, Maxine, in this setting.

I am grateful for a wonderful staff at the University of Miami, Judaic Studies Program. They have served this project in countless ways from typing drafts of hand-written chapters to transcribing oral histories, to collating material and tracking down citations, to photocopying and organizing my research schedules. Eileen Hirsch, my secretary, is unusually talented. Her commitment of support is a model for all those around her. Leah Medin Benchimol served as a research director and did much of the initial leg work including the conducting of oral histories. Lynn Schulte was keeper of the files. Stacy Roskin Masri oversaw the Israeli source material. Monique Hofkin served as proofreader. Linda Ruiz, a computer wizard, corrected draft after draft over several years.

This project is also indebted to the students that have shared with me the challenges of understanding Florida Jewish History. They have attended classes with a sense of purpose, raising dormant issues, exploring new veins of research as essay topics, and challenging normative conclusions. It is through their eyes that I have come to see much of greater Miami's Jewish history.

My thanks also go to Jacob Neusner, editor for South Florida-Rochester-St. Louis Studies in Religion and Society who has encouraged me without fail, and to Dennis Ford who has served as the publication editor.

The research, writing and publication of this project would have been impossible without the generous support of the University of Miami (a General Research Council Award and a sabbatical), the Florida Humanities Council, Temple Beth Sholom and the Miller Family Foundation. I am especially grateful to David Patterson, past President of the Oxford Center for Hebrew and Jewish Studies, University of Oxford, where I served as a Skirball Fellow during the Trinity semester of 1991. The warm hospitality of Yarnton Manor provided the nourishment for me to complete my first draft of the book.

Finally, I feel a profound sense of gratitude to my wife, Elizabeth, whose patience, support and insight have been invaluable in so many ways beyond the writing of this book; to my children, Jordan, Trevor and Fiona, who have tolerated my writing schedules and are sympathetic to the competing demands on my time, and to my parents, who taught me the meaning of being Jewish.

Henry A. Green
Founding Director, Jewish Museum of Florida
Director, Judaic Studies Program, Univ. of Miami

February, 1995
Adar 1, 5755
Coral Gables, FL

FOREWORD

by
Rabbi Alfred Gottschalk
President, Hebrew Union College-Jewish Institute of Religion

In every generation, there are individuals who, by virtue of their presence, make an indelible imprint on their communities and, by dint of strength of personality, upon the larger world as well. Such a man is Rabbi Leon Kronish–rabbi, teacher, compassionate pastor and Zionist leader *par excellence*. Rabbi Kronish has served as a paradigm for those who aspire to leadership because of his passionate commitment to the life and being of the Jewish people. Although he served as the spiritual leader and rabbi of a large congregation, he had a following that extended far beyond the confines of his exciting synagogue in Miami. I had the privilege of serving with Rabbi Kronish during several holiday periods when he was ill and saw at first hand the wonderful spirit that emanated from that sacred place. His sparkling, lustrous eyes, constant, ready smile, warm handclasp of friendship were the hallmarks of his personality.

Rabbi Leon Kronish has always possessed a great passion that animated him and defined much of his life. He directed his passion into many different pursuits during his growth and development as rabbi and as a caring human being. Influenced by the great thinkers and activists, Stephen Wise, Mordecai Kaplan, and Alexander Dushkin, Rabbi Kronish integrated their teachings and missions into his own personal vision for the direction Jewish civilization ought to take in the modern world.

Rabbi Kronish both celebrated and supported the ideals of Liberal Judaism. His commitment to the prophetic teachings on social justice hallmarked each of his professional successes. As a proponent of Liberal Judaism, Rabbi Kronish accepted and appreciated the value of traditionally ritual expressions of Judaism before it was fashionable to do so. From his educational experience at the Jewish Institute of Religion and from the sermons, lectures, and writings of Stephen Wise, Rabbi Kronish developed a most sincere commitment to both the Zionist and the theological aspects of *Klal Yisrael*. He understood that an ecumenical approach to Jewish civilization was crucial to its potential blossoming in both promised lands, the United States and especially the developing State of Israel.

Like his commitment to the whole of the Jewish people, Rabbi Kronish's passionate love for Zion and more importantly his commitment to Zionism, the movement whose goal was the building of the Jewish State, was ahead of its time within the leadership of the Reform Movement. Part of this sentiment stemmed from Rabbi Kronish's contact with Mordecai Kaplan and his writings. Rabbi Kronish adopted Kaplan's view of the Jewish people as a living organism subject to evolution in sociological, religious, and political realms. Kaplan's work in the area of liturgy which is vibrant and expressive of the ever-changing nature of Jewish identity was very appealing to Rabbi Kronish. The realization that Jewish civilization was a dynamic process served as an infinite source of energy which fueled Rabbi Kronish's incredibly diverse and dynamic career as a Reform rabbi.

Certainly Kaplan's teaching that Jewish civilization was alive and Wise's teachings about *Klal Yisrael* led Rabbi Kronish to believe that all Jews had a responsibility to participate in the rebuilding of a Jewish state in the Land of Israel. The fate of all Jews depended on a place of refuge and political, spiritual, and cultural regeneration. Life in the Jerusalems of America did not interfere with his, or in his opinion any Jew's potential support for the State of Israel. In fact, some might say that the greatest expression of Rabbi Kronish's passion was with regard to the actual rebirth of the land of Israel.

Rabbi Kronish was the spiritual leader and the voice of conscience for a Jewish population which quickly achieved prominence building and managing the famous Miami Beach hotels and resorts. From the seat of his institution, Beth Sholom, he nurtured interfaith relations with the Protestant and Catholic communities, which were in the beginning wary of the increase in the Jewish population on the Beach, where few Jews had lived before. Rabbi Kronish, hearkening to the ever-present voice of prophetic justice, was a pioneer of the civil rights movement and for the clear separation between church and state. Finally, as part and parcel of Beth Sholom's social, political, liturgical and educational programming, Rabbi Kronish developed a model for American Zionist relations with the State of Israel. He created within his congregation and among the Jews of South Florida a healthy compulsion to bond with the State of Israel and with the Israeli people.

I met Rabbi Kronish for the first time when I was dean of the California School of Hebrew Union College-Jewish Institute of Religion in the late 1950s and early 1960s. I knew I had in him a friend and supporter. He was devoted to the life of the Jewish mind and to the cause of Jewish education. This was his inner mandate to create a community of faith with knowledge and with love for one's fellow Jews and for the land and people of Israel.

Rabbi Kronish, a man devoted to liberal Judaism and a servant to *Klal Yisrael*, made a difference. His courage and his will to live and to serve stands as an example to all of his colleagues, his many friends and to all who have come within the orbit of his personality.

Chapter One

INTRODUCTION

Ever since the publication of Erik Erikson's pathbreaking *Young Man Luther*, those who would write biography cannot help but be aware of what a delicate task it is.[1] On the one hand, we are dealing first and foremost with an individual human being—someone whose unique talents and defects are embodied in a particular emotional and psychological package, one whose dynamics within a specific historical and institutional context must be examined with care and precision. On the other hand, what is significant for others in another person's life is the extent to which the subject's path has relevance for their own lives and concerns.

So it is when we consider the life of Rabbi Leon Kronish, who founded and built Temple Beth Sholom in Miami Beach and was a major presence in the communal life of greater Miami from the 1940s to well into the 1980s. A tireless activist on behalf of Israel from before its founding in 1948, through its decisive victory in the Six Day War and the dawning of peace with its Arab neighbors, he was a prominent exponent of the "Liberal" variant of Reform Judaism, not just in Miami and South Florida, but throughout the country during its American heyday in the aftermath of World War Two.

Throughout his career, Kronish exuded a compelling presence. Tall, handsome, energetic, an engaging public speaker, he was blessed with an unusually large capacity for rapport with his fellow human beings—a quality that led them to seek to enroll him in their projects, and not simply respond positively to whatever overtures he might make. Devoted husband, father of three children, spiritual mentor to one of the largest Jewish congregations in the Southeast, Kronish has always been a living example of the principles he has preached—a human being committed to bringing out the best, not just in himself, but in everyone with whom he came into contact.

In this introduction, the task is to outline the institutional contexts—religious, political, social and congregational—in which Leon Kronish was formed, and which he, in response, did so much to re-form. The following chapters will then turn to the main task of this biography: a detailed examination of the path Kronish took through these institutional contexts, how they molded him, and how he, in his turn, reshaped them—both for himself and, even more importantly, others, especially those in *Klal Yisrael*, the people of the worldwide Jewish community.

The first and most important of these institutional contexts is *Liberal Judaism*, a movement whose basic template was Reform Judaism's emphasis on "prophetic mission" and social justice, but which differed from standard Reform Judaism in two major ways:
a) from the beginning, Liberal Judaism was pronouncedly pro-Zionist; and
b) Liberal Judaism was considerably less hostile than Reform to traditional elements of the Jewish liturgy and custom.

Kronish had the great fortune to have as his teachers two of the major figures of twentieth century American Jewish life: Rabbi Stephen Wise, arguably the foremost activist and institution-builder of Reform Judaism, and exponent of co-operation with Conservative and Orthodox Judaism; and Mordecai Kaplan, founder of Reconstructionist Judaism, a ritually conservative movement that linked classical European social theory with a strongly cultural interpretation of the nature of Jewish identity.[2]

The second of these contexts was *Zionism*. For reasons discussed later, Reform Judaism in both Europe and America was initially hostile to the movement for a Jewish state. Stephen Wise, however, was one of the few enthusiastic advocates of both Reform Judaism and Zionism—a combination he bequeathed to his young student Leon Kronish, and a position Wise made tragically credible to many more by the devastating impact of the Holocaust. For Kronish, as for so many others, the Six Day War in 1967 evoked a marked expansion and intensification in his commitment to Israel, one that was to remain his lodestar from the late 1960s until the 1980s.

The third framework for Kronish was *Miami Beach*, which he termed "the American Negev"—a small town when he first arrived in 1944, but one whose potential he was able to foresee. Kronish's special genius was to sense from the beginning how the overall growth of the entire South Florida region could be especially rewarding to the Jewish community, not simply in Miami/Dade County, but also in Florida, the United States, and indeed, the State of Israel.

In Dade County, Kronish was a leading Jewish figure in the main social struggles roiling the 1950s and 1960s: civil rights and desegregation; the separation of church and state, especially in public schools; as well as the "ban the bomb" movement for peace and disarmament.

The final, but hardly least important, institutional context that both defined and was defined by Leon Kronish was the small congregation he turned into one of the major forces in South Florida Jewish life: *Temple Beth Sholom*. From the time he arrived in wartime Miami in the 1940s, Kronish managed to impart a strong commitment to both the open social values of Liberal Judaism—featuring a prominent and public role for women in Jewish community life—and, especially in the 1970s and 1980s, the "Israelization" of the synagogue:

the forging of deep personal links between members of his congregation and the wide variety of Israelis with whom he had become friends over the years.

The remainder of this chapter is devoted to examining these institutional contexts further, to assist the reader in navigating the streams and often-rushing torrents in the life of Leon Kronish. In the chapters to come, the reader will have the opportunity to scrutinize the intense interaction between Leon Kronish and these overlapping, yet complementary, institutional settings.

Liberal Judaism

The Reform Template

Ever since the onset of the Enlightenment, European Judaism found itself as mutable as did larger Christian society in which it was ensconced. Especially in Germany, several reform movements grew up that attempted to modernize Jewish tradition, to make it part and parcel of the new spirit sweeping through the whole of European life.[3]

As a wave of Jews emigrated from Central Europe to the United States during the third quarter of the 19th century, Reform Judaism became the dominant form of Judaism in America. Although a new wave of Eastern European Jews brought a revival of Orthodoxy at the turn of the century, Reform Jewry remained prominent in American Jewish institutions. Only during the religious revival of the post-World War Two period, did the Conservative movement become a competitive stream of American Jewish life.[4]

From a theological point of view, there is no Reform dogma, as might be expected. Rather, there are many different theologies, all combining similar elements in more or less distinctive ways. Reform rejects the idea of supernatural divine revelation of either the Torah (written law) or the Talmud (oral law). It sees scripture and tradition as human, time-determined reflections of revelation. As Michael Meyer, a leading expert on Reform Judaism, notes:

> Like other branches of Judaism, Reform recognizes the close connection between religion and ethics. It especially emphasizes the prophetic message of social justice, and seeks to act upon it both congregationally and as a united movement. Judaism is seen to exist for a higher universal purpose, which aims messianically at the biblical vision of world peace. Traditionally in Reform Judaism, this sense of purpose has been known as the "mission of Israel."[5]

Stephen Wise: Mixing Reform Judaism, Americanism and Zionism

In the life of Leon Kronish—who was born into an Orthodox family that had emigrated from the Ukraine in 1910—Reform Judaism was most dramatically embodied in the charismatic person of Rabbi Stephen Samuel Wise (1874 - 1949), a Budapest-born "rebel" who grew up in New York City.

In certain ways, Wise was a classic exemplar of an American Reform rabbi, a tireless advocate of the "prophetic mission" of social justice. He was an articulate and powerful ally of workers' movements agitating against exploitative conditions in the workplace.

In other ways, however, Wise was one to follow his own inner compass. He was never particularly interested in ritual. And while his sermons attracted huge crowds of Christians as well as Jews, their time—Sunday mornings, and their place—Carnegie Hall, were highly unusual, even for a Reform rabbi.

Perhaps most significantly, Wise dissented from the rejection of Zionism that dominated early Reform. Wise attended the Second Zionist Congress in 1898, and remained a fervent Zionist throughout his life. In his view, there was no contradiction between Zionism and an equally fervent embrace of Americanism. For Wise, support for Zionism did not imply the in-gathering of all Jews. Rather, it involved those who wanted to participate in a national revival of *Klal Yisrael*, in their ancient homeland, a task in which he felt all Jews should participate, even those for whom emigration was not an option.[6]

As might be expected from a rabbi who conducted services for both Jews and Christians on Sunday mornings at Carnegie Hall, Wise was an institutional iconoclast. After the board of trustees at Temple Emanuel in New York City —considered the most prestigious Reform synagogue in America—denied him complete freedom of speech from the pulpit, Wise founded his own congregation where he could speak freely. He called it the Free Synagogue where he would be untrammeled. Later, he created the American Jewish Congress in reaction to what he perceived as the conservative elitism of the American Jewish Committee.

Most important for Leon Kronish, Wise established the Jewish Institute of Religion (JIR) in 1922 as a dynamic, "modern" counterpoise to what had been, to that point, the historic American institution for ordaining Reform rabbis: the Hebrew Union College in Cincinnati. At the JIR, Wise took a distinctly ecumenical position on the differences among Jewish denominations: "I felt the time had come for the establishment of a school of Jewish learning without labels, without partisanship."[7] While the atmosphere was predominantly Reform, there were many among both the faculty and students who were either Conservative or Orthodox. Despite his own relative indifference to ritual, Wise felt that a "liberal" spirit in the Jewish context meant an openness to embrace all forms of Jewish religious practice—the theological basis of his commitment to *Klal Yisrael*.[8]

By the time Kronish came to JIR in 1938, Wise had become the leading figure in American Jewish life, due not so much to his scholarly activities but more to his tireless activism, driven by an enormous self-confidence, and buttressed by his undoubted intelligence, good looks and articulateness.

From Wise, Kronish—who was blessed with a similar self-confidence, and for many of the same reasons—inherited three main concerns: 1) a strong commitment to the Reform mainspring of the "prophetic mission" of social justice; 2) a fervent activist-oriented Zionism; and 3) an ecumenical approach, certainly to Christians, but even more so to those members of *Klal Yisrael* who were Conservative or Orthodox. These legacies were to become crucial for Kronish in his own rabbinic career.

Mordecai Kaplan: A Concern for Jewish Culture and Liturgy

The second major influence on Kronish was Mordecai Kaplan (1881-1983), the founder of Reconstructionist Judaism, a movement within Conservative Judaism until the late 1960s, when its adherents felt the diminution of Kaplan's personal energies required the formation of a separate institutional identity.[9]

Kronish encountered Kaplan in 1937 at Columbia University Teachers' College, where he taught courses similar to those at the Society for the Advancement of Judaism, which he had founded in New York in 1922, as a center for Reconstructionist thinking and scholarship.

Harold Schulweis, a longtime analyst of Kaplan's movement, summarizes Reconstructionism as follows:

> The Jewish people are a living organism whose will to live and fulfill itself often necessitates theological and institutional changes, a process that characterizes Judaism, in Kaplan's definition, as the evolving religious civilization of a living organism, the Jewish people. Kaplan's sociological and theological proposals are rooted in the matrix of the Jewish people and are responsive to its needs and aspirations. Jewish theology is responsible for the salvation, or self-fulfillment of the Jewish people. For Kaplan, there is no paradox in maintaining that continuity requires change.... Reverence for the creative innovation expresses no less a piety than does veneration of the past.[10]

Like Wise, Kaplan was a strong Zionist, a sentiment that is clearly compatible with his view of the Jewish people as a living organism, whose "needs and aspirations" are constantly changing, hence requiring new forms—political as well as sociological—as history progresses.

Unlike Wise, who had little intuitive empathy with ritual matters, Kaplan emphasized the religious civilization of Judaism, a concern that led him to seek to reinvigorate contemporary Jewish religious practices in a variety of ways.

For Kaplan, a living tradition could flourish in an open, democratic society only if it took a pluralistic approach to matters of dogma and ritual. Within that framework, Kaplan argued that it was crucial for all denominations of Judaism to revitalize their theological, ritual and liturgical dimensions.

His particular interests lie in the liturgy, and he produced two major—if controversial—texts. The first was the *New Haggadah* (1941), which was at the head of what later became a long line of Passover *seder* texts that attempted to meld the story of the Jewish exodus from Egypt with contemporary ideas about democracy and oppression. The second, the *Reconstructionist Sabbath Prayer Book* (1945), evoked angry responses from several Orthodox organizations who excommunicated Kaplan when it appeared.[11]

For Kronish, the legacy of Kaplan was two-fold. Zionism was, of course, one aspect, which Wise also shared. But even more important for Kronish was Kaplan's insistence on the centrality of a living liturgy, one that could express and re-express the simultaneous commitment of a living people to both change and continuity as part of a dynamic process of identity.

"Liberal" Judaism: Social Justice, Zionism and A Living Liturgy

While there were certainly others who influenced Kronish, there is no doubt that Wise and Kaplan were the most significant. From Wise, he took the profound commitment to the "prophetic mission" of social justice, principles he would apply in the context of the civil rights and peace/disarmament movements of the 1950s and 1960s.[12] From Wise too, he took the ecumenical notion of *Klal Yisrael*, the Jewish people as a whole, whose collective well-being was more important than the interests or concerns of any particular denomination within. From Kaplan, he took the idea of a vibrant Jewish people, whose identity was constantly evolving and could be authentically expressed by a living liturgy, a project that has consumed him throughout his five decades as a rabbi.[13] From both, finally, he took the idea of a politically active, spiritually infused Zionism—one that could be practiced as legitimately in America as in Israel, as long as the ties that bound the communities were nourished by constant care and attention.[14]

Zionism

As might be expected, the Zionism of Leon Kronish was rich and complex, a political identification, to be sure, but one that grew out of the multi-layered, multi-dimensional Jewish identity that combined his traditional upbringing with the wide-ranging activism of Stephen Wise and the dialectical theorizing of Mordecai Kaplan.

Zionism and Klal Yisrael

For Kronish, probably the most important concept for understanding his Zionism was that of *Klal Yisrael*, the idea emphasized over and over again by Wise that the Jewish people, whatever their differences (whether political, religious, or cultural), were all indissolubly bound together in a community of fate, and that this collective identity had to be at the forefront of the criteria by which any action was evaluated.

In the context of *Klal Yisrael*, Wise and others, including Kronish, saw support for the effort to build a Jewish homeland in *Eretz Yisrael*/Palestine as absolutely incumbent on all Jews, especially those for whom the concept of *Klal Yisrael* had special meaning.

For Wise, Kronish and other adherents of *Klal Yisrael*, Zionism was a political identification easy to embrace, one that flowed naturally from a profound and abiding concern for the fate of the Jewish people as a whole.

In this view, all Jews—whether they intended to emigrate to *Eretz Yisrael*/Palestine or not—had a real stake in the outcome of that effort. Success would be a major boon for Jews all over the world, while failure would be an equally devastating blow.

Zionism and Americanism

At the same time, Wise and his followers felt that the centrality of the notion of *Klal Yisrael* demanded strong and active support of the Zionist enterprise, they also saw no contradiction between being strong Zionists and strong Americans.

As Americans, Jews had access to the full panoply of political rights that was the hallmark of the American identity. The decision of Jewish Americans to exercise those rights on behalf of other Jews who were attempting to build a Jewish refuge, a homeland in Palestine, was a perfectly acceptable one for them to make.

Their support for that effort did not mean that they themselves felt compelled to move to Palestine. After all, they lived in America, which for many Reform Jews had become the "Promised Land" itself, a land where Jews were free to live like anyone else.

Wise and others recognized that: a) it was not practical for all Jews to come and live in America, although they certainly supported the right of any Jews who wanted to do so; and b) there were some Jews, who for one reason or another, preferred to live as Jews in Palestine, rather than in America.

In light of these realities, they saw their support of their brethren in Palestine as nothing more than a simple exercise of their rights as Americans, without feeling that they themselves were obligated to leave one Promised Land (in the New World) for another Promised Land (in the Old World.)

Nonetheless, the concept of *Klal Yisrael* did oblige American Jews to support those efforts at Jewish refuge and rejuvenation in *Eretz Yisrael*/Palestine. For Wise, Kronish and others like them, there was a positive *mitzvah* (commandment) for American Jews to use their freedom as Americans to help their fellow Jews whenever and wherever they were in danger, as well as to support whatever efforts they might make, as in *Eretz Yisrael*/Palestine, to end their conditions of oppression.[15]

Social Justice and Labor Zionism

For Wise, of course, the concept of *Klal Yisrael* was not the only fundamental principle guiding his political action, whether in an American or Jewish context. No less important was the Reform Jewish concern with social justice. For Wise and later Kronish, the commitment to a better, more equitable society was as strong a motive in the Jewish—specifically Zionist—context, as it was in America.

As Stephen Wise was known in his Sunday morning Carnegie Hall sermons for his thunderous attacks on the exploitation of workers in a rapidly industrializing American economy,[16] it is hardly surprising that he and his followers, like Kronish, were allied with the dominant, Labor tendency within the Zionist movement.

For Wise and Kronish, as well as for the movement's international leaders, like David Ben-Gurion, Chaim Arlosoroff, Yigal Allon, Golda Meir and others, the national redemption of the Jewish people could only be accomplished by their simultaneous social and economic transformation.

In principle, Labor Zionists argued that there was little point in eliminating the oppression of Jews as a people, simply in order to reproduce oppression in the workplace and economic relations of that new society they were involved in building.[17]

And as a practical matter, Ben-Gurion, Meir and other Labor Zionists argued, it was vital for the Zionist project in *Eretz Yisrael*/Palestine to establish a Jewish agricultural sector, and a Jewish working class. Otherwise, the inevitable claim to statehood would be lacking the crucial element of a Jewish infrastructure, which would render that claim utopian at best.

In this context, it is easy to understand why Kronish brought into being in 1965 the Histadrut Foundation of the United States, an American support group for the Histadrut umbrella labor Federation in Israel. He served as Chairman of the Board of the American Foundation as well as playing a leading role in the thinking and programming of the Labor Zionist Alliance in the United States, roles he maintained until his untimely stroke in 1984.

For all these reasons, then, Leon Kronish—whose father was a socialist—found himself situated quite comfortably in the egalitarian Labor Zionist stream that created the State of Israel, and guided it through the first four decades of its existence.

Alexander Dushkin and Cultural Zionism

While Stephen Wise created the political and ideological framework, it was Alexander Dushkin, another mentor—also from the Jewish Theological Seminary—who infused a strong cultural content into his Zionist identity.

A father of professional Jewish education in the United States, Dushkin believed that the teaching of the Bible as literature, and Hebrew as a living, modern language were major elements in the nuturing and maintenance of a strong Jewish identity.

Like Kaplan, Dushkin adopted the view of Ahad Ha'am (the Hebrew pen-name of Asher Ginsburg, the leading theorist of cultural Zionism), who argued that the most important outcome of Jewish re-vitalization in *Eretz Yisrael*/Palestine was not necessarily a politically independent state, but a worldwide Jewish cultural renaissance, and that teaching Jewish culture would impart a profound spiritual aspect to Zionism, one that would make it a viable alternative to assimilation.[18]

For Kronish, then, Zionism would have not simply the political aspect of Wise, but a strongly cultural dimension—one that highlighted Jewish education in general, and encouraged a direct encounter with the Hebrew language as a structural feature of the concept of the Zionist mission. Following Ahad Ha'am and Dushkin, Kronish's Zionism came to incorporate a distinctively cultural/spiritual presence, infusing both his theological point of view and his liturgical innovations.

A Zionist Activist

In this way, Kronish came to have a multi-faceted conception of what it meant to be a Zionist, one simultaneously collective (*Klal Yisrael*), egalitarian (social justice and Labor Zionism), and cultural (intimately connected to Hebrew as a living language).

As rabbi of Temple Beth Sholom, Kronish integrated all three aspects, imparting to his congregation a sense of not only what Zionism meant for the Jewish people and Jewish tradition—especially in the aftermath of the Holocaust, but also what the drama of Jewish history and tradition meant for Israel in the first two decades of its existence.

As a concrete way of making unshakable the connection between Diaspora Jewry and Israel, Kronish participated actively in the Israel Bonds program from its inception in 1951. By the 1970s, his success as a leader in the

Bond drives of the 1950s and 1960s had earned him the prestigious position as chair of the Rabbinical Cabinet of Israel Bonds in the United States. Under Kronish's direction, some twelve hundred congregations in the United States participated in Bond appeals throughout the decade. In the 1980s, in recognition of his efforts, Leon Kronish served as national chairman of Israel Bonds.

For Kronish, in short, Bonds quite literally became the way in which he could help achieve his long-sought goal of the redemption of Israel. Bonds were the strongest and most direct link that American Jews could make with the State of Israel, its people and its future.

The Six Day War: A Shift in Direction

With Israel's stunning military victory in the June, 1967 Six Day War, Kronish's Zionism, like that of many American Jews, underwent a profound transformation, a metamorphosis chronicled in two major documents he wrote: *Yisrael Goralenu* (Israel Is Our Destiny, 1968), and *What Are the 'Zionist Mitzvot'*? (1977).[19]

We will examine these texts in some detail in Chapter Six. Here, we will outline briefly the broad sweep of their arguments, thereby elucidating the changing dynamics in Kronish's relation to Zionism.

In *Yisrael Goralenu*, Kronish argues that the Six Day War had irreversibly altered the dynamics of Jewish life.

> Never before in the history of our movement has the oneness, the unity, the interlocking destiny of the Jewish people been so sharply and simply stated.... As Richard Hirsch has phrased it: "In June, 1967, it became clear that the destiny of *Am Yisrael* [literally, 'the people of Israel,' in the sense of *Klal Yisrael*] was inseparable from the destiny of *Medinat Yisrael* 'the State of Israel.'"[20]

For Kronish, the war brought an end to what he called the "equivocating" of the American Jewish community in general—and Reform Judaism in particular—with regard to relations with the State of Israel.

Henceforth, Kronish's mission would be to link with *gesher vakesher*—bridges and bonds—his congregation Beth Sholom, Reform Judaism as a whole, the entire American Jewish community, indeed the whole of world Jewry (*Klal Yisrael*), not simply to the State of Israel, but, in a very specific way, to the policies of the Israeli government, whatever its political coloration (a shift that became particularly important after 1977, when the leftist Labor Party lost, for the first time in Israeli history, to Menachem Begin and the rightist Likud).

The substantive aim of Kronish's new program was to re-focus the "prophetic mission" of Reform Judaism from social justice and *Klal Yisrael*, to the well-being of the State of Israel, and the aims of the Israeli government.

The strategy he chose to realize these new goals was to develop a myriad of close, personal connections—*gesher vakesher*—between the institutions of Reform Judaism in North America in general, and Temple Beth Sholom of Miami Beach in particular, with a wide variety of individuals and institutions—religious, political, social, and cultural—in Israel.

We term this program the "Israelization" of the temple, a calling Kronish pursued in the post-1967 period with his characteristic energy and enthusiasm as his agenda shifted from the Reform "mission" of seeking social justice in America to forging ever more numerous, tighter and intimate bonds between Jews in America, and the people and polity of the State of Israel.

Miami Beach

By the late 1960s, when Kronish made this fundamental move towards a more Israel-centered, Jewish-oriented agenda, he had earned a well-deserved reputation in the local and national American community as a leading figure in transforming Miami Beach from little more than a segregated, provincial southern town with a lot of potential, to an emerging international metropolis and one of the major centers of American Jewish life.

The Many Faces of Miami Beach

Since World War One, Miami Beach has experienced what might be termed a succession of different faces.

When John Collins, Carl Fisher, N. B. T. Roney and others arrived, and took an active role in establishing the city, it became known as "The Poor Man's Palm Beach" (not that those who came were in any way poor), a period that lasted up until the Depression. The face of Miami Beach during this period was decidedly upper-class WASP, and, as might be expected during that historical era, had both segregationist and anti-Semitic orientations.

Following World War Two, and lasting well into the 1960s, Miami Beach took on a much more pronouncedly Jewish face. While there had been a small Jewish presence on the Beach since the 1920s, the 1950s saw a huge explosion in both the Jewish population and the city as a whole, one that permanently and irrevocably changed its character.[21]

Having come to the Beach in 1944, when he became the rabbi of what he developed into one of the most influential and dynamic Jewish congregations in the entire Southeast, Leon Kronish was in the vanguard of this second face of Miami Beach.

After the coming to power of Fidel Castro in Cuba in 1960, Miami Beach once again took on a new face with the arrival of Cuban refugees, largely, although not exclusively, from the professional and middle classes. Many had supported Castro's anti-Batista efforts, but opposed his early turn towards Communism. The result was a Jewish face, with an ever-increasing Hispanic accent.

In 1979, this first wave of Cuban immigrants—who had fairly quickly moved to the Little Havana/Calle Ocho (SW 8th Street) area, and thence south and west through Coral Gables and into the growing reaches of suburban Kendall—was joined by a second wave, the so-called Marielitos (after the Cuban port from which they embarked). Many Marielitos stayed in the southern portion of the Beach, where they contributed to the early 1980s atmosphere captured by the groundbreaking television show *Miami Vice*.[22]

Despite the fact that one of the co-stars of that program was black, the Beach remained essentially hostile to African Americans. Up until the 1950s, there was a night-time curfew for blacks on the Beach, reflecting an attitude most dramatically manifested in a hard-fought, protracted, and often ugly struggle to integrate the public schools in the 1960s.

The Early Days of Miami Beach Jewry

When Leon Kronish arrived in 1944, with his wife Lillian and son Jordan, to become rabbi of the Conservative Beth Sholom Center (at that time, it was not yet constituted as either Reform, or a temple—a transformation we will examine fully in Chapter Three), he found a small Jewish community on Miami Beach which had been developing slowly since the immediate aftermath of World War One.

Jews had participated in the building of hotels in the Art Deco district in the lower part of the Beach, below Dade Boulevard (a far cry from the glitzy South Beach of the 1990s). Indeed, the institutional beginnings of what was to become the third largest Jewish community in the United States of America were laid during this period: Beth Jacob, for example, an Orthodox congregation and the first Jewish institution of any sort on Miami Beach, was chartered in 1927.[23]

Even so, upper-class WASP anti-Semitism kept the total Jewish population small, and their geographic domain limited to the lower reaches of the island.

World War Two: Dramatic Changes

Two developments changed this demographic profile, making possible the explosion of the 1950s.

The first was World War Two, when the armed services took over large sections of the Art Deco district. While the summer was hell on earth—lasting from early-mid May until well into October—the winter was paradise, and tens of thousands of soldiers, sailors and airmen glimpsed the possibility of a luxurious, tropical lifestyle still connected to the American political economy.

Among them, of course, were many Jews—many of whom either vowed to come back themselves, or told their loved ones about the place, or both.[24]

The second development was the coming onstream of the mass production of air-conditioners—both industrial-size, which made it possible to cool large buildings, and room units, which enabled the hotels to assure their patrons of year-round comfort (albeit at the cost of high electric bills for the grinding summer months).[25]

By the early 1950s, then, Miami Beach—which had first become known among Jews as the "Winter Catskills"—was starting to transform "snowbirds" (people who came down for the winter) into permanent residents.

Kronish and the "Jewish Explosion" of the 1950s

As the founding rabbi of the Reform Temple Beth Sholom, Kronish was well-positioned to take advantage of the unique Jewish demographics of Miami Beach. From his base of year-round congregants, during the "season," the handsome, personable, articulate Kronish was able to multiply several-fold attendance at his sabbath services by drawing on those snowbirds who wanted to maintain some sort of active Jewish identity while in residence on the Beach.

Not surprisingly, they told their friends up north about the charismatic, "Liberal" rabbi on Miami Beach, and the allure of Kronish and his temple grew by leaps and bounds. And when these snowbirds, or their friends, decided to become full-time residents of South Florida, their denominational allegiance had already been formed.

In this way, Kronish and Temple Beth Sholom, located on 41st Street (which was considered quite "uptown," especially when he first arrived), both encouraged and benefitted from the dramatic upward mobility of the Miami Beach Jewish community. As had occurred in Manhattan several decades before, the increasing socio-economic prominence of Jews was mirrored by a physical move from the southern towards the northern reaches of Miami Beach.

Located just a twenty minute walk from hotels like the Fontainebleau (1954) and the Eden Roc (1955), Beth Sholom became a visible symbol of the increasing prominence—both socio-economic and physical—of Jews in the life of Miami Beach.

Trouble in Paradise

At the same time this explosion of the Jewish population in Miami Beach marked the decisive defeat of the aforementioned WASP anti-Semitism, tensions were developing with some of the other communities on the Beach.

Most notable were those with the Catholic community that was also centered around 41st Street, symbolized by St. Patrick's Church, between Alton Road and Meridian Avenue. From the mid-1940s through the late 1950s, St. Patrick's was at the center of efforts to stop the building of three visible Jewish institutions in the 41st Street area.

The first was construction of Temple Beth Sholom itself, on an empty lot across from St. Patrick's, a project that eventually did come to fruition, albeit not without significant opposition and in a different location, a few blocks east and north of 41st Street on Chase Avenue. The second, which also went through, was the building of the mammoth Mt. Sinai Medical Center—now considered far and away the most distinguished medical facility on Miami Beach, and one of the best in all South Florida—just west of Alton Road at 41st Street. And the third was the proposed Hebrew Academy, an Orthodox educational center, which was unable to overcome Catholic opposition, and was finally completed much further south on Dade Boulevard.

In addition to these specifically Jewish projects, Catholic individuals and institutions, among others, also opposed the building of the Julia Tuttle Causeway, completed in 1959, which links the mainland to Miami Beach right at 41st Street, just south of the Mt. Sinai complex. Detractors argued the causeway would only increase the already (in their view) too-large numbers of tourists and others who were turning what had been a pleasantly sleepy backwater into a densely-populated, traffic-snarled urban neighborhood.

Implicit in this argument, many felt at the time, was hostility not just to the increasing Jewish presence, but a fear that a causeway would also give increased Beach access to Miami's large black population, centered in the Liberty City and Overtown neighborhoods just north of downtown Miami.

Those who held such fears felt them confirmed when the civil rights movement in the 1960s advocated busing children from schools in those black neighborhoods to Miami Beach.

While Jews (who by this time had become the majority of the Beach population) endorsed civil rights legislation in principle, they themselves became apprehensive at the thought of having their local schools integrated.

By the time Miami Beach High was integrated in 1970, black/Jewish relations were disintegrating—in the Jewish view, due to the lack of black support for Israel in the wake of the Six Day War and due to what black activists and then others in the black community saw as a paternalistic attitude on the part of Jews.

To compound this already turbulent situation on Miami Beach, the arrival of Cuban refugees in the 1960s, followed by the Marielitos in the late 1970s, further tended to heighten the often tense dynamics among the ethnic communities living cheek by jowl on an increasingly densely populated sandbar.

Temple Beth Sholom

During the 1950s, 1960s and 1970s, Leon Kronish was at the center—socially, spiritually and physically—of the tremendous growth of both Miami Beach as a city and as a Jewish community.

His base throughout was Temple Beth Sholom—a small Conservative center when he first arrived in 1944—and by the time of his stroke forty years later, a leading Reform congregation and a major center of Jewish life whose influence reached not just Miami Beach and South Florida, but all through the United States, and indeed, internationally, to the very heart of the Middle East.

Beginnings: From Conservative Center to Reform Temple

On June 3, 1942, a storefront was leased at 761 41st Street for the Beth Sholom Center, a Conservative oriented synagogue founded to serve not simply the twenty inaugural members, but, more importantly, the needs of the several hundred Jewish servicemen billeted in hotels in and north of the Art Deco Miami Beach district.

Despite its location in an anti-Semitic area, the Beth Sholom Center grew after its establishment, even though it had only a part-time rabbi, the much-loved Samuel Machtai, whose media career gave rise to the nickname "the Radio Rabbi."

Since its growing numbers came largely from the ranks of Jewish servicemen, the center was fairly ecumenical in its orientation, adopting elements of both Reform and Conservative practice. In this sense, the center embodied the basic principles of Liberal Judaism, although it was not articulated as such at that time.

Consequently, it was not surprising that, when members of the center decided they had grown enough to require the services of a full-time rabbi, they directed their first inquiries to the core institution of Liberal Judaism, the Jewish Institute of Religion in New York, founded by the charismatic Reform rabbi, Stephen Wise. It was in this way that the Beth Sholom congregation and the young Leon Kronish first met, and which led to his hiring as their first full-time rabbi.

After the usual initial period of mutual acquaintance, things began to move quickly and positively for the young rabbi and the new congregation. By April 1945, the Conservative Beth Sholom Center had become the new Reform Temple Beth Sholom, and plans were made to move from the storefront on 41st

Street, to a site just north on Chase Avenue, former home of the stables of Carl Fisher's Nautilus Club polo fields.

Building an Institution: 1945-1957

The next period saw explosive growth in the newly established Reform temple, nestled in what had been an anti-Semitic area of the Beach, now the vanguard in the rapid expansion of both the Jewish population of Miami Beach and the city as a whole.

Membership multiplied more than ten-fold during this time, from forty or so family units to more than seven hundred and fifty. Very quickly, the temple developed the whole panoply of institutional infrastructures characteristic of American Reform congregations during this efflorescence of organized Jewish life.

The Sisterhood, the Men's Club, an active adult education program, Zionist youth clubs for both girls and boys, a nursery school, a Sunday religious school, a weekly Hebrew school, a lecture series on Jewish current events, weekly library readings—all these seeds were sown, took strong root, and flourished during the first decade of Kronish's leadership of Beth Sholom.

The ideological matrix generating the flurry of productive activity was Kronish's unique mixture of Reform Judaism, Zionism and Reconstructionism—what he termed Liberal Judaism. Each week the *Temple Beth Sholom Bulletin* identified itself as "the Liberal congregation on the Beach."

During this period, which coincided with the end of World War Two, the stunning revelation of the Holocaust, the birth and early years of the State of Israel, the Zionist element received great emphasis. Linked to this focus on Zionism and Israel was what would become Kronish's continuing concern with the revival of Hebrew as a living language, embodied especially in his efforts—following in the footsteps of Mordecai Kaplan—to re-invigorate the liturgy and the educational curriculum.

The culmination of this era in the life of a new giant among religious institutions came with the dedication on November 29, 1957 of a completely new sanctuary on the Chase Avenue site. With this came the inauguration of a new period of activism in the life of both the Temple and its beloved and energetic leader.

The Era of "Prophetic Mission": 1957-1967

By the time Temple Beth Sholom consecrated its new sanctuary—the physical embodiment of its identity as a solidly-based, dynamic institution—America as a whole, and Miami Beach in particular, was about to enter a time of sustained social disequilibrium. While much of that change was positive, its intensity and rapidity left many people and institutions reeling. Fortunately for

Temple Beth Sholom, its roots had by then sunk sufficiently deep that it was able not just to survive these tumultuous times, but to channel them constructively and creatively.

The institution itself continued to grow. By the mid-1960s, it had become a large congregation, numbering in excess of twelve hundred households. Many were former snowbirds who had decided to relocate permanently to Miami Beach, and who made an easy transition from seasonal to full-time members of the Kronish following.

This new blood was of great help to Kronish and the synagogue as they together encountered three of the many great social challenges confronting American society at this time: 1) the civil rights movement; 2) the "ban the bomb"/peace and disarmament movement; and 3) the separation of church and state, especially relating to the issue of prayer in the public schools.

These challenges provided ample opportunity to test the congregants' internalization of Kronish's teachings of Liberal Judaism, and their commitment to this new meaning of prophetic covenant and mission.

Civil Rights

Kronish's attitude and behavior towards incidents of blatant racism was unequivocal, and he inaugurated social action programs in civil rights as a regular feature of Beth Sholom life. Members of the synagogue joined local black activists working to desegregate hotels and restaurants on the Beach, efforts crowned later by passage of municipal and state laws requiring the desegregation of buses (1957), beaches, parks and hospitals (1958), and public schools (1960).

In 1960, following the decision of the Reform umbrella Union of American Hebrew Congregations (UAHC) to build a Religious Action Center in Washington, D.C., Beth Sholom established an Interfaith Institute to encourage communication between Jews and non-Jews. In 1963, members of the Interfaith Institute actively participated in a unity march for civil rights jointly sponsored by the Rabbinical Association of Greater Miami, the Catholic Archdiocese, and local Protestant clergy.

Kronish became friends with the Reverend Theodore Gibson, head of the Miami chapter of the NAACP, and invited him several times to speak at Temple Beth Sholom. From the pulpit, Kronish criticized political figures, and especially Floridian national legislators, who spoke out against drives to register black voters.

For Kronish, the commitment to battle segregation had a religious basis.

> The story of segregation is a sordid and sinful one. Who is there among us who, in the tangled realm of race relations, is so righteous that he doeth good always, and sinneth not through his own acts of exclusion and segregation?

> .... If this problem has no relevance to Judaism; if we refuse, no matter how many statements we have previously made, to continue to "cry aloud and spare not," if we fail to take such action as may be within our power to end every vestige of discrimination, then Judaism itself really has no meaning or relevance to life itself.[26]

Nuclear Disarmament

Throughout the 1950s, Kronish took a visible public role in the campaign for nuclear disarmament. In 1950, he wrote a public letter to President Truman protesting the construction of the H-bomb, arguing that "the time has come for the American Eagle and the Russian Bear, and even the British Bull, to find a way of living together," sentiments he continually repeated from the pulpit, encouraging his congregants to write similar letters to members of Congress.[27]

By 1962, Kronish was one of a handful of clergyman interviewed by *Life* magazine for a cover story on "The Drive for Mass Shelters." Kronish's statement, published along with his picture, echoed his sermons. "Shelters delude people into accepting the inevitability of war... and the possibility of survival. Belief in safety is a hoax."[28]

In 1964, Kronish was invited to the "Washington Conference on Disarmament and World Peace," and in 1966, to the "National Inter-Religious Conference on Peace." The goal of both conferences—organized by the UAHC Religious Action Center—was to recommend how religion could play a role in governmental decisions affecting war and peace. Out of the 1966 conference came a declaration to promote peace in Vietnam, and to consider an "immediate halt to the bombing," both moves fully supported by Kronish and the social action committee on nuclear disarmament he had established at Beth Sholom.

Separation of Church and State

Throughout the 1950s, the question of a formal, Christian presence in public schools simmered both nationally and in Florida. In Miami, things came to a head when the American Jewish Congress, representing Jewish students, brought a suit challenging certain programs in Dade County Schools, such as the re-enactment of the crucifixion of Jesus as part of the Easter holiday programs and the morning recitation of the "Lord's" prayer.

As vice-president of the American Jewish Congress' South Florida chapter, Kronish had worked tirelessly behind the scenes to eliminate such practices. But when these efforts failed, he became a leading public critic of the mixing of church and state, a practice he repeatedly condemned from the pulpit.

The case was heard in July, October and November of 1960, attracting national media attention. Kronish was a prime witness for the plaintiffs, articulately and deliberately explaining why Jews considered unacceptable for public education such subjects as the divinity of Jesus, the dogma of the

Trinity, the New Testament and the Resurrection. The suit was successful in the Dade County Circuit Court, and two years later, was affirmed unanimously by the Florida Supreme Court.[29]

By 1967, Kronish had distinguished both himself and Temple Beth Sholom as being at the liberal forefront of the major social and political struggles that marked the 1960s.

A South Florida Cultural Center

At the same time, due to the heroic exertions of one congregant in particular – Judy Drucker – the temple began a cultural affairs program that would soon lead to its recognition as the foremost musical arts center in greater Miami, secular or religious.

The roots lay in both Drucker's unique talents and energy, as well as Kronish's long encouragement of musical innovations, part of his ongoing interest in creating a more emotionally powerful and spiritually uplifting liturgy.

From the late 1960s well into the 1980s, Temple Beth Sholom became known throughout South Florida for its prestigious winter concert programs featuring world-renowned instrumentalists, singers and dancers. Among those who appeared under the rubric of the Culture and Fine Arts Series – renamed Miami's Great Artist Series in 1970 – were Pinchas Zuckerman on his first U.S. tour, Leonard Bernstein, Itzhak Perlman, Luciano Pavarotti, Yehudi Menuhin, Zubin Mehta, Vladimir Ashkenazi, Richard Tucker and the Israeli Philharmonic, in addition to leading chamber music ensembles and others.

In addition, the temple established a unique art gallery featuring the work of Jewish artists from all over the world, and especially Israel. A Jewish cultural arts program was also integrated into the educational curricula.

The "Israelization" of the Temple and American Jewry

While Temple Beth Sholom was becoming known both regionally and, as a result of the continuing snowbird presence, nationally as a center of high culture, Rabbi Kronish was also leading it to a much deeper connection with a myriad of Israeli individuals and institutions.

As noted above, the stunning events of the Six Day War marked a significant shift in the political orientation of Leon Kronish and Temple Beth Sholom. From 1967 until his untimely stroke in 1984, Kronish became focused almost exclusively on linking the temple – via *gesher vakesher*, bridges and bonds – to many aspects of Israeli life, including, but not limited to, support for numerous policies of the Israeli government, even those not headed by the Labor Party.

Yisrael Goralenu (Israel Is Our Destiny, 1968), and *What are the 'Zionist Mitzvot'?* (1977) outlined the linking initiatives, and Temple Beth Sholom became Kronish's laboratory to exercise the programmatic features of the process we term here "Israelization."

One program was called "Pilgrimages (missions) to Israel," trips to Israel taken by teenage boys and girls following their religious confirmation at age fifteen. In Kronish's view, the best way to strengthen their sense of Jewish identity was to have them spend several weeks in Israel, getting to know first-hand the land and people. While parents were at first reluctant, the "pilgrimages" soon became extremely popular summer options, and were expanded to include adult missions and trips to sites in Europe of Jewish significance, especially, although not exclusively, Holocaust-related.

A second major program was the establishment in 1969 of an "Israelis-in-Residence" program, whose purpose was to expose Jews in the Diaspora to specifically Israeli (as opposed to merely Jewish) values. The idea was that an Israeli would come and live as a guest of the congregation at a member's home, while participating both formally and informally in a whole range of temple activities. In this way, Kronish argued, not only would American Jews come to understand Israelis better, Israelis would also have the chance to see how their American brethren saw the world.

In these and several other ways detailed at length in Chapter Six, Kronish moved to expand and extend the relations between American Jewry–especially Reform Judaism–and the State of Israel.

They all represented an Israel-centered focus for Jewish life in America. And they all went far beyond the traditional Zionist goal of bringing Jews to live in the Land of Israel.

Their purpose was to develop a wide array of interconnected relations between Israeli and American Jews–a web that would, in Kronish's view, redound not only to their mutual benefit, but also to the benefit of both Israel and the United States as interdependent, cooperating democratic nation-states.

"Re-Forming" Judaism in the State of Israel

At the same time Kronish was undertaking these, and indeed other, efforts to "Israelize" Temple Beth Sholom, and, by implication, all of American Jewry, he was also attempting to upgrade in a major way the status of Reform Judaism within Israel itself.

Without the credibility Kronish had gained in Israel as a result of his decades-long work with Israel Bonds, and his post-1967 efforts in particular, the drive to legitimize Reform Judaism in Israel would have been even more difficult. Even so, it was constantly challenging.

As one of the leading lights in binding Reform Judaism with Zionism, Kronish felt it was his duty to bring Reform rabbis to Israel. As chairman of the Committee on Israel of the Central Conference of American Rabbis in the heady days after the Six Day War, he asked his colleagues to consider joint pilgrimages to Israel, programs to encourage *aliya* (immigration) for Reform rabbis, and projects leading to the establishment of more institutions for American Jews to experience Reform Judaism in Israel.

Not surprisingly, these efforts to legitimize Reform Judaism in Israel aroused the antagonism of the Orthodox religious establishment there. They were especially bothered by what they considered the lax *halachic* (Jewish law) standards applied by Reform rabbis to those wishing to convert to Judaism, and the Reform insistence on recognizing the right of women to become rabbis.

Until his stroke in 1984, Kronish was a leading activist within the Reform movement in efforts to bridge the gap between the inclinations of the Reform movement towards the religious left, and the militant Orthodoxy of the Israeli religious establishment, a tendency reinforced by the existence of a right-wing government in Israel from 1977 on.

Leon Kronish: The Man

Energetic, charismatic, personable, dynamic, committed—these are the words that spring to mind as we consider the range of the activities that comprised Leon Kronish's life, and the depth of the intensity he has brought to his vocation.

But before we go on to examine in detail the life briefly outlined above, a slightly deeper look at the personal qualities that guided Leon Kronish on his unusual journey seems appropriate here.

Above all, Kronish must be seen as a man of the people. This is not to say that he pandered to his congregation, or tried to please the crowds he so regularly addressed. On the contrary, it was his conviction in the authenticity of his beliefs that carried them with him.

But it does mean that he possesses a rare quality—often simulated, rarely found—that enabled people of all sorts to be comfortable in his presence, to feel that, whatever his erudition, achievement and standing, Kronish is genuinely interested in what they had to say, be it about their ideas, their problems, their dreams. For Kronish, this is a vocation that he has renewed each and every day and that he continues to demonstrate even with the severe handicaps of a debilitating stroke.

In this context, he was able to be an effective, not to mention tireless, organizer. From the reactions in the faces of those he has affected, he has been able to see the power of his own initiative—a reflection that served to replenish the wellsprings of his own authentic commitment to the principles he strove so mightily to serve.

Similarly, Kronish has been a great conciliator. As we have seen, he was hardly loath to confront the great issues of the day, and to do so with a truly

Biblical—indeed, prophetic—fervor and passion. At the same time, he has never let these great passions get the better of him, and lead him to condemn those whose position he opposed, and who opposed him. Rather, he has striven—so often successfully—to find the common ground, even with his enemies, that would enable them all to move beyond the issues of contention and towards more harmonious relations.

This ability to find common ground, to reconcile opposing positions was undoubtedly influenced by the work he did to overcome the crises in his own life. Although the story we tell is so frequently one of triumph and transcendence, there was tragedy, too—experience Kronish has used to inspire him further. His grandfather was lost during the Holocaust, his first child was challenged in a variety of ways and died before reaching adulthood, he suffered a major heart attack in 1978, yet he persevered on until a stroke in 1984 finally began to slow his great energies.

Throughout it all, Kronish has never lost his own sense of mission, especially with his congregation, whom he sincerely saw as the members of his extended family, and those he encountered—whether in Miami, elsewhere in the United States, or particularly Israel—in the whirl of activities that both consumed and nurtured him. Indeed, Kronish has been and continues to be a role model for a whole generation of religious, political and community leaders—locally, nationally, and globally—who see in him a person worth emulating, and whose work was of such transcendent import that they feel themselves called upon to continue it.[30]

All this is admirable. But it is only what we've come to expect in those we call "great men." The public self shines, but the private person is so often quite different. What makes Leon Kronish so unusual, therefore, even within the vaunted circles he frequented, is not simply his magnetism to outsiders, but the extent to which he was able to pass on his own brand of principled commitment to values to his own children.

His son Ronald Kronish followed in his father's footsteps, without ever feeling that such a path was pre-ordained for him. He became a rabbi at the Hebrew Union College-Jewish Institute of Religion, after completing his degree in humanistic psychology at Brandeis. In addition, he earned a Ph.D. in education from Harvard University—testaments to his desire to carry on the tradition of teaching that he learned at his father's feet.

Most importantly, Ronald Kronish lived out his father's deep commitment to the State of Israel, and made *aliya* in 1979. Since then, he has served in several positions, including as Co-Director of the Melitz Centers for Jewish Zionist Education in Jerusalem, the Director of the Israeli office of the American Jewish Committee, as well as a lecturer at both the Hebrew University of Jerusalem and Tel Aviv University. At this writing, he is Director of the Inter-Religious Coordinating Council in Israel. All this activity reflects a wholehearted embrace of the principles for which his father, Leon Kronish, so strongly stands to this day.

And, finally, as his daughter Maxine Kronish Snyder—one of many beneficiaries of Kronish's deep commitment to the equality of women in the Temple, and the notion that a loving family life is the basis of a vibrant Jewish identity—so eloquently put it in a volume of essays in honor of her father:

> With all my father's commitments and activities as a rabbi and communal leader, I am sure that I—and the rest of the extended Kronish family—revere him most as the patriarch of our family. And we know that the feeling is mutual, that family for him is always the top priority—it always has been, and it is so now, more than ever before.... It is my privilege to share in his dreams—for our family, for the Jewish people, and for all of God's children—and I fervently pray that I will be able to continue to fulfill many of his dreams and hopes for the future, along with the rest of his family and his many friends and followers, who have become his devoted disciples in the Jewish world.[31]

Chapter Two

NORTHERN ROOTS

Introduction

Leon Kronish, the man, embodied many of the typical traits of his generation of American Jews.

His father, Max, had been born to an Orthodox family in the Ukraine. Anti-Semitism drove him to the New World, first to Toronto, and then, three years later, to New York. Like many of his co-religionists, Max Kronish worked for a union in the garment industry, where his combination of socialist and Zionist views were common.

Similar to most Jewish women of that era, Max's wife Lena fulfilled the traditional roles of child-rearing and housekeeping.

Born in 1917 as the first child of Max and Lena Kronish, Leon Kronish grew up in New York, then as now the center of American Jewish life. He was sent by his father to a talmud torah, where modern Hebrew was an important part of the curriculum. By the time he finished high school, his education was a lively mix of Orthodox, *Yiddishkeit*, socialist, Zionist and assimilationist tendencies typical for so many families of his generation.

Growing up in the hard years of the Depression, Kronish personally felt the bite of anti-Semitism while walking from home to school, and the fear that resulted from being "ganged up on" by hostile Gentiles. A teenage member of the *Hashomer Hatzair*, a socialist Zionist youth movement, he experienced both the aspirations for a Jewish homeland of Zionism and the threat to all Jews represented by the brutal realities of Nazi Germany.

After graduating from college, Kronish made the decision to become a rabbi. First, he attended the Jewish Theological Seminary, where he encountered Mordecai Kaplan, the founder of the dynamic movement of Jewish revitalization, Reconstructionism. Then, he was ordained at the Jewish Institute of Religion, where he became a close disciple of the Institute's founder, Stephen Wise, the dominant figure in American Jewish life during the first half of the twentieth century.

These "northern roots" molded the man Leon Kronish. His personality and Jewish consciousness were intensely shaped by these intertwining elements—his family's background, the Williamsburg milieu of intensive *Yiddishkeit*, his father's socialist leanings, his talmud torah/Zionist education, his involvement with Zionist youth movements, his rabbinical school training, and his first professional vocational calling.

These formative influences—all in the New York area—shaped the man who was to become a major figure in the development of a city many considered a tropical suburb of New York: Miami Beach.

Max Kronish Comes to America

The story of Leon Kronish of Miami Beach begins with the journey of his father Max from the steppes of the Ukraine to the teeming Jewish slums of Toronto's Lower Spadina and Cabbagetown districts in 1910, and then, in 1913, on to the Jewish mecca of the New World, the East Side of Manhattan.

Between 1894, when the Dreyfus case erupted upon France, and 1917, when revolution devastated the Russian Empire, a steady stream of immigrants—nearly one-tenth of them Jewish—came to North America. Of the approximately one and a half million Jews seeking shelter and freedom, a majority originated from the Ukraine, Poland and Lithuania. Among these was Max Kronish, Leon Kronish's father, a young man from Zborow, a small Ukrainian community of two thousand Jews.[1]

Max Kronish's decision to emigrate and leave Zborow was the same as it was for masses of Jews leaving eastern Europe. They dreamed of earning a livelihood, of practicing Judaism, and of gaining political freedom. Many envisioned these dreams materializing in the United States, their *goldene medina*, a land filled with endless economic opportunities.

In 1910, following the trail of others from Zborow, Max crossed the border into Germany, proceeding first to Berlin, and then westward to Hamburg. Although the Czarist regime made it hard for the Jews to obtain legal passports, corrupt border guards could be "encouraged" to tolerate illegal crossings. Bribes of various sorts, plus border crossing fees, and the purchase of steerage class tickets, cost a small fortune for the emigrating eastern European Jew.[2]

Max learned before embarking in Hamburg that he would be refused entry into the United States due to a health problem.[3] The emigré community of central Canada became his next choice. A significant percentage of the Toronto, Ottawa, and Montreal Jewish communities were people who had been rejected or discouraged by American authorities and who had emigrated from the Ukraine.

Travelling by steerage was claustrophobic. Passengers were huddled together like cattle. Everywhere the smell of vomit soured the air, and anxiety crackled like electricity. To keep their spirits high, several would sing Yiddish songs together to tide them on their way: "*Geyt, yidelelch, in der vayter velt;*

in Kanada vet is ferdinen gelt" (Go little Jews into the wide world; in Canada you will earn money).[4]

First Stop: Toronto

In 1910, at the age of nineteen, Max Kronish arrived in Toronto. There he found familiar *landsmannschaften*, fellow countrymen, who created chains of social networks of great benefit. They helped to absorb new immigrants, found them housing, and put them in touch with others who shared their interests and plight. Max settled in Lower Spadina, Canada's equivalent in the early decades of the twentieth century to New York City's Lower East Side.[5]

During the day many of Toronto's immigrant Jews worked in an area close to Lower Spadina called Cabbagetown. Cabbagetown, known to all as peddler's row, swarmed with Jews: some were bottle-washing laborers; others sold rags and scraps, cast-off clothing and used furniture. The extreme cold in winter, rife competition, and anti-Semitic occurrences caused a high turnover of peddlers.

Many sought out higher-status jobs, particularly in the ready-made clothing industry. By 1911, twelve-hundred of Toronto's eighteen-thousand Jews were engaged in the clothing industry.[6] Max peddled briefly in Cabbagetown before he found employment in the garment industry as a tailor.[7]

At night, Max Kronish returned to the Kensington Market district of Lower Spadina, a neighborhood that resounded with a cacophony of Yiddish dialects. Once a middle-class residential area, it was about a thirty minute walk from Cabbagetown and the garment industry district. Over time, as immigrants settled in the area, the housing stock deteriorated. Frame houses on narrow streets with disreputable rear structures offered cheap accommodations. Single-family dwellings were subdivided again and again, and landlords crowded more and more tenants into smaller and smaller living spaces.[8]

As a child in the Ukraine, Max Kronish had followed the folkways of Orthodox Judaism. In Toronto, Max's choices were the Orthodox University Avenue and McCaul Avenue synagogues.[9] Nearby, Jews who tried to recreate the Orthodox education of their childhood *shtetls* and who supported Zionism formed the Simcoe Street Talmud Torah. There was also greater opportunity than in Zborow to practice a more liberal Judaism. Holy Blossom, a Reform temple on Bond Street founded by German Jews, catered to the less traditional members of the growing community.

In 1911 Max sent for his sister, Shendel, and his brother, Itzik, to join him in Toronto.[10] Like so many of the Jewish immigrants of that period, their decision to leave Europe depended on having an already-transplanted family member who would help them defray expenses and find housing and employment. Max's parents, Reuven and Leah, did not emigrate from Zborow, the result of which was to prove tragic later on.[11]

Migration to Manhattan and The Yiddishkeit *Network*

Garment industry work in Toronto was frequently disrupted by seasonal dislocations and labor unrest. The failure of workers to form a union in 1912 in Toronto led some strikers to set up their own rival shops and fight for unionization. This created in Max Kronish, and many others, a state of high anxiety regarding future employment.

In 1913, at the age of twenty-three, shortly before Canada entered World War One, Max left his sister and brother in Toronto and resettled in the lower east side of New York.[12] Because New York was the largest garment center, Max believed it would offer better employment opportunities. Ninety percent of New York City's garment industry population at that time were Jews.[13]

Assisted by a social network of *landsleit*, people from his region of the Ukraine, Max quickly gained employment as a tailor. Their advice led Max to seek out the Hebrew Immigrant Aid Society (HIAS). That year he was among the tens of thousands who stopped by the HIAS information bureau at 229 East Broadway. There Max learned of American naturalization and aid programs.

The Lower East Side replicated for many Jewish immigrants the old communities in eastern Europe. Traditional customs and mores formed the foundation of its culture. Synagogues, talmud torahs, and *landsmannschaften* societies were oversubscribed. Each synagogue provided continuity with historic traditions, often as a link to a particular homeland. They served as houses of prayer and learning, as halls for socializing and gossip, and as centers for networking and mutual aid.

Within the neighborhood thrived a Jewish economy where Jewish workers supported storekeepers and landlords, kosher butchers and restaurants. Life was arduous, and poverty was widespread. Between 1890 and 1914 Jewish workers received only a modest raise in real wages.[14]

Slowly, the pervading attitude of pessimism brought over from Europe by the immigrant Jews, changed along with their skills. Traditional habits and non-urban labor vocations were replaced by those more in tune with the American industrial ethos. Newly emerging trade unions allowed a sense of dignity. Night schools provided instruction in English.

Brooklyn: Marriage and Children

With the opening of the Williamsburg Bridge in 1903, the subway to Brooklyn in 1908, and the Manhattan Bridge in 1909, Jews found access to better living conditions across the East River. In the next decade there was an exodus of thousands of Jews from the lower east side to Brooklyn, including Max. An immigrant bourgeoisie began to emerge.

A year after his arrival (1914), Max was introduced to Lena Seligman,[15] the daughter of Moses and Jennie. Two years later Lena and Max were married and they moved to Williamsburg across the East River. Still employed as a tailor and a member of a union, Max was fortunate to work a step above the infamous sweatshops that demoralized the soul with every stitch. He took advantage of the wide-range of socio-economic services his union provided.[16]

Max and Lena participated actively in Yiddish cultural activities and theater. They enjoyed productions, and strongly empathized with New York's Yiddish poets and writers who both celebrated and agonized over coming to a new land. They attended concerts by cantors, who a few years previously had sung to select parochial gatherings, but were now vying for audiences in the growing cosmopolitan environment. Avid readers of *The Forward*, a Yiddish newspaper, Max and Lena eagerly read the letters in *Bintel Brief* and searched for names of extended kin who may have settled in New York.[17]

On February 21, 1917, Max and Lena Kronish celebrated the birth of their first child, Leon. He was given the Hebrew name, Asher. That year was a watershed for both the United States and the Jews. America entered the war against Germany, the Balfour Declaration committed the British government to support the establishment of a Jewish homeland in Palestine, and the Turks surrendered Jerusalem.

Sylvia, Leon's sister, was born in 1920, followed five years later in 1925 by a brother, Zev.[18]

Leon Kronish and Judaism: The Early Days

The Williamsburg neighborhood in which the Kronish *kinder* (children) grew up was marked by Yiddish culture and an easing of the deprivations of the World War One period. Lena accommodated herself to American-style manners and habits.

The children grew up with Jewish street culture, the synagogue, and the talmud torah. Each sabbath, Leon attended the local Orthodox synagogue and observed sabbath rituals. The Kronish South Second Street residence was kosher and exhibited the traditional Jewish artifacts such as a *mezuzah*, a Hanukkah menorah, sabbath candlesticks, and *havdalah* candle. On the High Holy Days, the family would go to synagogue and return to enjoy Lena's cooking. Family friends often accompanied them.

Max spoke Yiddish more often than not, and the children, Leon, Sylvia and Zev, quickly learned it as their first language. Grandfather Seligman, Lena's father, demanded it. An avid reader of Yiddish and the owner of a large library of Yiddish books and newspapers, he re-created for his grandchildren the Yiddish-centered home of eastern Europe. He particularly loved writers such as Sholem Asch who brought to life the colorful experiences of the Jewish community in the United States. Frequently, articles in the Yiddish newspapers *The Tageblatt* and *The Forward* became topics of conversation,[19] with the viewpoints expressed in Abraham Cahan's socialist *The Forward* usually winning the day.[20]

Max Kronish: A Socialist Zionist

Economically, the Kronish family benefitted when Max moved from being a tailor to a cutter in the manufacturing of dresses and other garments.[21] As a committed union member in the mid-1920s, Max actively participated in his local. In the 1920s the clothing industry yielded, in terms of value, the fourth largest product in the United States and the Jewish proletariat of New York was a significant feature of urban economic life.[22]

Leon Kronish listened to his father's changing attitudes as a union member. As a child he heard his father, the first-generation Jewish American, discuss the socialist ideals for adjusting to society. As he grew older, his father became more concerned with how his union and others, especially those with significant Jewish membership, could contribute to the transformation of American unionism.

Max Kronish's interest in expressing socialist values and advocating better working conditions was in large measure due to union leaders like David Dubinsky, Sidney Hillman, and Samuel Gompers who were actively designing the socialist blueprint for Leon's generation. Attending union events, Max saw Republican and Democratic politicians court Jewish union leaders wherever they gathered: meetings, lectures, social events, parades, and soapbox speeches.[23] Max's support of a socialist ethic complemented his religious beliefs. Social justice was paramount.

In addition to his union activities, Max was attracted to Zionism during the 1920s.[24] Louis Brandeis, the renowned Supreme Court Justice, and one of the early American Zionist leaders, presented Zionism as an outgrowth of the inherent dynamism of Jewish history, not of its religious traditions. "My approach to Zionism is through Americanism. To be good Americans, we must be better Jews and to be better Jews, we must become Zionists."[25]

Although the appeal of the Zionist Organization of America was weak during the 1920s, declining from one-hundred-and-fifty-thousand members in 1917 to eighteen-thousand in 1929, a handful of Zionist youth movements found fertile ground in the crowded halls of talmud torahs and afternoon Hebrew schools.[26]

Max's interest in Zionism rubbed off on his son. Shortly before his bar mitzvah Leon Kronish became a member of *Hashomer Hatzair*, a socialist-Zionist youth movement, whose goal was to prepare boys and girls for *aliya* (immigration) to Palestine. Some of the movement's leaders had served in the Jewish Legion during World War One. One evening a week he attended meetings and participated in their activities. Several of his close friends were active in other Zionist youth groups, such as Junior Hadassah, Young Judea and Habonim.

As a member of *Hashomer Hatzair*, Leon Kronish met Julius Freeman. They spoke modern Hebrew, sang songs together, argued about Zionist ideology and shared dreams of what a future state of Israel might be like.[27] With their peers they formed the first generation of American-born youth in the movement. Over the next decade a number of American *halutzim* (pioneers), products of *Hashomer Hatzair*, would settle in Palestine and become an integral part of the agricultural colonization program of Palestinian labor.

Leon's Kronish's gravitation to a socialist Zionist youth group was due also to the rise of anti-Semitism in the 1920s. The 1920 publication of the notorious *Protocols of the Elders of Zion* in Henry Ford's newspaper, the *Dearborn Independent*, continued to stir old fears a decade later.[28] Through a series of articles, Jews were viciously attacked in all areas of life including baseball ("Jewish Degradation of American Baseball"); music ("Jewish Jazz"); and community organization ("The Jewish Kehillah Grips New York").[29]

Moreover, Kronish had personally felt the teeth of anti-Semitism:

> As a child I lived and grew up on the edge of a non-Jewish neighborhood. To walk to public school or to go to talmud torah meant walking through "the enemy camp." I was afraid because I had already been beaten up many times by non-Jewish children who ganged up on me.[30]

The Zionist position that Jews had to liberate themselves and create a Jewish state as a response to anti-Semitism was appealing to him and many others who joined Zionist youth movements.

Religious Education and Bar Mitzvah

Talmud torah education had a profound influence on Leon Kronish's formative years. He went from public school to the Talmud Torah of Williamsburg daily. Stamped by the *Haskalah* (Jewish enlightenment) and Zionism, the Bible rather than the Talmud, was the central subject at his talmud torah. Modern Hebrew literature also was an important part of the curriculum, and Hebrew was studied as a living language. Students read the Hebrew bi-weekly youth newspaper, *Hadoar Lanoar*, and material prepared by the *Histadruth Ivrith*, an organization of American Hebraists. Influenced by Samson Benderly, a Zionist Hebrew educator, the Williamsburg Talmud Torah introduced into the curriculum Zionist songs and the study of the history and the geography of Palestine.[31]

Jewish tradition was more than just the teaching of the traditional subjects of Torah, Talmud, and ethics, as in the *Pirke Avot* (Ethics of the Fathers); for Samson Benderly, Jewish tradition also meant a firm commitment to the reconstitution of Palestine as a home for the Jewish people and as a center of spiritual influence.

In February 1930, Leon Kronish and his family celebrated his bar mitzvah. *Yitro*, his *sedrah* (portion of the Torah), culminates in God's revelation to the Jewish people through the Ten Commandments. It includes honoring one's parents, not solely as a social norm, but also as a religious obligation. The Haftorah (the prophetic portion), *Isaiah* chapter 6, recounts how the prophet is consecrated when a seraph touches his lips and prepares him to speak the word of God. The Torah and Haftorah portions reinforced Leon's religious beliefs. The bar mitzvah symbolically took on the meaning of affirming his ancestry and committing him to be a son of the covenant.[32]

During his high school years, Leon Kronish spent his free time earning extra money teaching bar mitzvah classes.

Lillian Austin: The Future Mrs. Leon Kronish

Leon Kronish also spent his time courting Lillian Austin. The Austins lived on Second Street South, a few houses from the Kronishes.[33] Like Leon Kronish, Lillian Austin attended Eastern District High School, and they had mutual friends. According to Lillian, "Leo was tall, thin, and handsome, the kind of guy who was fun to be with."[34] Known for his sense of humor, Leon often composed songs with clever rhymes. Lillian Austin and their friends vied to be recognized in one of his couplets.

Lillian's parents, Sarah (Marcus) and Adolph Austin, immigrated to the United States from east central Europe before World War One. The Austin family's integration into America was less traditionally religious than the Kronishes' and it led to more rapid social mobility. Adolph had matriculated to be a doctor in Austria. He changed course when he immigrated, and opened a successful vegetarian restaurant, the *Pine Tree* at 38th Street and 6th Avenue, on the outskirts of Manhattan's garment district.

Many of Manhattan's garment workers ate at the *Pine Tree* where Yiddish was the dominant language of the clientele. Articles from journals such as the socialist *Tsukunft* and the Labor Zionist *Yiddisher Kemfer* were debated between servings of blintzes and borscht.

Like Leon Kronish, Lillian Austin was well-versed in Yiddish. Her father, Adolph, frequently bought tickets for the Yiddish theater and brought his wife Sarah, and his four girls, along for the shows. These productions included I. J. Singer's *Yoshe Kalb* and *The Brothers Ashkenazi*, S. Ansky's *The Dybbuk*, and Peretz Hirschbein's *Greenfields*.[35]

Leon and Lillian and the Bridge Between Past and Future

The Kronishes and the Austins practiced different Jewish lifestyles. But both were first-generation immigrant Americans strongly connected to a European Jewish past. Their children, Leon and Lillian, born in the United States, looked to America to forge their futures.[36]

During the 1930s, Jewish youth, like Leon Kronish and Lillian Austin, were buffeted by rapidly changing economic conditions and foreign policies. There was neither the economic optimism of the previous decade nor the idealism fostered by the young League of Nations. The Depression, with its high unemployment and bankruptcies, retarded economic growth.

The rise of Hitler and the Nazis brought foreboding. Jewish refugees frequently were unable to enter the country as the United States dug into its increasing isolationism. Changes in British policy towards a Jewish homeland demonstrated the impotence of American-Jewish lobbying in trying to influence British foreign policy.[37]

Although American Jews had little influence on President Roosevelt's foreign policy regarding European and Palestinian Jews, the increasing number of Jewish youth reaching voting eligibility began to have an impact on domestic issues. Eastern European Jews, as a collective entity, had enough political clout to lend weight to state[38] and presidential elections.

FDR and the Changing Political Allegiance of Jews

American Jewry's alliance to national parties at presidential elections in the twentieth century changed in 1932. With the exception of 1916, more Jews voted Republican than Democrat. Since 1932, the Democrats have received the majority of Jewish votes.[39] One immediate difference was that several of the new president's advisors were Jewish. They would come to play a significant role in developing Roosevelt's various New Deal policies.[40]

Leon Kronish observed these changes on the political landscape and discussed the consequences with family and friends. Would Roosevelt's advisors Henry Morgenthau, Jr. and Felix Frankfurter assist in developing policies to aid European Jewish refugees? Would David Dubinsky, president of the International Ladies Garment Workers Union (1932) and vice-president of the American Federation of Labor (1934) lend his union weight to Jewish concerns? Would the fostering of new Jewish organizations – American Jewish Congress (1917), the United Jewish Appeal (1925) and the Council of Jewish Federations (1932) – galvanize Jews to support Jewish causes?[41]

Kronish typified the youth of second generation American-Jewish voters: "earthy... ethnic but rarely ethnocentric [and proud] of a Jewish presence in the congressional delegation and political offices, enumerated annually in the Anglo-Jewish press."[42]

Brooklyn College

When Leon Kronish graduated from high school in 1932, he was competent in Greek, Latin and Hebrew. Hebrew had been transformed from the language of the Bible to the language of modern Palestine. Through *Hashomer Hatzair*, his Zionist youth movement, and the talmud torah, he met youth leaders and teachers who knew first-hand about Palestine. Leon in turn, coached his brother, Zev, in Hebrew studies.[43] Zev applied to the Herzliyah High School in Manhattan. In due course, Zev would join *Hashomer Hadati* (later *B'nai Akiva*), the Zionist organization for Orthodox Jewish youth.

Between 1932 and 1936 Leon Kronish and Lillian Austin both attended Brooklyn College. Leon majored in the classics, Greek and Latin, and also took electives in psychology and archaeology. Lillian majored in English literature.

Leon Kronish's courses in psychology led him to Freud's *Introduction to Psycho-Analysis*, first published in English in 1917, the year Leon was born. By the mid 1930s, Freud's work had motivated psychologists to try to understand the relationship between the psyche, totalitarianism and Nazism. Leon Kronish's father's family still lived in Zborow.[44]

To improve his knowledge of Palestine, Kronish studied archaeology. Archaeological discoveries created excitement for the handful of faculty at the new Hebrew University in Jerusalem and were popularized in Zionist publications.[45] His archaeological studies were complemented by extra-curricular activities with the campus-based Menorah Society[46] and the university's Zionist programs.

Leon Kronish's interests in psychology and archaeology were related: an understanding of what motivated Jewish people was as important as comprehending the connection to the past. By viewing Judaism through lost fragments, Kronish hoped to understand and recapture parts of a tradition that had long remained dormant.

The Decisive Turn

Graduating from Brooklyn College in 1936, Leon Kronish taught in various Jewish schools the following year.

In 1937 Kronish turned from secular to parochial studies and enrolled at the Teacher's Institute of the Jewish Theological Seminary in New York City.

Kronish's decision to enter a program leaning towards a Jewish vocation came after much consideration. As a first-generation American Jew who grew up in New York in the 1920s and 1930s, he felt pulled between his immigrant parents, on the one hand, who represented old-world traditions transplanted from eastern Europe, and by his peers, on the other hand, who sought achievement of the American dream through acculturation.

Kronish was part of a generation that demonstrated a strong desire to assimilate into the mythic melting pot. Yiddish parodies, mimicking talmudic style, captured the spirit of Jewish Americans who salivated at acculturating. "Akabiah, the son of Charlie said: Consider three things and you will be able to exist in America: forget who you are, wear a mask before those who know you, and do anything you can."[47]

But joining the American melting pot and becoming an integrationist had its price. Abraham Cahan, editor of *The Forward*, a Yiddish newspaper, and considered by many to be the finest Jewish-American writer of the early twentieth century, illustrated the moral costs of success in his novel *The Rise of David Levinsky*, which was read by the young adult, Leon Kronish. This theme was echoed over and over in the Jewish literature of the period.

At the same time, like many of his generation, he felt instinctually Jewish. His life remained infused with *Yiddishkeit*. In his neighborhood there was little choice. If he was to have a social and religious life, he was compelled to practice the Judaism of his parents. Living in a homogeneous residential area, Leon met his peers on the stoops in front of their houses and apartment blocks and in the corner stores. Each life-cycle event he attended, each *bris* (circumcision), bar mitzvah, or wedding, reinforced his Jewish lifestyle and his commitment to preserving Jewish tradition.

Moreover, Kronish felt that his opportunities for higher secular education were limited. University admissions quota policies that discriminated against Jews were the norm in those days.[48] Many of his generation that were able to enter these institutions quickly divorced themselves from their heritage, a reaction he considered deplorable. The enrichment of Jewish identity was foremost for Leon Kronish.

The Influence of Mordecai Kaplan and the Jewish Theological Seminary

During his years at Brooklyn College, Kronish had grown increasingly attracted to the writings of Rabbi Mordecai Kaplan of the Jewish Theological Seminary—one of the major intellectual/spiritual activists of twentieth-century American Jewish life.

As a student member of a Menorah Society, Kronish had read several of Kaplan's articles published in the *Menorah Journal* (e.g., "On Creeds and Wants," 1933) and his 1934 book, *Judaism as a Civilization: Toward a Reconstruction of American Jewish Life*, Kaplan's most important work.[49]

Leon Kronish entered the Jewish Theological Seminary Teacher's Institute in the fall of 1937 and, there, came into direct contact with Mordecai Kaplan, Dean of the Teacher's Institute and founder of Reconstructionism, a movement for Jewish cultural revitalization.

Kaplan had immigrated to New York as a young boy in the late 1880s. The son of a distinguished rabbinic scholar, he was ordained a rabbi by the

Jewish Theological Seminary in 1902. Complementing his theological training, Kaplan studied at Columbia University and embraced the philosophy of pragmatism taught to him by John Dewey.

In 1917 Kaplan became the rabbi of the first New York Jewish Synagogue Center and established a movement where ethnicity and Judaism would be enmeshed and enriched through recreation and culture. Influenced by Horace Kallen's notion of cultural pluralism as a rationale for ethnic identity reinforcement, Kaplan understood that many Jews no longer held orthodox beliefs but still desired to retain Jewish affiliations and serve the Jewish people. His vision generated the formation of many centers, some attached to synagogues, others "reconstructed" as secular expressions of Jewish ethnicity with no religious face.

In *Judaism as a Civilization*, Kaplan conceived of Judaism as an evolving civilization with its own culture and ethos which needed to fit into American society. Theology is replaced with cultural anthropology, and Judaism is reconstructed by sociological thinking.

Kaplan viewed God as "natural," the sum of the community; Judaism's function was social and centered on the idea of peoplehood. The God that spoke at Sinai continued to reappear and be reinterpreted in every generation. There was no "supernatural revelation or supernatural 'choosing' of the Jews."[50]

Rather, the Jewish experience is one of an "organic community," with each element (language, literature, art, folkways, values, homeland, identity) interdependent. The social function of rituals and traditions is to ensure continuity. Kaplan's ideology allowed for American Jews, even those who are secularized, to possess a vibrant, dynamic Jewish identity within a pluralistic society. America did not have to be a melting pot.

Kaplan expanded these ideas in his lectures to his students at the Jewish Theological Seminary and debated with them the meaning of concepts such as "chosenness," "peoplehood," "prayer" and "Zionism."

For Kaplan, Zionism could be viewed instrumentally. Following the lead of Ahad Ha'am, an early Zionist theoretician, Kaplan took the position that one could support Zionism without *aliya* (immigration). Kaplan refused to accept the Zionist notion that it was necessary for a Jew to live in his own community in Palestine, in a majority culture, rather than in a minority culture, even in the United States, a democracy.

In Kaplan's view, political allegiance for American Jews was to America, religious allegiance was to Judaism. Culturally they overlapped: Jews could combine the culture of an American homeland with the Jewish culture of their ancestry, and support a Jewish homeland in Palestine.

Kaplan taught Leon and the other students that Reconstructionism was a way of thinking, not another religious denomination.[51] Its mandate: democratize the Jewish community, intensify Jewish education, cultivate the Jewish arts, re-

Judaize the Jewish home, rebuild the Jewish homeland in Palestine, enrich the content of Jewish worship, and raise the ethical standards of the community.[52]

In Kaplan's Society for the Advancement of Judaism, women participated in religious services as equals to men and were among the first women to become bat mitzvah. Women also took part in concerts, plays, forums, study circles and sports programs. Leon and his fellow students learned that a synagogue had the potential to be in the forefront of transforming Judaism to match the social, educational, recreational and religious ethos of Americans.

Alexander Dushkin: A Second Mentor

Leon Kronish was also motivated by the presence of Alexander Dushkin.[53] Dushkin, a disciple of Samson Benderly, the father of professional Jewish education in the United States, was a strong Zionist educator. Dushkin believed in the communal sponsoring of Jewish education as an instrument for Jewish and ethnic (Zionist) survival.

Kronish had come under the spell of "the Samson Benderly Boys" (Alexander Dushkin, Isaac Berkson and Emmanuel Gamoran) while teaching in Jewish schools the previous year. Dushkin had been the assistant of David de Sola Pool in 1910 when the New York Kehillah established a Jewish Board of Education. Over the next three decades, he helped to establish the School of Education at The Hebrew University of Jerusalem, was the head of the Board of Jewish Education in Chicago, and was named the director of the Jewish Education Committee of New York City in the late 1930s.

Dushkin extended Horace Kallen's notion of cultural pluralism by combining it with John Dewey's idea that education itself was a process. For Dushkin, the teaching of the Bible as literature and Hebrew as a modern language was academically justifiable. Dushkin adopted Ahad Ha'am's perspective that teaching Jewish culture as a means to support Zionism is the best way to fight assimilation.

Dushkin was interested in creating a "state of mind" first, then filling it with content. Synthesizing Hebraism, Zionism and pedagogical methods was only half the lesson. The other half was animating the community to become responsible for developing Jewish education. These two components were the building blocks, and were vital for the survival and renewal of Jewish life in America.[54] From Dushkin and his colleagues, Kronish was inspired to believe that it was his personal task, if he chose a leadership role, to galvanize the community to enhance Jewish education.

The Kronish Synthesis

Both Mordecai Kaplan and Alexander Dushkin opened Kronish's eyes to the regenerative ideas that would shape second-generation American Jews. The tensions between cultural pluralism and religious-ethnic parochialism, Zionism and American patriotism, would occupy Leon Kronish's thought and action in the decades ahead.

During his year at the Jewish Theological Seminary Teacher's Institute, Kronish experienced first-hand the struggle between the Reconstructionists (cultural pluralists) and traditionalists over Judaism. Kaplan's changes in the prayer book, and alteration of the content of prayers and the order of worship, were challenged continuously.

Kaplan's deletion from the prayers of references to salvation, the resurrection of the dead and the popular *Kol Nidre* prayer chanted on Yom Kippur, were viewed as contrived by the more "orthodox" arms of Judaism.[55] With the emergence in book form of this creative religious literature, the conflict between the two groups intensified. In 1945 the Union of Orthodox Rabbis excommunicated Kaplan for "expressing atheism, heresy and disbelief in the basic tenets of Judaism."[56] In their view, modernization and secularization of Jewish tradition skirted heresy.

Despite their great impact, both generally and on Kronish in particular, neither Kaplan nor Dushkin spent a great deal of time at the Institute. Dushkin spent most of his time in Jerusalem as a professor of Educational Method at the Hebrew University. Kaplan's rivalry with Cyrus Adler, president of the Jewish Theological Seminary, and Louis Ginzberg, its most noted scholar, provoked "considerable discomfort [for him] at the seminary."[57] Their absence had a profound influence on Kronish, pushing him in unanticipated directions for his own life.

The narrowness of a sectarian approach to Jewish life experienced at the Jewish Theological Seminary and the inability to meet face to face with his mentors on a regular basis caused Kronish to examine other options.

Kaplan's and Dushkin's ideas pushed Kronish to think of America and Zionism as complementary. *Aliya* (immigration) was not necessary, although it was an option. Leon Kronish wanted "to serve the Jewish people" in the United States of America.

Adopting an ethos where American Judaism was liberating rather than confining, Kronish looked downtown to Stephen Wise for guidance and for the opportunity to fulfill his vocation: to become a rabbi. He enrolled as a rabbinical student at the Jewish Institute of Religion, the other major non-Orthodox seminary in New York.

Stephen Wise: A Prophet for Twentieth-Century American Jewry

Rabbi Stephen Wise was a towering figure who played a dominant role in reshaping the landscape of American Jewry during the first half of the twentieth century. Living in a time of imposing political figures—Winston

Churchill, Franklin Delano Roosevelt and David Ben-Gurion—the magnetic Wise was equally formidable and knew the others personally.

I. F. Stone, in an article in the *Post-Home News* wrote, "I am afraid I never got over seeing Rabbi Wise through the eyes of a hero-worshipping small boy."[58] No pulpit resembled his; no Jewish religious institution could match his program founded on social vision and social service. He was one of America's foremost Zionists in the first half of the twentieth century.[59]

An apocryphal story describes Wise's stature in America. When a letter addressed to "Rabbi, United States" arrived from Europe, postal authorities had no hesitation in delivering it to Wise.

In 1897 Wise was a co-founder of the Federation of American Zionists and attended the Second Zionist Congress in Basel in 1898. That year, Herzl appointed Wise, at the age of twenty-four, as the American Secretary of the World Zionist movement. For the next fifty years Wise was relentless in prodding and cajoling American Jews to make Zionism an American Jewish issue. In 1917 he helped found the American Jewish Congress as a Zionist forum and an alternative to the American Jewish Committee which he viewed as elitist and weak on Zionism.

Time and time again Rabbi Wise emphasized the importance of *Klal Yisrael*—the collectivity of the Jewish people. For Wise, like Kaplan, peoplehood was primal. And like Kaplan, Wise believed that Zionism was compatible with American loyalties.[60]

Rabbi Wise was a maverick when it came to religion. He was privately ordained and moved from Orthodoxy to Reform into his own independent synagogue in less than a decade and a half. Offered the most prestigious Reform congregation in New York, Temple Emanuel in 1907, he turned it down over a "free speech" dispute with the board of trustees.

In its place, Wise established The Free Synagogue of New York and abolished pew rents and regular dues. Frequently he travelled to the Lower East Side on Friday nights on missions of converting traditional Jews to Reform Judaism. Holding meetings in Clinton Hall, he attracted thousands of second-generation Jewish Americans whose parents often castigated him for "practicing a foreign religion."[61]

Stephen Wise and The Jewish Institute of Religion

The same year Mordecai Kaplan established the Society for the Advancement of Judaism (1922), Wise founded The Jewish Institute of Religion (JIR) to train rabbis for a career that crossed denominational lines. Dissatisfied with the anti-Zionism that pervaded the Reform seminary, Hebrew Union College (HUC), Wise reached out to those with Zionist sympathies.

Although Rabbi Wise removed himself from the inner circle of the Reform movement and did not take a leading role in the Central Conference of

American Rabbis (CCAR), he remained influential and considered himself within the Reform camp. Wise's disenchantment with the movement's lack of recognition of the needs of the times and its disinterest in Zionism fueled his determination to confront Reform Judaism from his own organizational base. For Wise, the unity of the Jewish people, *Klal Yisrael*, was foremost. American Jewry could not afford the luxury of alienating committed Zionists.

Wise was a Democrat in politics. His social conscience aligned him to policies advocating social welfare and human dignity. Jewishness meant a sense of oneness with all Jews in all lands whatever the circumstances and their ways of practicing Judaism.

The Jewish Institute of Religion stressed "the prophecy of tomorrow" rather than "survival of yesterday."

In 1908, Wise had campaigned for women's suffrage. In 1909, he was a founder of the National Association for the Advancement of Colored People. In 1914, he labored to introduce social welfare legislation. In the 1920s, he fought Henry Ford and his anti-Semitic mouthpiece, the *Dearborn Independent*. In the 1930s, he criticized America's restrictive immigration policies, while supporting Roosevelt's New Deal agendas. And in the 1940s, he spearheaded Madison Square Garden rallies against Nazism.

Understandably then, Rabbi Stephen Wise was hailed in his own lifetime as the twentieth-century American embodiment of the prophetic tradition.

Leon Kronish Meets Stephen Wise and Other Luminaries

In 1938, Kronish entered the Jewish Institute of Religion. Most of the fifty-four matriculated students were also sons of first-generation eastern European immigrants and shared the ideals of American Zionism. Nearly all were college graduates. Wise, now an elder statesman of American Jewry, was the magnet that drew them and linked them.

During Kronish's years of study at the Jewish Institute of Religion, 1938 to 1942, Rabbi Wise was president of the American Jewish Congress, the World Jewish Congress and the Zionist Organization of America. He served as chairman of the United Palestine Appeal and as a member of President Roosevelt's Advisory Committee on Political Refugees. Students modeled themselves after him and "conceived the rabbinate as committed to Zion, to the people of Israel, and to social justice."[62]

The faculty of the Jewish Institute of Religion included Henry Slonimsky, Dean and Professor of Ethics and Philosophy of Religion, Chaim Tchernowitz, Professor of Talmud, Shalom Spiegel, Professor of Hebrew Language and Literature, Ralph Marcus, Professor of Semitic Philosophy, Guido Kisch, Professor of Law and Jewish History, Sidney Goldstein, Professor of Social Service and John Tepfer,[63] Lecturer in Jewish History.

Samson Benderly and Isaac Berkson served as Lecturers in Education and Salo Baron acted as the Director of Advanced Studies, while still a professor of History at Columbia University. Harry Wolfson, of Harvard University, had served as Professor of Jewish Philosophy at the Institute in the 1920s and continued to visit and deliver guest lectures. Abram Granison was the director of rabbinical placement and field activities.

The curriculum emphasized Bible, *midrash* (exegesis of scripture) and Hebrew literature. Courses were taught in English and Hebrew, and there was a community service component sponsored by the Free Synagogue. Graduation with the title of rabbi and a Master of Hebrew Literature required 130 hours of classroom work, a comprehensive exam, and a thesis.

Wise the Teacher

Every week, Kronish accompanied Rabbi Wise to the chapel on the fourth floor, where students led morning prayers before classes.[64] Rabbi Wise would then hold a lively colloquy with his students, frequently in his study, a large room with stone walls and wooden bookcases, tall chairs around a table, and plain wooden benches for the latecomers.

Wise talked about many things: his conversations with Roosevelt, Ben-Gurion, and other political leaders; his suffering when he talked to bereaved families; his correspondence with rabbis, friends, and congregants; his joy at attending the bar mitzvah of the son of the policeman who patrolled the Institute's beat.[65]

From the students, he elicited ideas for weekly sermons and explored their thoughts and their feelings on a wide variety of issues on the American-Jewish agenda.

At 11 a.m., Rabbi Wise would lecture on homiletics, the art of preaching. Each student was responsible for preparing a sermon, and its content and delivery were carefully evaluated. Kronish found this experience challenging and quickly found that he had a natural flair for the art of oratory. Rabbi Wise complimented him on his abilities and worked with him to polish his style.[66] It was here that Leon developed his oratorical skills, which was later to become one of his dominant characteristics as a rabbi and communal leader.

In tribute to Rabbi Wise's people skills, Samuel Karff has written that "nearly all of the Institute's graduates harbored a lasting affection for their one-time mentor."[67] This was certainly the case with Leon Kronish. Much of his rabbinical style and substance for decades to come was molded in the image of Rabbi Stephen Wise.

Observing Wise through periods of crisis, Kronish came to understand the complexity of the man and the rabbinical vocation. Each critical period carried moral dilemmas, calls to social action, and tensions in searching for solutions to problems. From Britain's White Paper on Palestine in 1939, to

Pearl Harbor in 1941, to the recognition by the U.S. State Department of the liquidation of Jews in 1942, Kronish learned that each crisis initiated a process of self-discovery.

Many years later, Leon Kronish remembered Wise sharing a cable with his students that illustrated this process. Wise was preparing to send the cable to President Roosevelt. It concerned Britain's policy shift, the 1939 White Paper that would restrict legal immigration to Palestine and reject the recommendation of the Peel Commission and the terms of the Balfour Declaration.

Debate ensued about the impact the policy would have on European Jews living in the dreadful shadow of Nazism. The discussion extended into the anti-Zionist position of some components of American Jewry, and contradicted Roosevelt's isolationist policy regarding political refugees. Later that day, when Kronish left the Institute to return home, he was struck by the awesome challenges of becoming a rabbi and communal leader under the influence of Stephen Wise.[68]

The Jewish Institute of Religion and Contemporary Scholarship

The other teachers at the Jewish Institute of Religion similarly opened new horizons for Kronish.

Henry Slonimsky profoundly influenced his students. An inspiring teacher, he was described by Richard Aldington in his memoir, *Life for Life's Sake*, as "a personality [that] stands along side with Yeats and Lawrence.... Slonimsky talks books better than most people write them.... We would sit for hours while he talked of Hellenism and Plato, of Homer and Thucydides.... We [were] moved by the beauty and grandeur of what he set before us."[69]

Chaim Tchernowitz was an internationally acclaimed talmudic scholar who combined traditional studies with modern empirical research as a means to rejuvenate Jewish learning. He had founded his own yeshivah and rabbinical seminary in Odessa (1907) which attracted the Russian Jewish intelligentsia including Hayyim Bialik and Joseph Klausner. He was friendly with Ahad Ha'Am, and a strong advocate for Jewish political independence and Zionism.

Studying with Professor Tchernowitz, Kronish's thinking matured regarding the link between today's contemporary Jewish problems and those in the era preceding the late Second Temple, a time when the last Jewish sovereign state was established. Tchernowitz was a man of ideals and founded in 1940 the Hebrew monthly, *Bitzaron*.[70]

Professor Guido Kisch, a historian of law, was a victim of Nazi persecution and was forced to flee Germany in 1935. He also founded and edited a journal while Leon was a student (*Historia Judaica* in 1938.)[71] Kronish studied European Jewry and Zionism with Kisch, and on his counsel read Herzl's diary.

Discussing an essay Kronish submitted to Kisch on "Herzl and Palestine," Kisch wrote: "Mr. Kronish's essay is more a sermonic than an historical appraisal of Herzl. The main problem, being Herzl's attitude toward the Palestinian question, is touched upon only superficially."[72] Indeed, Kronish was destined to become a rabbi and Zionist activist, rather than a historian.

Like many of the seminary students of his day, Kronish tended to ignore the Palestinian-Arab viewpoints and the Zionist reactions to them. Kisch, who knew first-hand the bite of Nazism, appealed to his students to look at both sides. As Amos Elon, an Israeli historian, has poignantly pointed out in *The Israelis*, before the Holocaust Herzl and most Zionists drew a utopian picture of the future Jewish commonwealth. There was little awareness and credibility given to the "anti-Zionist nationalism among the Palestinian Arabs."[73]

The World – Good and Bad – Comes to JIR

Students at the Jewish Institute of Religion, in addition to their regular faculty, were treated to visiting scholars. In 1938 Gershom Scholem served as Stroock Lecturer and delivered a series of seven lectures, six in English and one in Hebrew, on the nature and development of Jewish mysticism. Three years later when the first edition of *Major Trends in Jewish Mysticism* appeared, Scholem thanked Professor Henry Slonimsky and Ralph Marcus, Dr. Stephen S. Wise, "not only for the invitation... but also for his generous consent to their publication in the present form," and Shalom Spiegel "for his unfailing friendship and readiness to give of his time and help."[74]

Kronish served as Director of Student Activities during 1938-1940 and was responsible for arranging the programs for students when guests were invited to lecture. In this capacity he met Professors Gershom Scholem, Harry Wolfson and Salo Baron. He also helped to coordinate events off campus. In November 1939 he coordinated a group visit to the Palestine Pavilion of the World's Fair and heard Louis Lipsky of the American Jewish Congress plead the Zionist case. In 1940, he marched with his fellow students throughout the streets of the city rousing attention to the menace of Nazism.[75]

The full dimensions of this menace were revealed to the students at JIR shortly before Kronish's graduation, when Wise informed them of the Nazi death camps. The World Jewish Congress had notified the American Jewish Congress that Hitler was annihilating European Jewry in crematoria.

Henry Morgenthau, Jr., Secretary of the Treasury, some years later spoke of the debilitating effect of Rabbi Wise's report:

> I will never forget the day in '42 as long as I live when Dr. Wise and his son James came to call on me in the Treasury and read me that unbelievable cable telling about the crematoria in Europe. That day changed my life. I will never recover from it....[76]

Marriage, a Son and the First Congregation

During his second year of rabbinical studies, Leon Kronish and Lillian Austin were married on January 19, 1940. They then moved north to the Bronx from Williamsburg.

In the summer of 1941, while Kronish was still in rabbinical school, Dean Slonimsky offered him the position of student rabbi at the Huntington Jewish Center on Long Island. The congregation's rabbi, Sidney Hoenig, was leaving to serve as chaplain in the army.

From 1941 to 1944, Leon and Lillian Kronish lived in Huntington—where their first son, Jordan, was born on August 3, 1942—and experienced first-hand the transformation undulating through American synagogues. The Huntington Synagogue-Center had functioning adult education classes, a junior congregation, after-school Hebrew classes, and auxiliary associations such as sisterhoods and men's clubs. It served the needs of the growing number of middle class families by functioning as an "arena for ethnic-based socializing and group mobilization."[77] And it reinforced Leon Kronish's understanding of Kaplan's notion of vocation for those who chose rabbinical careers.

Finishing the Thesis

While serving as rabbi at the Huntington Jewish Center, Kronish completed his thesis, *Educating Children and Young People for Jewish Public Worship*, under the supervision of Rabbi L. Schwartz. He examined Morris Silverman's *Junior Prayer Book*, the current field of youth worship, and experiential services developed by Nathan Brilliant and Lillie Braverman at the New York Euclid Temple. He concluded that youth services had to be more experiential, dynamic and aesthetic.

> Children should be motivated to utilize their creative powers (art, dance, poetry, pageantry).... The intensification of Jewish consciousness should be considered the primary objective of public worship, [and should include] expressions of hope for national restoration.[78]

This line of thinking became very prevalent in his early years in the rabbinate in which he wrote many innovative liturgical prayers.[79] It also pointed to a theme that would take increasing prominence in the years to follow: the redemption of *Eretz Yisrael* through Zionist activism.[80]

Leon Kronish graduated from the Jewish Institute of Religion in June 1942 with a Masters of Hebrew Letters and rabbinic ordination. He and Lillian celebrated their exceptional good fortune—together they would dedicate themselves to the service of the Jewish people.

1937-1944: A Life is Launched

By the time he left for Miami Beach in 1944, Kronish had become an exemplary representative of the generation of American Jews from New York between the two world wars.

His parents were Orthodox Jews, born in Europe, who made their start in America as socialist Zionists working in the garment industry. As the first son of these parents, his first language was Yiddish—supplemented, from the Jewish perspective, by the modern Hebrew he learned in talmud torah.

Educationally, he was formed by a not-unusual mix for his generation of Orthodox, *Yiddishkeit*, and assimilationist tendencies, following particularly the socialist Zionist inclinations of his family.

Perhaps most importantly for the path he would blaze for himself in the tropical environs of Miami Beach, Kronish had the privilege of encountering directly two of the leading lights of twentieth-century American life.[81]

The most important was Rabbi Stephen Wise, the founder of the Jewish Institute of Religion, where Kronish was ordained in 1942. Only slightly less important was Rabbi Mordecai Kaplan, the founder of Reconstructionism, a movement of Jewish cultural and spiritual renewal, whom he encountered at Teachers' Institute. In their view, there was no conflict between a complete political devotion to the United States and a complete religious and cultural commitment to world Jewry (*Klal Yisrael*) in general, and the Zionist community in *Eretz Yisrael*/Palestine in particular.

Personally, he had the joy of a happy marriage to a woman he had known since high school, as well as the birth of a son.

Thus prepared, Leon Kronish was about to embark on his fateful meeting with the people, both Jewish and Gentile, and politics of Miami Beach—a city he would come to call "the capital of the American Negev."

Max and Lena Kronish, Leon's parents.

Leon Kronish, age 2.

(Right) Bar Mitzvah, 1930.

(Below) Talmud Torah Graduation, 1931.
(Leon is standing, 2nd on right).

(Left) Lillian Austin and Leon Kronish, late 1930s.

(Below) Marraige, 1940.

Ordination of Rabbi Leon Kronish (back row, second from the right), Jewish Institute of Religion, 1942.

(Left) Leon Kronish with son, Ronald, celebrating Purim, mid-1950s.

(Right) Jordan Kronish's Bar Mitzvah, 1955.

(Above) Ordination of Rabbi Ronald Kronish, 1973. (Left to right) Rabbi Leon Kronish, Rabbi Ronald Kronish, Rabbi Alfred Gottschalk, President HUC-JIR.

(Below) A Family Reunion, 1989. (Back row, left to right) Sari Kronish, Ronald Kronish, Maxine Kronish Snyder, Eddie Snyder, Ariella Kronish (in front of Eddie), Amy Kronish. (Front row, left to right) Davida Snyder, Leon Kronish, Dahlia Kronish and Ami Snyder.

Chapter Three

MIAMI BEACH: "AMERICA'S NEGEV"

Introduction

Leon Kronish's decision to move to Miami Beach in 1944 came at an important juncture in United States history. The entry of Americans into World War Two in December 1941, led to decisions regarding locations for the training of troops year-round. Miami Beach—with its hotels, climate and miles of beaches and ocean water—was a natural site for such activities.

It was also an important moment in Miami's Jewish history. Until the Second World War, Miami's Jewish population had hovered around three thousand households, approximately eight thousand residents, evenly divided between the mainland and the island.[1] The presence of Jewish soldiers on the Beach led to the establishment of new synagogues: the Miami Beach Jewish Community Center and Congregation Jacob Joseph (1941, renamed Temple Emanu-El in 1954), and Beth Sholom Center (1942, renamed Temple Beth Sholom in 1945).

The development of these Jewish institutions on Miami Beach was not predicted by local or national leaders/policy planners before World War Two. Miami Beach was perceived as an island that was blatantly anti-Semitic and racially segregated. Jews and blacks were "outsiders."

The founding of the Conservative Beth Sholom Center in 1942 in the "uptown" section of the Beach—the area most noted for its "restricted clientele"—was a bold move, and one that appealed to Kronish. His experiences growing up in Williamsburg, and his association with Rabbi Stephen Wise, Jewish social activist par excellence, between 1938-1942, had prepared him for the challenge.

Over the next decade (1945-1955) Kronish would lead a forty-member congregation towards affiliation with Reform Judaism, bring Liberal Judaism to Miami Beach, increase membership some twenty-fold, confront the Holocaust and anti-Semitism, introduce liturgical innovations and educational programs for youth and adults, promote Israel Bonds drives and Zionism, and preach *Klal Yisrael*.

The Kronish family grew with the birth of a second son, Ronald, in 1946, and a daughter, Maxine, in 1951. With the family's growth, new friendships developed and a rhythm of life evolved that typified the Jewish American family of the post-World War Two period. Synagogue was at the center and affiliation with Jewish organizations reverberated in all directions.

The Growth of Miami Beach, 1915-1944

Joined by a bridge to the mainland in 1913,[2] Miami Beach was incorporated as an independent town in 1915, with thirty-three white registered voters. Kronish's migration to Miami Beach in 1944 reflected the changes that had occurred in the most southeastern state of the Union during the previous three decades.

The Beach's growth was slow. The tourist industry would not be transformed to cater to middle class dollars until after World War Two. There were no planes to shuttle holiday-makers to Miami or air conditioned hotel rooms to cool them. Restrictive covenants in leases limited the availability of properties. Jews who wanted to retire to the south found it difficult to secure lodgings. Hurricanes in the mid- and late 1920s, followed by the Depression in the 1930s, also did nothing to encourage northerners to migrate to Florida.

Miami Beach in the 1920s and 1930s bore the imprint of Carl Fisher's and John Collins's policies. Fisher, the president of Prest-O-Lite, the first corporation to manufacture carbide gas headlights for automobiles, and creator of the Indianapolis Speedway, joined forces in 1919 with Collins, a Quaker, farmer and scientific horticulturalist, to form the Miami Beach Bay Shore Real Estate Company. Collins owned all the land between 20th Street and 67th Street. During the 1920s, Fisher owned everything below 20th except for a narrow stretch along the ocean, south of 15th Street, and the southernmost tip of the island south of 5th Street, which was owned by the Lummus brothers.[3]

The Lummus brothers had bought property before the city of Miami Beach was incorporated (1917). Real estate developers, they sold land to Jews. In contrast, Fisher and Collins, following standard real estate procedures, put restrictive covenants into all their deeds to their property.

> Said property shall not be sold, leased or rented in any form or manner, by any title, either legal or equitable, to any person or persons other than of the Caucasian Race, or to any firm or corporations of which any persons other than of the Caucasian Race shall be a part or stockholder.[4]

Jews were defined as non-Caucasian. In 1920 Fisher proclaimed "we don't want Miami Beach ever to become a Jewish outfit—it would not only ruin the Hotel [his], but ruin the property [Miami Beach]."[5]

Fisher's determination to transform Miami Beach into a winter playground, comparable to Palm Beach, initially attracted a ripple of northerners: Parker (pens), Champion (spark plugs), J. C. Penney (retail), Hopkins (Coca Cola), Firestone (rubber) and Gar Wood (speedboats). They came to the balmy shores of Miami Beach after World War One to gamble, play polo, yacht and relax. But Miami Beach could never compete with the socially exclusive Palm Beach. Miami Beach catered to anyone who had money—or nearly anyone.

Carl Fisher's promotional campaign in 1922 to sell Miami Beach to New Yorkers by illuminating a winter-time sign at the corner of Fifth Avenue and 42nd Street flashing "It's June in Miami," was parodied by Miami Ku Klux Klan members to read, "It's Jew'n in Miami."[6]

The Jewish Presence On Miami Beach

In spite of the hostile welcome Miami Beach real estate developers offered Jews, a trickle migrated to Lummus-owned property—today, the well-known international tourist district called South Beach.

In 1913, Joe and Jennie Weiss migrated from New York and opened up a lunch counter at Smith's Casino, a popular bathing spot for both Miamians and tourists. Five years later they moved to their own quarters, Joe's Stone Crab restaurant (227 Biscayne Boulevard).[7]

The Granats came immediately after the war (1919) and built the David Court Apartments (56 Washington Avenue). New Yorkers Rose and Jeremiah Weiss arrived in 1920, and moved into the Royal Apartments (221 Collins Avenue).[8] Both Joe Weiss and Rose Weiss (no relation) were asthmatics who had come to Miami Beach for health reasons.

Others came to cater to the handful of Jewish tourists. The Goodkowskys arrived in 1920 and constructed the Nemo Hotel at 101-106 Collins Avenue, the first kosher hotel. By 1922 there were a score of Jewish families living on South Beach.[9]

Rabbi Stephen Wise, invited to Miami in 1920 to speak to its handful of Jews confirmed this observation first-hand. Writing to his wife, he asks, "And, what of Miami?... The Jews are in a small minority."[10]

During the "land fever" epidemic of the mid-1920s, Miami lured thousands by the prospects of immediate wealth. The state passed an amendment to its constitution prohibiting state personal income and inheritance tax in order to encourage investors. One of the immediate results was that it was not uncommon for real estate values to double and triple within a very short time period.

Many of the Jewish community's future leaders, including those who established the communal infrastructure, arrived during these boom years: Sam Blank, Stanley Myers, Baron de Hirsch Meyer, Max Orovitz and Harry

Simonhoff. Hundreds of other small Jewish retailers, white collar and blue collar workers, also flocked to Miami.

By 1926 the "binder boys," real estate speculators, helped send the price of real estate spiraling out of control by trading "binders" (land options) over and over again. Many Miamians, including the socio-economic elite, perceived (incorrectly) that the "binder boys" were largely northern urban Jews.[11]

A number of the Jews who arrived in South Florida during the mid-1920s real estate boom gravitated to Lummus' property on South Beach. Children had fun "hanging out" at the *Yededum* (Jewish) social club at Smith's Casino. Gradually, members of the small Jewish community began to meet for religious services on the top floor of the David Court Apartments in 1925.

Two years later in 1927, the Orthodox Beth Jacob congregation was legally incorporated as Miami Beach's first synagogue. Over the next two years they met at the Leonard and Sea Breeze Hotels and the Penway. The Royal Apartments served as the setting for organizational meetings. In 1929 a modest Beth Jacob opened its doors on Washington Avenue near 3rd Street, boasting sixty family and one hundred fifty tourist units.[12]

Seven years later, in 1936, Art Deco architect Henry Hohauser, designed a grander Beth Jacob edifice.[13] Plaques honoring the donors included the name of Meyer Lansky, "architect of organized crime in the United States."[14]

Hohauser's office designed nearly one thousand structures between 1932 and 1949, including the more well-known Art Deco hotels—The Park Central, Cardozo, Essex and Colony.

In 1938, several members of Beth Jacob split off and organized a new Conservative congregation, Jacob Joseph, converting a house on Euclid Avenue. Chartered in 1940, the congregation changed its name to the Miami Beach Jewish Community Center and Congregation Jacob Joseph in 1941. In 1954 it changed its name again to Temple Emanu-El.[15]

During the Depression years, relatives, friends and *landsleit* (Jews from common origin points) came to join the South Beach Jewish community seeking a more hospitable climate and economic investment opportunities. Some who migrated south purchased with their Miami partners commercial properties from debt-ridden owners who were only too happy to sell them.

Others bought residential lots and hotels where restrictive clauses proved impossible to enforce after the property had changed owners several times. Among these were Harry Sirkin (Triton, Atlantic and Di Lido hotels), Harry Koretsky (Grand Plaza and National Hotels), Nathan Stone (The Blackstone Hotel), Walter Jacobs (Biscayne Collins Hotel), Samuel Friedland (Shelbourne Hotel and Food Fair markets) and Bernard Schoenberg (Strath Haven Hotel).

Throughout the 1930s most Jews living on Miami Beach were a mixture of first- and second-generation Americans. They leased apartments south of Lincoln Road (between 16th and 17th Streets), were active in the mercantile trade and spoke Yiddish. Along with other Beach residents, they were awed by the new Art Deco architectural styles—Mediterranean revival, Zig Zag Moderne, Streamline and Depression Moderne—that were rising around them.[16]

Their neighborhood, surrounded by water on three sides, took on all the trappings of a Jewish enclave. By the 1930s there were a few kosher groceries, delicatessens and restaurants. A number of hotels served as interim places of worship, and catered largely to members of the tourist traffic that demanded a place to pray. Some apartment buildings that were owned by Jews, such as the Mare Vista, advertised for more long-term tourists. The Tides Hotel offered its facilities to the YMHA.

Jewish families during the late 1930s and early 1940s frequently spent their evenings around a radio listening to comedians like Jack Benny, serials like Buck Rogers or tuning to the Big Bands like Benny Goodman's. For those more mobile, with business and pleasure interests outside Florida, they could reach New York in thirty hours on the Silver Meteor express or travel to Havana by taking a "flying boat" in just two and a half hours.

Between World Wars One and Two, the greater Miami Jewish community in many ways resembled the Jewish community in New York institutionally, but with fewer organizational spin-offs, frills and members. National philanthropic, social and cultural institutions had offices in Miami: the United Jewish Aid Committee (1920, later the Jewish Welfare Bureau, today's Jewish Family Services); the Zionist Organization of America (1926); a Jewish press—*Jewish Unity* (1927) and *Jewish Floridian* (1928); the Anti-Defamation League (1933); the Jewish War Veterans (1937); the Greater Miami Jewish Federation (1938); and the American Jewish Congress (1939). A *vad ha-kashrut* (dietary supervision) was instituted for the more traditional members of the community in the 1930s. In addition, there were local chapters of B'nai B'rith, Hadassah, Young Judea, Workmen's Circle, the Menorah Association and the National Council of Jewish Women.[17]

But in other ways, there were no comparisons between the Jewish communities of New York and Miami. Jewish cultural life in Miami was minimal. There was no Yiddish theater or press. The college-bound student looked elsewhere to be educated.[18] Bundists and Marxists had little future in a segregated community that preached an anti-trade union rhetoric. Orthodox Jews viewed Miami as a hinterland, void of *yeshivot* (parochial seminaries) and traditional support systems. A vibrant intelligentsia debating current issues in the press was absent. Hester Street South did not exist.

These shortcomings were compounded on Miami Beach. The YMHA, lodges of B'nai B'rith and chapters of organizations such as Hadassah and the National Council of Jewish Women were on the mainland. To attend meetings meant arranging drives or public transportation. Similarly, national Jewish organizations were mainland bound. Although branches began to surface on the Beach, their institutional base was on the mainland. The community's perception in the 1930s was that Miami was the center of gravity.

Discriminatory practices by the Beach tourist industry and hoteliers affected the ability of Jews to capture tourist trade dollars. In the hungry 1930s, competition was fierce. Visiting Jews were often perceived by Miami Beach's population as "lacking American ways and limited by their eating habits and religious practices."[19] With only finite accommodations for northern Jews because of "restricted clientele" signs, and lack of jobs because of discriminating practices in the industry, Miami Beach Jews were at a considerable disadvantage.

Resolved to tackle this, a handful of Beach Jews organized in 1932 a Jewish Voter's League named after David Levy Yulee, who was the State of Florida's (and America's) first Jewish U.S. Senator.[20] The League proposed to guarantee proportional representation for Miami Jewry in the attainment of jobs. With the support of the *Jewish Floridian* encouraging Jews to vote as a block, Baron de Hirsch Meyer was elected city councilman in 1934.[21] With his election, the balance of power in the greater Miami Jewish community began to shift from the mainland to the island. Miami Beach Jews' campaign for Jewish politicians to serve on the city council came two decades earlier than in the City of Miami.

Assimilationists and early Miami pioneers like Isidor Cohen found the Yulee League embarrassing. Cohen, five years earlier, had criticized members of the Jewish community and held them responsible for anti-Semitic sentiment: "[this] energetic and vociferous crowd of co-religionists made themselves obnoxious to the local non-Jewish conservative realty operators and to the rest of the community."[22]

Cohen and other Miami Jewish "fathers" petitioned national Jewish leadership to lend support for their opposition to the strategy of political action committees as a means to achieve goals. Rabbi Stephen Wise and Dr. Cyrus Adler, leaders of the American Jewish Congress and the American Jewish Committee respectively, replied that the appropriate course of action was not to link the Jewish name with partisan political organizations. "We would regard such a move as thoroughly reprehensible, un-American and in conflict with the best interests of the Jewish people" was Adler's opinion of the Yulee League.[23] Ironically, the idea of a political action committee (PAC) was vetoed.

Coincidentally, the election of Baron Hirsch de Meyer to the city council overlapped with David Sholtz's term as the only Jew to serve as the Governor of Florida (1933-1936). Both were Democrats, northern transplants and second-generation American Jews.

In 1939 Mitchell Wolfson (of Wometco fame) joined Meyer as a council member. Four years later, in 1943, the citizens of Miami Beach elected Wolfson as their mayor.[24]

The breakthrough in local politics resulted in increased employment opportunities and Jewish tourist trade dollars, but had little impact on housing practices north of 17th Street. Visiting Jewish fundraisers, nonetheless, recognized this changing situation on the island, and began to tailor their activities to the growing tourist population.

The *Jewish Floridian* captured their buzzing poignantly:

> Hath it not been said "from Miami Beach there shall go forth the voice of the law and the shekels of the blessed roll forth into the pockets of the seekers."[25]

By the early 1940s, Miami Beach replaced Miami as the preferred choice of residency for Jews.[26] At the same time that the demographic shift was tilting to the island, Miami Beach Jews began to lead initiatives in lobbying for national Jewish causes.

In 1939, many stood on the Beach protesting the United States' immigration policy that refused admittance to Jews fleeing Nazi Germany. Helplessly, they watched the *St. Louis*—a Nazi-chartered ship carrying nearly one thousand Jewish refugees—slowly cruise off the American coast, only to be turned away and sent back to Germany—most of the passengers later to die in Nazi crematoria.

In 1942, the year Beth Sholom Center was inaugurated, Miami Beach Jews were touched by Nazism directly. U-boats loaded with torpedoes shadowed the coast. Each evening blackouts were necessary. It was common to walk along the beach by the light of fires burning and to assist cargo ships that were attacked.

The Founding Of Beth Sholom Center

While Leon Kronish was completing his last year of rabbinical studies at the Jewish Institute of Religion, fifteen hundred miles away on Miami Beach, a handful of Jewish men met in the home of Louis Nauhaus during Passover. Among them was Benjamin Appel and Abraham Zinnamon.

Zinnamon had seen Appel reading a Yiddish newspaper on the beach one day. In due course, the conversation led to the subject of why there was no congregation north of Lincoln Road. Joining together, they solicited Samuel Dubin, Julius Goldsmith and Louis Nauhaus, among others, to consider establishing a "Center" to meet the needs of those who lived in the area then referred to as "North Beach."

United States' entry into World War Two in December 1941 had led to the federal government sequestering hotels on the Beach the following year for the training of servicemen. A significant number of recruits were Jewish. Several stationed in hotels north of Lincoln Road desired a place for worship and had mentioned their need to Appel and Zinnamon.

Julius Goldsmith, Samuel Dubin, Isidor Pearse, Isaac Robinowitz, Abraham Zinnamon, Max Ellis, Jacob Cohen, Bernard Ordover, Louis Nachaus, Morris Perrell, Samuel Appel and David Rott assembled for the

Founders meeting in the home of Benjamin Appel, 4430 Royal Palm Avenue, on April 6, 1942 to remedy the situation. Those present unanimously decided that "the spiritual ritual of the Center would be conducted as 'Orthodox-Conservative.'"[27] At the second meeting, three days later, the congregation was named "Beth Sholom Center," women were invited to attend (but not vote) and the yearly membership dues were fixed at ten dollars.[28] By the fourth general meeting on April 23, 1942 the decision to incorporate as an "Orthodox-Conservative" congregation was challenged.

On May 28, 1942 a sisterhood was formed at the home of Mrs. Isidor Pearse.[29] One week later (June 3, 1942), a storefront was leased at 761 41st Street (Arthur Godfrey Road) to serve as the synagogue and a draft of the charter was circulated. It was approved including the designation as a "Orthodox-Conservative" congregation.[30] A charter of incorporation was issued by the state of Florida on June 10, 1942.[31]

At the thirteenth general meeting on July 14, 1942, of the young Beth Sholom Center, held in the new quarters on 41st Street, the nomination and election of officers were conducted. Alfred Rosenstein was elected president, Max Ellis, first vice-president, Irving Applebaum, second vice-president, Raymond Rubin, third vice-president, Hazel Haber, recording secretary, Isidor Pearse, Treasurer, Ann Zinnamon, financial secretary and Charles Tobin, Chairman of the Board of Trustees. Forty-three family units were listed as members.[32] The official installation took place the following week, July 23, 1942. Rabbi Max Shapiro of Beth David Congregation served as the inducting officer with the assistance of Rabbi Colman Zwitman of Temple Israel.[33]

The congregation received the funds for its first permanent Torah scroll from Mr. and Mrs. Morris Perrell on August 12, 1942.[34] The first sabbath services were held on August 5, 1942 and were conducted by Benjamin Appel and Lewis Green. Ten days later, Lewis Green was hired as Beth Sholom's first Activities Director.[35] Rabbi Samuel Machtai, affectionately known in the community as "The Radio Rabbi," presided over High Holy Day services that fall, and served as a part-time interim rabbi. Soldiers were offered free seats and fifty-eight attended High Holy Day services.

Like many congregations surfacing in the United States in the 1940s, the Beth Sholom Center adopted several characteristics of Mordecai Kaplan's synagogue-center "reconstruction" of American Judaism. The novelty of the location, a storefront, added one more element to the concept of "reconstruction." The synagogue-center provided a convenient place to gather for the forty-three Beth Sholom Miami Beach family unit members and for Jewish servicemen billeted in nearby Miami Beach hotels along Collins Avenue.

Soon a Sunday school was established (September 20, 1942) and adult education classes were instituted both for the local residents and soldiers. During 1943 and into 1944, the Beth Sholom Center benefitted from an open air army theater set up on the southwest corner of 41st Street and Chase

Avenue. Before and after the shows, scores of young men dropped in for refreshments and conversation, and tasted Jewish cooking. Frequently, members would invite these soldiers to their homes to share in Jewish holiday festivities.

At the first Passover *Sedorim* (meals) in 1943, two hundred and fifty meals were served and seven hundred Passover lunches were prepared at the Beth Sholom Center.[36] Similarly, when the congregation held its first confirmation service on June 6, 1943, many servicemen were in attendance to celebrate the joyous occasion. Eve Naomi Machtai, Charles Greenberg, Nelson Kemp, and David Tobin were confirmed that sabbath.[37]

Camille Baum frequently served as hostess for synagogue-center events, and became identified as "Mother Baum." During holiday social functions, Mother Baum and other volunteers had great success in having servicemen and their visiting families drop by the center. They coordinated their activities with Chaplains Freund, Gordon, Deitch and Kraft who served Jewish servicemen on the Beach. The center's Red Cross chapter knitted and sewed clothes for the American servicemen and the women offered to share their homes during Jewish festivals.

Between the hosting of Rosh Hashanah services in the fall of 1942 and the spring of 1944, Beth Sholom's membership remained at about forty family units.[38] Increasing numbers of Jewish servicemen and servicewomen found their way to the synagogue-center for religious and social functions. Synagogue membership came from both the Conservative and Reform streams of Judaism.

In the spring of 1944 the Board of Directors resolved to hire a permanent rabbi who could guide and lead the young congregation.

Rabbi Leon Kronish: Beth Sholom Candidate

When the board members began to search for qualified candidates, the Jewish Institute of Religion (JIR) in New York was uppermost in their minds. Beth Sholom Center members wanted someone with fresh ideas, dedicated to the American ethos and who was a social activist. Candidates from the Jewish Institute of Religion, even if not tested south of the Mason-Dixon line, had at least been trained for such a role by their teacher, Rabbi Stephen Wise. Wise's vision, dedicated to combining the American ethos and Zionism, seemed the wave of the future. Charles Tobin, Chair of the Search Committee, was commissioned to contact the Dean, Henry Slonimsky.

Tobin's interview with Dean Slonimsky at JIR coincided by chance with a visit by Kronish—at that time ensconced in Huntington, Long Island. Tobin and Kronish were introduced. That evening Kronish invited Tobin to dinner at Lillian's father's vegetarian restaurant, the *Pine Tree*, in midtown Manhattan. During dinner they discussed the new congregation and soon afterwards Kronish was invited to travel to Miami Beach for an interview.

In August 1944, Kronish arranged to travel to Miami Beach. The train ride to the most southern terminus in the continental United States was uncomfortable. During the war years the majority of travelers were soldiers and most passengers slept upright. It was Kronish's first trip south, and the flat terrain, oppressive summer heat, and semi-tropical climate, powerfully reminded him of how different this was from his northern roots.

It was a typical summer day, hot and humid, when Charles Tobin and Morris Berick, president of Beth Sholom Center, greeted Kronish at the Florida East Coast Railroad terminal in downtown Miami. Driving to Miami Beach, they were refreshed by the breezes of the ocean. Crossing from the mainland to the island the temperature dropped a few degrees, and bougainvillaea and royal palms, mangroves and alligators, were part of the landscape.

After Kronish rested, Tobin took him on a short tour of the island. The Tobin-Granat families were early Miami Beach pioneers. Charles Tobin came to Miami in 1918 and moved to Miami Beach in 1935. Rellietta Granat Tobin, his wife, had moved to Miami Beach as a child in 1919 and had grown up watching the encroaching developments. Their family had been instrumental in establishing Beth Jacob Congregation on the southern tip of Miami Beach where most of the Jewish beach population lived in the 1920s and 1930s.

The Tobin family home on North Bay Road was within walking distance of the storefront synagogue-center. Rellietta charmed Rabbi Kronish with vivid descriptions of the beauty of the island: "the beautiful wild birds, the orchards of avocado and mango and winding paths that led from bay to ocean."[39]

During Kronish's short visit, other members of the center escorted him around the island. Morris Berick served as the rabbi's house host and guided him to non-restricted Beach residential locations and other Jewish areas in Dade County which offered rental accommodations.

Kronish requested to meet with Rabbi Irving Lehrman of the Conservative Miami Beach Jewish Center (Temple Emanu-El). They had been classmates under Rabbi Wise's tutelage and shared the Jewish Institute of Religion New York experience. Both were committed Zionists and advocates of infusing more Jewish education into synagogue life. Lehrman, also a graduate from JIR in 1942, had migrated to Miami Beach in 1943, and was in the process of changing the orientation of his congregation from transient soldiers to permanent residents. He was optimistic about Miami Beach's future, and recommended his colleague seriously consider the challenge of serving as a rabbi in this new and growing community.[40]

At group meetings and during private conversations with center members, Kronish was asked what he could bring to Miami Beach. He spoke of his vision: to create a Jewish heartland in "the Negev of America."

> The beauty of Miami Beach has the potential to attract [second generation] Jews like myself, retired people from the garment industry and military

> personnel who have passed through on their way to European and Pacific war theaters. Our task [is] to bring Liberal Judaism to Miami Beach and to bring Miami Beach to Zionism.[41]

He talked of the future and of the promise of *Klal Yisrael*, bringing Jewish people together to build a community to redeem Israel.

The thirty-sixth meeting of the Board of Directors of the Beth Sholom Center was held on August 9, 1944, at the home of the Chairman, Charles Tobin, with Kronish present. The board was impressed by his enthusiasm, personality and commitment to a new congregation. The young rabbi exhibited the qualities they thought necessary for the post-war period. His vision, of building a Jewish heartland in "the Negev of America" was most appealing, plus he came highly recommended by Rabbi Stephen Wise, Dean Henry Slonimsky, the Huntington congregation, and Rabbi Irving Lehrman. An invitation was extended to Rabbi Leon Kronish to return with his family for Rosh Hashanah, less than six weeks away. The board offered him four thousand dollars per annum, moving expenses and rent-free accommodations for the first two months of his service.[42]

A Decision

Returning to Huntington, Kronish described to Lillian in detail the congregation, Miami Beach and the tropical climate. Despite the small size of the congregation and the lack of children Jordan's age, he envisaged it "within several years as a place where many children will be."[43]

Lillian's parents, who had visited Miami Beach previously as tourists, asked their son-in-law "if there really were Jews on 41st Street." Lillian remained apprehensive about Miami Beach, despite the fact that the position at the Huntington Center was temporary. Her family and sisters were in New York. Kronish calmed her with his characteristic humor: "What do you mean you don't want to leave? Some men take their wives for two weeks to Miami. I am taking you for twelve months!"[44]

Kronish tendered his resignation as rabbi at the Huntington Jewish Center on August 28, 1944.

> My dear Friends,
>
> It isn't easy for me to take my leave of you, with whom I have shared every family occasion of joy and of sorrow. I have laughed and danced at your *simchos* [joyous occasions] and my heart has gone out to you in your moments of anguish and pain.... I have derived an immense spiritual satisfaction from my leadership and service.... While the Jews of Eastern Europe were being slaughtered by the millions, I have made an ever-increasing number of Jewish families conscious of their Jewishness and conscious of their responsibility to their own Jewish Center.... I regret that I

> cannot accept the invitation of the Congregation to serve as your Rabbi for the coming year.[45]

1944-1945: Kronish's First Year at Beth Sholom

The blackouts of 1942 had become memories when the Kronish family—Leon, Lillian and son Jordan—steamed into downtown Miami aboard the Florida East Coast Railroad. Soon the Kronishes were settled in their new home, above the storefront synagogue-center on 41st Street.

The store owners had contributed some office space upstairs for an apartment, but there was no kitchen and it could hardly have been described as an apartment. Conditions in Miami were very different from those in New York. Their first guests were the black palmetto bugs of South Florida. Early September in Miami Beach meant ninety degrees on the streets and in the apartment, as air conditioning was still foreign to most Miamians.

Blacks were restricted from coming to Miami Beach unless they had identity cards. Public facilities were segregated. Signs clearly visible from Kronish's second story windows boldly read "White" and "Colored."

Within a week it became apparent that the Air Force paraded across the street every afternoon (near the future Roosevelt Theater) just when Jordan was about to nap. Lillian was becoming desperate.

Miami Beach had few, if any, vacant apartments and could not meet the demands of military families arriving to be with their husbands. Landlords exploited the situation and rents were raised to extortionary levels. A preponderance of "restricted clientele" notices further limited the selection in the Beth Sholom Center's neighborhood. The election of Jewish politicians in the early 1940s to City Hall had little impact in changing the behavior of the residents around 41st Street.

In spite of these handicaps, Kronish saw as his personal mandate the "colonization" of Miami Beach north of Lincoln Road, using Jewish prayer, education and culture, the building blocks of Liberal Judaism. Over fifty percent of Dade County's Jewish population lived on the Beach—about fifteen hundred permanent Jewish residents, most (eighty percent) of whom lived south of 23rd Street.[46]

In addition to Miami Beach's permanent Jewish residents, there were thousands of Jewish soldiers stationed there. Approximately one-fourth of all United States Army Air Force officers and one-fifth of its enlisted men were trained on Miami Beach.[47]

Rabbi Leon Kronish and Cantor Louis Hyman conducted the 1944 High Holy Day services. In his first Yom Kippur *Kol Nidre* sermon, (September 26, 1944) Rabbi Kronish addressed the nature of sin. "Sin is not just a product of action, but non-action." The themes of his teacher, Rabbi Stephen Wise, echoed in his words:

> I had felt from the beginning that a synagogue should be more than a gathering of divine worshippers, and that within the synagogue life worship should be formulated into collective and organized human service.[48]

Kronish explained to his congregation that service was dependent on their commitment to education and their ability to translate these values into community programs. He asked them to work with him in building a "new center to replace those which are no more; to replace those which have burnt. By salvaging the remnants of European Jewry we serve God by strengthening our Jewish identity."[49] Soldiers and their families sitting in the storefront synagogue-center knew that the images of fire were more than metaphorical.

Major Herbert and Rose Lapidus, for example, were present for the *Kol Nidre* service, and wrote to Rabbi Kronish in appreciation of his thoughts.

> Please accept our check for $25.00 for your Building Fund. We were deeply moved by your keen desire to perpetuate the memories of our fallen martyred brethren.[50]

Some of them would return with their families after World War Two and join the congregation.

After Yom Kippur, Kronish turned his attention to reshaping the synagogue-center in the image of Liberal Judaism while at the same time supporting the view that the Beth Sholom Center was "a Modern Conservative Jewish organization."[51] His vision was to mirror the transformation taking place among several congregations across America. For two decades, rabbis under the tutelage of Rabbis Mordecai Kaplan and Stephen Wise had recast the landscape of American Judaism.[52]

To share these changes with congregants, Kronish believed personal example was the best publicity. Revitalization of tradition by Liberal Judaism began with worship. Thus, Kronish set the tone by wearing a *Kippa* (skullcap) and a *tallit* (prayer shawl). Sabbath services included a Friday and Saturday component. Reading of the weekly Torah portion every Saturday morning became the norm and individuals called to the torah had to wear a *tallit*.[53]

Bar mitzvah and later, bat mitzvah (1948), became integral elements of temple life.[54] Festivals with a Zionist orientation such as *Tu'B'shvat* (Arbor Day) were adopted. Established holidays like *Purim* were given new religious touches and a full reading of the *megillah* (*Purim* story) was expected. Kronish also made appeals to congregational parents to keep their children at home for Jewish religious holidays.[55]

Increased congregational participation increased attendance in educational programs. Meeting with the board of directors and the newly instituted Beth

Sholom Religious School Board, chaired by Louis Goldman, Kronish offered a new strategy that was more aggressive and more in line with Liberal Judaism. In Kronish's view, members must be encouraged to commit their children to intensive Jewish education. There should be a more Zionist orientation for syllabi with modern Hebrew a regular feature of the curriculum and courses about Palestine and Zionism, as well as Bible, religious customs, history and American Jewry.[56]

Extending the conclusions of his thesis, *Educating Children and Young People for Jewish Public Worship*, Kronish advocated new patterns of religious worship for the students. Ceremonies and services were to be transformed into dramatic, vibrant, poetic religious pageants. "The prayer book is the mirror of the spirit of the Jewish people and its development... [and] should be co-terminous with life."[57] Within a few months the number of students in the religious/Sunday school jumped from fourteen to forty-two.[58]

The 1944-1945 religious/Sunday school staff included Rebecca Kelemer (graduate of the Herzliyah Secondary School in Tel Aviv), Belle Goldstrich (University of Chicago), Emma Rosenberg (University of Miami), Natalie Frankel (University of Miami), Phyllis Kohn and Cpl. Louis Fox, as well as Rabbi Kronish. The culmination of these classes led to Rabbi Kronish's first confirmation class in May 1945 comprising Carol Adler, Joy Berick, Pauline Markes, Florence Settlow, Stewart Kohn, Mynhard Tobin, and Carol Solmon.[59]

Cultural outreach programs were organized for adults and included Zionist themes. A series was introduced on "Jewish Current Events," which concentrated on how members could play a more active political role in their society and in furthering the cause of Zionism. The men's club and sisterhood were reorganized and offered a variety of activities. There were forums, adult education classes on current Jewish problems, and musical programs. These programs were often followed by mah jong, and weekly library readings of contemporary literature, led by Lillian.

With a program in place for youth and adults, the board began an initiative to recruit new members to join its community, described by the *Beth Sholom Center News* as "a modern and Liberal Conservative synagogue."[60] The embryonic congregation consisted of forty families.[61] According to popular legend and Kronish's own testimony, he would walk his neighborhood looking for *mezuzot* on doors. Dr. Max Gratz remembers Kronish knocking on his door on Nautilus Drive to invite him and his family to join the congregation.[62]

Across the street lived the Arkins, who received the same invitation. Each time, Kronish would explain the meaning of Liberal Judaism and the importance of participating in the future of American Jewry. Stanley Arkin, a member since that visit, says it was "his warmth and humor, his emphasis on Jewish renewal" that appealed to them.[63] These personal qualities, first manifest at the Huntington Jewish Center, came naturally to the young rabbi.

Over the next six months Kronish solicited one hundred new members.[64] Each Friday service, Kronish took advantage of the moment to forge ahead on issues—anti-Semitism, Jewish education, social justice, Zionism—that he felt would play a dominant role in the post-war period. Among these, Zionism was the most pronounced.[65]

A New Home for Beth Sholom

In February 1945, the board of directors expressed its enthusiasm for Rabbi Kronish's leadership by announcing plans to erect a permanent synagogue on the corner of north Meridian Avenue and 40th Street. In a sermon two weeks later, the February-born Kronish responded to the idea of a new house of prayer: "What would the Big Two, [Presidents] Washington and Lincoln, say to the Big Three?"[66]

Both Presidents had led the nation in time of great peril. Kronish viewed the fate of the Jewish people as of equal magnitude. Zionism demanded that Jews stand up and be counted. Recalling Rabbi Wise's words, he challenged the congregation, "I have been an American for three decades—I have been a Jew for four thousand years."[67] For Kronish the value of being Jewish in America lay in the freedom to be Jewish.

As an American Jew, Kronish had internalized the teachings both of Kaplan and Wise that American Zionism did not have to translate into *aliya*. A commitment to furthering the realization of an independent sovereign state was of equal value to building the Jewish community in America. Furthermore, support for Zionism did not tarnish one's loyalty to America.

The highlight of Kronish's first year at Beth Sholom Center was the visit of Rabbi Stephen Wise in March to install him officially. Arriving a week before the event, Wise spent the time meeting with select groups and giving public speeches to support Zionism. Kronish attended these events and served as Wise's liaison.

On March 9, 1945, the installation of Rabbi Kronish took place not at the synagogue, but down the street at the North Beach Elementary School Auditorium, due to the overflow crowd which had come to hear Rabbi Wise. Wise charged him with the responsibility of building a new congregation where none had gone before (north of Lincoln Road). He stressed the God of social imperative, and challenged the young rabbi to follow the prophetic tradition of social reform.[68]

Wise's visit also provided the opportunity for Kronish to speak privately to his mentor about a pressing concern that appeared to have no immediate solution without alienating part of his congregation.

When the Beth Sholom Center announced in February that it planned to erect a new synagogue on the corner of North Meridian Avenue and 40th Street, the land stood vacant. Its only immediate neighbor was the Catholic

Church, St. Patrick's, across the street. The church faced the bay and monopolized a large tract of land.

To publicize the new building and increase membership, the board of directors placed a prominent sign on the vacant lot which read, "Future Home of Beth Sholom Center." Each evening when no witnesses were present it was knocked down.

After repeated occurrences, Kronish decided to visit Father William A. Barry, the director of St. Patrick's and an influential leader of the Catholic Miami Beach community. Kronish inquired if Barry knew anything of these occurrences. While Barry denied specific knowledge, he made plain—according to early Beth Sholom members Max Gratz and Shepard Broad—that he did not support the construction of a synagogue next door. Kronish was astounded by his reaction.[69]

Kronish informed the board of his conversation. Long discussions were held with many of the board members concerning how to proceed. Deep-seated emotions divided the congregation into two camps. Some were uncomfortable in confronting the Catholic Miami Beach community. Others adopted a position of defiance and argued that America was founded on the principles of religious liberty and therefore such behavior should not be tolerated.

Stephen Wise listened to the various possible responses that the board was considering. He offered to help negotiate with the church, but the board, fearing national attention, gratefully declined his offer. Wise then advised the board of directors to look for a third way that could meet the needs of both camps within the congregation.

While board members contemplated the congregation's choices, Beth Sholom was offered, and accepted in exchange for the Meridian Avenue property, another attractive piece of land with a two-story building further east on Chase Avenue. Ironically, the exchanged property was a parcel of land formerly owned by the anti-Semitic Carl Fisher.

The first floor of the Chase Avenue property was then being used as a warehouse for a number of Beach hotels temporarily converted to Air Force barracks. The upper story served as a temporary lodging for transient GIs and their wives. In an earlier decade the building had been used to provide stables for Fisher's Nautilus Club's polo fields before being reconverted into the Chase Hotel for "restricted clientele."[70]

For Kronish the decision to move to a different location, while solving the immediate problem, still did not answer certain fundamental questions of principle. Shepard Broad, recalling this incident many years later, summarized the thinking of the rabbi during this crisis:

> At what juncture is it appropriate to attack discrimination and prejudice publicly? Can one move forward with such an agenda before a congregation has inculcated the values of Liberal Judaism? If discrimination is addressed

now, will it affect our efforts so desperately needed to save Nazi victims? Should the congregation's political efforts be focused on international or local issues?"[71]

The Founding of Temple Beth Sholom

Selection of the new site for the congregation on Chase Avenue coincided with the election of a new Board of Directors and the passage of by-laws that amended the charter of the Beth Sholom Center. The congregation adopted the new name, Temple Beth Sholom, on April 24, 1945. The Conservative center became the Reform temple. Temple Beth Sholom, House of Peace, was inaugurated two weeks before V.E. (Victory in Europe) Day.

The shift to a Reform Temple from a Conservative Center reflected both the personal inclination of Kronish to affiliate with the Reform movement, and the changing membership during his first year of tenure.

His traditional orientation to ritual had already been tempered by Kaplan's "reconstructionism" before he arrived at the Jewish Institute of Religion in 1938. As a student at JIR, Kronish was encouraged to explore the different denominations in American Judaism. Wise's policy was to facilitate the ordination of rabbis to serve the American Jewish public, not one particular denominational development. Although Wise viewed himself as Reform and his allegiance was to the Reform movement, a number of rabbis trained at the Institute affiliated with the Conservative movement.[72] Most rabbis ordained by Wise, however, chose affiliation with the Reform movement.

As a rabbi committed to Liberal Judaism, Kronish was also more akin to the Reform movement's philosophy. He had a strong commitment to social justice. His faith was a community-centered one in which Judaism fulfilled a particular way of life. The concept of the people of Israel, *Klal Yisrael*, bonded every Jew to the other and directed them to a common objective as a people: the establishment and enhancement of *Eretz Yisrael* as the homeland of the Jewish spirit.

Kronish's brand of Reform Judaism, Liberal Judaism, was tailored to meet his Miami Beach community and stood in sharp contrast to his crosstown Reform colleagues, Rabbi Colman Zwitman (1936-1949) and Rabbi Joseph Narot (1950-1972) of Temple Israel in downtown Miami, the oldest Reform congregation in the county (1922).[73]

Zwitman's and Narot's interpretation of *Klal Yisrael* still had the characteristics of classical Reform Judaism: non-Zionist, anti-ritual and anti-centralized organization. Congregants were not encouraged to wear *kippot*, attend services on Saturday morning and read the Torah. They were also discouraged from celebrating the less popular holidays, especially those with a nationalist/Zionist orientation, such as *Tu'B'shvat*. Israel did not feature in the weekly sermons and the suggestion of living there (*aliya*) was an anathema. Narot's theology, in particular, had an affinity to religious existentialism.[74]

Although Kronish would challenge Narot to move forward with the times and adopt Liberal Judaism, both men were steadfast in their approach.

Examining the membership rolls during 1944-1945, Kronish believed that the majority of his congregants also felt comfortable in moving towards Liberal Judaism. Although there were some who perceived affiliation with the Reform movement as undesirable because of its elitism, lack of tradition and lukewarm attitude towards Zionism, Kronish urged them to consider affiliating with the Union of American Hebrew Congregations.[75] The rolls resonated with second-generation American Jews seeking less traditional orientations than those offered by the Orthodox and Conservative movements. Reared in homes where they rejoiced in Jewish ritual, they wanted to recapture this positive religious expression and at the same time reflect their acculturated lifestyle.

The newly elected President, Harry Cornblum, and the board of Temple Beth Sholom articulated the temple's philosophy and relationship to its rabbi in the preamble to the new constitution. The synagogue was to be democratic with a fair-share dues system, no assigned pews and no tuition fees.

> Temple Beth Sholom is a Liberal Congregation, desirous of re-asserting the fundamental ideals of Israel, believing that Judaism is a religion of perpetual growth and development, we hold that while loyal to the fundamental teachings thereof, we are by virtue of the genius of Israel, free to interpret and re-state the teachings of Israel of the past in the light of the present; and that each succeeding generation in Israel is free to reformulate the truths first entrusted in the providence of God to our Fathers. And, whereas we believe that the power of the Synagogue depends, in part, upon the inherent right of the pulpit to freedom of thought and speech, the members of the Temple Beth Sholom resolve that its pulpits shall be free to preach on behalf of truth and righteousness in the spirit and after the pattern of the prophets of Israel.[76]

The erection of a new Conservative synagogue less than two miles away at the intersection of Washington Avenue and 17th Street was also a consideration. Under the able guidance of Rabbi Irving Lehrman, the Conservative Miami Beach Jewish Center (Temple Emanu-El) offered an alternative approach to the practice of Judaism. For the next four decades Temple Beth Sholom and Temple Emanu-El remained friendly competitors that offered two different streams of Jewish religious worship.[77]

The word *sholom* had special significance for Kronish. During his first year on Miami Beach there were many occasions when he was called upon to comfort congregation members who lost sons in the war.[78] Peace was always in his prayers. Throughout 1944-1945 Kronish announced in the bulletin that when peace would be declared, "when the surrender of the enemy is announced,"[79] Victory Day services would be held at 8 p.m. For Kronish, peace was synonymous with religious renewal.

Preparing the congregation for *sholom*, Rabbi Kronish drew from the prophets and vowed to work towards creating a world where lion and lamb would have respect for one another. The new temple symbolized a stronghold against the atrocities of humanity.

The summer of 1945 was spent renovating and preparing the purchased property. Ten classrooms, a library, an arts and crafts workshop, a scout's room, an assembly hall and school administration offices were built on the second floor. On the first floor stood the kitchen, a banquet hall, the rabbi's study and offices and a chapel.

When the new temple opened its doors on Chase Avenue in the late summer of 1945, Samuel Kelemar joined the congregation as cantor. His musical talents, combined with Kronish's interest in liturgy, led to a fruitful collaboration on several occasions. Rabbi Kronish wrote and Cantor Kelemar musically arranged *Purim* songs, hymns in honor of Rabbi Stephen Wise and a cantata for *Hanukkah*, among other works.[80]

The formal dedication of the new Reform congregation, Temple Beth Sholom, took place on November 28, 1945. Rabbi Abraham Feldman, vice-president of the Central Conference of American Rabbis and chair of its committee on ritual for children's Holy Day services, led the ceremony. He spoke of "a sanctuary of peace, youth with a vision, [and of] prophecy in Miami Beach."[81]

In the Shadow of the Holocaust

In the aftermath of V.E. Day, May 8, 1945, the horror of the Holocaust was bitterly revealed. Kronish had frequently preached on the evil of Nazism and totalitarianism. He had comforted parents, soldiers and loved ones. But the fate of his own European family was still a mystery.

Germany had invaded Zborow, Ukraine in July, 1941. By the end of the war only twenty-five of the town's eighteen hundred inhabitants were still alive. Rabbi Kronish's grandfather, Reuven, was not one of them. At age ninety, he had been killed by the Nazis when the ghetto was liquidated in April-June, 1943. The *Yizkor Buch* (memorial book) for the town of Zborow, published in Israel, lists forty names of the family that became martyrs. Zborow, "*aklein shtetle vos hot aroisgegeden groisse mentschen*, a little town that had produced great people," was no more.[82]

Part of the pain of losing a link in the chain was diminished by the birth of Ronald, their second child, on June 17, 1946. Named Reuven in Hebrew after Leon's grandfather, the tradition of passing on family members' names after their deaths took on greater significance. The concept of *dor l'dor*, generation to generation, gave meaning and life to a Holocaust victim. Born in a century where state policy granted Jews religious liberties, and into a new synagogue dedicated to peace, Temple Beth Sholom, Ronald was a bridge to carry forth the historical memory of his European family's heritage.

Post-World War Two Developments: A New Miami Beach

The second half of the 1940s was a time of phenomenal growth in Dade County, Florida.

The Jewish population of Miami Beach alone grew by over six hundred percent—four thousand in 1940 to twenty-five thousand in 1950—and Jewish families moved more frequently north of 41st Street.[83] Only one in five had lived in greater Miami for more than twenty years. The average length of residence on Miami Beach was less than five years. Half of the immigrants came from New York City. One in four professed an affiliation to Reform Judaism. Between Kronish's arrival in 1944 and the end of the decade, the area from 41st Street to 71st Street climbed from fifteen percent of the Beach's Jewish population to nearly thirty percent.[84]

In the following decade the Miami Beach Jewish community continued to grow at a galloping pace. Between 1950 and 1955 the population doubled from twenty-five to fifty thousand.[85] Northerners were drawn to the area by the climate, the lifestyle and economic opportunities. A large percentage were elderly, fixed-income retirees, first-generation immigrants, who were reaping the rewards of their garment industry pensions. A number were enticed by the hungry tourist industry's advertising campaigns, liked what they saw and did not leave.

Miami Beach was packaged as the winter Catskills.[86] The city with the "superior climate all year long" was touted by its publicity department as "one of the most magnificent mainstream cities in the world."[87]

Mass-manufactured air conditioning, and the transfer of aviation technology from military to civilian life, made Florida an extremely attractive and accessible proposition to middle-class tourists. New hotels were constructed year after year to the adulation of Miami Beach residents: the Saxony (1950), Nautilus (1951), Algiers (1952), Di Lido (1953), Fontainebleau (1954), Eden Roc (1955), Casablanca, Americana and Seville (1956).[88] Miami Beach was crowned as the Jewish winter playground in the United States.

Confronting Anti-Semitism

On April 19, 1949, Rabbi Stephen S. Wise—the teacher of Leon Kronish and the leading figure of 20th century American Jewish life—died during the Passover holiday.

Temple Beth Sholom mourned with Kronish. They had met him on several occasions and felt his spirit. Kronish dedicated his Passover sermon to both personal recollections and Wise's contributions to American Judaism and *Klal Yisrael*. Kronish spoke of the human side of the man, his generosity, his capacity for work, his penchant for phrasemaking and for indignation. "I count as one of the good fortunes of my life that I was among those who were privileged to have known his friendship, to have had his instruction and counsel, to have been blessed by his concern as his student."[89] He recounted Wise's re-Judaization of Reform Judaism, the democratization of the American Jewish community and his place in the establishment of the State of Israel. Rabbi Stephen S. Wise, Kronish proclaimed, "taught my generation the meaning of loyalty to *Klal Yisrael*."[90]

As if in tribute to Wise's activist spirit, the Miami Beach Jewish community began new efforts in 1949 to stop the island's discriminatory sign practices. Beach city councilmen, D. Lee Powell, a Presbyterian, and Burnett Roth, a Beth Sholom member,[91] co-introduced anti-discriminatory sign ordinances making it illegal to

> maintain or display any advertisements, notice or sign which is discriminatory against persons of any religion, sect, creed, race or denomination in enjoyment of privileges and facilities of places of public accommodation, amusement or resort, including hotels, apartments, restaurants, bars, stores, theaters, hospitals, golf courses, public libraries, public conveyances and terminals.[92]

After the war (1945-1947), Roth's efforts with sixteen other ex-servicemen, calling on managers of hotels and apartment houses displaying or advertising "Gentile Only" policies to remove their signs, had proven only partially successful. The anti-discrimination legislation curtailed further anti-Semitic practices. Kronish worked behind the scenes with others, and in particular the Anti-Defamation League, to build a coalition of forces to confront those who had restricted Jews from housing, work and recreational facilities.

In 1951 he again assisted Powell and Roth in their efforts to draw up anti-Ku Klux Klan legislation for the Florida State Legislature prohibiting the burning of crosses and the wearing of masks and hoods.[93]

The Zionist Community in Miami

Shepard Broad, (president, Zionist Organization of America, Miami Beach chapter), Abraham Goodman (treasurer, Zionist Organization of America) and Ed Kaufmann (president, Zionist Organization of America) were part of the crop recruited in Kronish's first year at the Beth Sholom Center. Veteran Zionists all, they constantly were seeking ways for the rabbi to assist them in their efforts.

On July 1, 1945, Broad was chosen to be one of a select group of men to meet with Ben-Gurion in New York at a secret emergency meeting.[94] This group, later known as the Sonneborn Institute, after Rudolf Sonneborn, a Baltimore industrialist, helped to organize the underground network to supply the machinery for Israel for the War of Independence.

Four years earlier Broad assisted in the organization of the Miami branch of the Jewish National Fund (1941). The following year (1942), Broad, with Kaufmann's urging, organized the first Zionist chapter on Miami Beach.[95] By 1945 the chapter had swelled to thirteen hundred members.[96] Broad also was a founder that year of the Miami branch of the American Zionist Emergency Committee. The following year, 1946, Broad was a delegate to the 22nd World Zionist Congress in Basle, Switzerland.[97]

In the 1940s, Zionism did not receive wide support from Miami's Jewish community. "Federation leaders thought Zionism was too controversial because it raised the specter of dual loyalties."[98] Consequently, Broad gravitated to individuals like Kronish whose fervor and outspokenness for Zionism made him an immediate ally. In the aftermath of World War Two, local sentiment was directed to assist Holocaust survivors, fund local agencies and advocate changes in policies discriminating against Jews.

In September 1945, several Jewish Miami residents organized a chapter of the anti-Zionist American Council for Judaism.[99] Benjamin Bronston, a past president of the greater Miami Jewish Federation, was elected president. According to Roth, "even in [Miami's] B'nai B'rith, it was difficult to find supportive leadership [for Zionism], particularly when men like Louis Heiman, the law partner of Stanley Myers, president of the Council of Jewish Federations in 1947, voiced opposition."[100]

Broad was asked by Yaakov Dori in 1946 (later to be the first chief of staff of the Israeli Defense Forces) to buy two freighters, tow them up the Miami River and outfit them to carry illegal Jewish immigrants from the French port of Marseilles to Palestine past the British blockade. Roth was Broad's field officer, recruiting youth to help the Haganah and secure items for the ships.[101] He, like Broad, was totally devoted to the Zionist cause. Roth's father was a friend of Naphatali Herz Imber, the author of *Hatikvah*.[102]

Broad, Roth, Kaufmann and Kronish assisted dedicated followers to procure identity cards, passports and visas.[103] They solicited veteran Zionists who had migrated south and organized a group of devoted couriers to carry information and supplies. They arranged for Stephen Wise to deliver the keynote address at the American Zionist Emergency Committee gathering in Miami at Bayfront Park. They organized Temple Beth Sholom congregants, as well as others, to picket the British Consulate in front of the Pan American building and to join rallies at Flamingo Park (South Beach) to support Zionism (1946 and 1947). They spoke before civic groups and businessmen, and at church meetings. They delivered books on Zionism to public libraries.[104]

These activities were instrumental in helping to procure in America people, dollars and arms for Palestine. A member of the Administrative

Committee of the Southeastern Zionist Region, Kronish felt a personal responsibility to help in the creation of a new Jewish state. He even went so far as to appeal for guns from the pulpit.[105]

In May 1948, the Zionist goal of an independent Jewish state came to fruition. Kronish and his congregants joined with thousands in Flamingo Park to celebrate the creation of the State of Israel. They danced and sang Hebrew-Zionist songs into the early hours of the morning.[106]

Kronish Visits the Newborn State of Israel

During the Israeli War of Independence, Rabbi Kronish visited Israel with Rabbi Max Shapiro (Beth David Congregation) and William Singer (Greater Miami Jewish Federation Campaign Chairman) as part of a United Jewish Appeal Federation fact-finding mission.

In 1949 Israel was still an underdeveloped country. When they arrived in January, the weather was cold, windy and rainy. Thousands of immigrants lived in tents, knee deep in mud. The mission toured the country and saw first-hand Israel's immense needs.

From the military front lines to *kibbutzim*, from the cities to the *ma'abarot* (tent cities), they talked to Israelis and listened to their comments. The mission met with Israeli leaders and observed the new state's first democratic election. Kronish spoke in Hebrew, realizing a dream that had begun in his youth while active in *Hashomer Hatzair*.

On a day off in Tel Aviv, Kronish contacted the Government Tourist Office (previously the Zionist Information Bureau). His younger brother, Zev, while stationed overseas had seen a picture of an old friend of Leon's from Williamsburg, Julius Freeman, and had informed Leon he was a member of Kibbutz Kfar Menachem. Julius had changed his name to Yehuda Ben Chorin and was on loan to the Tel Aviv Tourist Office from his kibbutz, serving as a guide for missions from English-speaking countries.

Yehuda Ben Chorin had made *aliya* in 1939 and had helped to found Kibbutz Kfar Menachem (between Tel Aviv and Beersheba). He had fought in the War of Independence and knew the country intimately.

With Ben Chorin as guide, Kronish saw Israel as an Israeli as well as a United Jewish Appeal leader. Ben Chorin introduced him to the political elite, such as Joseph Sprinzak, the Speaker of the Knesset, among other political and economic personalities.[107]

While in Israel, Kronish met with the Ambassador of the United States to Israel, James McDonald, at the Ambassador's residence. Kronish's friendship with Ambassador McDonald went back to his days as a student at the Jewish Institute of Religion, when Stephen Wise served on President Roosevelt's Advisory Committee on Political Refugees and McDonald chaired the Committee. The friendship continued in Miami and on several occasions McDonald had spoken at Temple Beth Sholom.[108]

To mark Kronish's visit, a picture of Kronish and McDonald was taken on the rooftop of the American Ambassador's residence. A few days later McDonald made Kronish an international celebrity by circulating the picture to the press.[109]

Returning from Israel in early February, Kronish was physically exhausted. The three week trip had been grueling, with few comforts. At a gala buffet dinner in the temple dining hall, Kronish gave his congregation an eyewitness account of his trip and circulated photos he had taken. With rolled-up sleeves, he spoke with passion of the plight of the Middle Eastern Sephardic Jews and the Holocaust survivors that were arriving in Israel. Quoting a phrase of his mentor, Stephen Wise, he called on those listening to help the "DPs," those "destined for Palestine."[110]

He conveyed the mood of Israelis, their enthusiasm for living in a Jewish state in spite of the hardships. He discussed the recent elections[111] and the nature of coalition politics and he asked his congregation to help him lobby the American government by writing letters to their congressmen to give greater support to Israel. All during February he was busy giving speeches at Jewish functions throughout the city about his experiences in Israel.

Kronish's brief encounter with Israel in 1949 created a sense of anxiety as well as satisfaction. Socialized with Zionist values, he compared himself to his friend, Yehuda.

> Was the planting and nurturing of a Jewish temple as valid as establishing a kibbutz and rebuilding the state of Israel? Was migration to Miami to colonize a Jewish tropical oasis of equal significance in perpetuating *Klal Yisrael* as making *aliya* to the new Jewish state? What is my role as an American Zionist?[112]

Throughout the coming decades, Kronish was able to give positive answers to these questions by building one of the most vibrant synagogues in American Jewish life, one that was equally committed to developing the synagogue and the State of Israel.

Israel Bonds

Given the array of problems that Kronish witnessed on his 1949 trip to Israel, it is hardly surprising that the Israeli government urgently felt the need for a massive capital campaign to promote social and economic development. By far, the most successful of these was the Israel Bonds policy initiative of 1950. The basic idea was that Jews in the Diaspora, especially the United States, who may have been lukewarm about Zionism in its pre-state phase would be much more willing to invest in the non-partisan development of a Jewish state.

In 1951, when Kronish inaugurated what was to become a phenomenal career as an advocate for investment in Israel through the Bonds program, he appealed to his congregation with example and prophetic passion:

> I have already purchased my Bond for Israel. Every Jewish family ought to purchase one or more Bonds for each member of the family. The cornerstone of aid to Israel is the purchase of Bonds. I pledge to the Government of Israel that every one of our more than 500 families will purchase at least one Bond for every individual within that family.[113]

Within a few months, Temple Beth Sholom members had bought over $300,000 of Israel Bonds.[114] Members were solicited at the temple, during organizational meetings, in their homes and when relaxing at Beach hotels. They also were encouraged by visits from such Israeli luminaries as Golda Meir, Israel's Minister of Labor, Abba Eban (Ambassador to the United States) and Avraham Harman (Ambassador to the United States in the 1960s) who visited Miami Beach in 1951. Meir's visit alone helped raise over $500,000 of Bonds in Miami of what would become an annual drive.[115] This set a precedent for many such visitors from Israel, who would ask congregants to be a partner in state building and help redeem Jews wherever in need.

In the years to come, Israel Bonds became the focal point of Kronish's manifold activities on behalf of Israel. He vehemently opposed the views of the American Council for Judaism and others that argued that it was "presumptuous to suggest to any citizen that because he is of Jewish faith he has a unique duty to buy these Bonds."[116]

For Kronish, Bonds were a means to inspire his congregants and focus their attention on events in the Middle East. Moreover, Bonds were a way not only to show support for Israel that was completely compatible with American patriotism, but also an opportunity to express commitment to *Klal Yisrael* and *Eretz Yisrael*.

Family and Temple Life

Between 1945 and 1951 the Kronish family moved three times, all within the neighborhood of the site of Beth Sholom on Chase Avenue just north of 41st Street. The first was to 4812 Pine Island, northeast of the temple. Ronald's birth in 1946 precipitated a move in 1947 to Sheridan Avenue. Maxine's[117] arrival on January 27, 1951 prompted yet another relocation, to a new accommodation on Prairie Avenue, less than a five minute walk to the temple.

With three young children under the age of seven, Lillian had to juggle home and temple responsibilities. Jordan required special medication regularly, and had difficulty keeping up with children his own age. To host the steady stream of out-of-town guests invited by the congregation, Lillian frequently had to arrange babysitters on short notice.

To maintain a sense of familial privacy, Lillian insisted that her husband reserve the early part of the evenings for the family. He accommodated willingly, reserving the evening meal time with his family as holy time, to be interrupted only by urgent telephone calls.

During the summers they traveled north to Spring Valley, New York, (Rockland County, north and west of Manhattan), relaxed at "bungalow colonies" and visited their northern families.

With each passing year, Kronish's institutional obligations increased. Invited to serve on local and national committees, he began to take a more active role in their undertakings.

In the 1950s, he served as chairman of Brandeis University's Camp Committee of greater Miami, editor of the *Miami Beach Zionist* and sat on the administrative committee of the southeast region of the Zionist Organization of America. He devoted time to the American Jewish Congress and the Central Conference of American Rabbis (CCAR), the national rabbinic movement of Reform Judaism. Kronish was also a member of the board of directors of the Miami Bureau of Jewish Education, the Miami Beach YMHA and the Miami State of Israel Bonds organization.

Kronish's congregational responsibilities also expanded because of increased membership. There were more births and deaths, bar and bat mitzvahs, and weddings. There were more administrative details and temple interests competing for his time. He was advisor and teacher, confidant and comforter, spokesman and sociologist, father and husband.

A Growing Congregation

The congregation membership climbed from one hundred and forty families in 1945 to five hundred families in 1950. By 1955 there were over seven hundred and fifty family memberships.[118]

A brochure prepared by the Membership Committee of Temple Beth Sholom for a "welcome service" during this period encapsulates the spirit of the congregation and its ideals of Liberal Judaism:

> We want a Temple that will be a live and living thing. We want a Temple that will speak our language and talk to us in present-day terms. We demand that it be democratic [with] an equitable dues system. At no time shall any family be barred from joining the congregation because of financial circumstances. Democracy means also that we have no assigned pews or seats... even on the High Holy Days. Democracy also means that we shall have no restrictive tuition fees. Jewish education is as much a communal responsibility as general education is a public responsibility. We shall hang on to every shred of Jewish tradition or ceremony that has any beauty or meaning to us.[119]

Betty Malakoff, Kronish's administrative secretary, was assigned the task of welcoming new members.

To cope with this influx and develop the goals of Liberal Judaism, Kronish engaged the sisterhood and men's club to take a leading role and work to establish programs for new members. Over the years, several of the programs arranged focused on the themes Kronish developed during his first year at the Beth Sholom Center—anti-Semitism, Zionism and social justice.

At one of the sisterhood programs in the late 1940s, Laura Hobson's *Gentleman's Agreement* was reviewed by Kronish. The book describes how people [i.e., Jews] are stereotyped and denied their individual freedoms because of prejudice. A week later he followed-up the sisterhood program by preaching from the pulpit on "Hollywood's Exposure of Hatred." Discrimination based on religious and ethnic affiliation ran counter to everything Kronish had come to believe. Jews would no longer tolerate anti-Semitism in any fashion.

The men's club especially took a pro-active Zionist role. For example, they organized scholarship support for Tel Yehuda (a Zionist summer camp) and offered assistance to Beth Sholom's Young Judea group. Beth Sholom's Young Judea group was divided into the Haganah Boys' Club and the Hadera Girls' Club and was the largest Young Judea youth group in the state. Their advisor was Miriam Scheinberg (Zatinsky), who had grown up in Miami.[120] There was also a Masada group headquartered at the temple.

The success of Young Judea led to the formation of a Jewish Boy Scout troop, with a strong Zionist emphasis and the sponsoring of B'nai B'rith AZA and BBG youth clubs that featured Israel programs.

As the congregation grew, cultural, interfaith, and social programs were introduced on a regular basis. For example, Senator Estes Kefauver, chair of the Senate Crime Investigation Committee, was invited to the men's club to speak on the "Citizen's Responsibility in Law Enforcement." In Kefauver's view, social justice depended on citizens serving their communities in the interests of justice.[121]

In a similar vein, the Greater Miami Interfaith Council, a women's organization sponsored by the Miami Council of Church Women, the Negro Branch of the Council of Church Women and the Conference of Jewish Women's organizations, was invited by the sisterhood and met in 1953 at temple. They addressed the issue of "Social Justice and Basic Beliefs."[122]

Religious Education

These themes were also evident in the religious school, although Zionism had the dominant role.

With the expansion of the religious school from nearly four hundred students in 1950 to just under seven hundred by 1955, there was an eager audience waiting for Jewish education.[123] A pre-school program, the Hebrew

Nursery School, opened for children ages two-and-one-half to five. With the growing Jewish population north of 41st Street, a taxi service was arranged to bring students to classes. Children who lived on Normandy Isle, North Beach, Biscayne Point and Surfside were provided bus service.

Tuesday afternoons became designated for religious education in addition to Sundays. It became compulsory for children to attend sabbath worship every week for three years before becoming confirmed and to have a minimum knowledge of Hebrew.

A few of the confirmands of these early years were the children of first-generation Miami Beach residents. For example, Stanley Arkin, Rhoda Granat and Harriet Ginsberg were members of the 1947 class. By the mid-1950s, it was not uncommon to have fifty bar mitzvahs in a year, a score of bat mitzvahs and two dozen confirmands. Among the many who passed through Temple Beth Sholom's doors during these years was Robert Rubin, Secretary of the Treasury in President Clinton's administration. Rubin had a bar mitzvah in the early 1950s, but refused to be confirmed. He sought out Kronish with a few of his friends and asked if they could meet with him in his office on a regular basis to further their Jewish education. According to Rubin, Kronish taught him the meaning of "humanistic Judaism."[124]

Under the able Educational Director, Sydney Greenberg, who joined Beth Sholom in 1947, Hebrew-Zionist education was further enhanced.[125] The emphasis on Hebrew was not only part of a national trend to revitalize religious heritage in Reform congregations but also a bond to *Klal Yisrael*, the people of Israel, and Zionism.

Liberal Judaism: American Jewry's Future

Throughout these years Kronish's overall theme remained constant: the need for Liberal Judaism. He asked his congregation rhetorically what they expected of the synagogue, and would answer the question himself: "meaningful faith, a philosophy of life, a Torah for twentieth century Jews and a sense of belonging and love."[126]

Each week in the *Temple Beth Sholom Bulletin*, he provided temple members with information on the particular features of Liberal Judaism: what it means to be Jewish, how one should celebrate a festival, an explanation of Jewish symbols and editorial comments by colleagues on the importance of practising tradition.

David Goldstrich, a grade six student, succinctly summarized the essence to his fellow students after hearing Rabbi Kronish talk to his class on the theme of Liberal Judaism:

> It's exciting to learn what Moses and David and Isaiah said—and in the very language they spoke. I'm learning the meaning of the Jewish holidays.... and

> what it means to be a good American, because Americanism and Judaism have much in common.[127]

Kronish understood Liberal Judaism as being dedicated to the principle that each generation of Jews was free to interpret tradition in the light of its own historical moment. It was the integration of "old-new" culture.

> Torah should be honored but it should not tyrannize. A return to ritual, to ceremony, strengthens Judaism. To separate the sabbath from the rest of the week increases attendance at temple services. [But] Liberal Judaism is democratic. There is an equitable dues system. No family is excluded because of financial circumstances. There are no assigned seats and no tuition fees for Jewish education.[128]

Liberal Judaism for Kronish was the prophetic legacy of Rabbi Stephen Wise. By fortifying tradition he revitalized Reform Judaism and made it more meaningful to his congregants. The Central Conference of American Rabbis had similarly moved towards advocating more ritual and customs. In the mid-1950s, authors such as Will Herberg, in *Protestant, Catholic and Jew*, spoke of a return to tradition and synagogue.

Conclusion

The unprecedented growth of the Reform movement in North America transformed it from a movement of three hundred and sixty-four congregations, with one hundred thousand families in the late 1940s, to five hundred and thirty-six congregations—with seven hundred thousand families by 1956.[129] At one point, "fully one in two Reform congregations were contemplating or engaged in a major building project."[130] In 1955, Temple Beth Sholom, with nearly eight hundred families, was bursting at the seams. They, too, voted to build a new sanctuary, and renew their covenant with *Klal Yisrael*.

Reconsidering the meaning of the covenant, Kronish re-interpreted it to meet the particular needs of his membership at that moment in history: American Jews confronting simultaneously the appeals of assimilation into an open society, and the desire to maintain an identity forged by 4,000 years of history:

> To be an American Jew and to preach Liberal Judaism is to live an American religious life. To construct a new sanctuary is to renew the covenant between congregants and rabbi. To worship in it is a celebration of living faith and collective service.[131]

Beth Sholom Center, 1942.

Beth Sholom Center seder for servicemen, April 1943.

(Above) Breakfast for 8th grade, early 1950s. Sol Lichter (bow tie) is seated at the table on the extreme left. Leon Kronish is standing, third from left. Sydney Greenberg, Educational Director, is standing, seventh from left.

(Above) Temple Beth Sholom, 1945.
(Below) Temple Beth Sholom school, 1947. Leon Kronish is on the extreme left. Harry Cornblum, president, is on the extreme right.

(Above) Confirmation Class, 1949. (Back row, left to right) Ann Broad, Carol Wien, Gilda Goldstein, Barbara Rothman, Barbara Hillman, Geraldine Taran. (Middle row, left to right) Rabbi Leon Kronish, Ruth Robbins, Gloria Silverman, Diane Silverman, Carol Ciralsky, Sylvia Perlman, Charlotte Glyck, Diane Wolfe, Shepard Broad, Alyce Ell and Cantor Samuel Kelemer. (Front row, left to right) Suzanne Stahl, Barbara Levinson, Alan Levy, Helene Rosenthal, Barbara Pallot.

(Below) Sisterhood Luncheon, 1949. Lillian Kronish is standing, fourth from the left. Leon Kronish is standing between the flags.

(Above) Checking the sanctuary blueprints, 1954. (Left to right) Harry Greenberg, Morris Burk, Leon Kronish, Izzie Hecht.

(Above) Breaking ground for a new sanctuary 1953. (Left to right) Tommy Kravitz, Ralph Spero, unknown, unknown, unknown, Joseph Arkin, Ben Reimer, Harry Greenberg, David Pollack, Jack Abbot, Alexander Rubin, Louis Snetman, James Albert, Norman Russ, Murray Rothman, unknown, unknown, William Bailey.

(Right) 1956
Temple Beth Sholom.

(Above) Bar Mitzvah of Michael Oritt. (Left to right) Rabbi Leon Kronish, Michael, Sam Oritt, Cantor Kelemer.

(Below) Cinderella Ball Committee. (Back row, left to right) Millie Ser, Hilda Zaiac, Maria Perez, Kathy Farber, Mickey Granoff, Jodi Morgan, Beth Nathenson, Sandra Deckerman, Jeanette Stark. (Front row, left to right) Judy Drucker, Lin Arison, Audre Mendel, Dolores Goodstein.

(Above) Mission to Israel. (Left side, front to back) Leon Kronish, Sue Miller, Irving Miller. (Right side, front to back) Lenny Miller, Shirley Miller, Lillian Kronish.

(Below) Planning committee CJA-IEF, 1967. (Left to right) Max Gratz, Robert Rosen, Leon Kronish, Harry Smith, Mike Cooper.

(Above) Decades of leadership, 1984. Shula Ben-David, Hebrew Education Director, Rabbi Leon Kronish, Rabbi Harry Jolt.

(Left) Breaking ground for the new school, 1983. (Left to right) Malcolm Fromberg, James Knopke, Dennis Rice, Leon Kronish, Teena Weiss, Jack Gordon, Harold Vinik.

(Above) Temple Beth Sholom presidents, 1986. (Left to right) Lenore Gaynor, James Knopke, Rabbi Gary Glickstein, Neal Amdur, Harold Vinik, Rabbi Leon Kronish.

(Below) Dedication of Kronish Plaza, 1988. (Left to right) Rabbi Gary Glickstein, Rabbi Leon Kronish, Lillian Kronish.

Chapter Four

CONSOLIDATION AND EXPANSION: TEMPLE BETH SHOLOM AND MIAMI BEACH, AMERICA AND ISRAEL

Introduction

The years between 1955 and 1967 were marked by consolidation and expansion of the institutions to which Leon Kronish had dedicated his life.

As he celebrated his first decade at Temple Beth Sholom, plans were being made for the construction of a new sanctuary, one better able to handle a congregation that had grown from forty households to more than seven hundred and fifty by 1955, and would, by the late 1960s, embrace more than twelve hundred families.[1]

The growth of the temple during this period mirrored that of Miami Beach in general, and its Jewish population in particular. By 1960, more than 140,000 Jews lived permanently in the greater Miami area – comprising some fifteen percent of the entire population of Dade County – with a little more than half living in Miami Beach alone.[2]

But these numbers understate the Jewish influence on the "island sandbar" when one takes into account the large number of Jewish tourists and – even more importantly for Kronish and Temple Beth Sholom – "snowbirds," people who lived in Miami Beach for several months during the winter.[3]

The Liberal Judaism that Kronish preached to this ever-growing audience was of particular relevance during this period, as America was just entering a tumultuous period in its history, one marked by disequilibrium in several areas of life. As will be seen shortly, Kronish took a leading role in espousing a muscular American version of the Reform notion of "prophetic mission," especially in the areas of separation of church and state, civil rights, and the nuclear disarmament movements.

Perhaps even more important, this period saw a major consolidation in Kronish's profound commitment to the State of Israel. His active role in the first Israel Bonds drive in 1951 has been noted before.[4] By the time the Six Day War broke out, Kronish had become a major figure in the national leadership of Israel Bonds in America, a status that would become even more elevated in the aftermath of that seminal conflict.

Kronish's family life also underwent profound change during these years. Tragically, his first-born son died in 1959. At the same time, his two surviving children—Ronald and Maxine—flourished, growing into young adults able and eager to follow their own compass into the pathways blazed for them and many other young Jews by their energetic and devoted father.

Leon Kronish and Beth Sholom: Celebrating the First Decade

Temple Beth Sholom, in the mid-1950s, was viewed by Miamians as "The Liberal Congregation on the Beach."[5] It was distinguished by its restoration of traditional and religious practices, its unwavering support of Zionism and use of modern Hebrew, and its innovative programming in Jewish education. Leon Kronish was respected as a pulpit rabbi and as a spokesperson for the Jewish community. Committed to social action, the congregation attracted new members from throughout the city as well as snowbirds who lived on Miami Beach during the winters and tourists who regularly vacationed there.

On April 23, 1955, the congregation of Beth Sholom held a dinner at the Hollywood Beach Hotel to honor their rabbi at the end of his first ten years of service. In tribute to his enduring concern for peace, education director Sidney Greenberg prepared a dramalogue, "A Rabbi Builds for Peace," and Cantor Samuel Kelemer arranged the music. The dramalogue highlighted Kronish's love for Israel, his passion to renew Jewish traditions, and his philosophy of activism in behalf of the Jewish people. Rabbi Barnett Brickner, president of the Central Conference of American Rabbis (CCAR), commented on the symbolism of the event by saying that "this is a *shidach* (marriage) that will deepen with the years."[6]

Building the New Sanctuary

Enthusiasm to build for the future escalated when the congregation invited Percival Goodman, a "people's designer," to be the architect of the new sanctuary. Architect of many sanctuaries in the United States after World War Two, Goodman was known for his integration of contemporary art with the symbolic foundations of Judaism.[7] His objective was to capture the collective spirit of the congregants in the design. Goodman's book, *Communitas*, co-authored with his son, Paul, had achieved national fame as a commentary on community living.[8]

Percival Goodman was selected by Beth Sholom for his past record as an architect of synagogues who was sensitive to Jewish tradition and subordinated his own theological ideas to those of the congregation. When invited to design a "tent for the people of Israel in Miami Beach," Goodman responded with the 108th Psalm, "I will praise Thee, O Lord, among the people."[9]

To meet the challenge of building a new sanctuary for Temple Beth Sholom, Goodman met with Kronish. They discussed the meaning of *Exodus* 25-27:19—the biblical chapter of *Terumah*—where God instructs Moses in the building of the tabernacle. Both interpreted the instructions as an obligation to create an edifice that would fortify Jewish values and familiarize modern Jews with their heritage and culture. To determine which features would most enhance prayer, ritual, and customs, they examined Jewish tradition through the expression of Liberal Judaism.

The Design

The architectural design was in part, a product of their dialogue. The sanctuary was designed on an intimate, human scale. Tent-like and rustic, the synagogue evokes the memory of a meeting place for a wandering people, in Hebrew, an *ohel mo'ed*. The self-supporting canopy overspreads and connects the rabbi with the congregation. Opaque stained-glass windows set a glow upon the sanctuary and illuminate it in a tapestry of colors. At the center rises the Ark, encased with gilded figures representing the Ten Commandments and surrounded by symbols for the sabbath and religious holidays. The design evoked respect for observances and linked tradition to twentieth-century American Jewry.

The board of directors actively participated in all phases of planning and design. Some members of the congregation undertook particular leadership roles while others made significant personal contributions. Charles Silvers, as chair of the gifts and building committee, organized members for pledges and resources. Morry Morris donated wood and aluminum. Joseph Arkin took responsibility for laying the foundation for the sanctuary. Morris Burk constructed the dome. Many board members held congregational dinners and parlor meetings. Others extended special appeals at temple functions.

Building new sanctuaries was common in the 1950s and 1960s. Hertzberg has commented that "at least a billion dollars was raised and spent building a thousand new synagogue buildings."[10] These endeavors frequently resulted in large mortgages as building campaigns did not generate enough funds over a short period. Temple Beth Sholom also fell prey to a cash shortfall.[11]

The Dedication

The dedication of the sanctuary on November 29, 1957, inaugurated a new phase of activism for the members of Temple Beth Sholom and for their rabbi. Over eighteen hundred congregants shared in this festive celebration.

Under Cantor David Conviser's direction, the newly inaugurated Temple Beth Sholom choir led the congregation in hymns and prayer.

Rabbi Maurice Eisendrath, president of the Union of American Hebrew Congregations (UAHC), was present to deliver the dedicatory sermon.[12] Kronish responded by urging the congregation, "Forward, Forward to the Future," in a song he wrote especially for the occasion.

> Forward, forward to the future
> Building our Religious School
> Building this testament of Hope and of Faith
> We shall build our Beth Sholom!
>
> From every member of our Temple
> We shall find the strength to build
> This house of learning for tomorrow
> Where God's word will be instilled.
>
> All the teaching of our sages
> All that's holy must survive
> All the spirit of the ages
> We shall try to keep alive.

Preaching, he asked his congregants "to share with me your understanding of messianic redemption so that I may labor for a Jewish future."[13]

Temple Beth Sholom and "The Season"

By the mid-1960s Miami Beach's Temple Beth Sholom became as popular among Jewish snowbirds as the Fontainebleau Hotel was for tourists. Membership consisted of Reform Jews from every part of the United States and from Canada, the Caribbean, Cuba, Central America, South America—and even Israel.

Kronish wondered whether the Jewish tourists to Miami Beach—now coming in record numbers—might also appreciate his revitalized education package of programs and informal social-cultural groups.

Miami Beach, "the southern borscht belt," had become the winter Catskills and the Hollywood of the East. In 1960, the Miss USA and Miss Universe pageants were moved to Miami Beach. Five-and-one-half million tourists visited the Miami area in 1962.[14] In 1963, the Jackie Gleason television show opened, and the following year, 1964, Cassius Clay (Muhammad Ali) became heavyweight champion on Miami Beach.

The Fontainebleau and the Latin Quarter, a night club operated by Barbara Walters' father Lou, and other fabulous watering holes on the Beach brought a continuous procession of big time stars to dazzle tourists. Red Buttons, Judy Garland, Frank Sinatra, Lucille Ball, Ed Sullivan, Louis

Armstrong and Sophie Tucker were among the star attractions. Beach cabanas, deep sea fishing, golf, and gambling off-shore and at jai alai frontons and at the numerous horse and dog tracks were depicted in the advertisements and the news stories that were beamed across the country.

Middle-class America got the message. Hollywood stars vied to be seen as part of the Miami scene. The superstars who converted to Judaism—Marilyn Monroe, Sammy Davis Jr., Carroll Baker and Elizabeth Taylor—were lured to the Beach by Jewish hotel owners who also hustled them to be photographed with their Jewish clientele.

Kronish began to meet with tourists at their hotels—the Saxony, Sans Souci, Eden Roc, Deauville, and Fontainebleau. He invited them to participate in Temple Beth Sholom's sabbath services and activities. Those tourist who attended services or congregational programs were often greeted by World War Two veterans or former tourists who had returned to Miami Beach to settle down permanently.

Within a short time, many tourists became accustomed to praying at the temple on Friday nights. Among the visiting tourists were Rabbis Jacob Rudin, Richard Hirsch and Alexander Schindler.[15] Others came because they had heard about Kronish's stands on nuclear disarmament and civil rights and were curious to hear him preach. Sometimes they came for no particular reason other than having noticed the temple through the taxi window on their ride from the airport to the Beach, over the Julia Tuttle Causeway and along 41st Street.[16] Gradually Kronish earned a well-deserved reputation as a dynamic speaker who preached on relevant topics. These visitors, in due course, assisted Kronish in establishing a nationwide support network for his organizational efforts on behalf of many Jewish causes, and especially the State of Israel.

Snowbirds

Over the years Kronish noted changes in the behavior and habits of those who visited Miami Beach. Beginning as tourists who spent a month or two in a hotel, many bought or leased condominiums, stayed for six months and called themselves "snowbirds." In the 1960s, thousands of Jewish northerners bought condominiums on Miami Beach.

Deborah Dash Moore has described this phenomenon as representing an alternative to suburbanization and one that disproportionately attracted Jewish seniors. "The mass majority of elderly Jews in Miami Beach received an impetus from the steady decay of the inner cities, accompanied by the rising rate of crime, the high cost of living and the arrival of new, poor immigrants. The portability of federal social security benefits and union pensions encouraged mobility."[17]

Kronish sensed that many of these winter residents would be interested in participating in the programs offered by the temple. He saw many of them as socialized with Jewish values, hungry for Jewish culture, and eager to share their life-experiences. Theirs was a unique opportunity for one another and for the others in the congregation. David Scheinbaum, a new member during this period and a *zayde* (grandfather), succinctly summarized the situation: "Mine is the last generation of its kind. What we have here is a cumulative 800 million years of experience walking around. Surely all that experience can still make a contribution."[18]

Kronish's sensitivity to this senior citizen population was rare in the Reform movement. According to a 1966 UAHC report on Senior Citizen Programs, less than ten percent of congregations offered programs to this group and "the prospect for future expression is not encouraging. Thus far, [congregations] have not felt the need for such a program, and have not grasped the philosophical concept of a retirement program."[19]

In contrast, for Kronish, everywhere he looked was the "world of his fathers and mothers." Polly Redford in her *Biography of Miami Beach*, describes demographically this world south of Lincoln Road—"forty thousand people, 85 percent of them Jewish, 80 percent over sixty-five." By the late 1960s, Jews made up seventy percent of the Beach population and over half of all households were over the age of sixty-five.[20]

A significant number of these condominium "season" residents and snowbirds sought membership at Temple Beth Sholom. Many were first-generation American Jews and Holocaust survivors. Some were former garment workers including former *Bund* members, who were now strong supporters of Israel.

Kronish looked to them as his in-house ambassadors to Beth Sholom youth. They were to be role models as social activists who combined their American loyalties with Zionist sentiments. By adopting Israel as their spiritual homeland without making a commitment to *aliya*, they also illustrated, ironically, the meaning of American Zionism for the younger generation.

The Life of an Activist Rabbi

Given his wide-ranging efforts at attracting and organizing tourists, snowbirds and residents, Kronish was often absent from home. He was at the beck and call of his congregation whom he served as teacher, theologian, preacher, pastor, administrator, community spokesman and fundraiser.

He taught bar mitzvah, bat mitzvah and confirmation classes, prepared new liturgical pieces, composed sermons, wrote public speeches, conferred with his board, counseled the distressed, visited the sick, met with committees, arranged life-cycle events, and officiated at weddings and funerals.

He was aided by the congregation's dedicated administrative staff, Betty Malakoff, the Executive Director, and Dorothy Jacobson, his administrative secretary. They described him as a "whirlwind of activity." In 1966 the board voted to hire assistant rabbis to help him with his workload. Rabbi Daniel Franzel was the first of many who joined the congregation.

Kronish made it a practice to meet in his study with members as frequently as possible. The office-study mirrored the rabbi's personality and interests. Behind the desk was a large, nine-by-four foot map of Israel, that detailed the history of the patriarchs of Judaism. Their teachings – the teachings of the biblical patriarchs – was where Rabbi Kronish had begun his lifelong quest into the relationship between God and *Klal Yisrael*. Astute visitors could see Kronish's personal commentary on the map. There was, for example, a sign on Babylon, today's Iran and Iraq, that read "Danger, Unsafe for Travelers."

The study's walls also held bookshelves, stacked and crowded with a Judaica library: Rambam's *Commentary on the Torah*, Weizmann's *Trial and Error*, Hiller's *Isaac M. Wise*, and liturgical volumes, devotional works and popular literature. On the walls between shelves and windows were paintings and religious artifacts, family portraits and signed documents, including David Ben-Gurion's portrait signed, "To my friend, Rabbi Leon Kronish."

Despite his demanding schedule, Kronish still managed to set aside certain moments of the day for his own personal, reflective time. Quiet and alone, he would prepare his sermons and public speeches by dictating them on a microphone. Rocking on his chair in the study, listening to soft music in the background, he could look out at the beautiful Atlantic Ocean inlet, and watch the intracoastal waters flowing by his window.

Often a moment of meditation would be interrupted by a telephone ring. Maxine or one of his sons demanded his attention. Or, as often happened, the telephone rang with a "can't wait" message from Dorothy Jacobson, his secretary. Temple Beth Sholom presidents of the 1950s and 1960s, Ralph Spero, John Serbin, Harry Greenberg, James Albert and Louis Snetman, were the "can't wait men."

In addition to his responsibilities to his congregation, Kronish developed increasing obligations to the greater Miami and national organizations, which he served. Service to the larger community was always part of his rabbinic vision, and it was supported and encouraged by his congregational leadership who took pride in his growing local, regional and national prestige.

During the 1960s he was chair of the Greater Miami Rabbinical Association, a vice-president of the Greater Miami Jewish Federation, a vice-president of the Florida chapter of the American Jewish Congress, and chairman of the national board of the Histadrut Foundation. He was also on the national board campaign cabinet of Israel Bonds, a member of the executive committee of the Hebrew Union College-Jewish Institute of Religion and a member of various Central Conference of American Rabbis committees.

Liberal Judaism and Liturgical Innovation

Part of Kronish's attractiveness to Miami's Jewry during these years was his response to his congregant's spiritual needs. They sought out a liturgy that was thoughtful and contemporary. In the 1950s several guidebooks to the ceremonies and observances of Reform Judaism were published.

Perhaps the most influential of these, *A Guide for Reform Jews*, was co-authored by Rabbis David Polish and Frederick A. Doppelt in 1957. Polish and Doppelt, rabbinical colleagues of Kronish, argued that "the authority or criterion for observances ought to be the Jew's historic memory.... *Mitzvot* [commandments] have the goal of leading the Reform Jew to the 'self-imposed discipline of observance.'"[21]

Polish, one of the foremost Zionist leaders of the Reform movement, strongly urged the Reform movement to rekindle Judaism's spiritual intimacy with Israel, "to remember the spiritual roots of its being [and] recognize and accept a *Halachic* existence."[22]

Shortly after World War Two, Polish had instituted more traditional practices in his congregation, Beth Emet, in Evanston, Illinois, and advocated greater attention at meetings of the Central Conference of American Rabbis (the national body of Reform Rabbis in North America), to the voices of non-rabbinical Reform Jews. In 1946 Polish had suggested that *Tisha be-Av* be revived as a religious holiday, and in 1953 he put forward the idea of a commemoration day for the Holocaust.

Although these suggestions were not quickly accepted by the Reform movement, they immediately struck a positive response from Rabbi Kronish. He, too, strongly wanted to link the past with the present, to restore Jewish tradition to the twentieth century, and to connect American Jewry with Israel.

When Polish co-authored his *Guide*, many of the *Mitzvot* he highlighted were already part of the standard observances in Temple Beth Sholom. The observance of *Tisha be-Av*, a memorial day for martyrs, and a religious celebration for Israel Independence Day, had been accepted by members of Temple Beth Sholom as obligatory for the renewal of a living Judaism.

At Central Conference of American Rabbis (CCAR) meetings and other occasions, Kronish shared with Polish his own congregants' responses to these innovations of Liberal Judaism.

Kronish shared the lead with a handful of other Reform rabbis committed to introduce innovative liturgies that captured both the Zionist and Jewish experience to meet the personal needs of their congregants. These liturgies also made the prayer books more responsive to the issues of the day. They focussed on current political events, and topical moral issues frequently infused with a Zionistic bent. More traditional Hebrew prayers, praying for Zion, and strengthening the bond between American Jewry and Israel were common features of this effort.

Following the lead of Polish, Kronish articulated the need for new worship forms.[23] "It is my conviction," he wrote, "that we can develop a creative *'Minhag* America' that reflects both our timeless tradition and present times; [that reveals] the tensions between the Twentieth Century, the teachings of our tradition, the timeless ties of the faith and the people of Israel."[24] Messianic redemption was linked to the future of *Klal Yisrael*.

To reach the goal of a "*Minhag* America," Kronish drafted several innovative liturgies. A *Shofar Service for Rosh Hashanah*, written in 1948 and revised in 1955, complemented the regular *shofar* service in the *Union Prayerbook*. A special *Hanukkah Candlelight Service*, first published in 1949, was revised and rededicated each year to the liberation of Jews and to the preservation of the Jewish state, and *The New Haggadah in Israel*: *Passover Supplementary Haggadah*, composed in 1950, added contemporary interpolations to key passages and was revised annually.[25]

Jewish Education

One of the *mitzvot* identified in the Doppelt-Polish *Guide* was the enhancement of Jewish education, "in the heritage of Israel [and]... thereby fulfilling the spiritual destiny of the Jewish people."[26] Kronish interpreted this *mitzvah* for his congregation and American Jews in terms of creating a synthesis of Liberal (Reform) Judaism with Zionism.

Such were the pillars of his vocation. The foundation blocks of this synthesis were covenant, *Klal Yisrael* (people of Israel), and *Eretz Yisrael* (the land of Israel). The covenant, the "chosen people" concept, between God and the people and land of Israel, was the cement that bonded Reform Judaism in the United States to Zionism.[27]

Throughout the 1950s, more and more Jewish parents enrolled their children in religious education programs in North America. With the increasing numbers of Jewish baby boomers growing up, and with demands by young parents for parochial education, new and expanded options for religious instruction were developed.

In Miami, these needs were more urgent than in most Jewish communities. Greater Miami's Jewish population grew from 55,000 in 1950 to 140,000 in 1960.[28] Although a Miami Bureau of Jewish Education was formed in 1944, it could not keep up with growing number of parents requesting a Jewish education for their children.[29]

In a national study conducted in 1956, the American Association of Jewish Education calculated the "growth in enrollment in classes [in Miami] during the post-war decade to be 485 percent, four times higher than the population growth."[30] At Temple Beth Sholom, school registration had increased from eighty-one in the fall of 1945 to six hundred and seventy-nine ten years later (1955).[31]

Kronish served on the Commission for Jewish Education of the Central Conference of American Rabbis for nearly a decade. The Commission's recommendations combined with Kronish's own reformulation of Kaplan's concept of synagogue-center, provided fertile soil for his educational directors of the 1950s and 1960s, Sidney Greenberg, Herb Bloom, and Sol Lichter,[32] to develop new programs and curricula. They also incorporated Kronish's liturgical innovations and commitment to covenant, peoplehood, and Zionism.

Following Doppelt's and Polish's *Guide*, each educational phase of the life cycle—from pre-school to advanced adult learning—had a *mitzvah* component;[33] and each new program had to pass a battery of questions regarding its effectiveness in linking Liberal (Reform) Judaism to Zionism.

These questions included: How did the existence of the modern state of Israel affect the relationship between American Jews and God? How does a Jew, living in America, participate fully in the "chosenness" partnership with God? What are the spiritual dimensions of "chosenness" for the Reform Jew in the United States of America?[34]

From Pre-school to Seniors

Programs developed were to touch all age groups from pre-schoolers to the octogenarians.

The Foundation pre-school program, inaugurated in the late 1940s, was expanded to include more Israeli songs, Hebrew words, and traditional Jewish observances. The first years of afternoon Hebrew school and Sunday school were altered to reflect the changed emphasis on Zionism. Greater concentration was given to developing modern Hebrew skills and to understanding the most recent archaeological discoveries within the context of Jewish history and of the words of the Torah and the Prophets.

The history of the 1948 War of Independence was given equal importance to that of Joshua and David conquering Canaan. Religious study integrated with modern history and culture—with a focus on developments both in America and in the land of Israel—was Kronish's formula for education.

Bar and bat mitzvah preparation and confirmation and post-confirmation classes emphasized interpretation of texts, practice of rituals, and learning the Hebrew language. Cantor David Conviser, a graduate of the Juilliard School of Music and the Hebrew Union College School of Sacred Music in New York, who joined the congregation in 1957, contributed musical features to these lessons, and taught his pupils to sing Israeli songs.[35]

Each bar or bat mitzvah was viewed as a collective educational opportunity where everyone joined in renewing the covenant of Judaism. The bar or bat mitzvah child, or children, standing on the *bimah* with his or her parents, symbolized to the congregation the unity of the Jewish people and the passing of tradition from generation to generation.[36]

Rabbi Kronish, spreading his *tallit* over the bar or bat mitzvah's head, recited the priestly blessing that has been repeated by Jews since biblical times:

> May the Lord bless you, and keep you;
> May the Lord make his face to shine upon you
> and be gracious unto you;
> May the Lord lift up his countenance upon you,
> and give you peace.[37]

The Kronish children celebrated their *b'nai mitzvah* at Temple Beth Sholom: Jordan in 1955; Ronald in 1959; and Maxine in 1964. These were especially meaningful events for the rabbi, as they intertwined his personal family celebrations with that of his "congregational" family.[38]

At the age of fifteen, children who had celebrated their bar and bat mitzvah were confirmed—the ritual practice in Reform and Conservative Judaism in which young adults, of both genders, re-affirmed their individual commitment to the Jewish faith and people.

Confirmation occurred on the holiday of *Shavuot*, the day of tradition that God gave Moses and the Jewish people the Ten Commandments and the Torah. In preparation for confirmation, Rabbi Kronish personally taught the teenagers more advanced Judaica and concentrated on subjects that deepened their knowledge of American Zionism and Liberal Judaism.

Kronish devoted a great deal of attention to the confirmation of Temple Beth Sholom youngsters. Each year he would write a special service, introduce liturgical innovations and work with the choir to prepare something special. Observing the students, he would identify those most committed to Jewish education and invite them to return and serve as counsellors in the temple's youth programs.

All students were also encouraged to join post-confirmation classes. When *Shavuot* approached, he would personally seek out the children's parents to participate in the service. Confirmation was a beautiful, meaningful and collective celebration for the temple "family." When Jordan, Ronald and Maxine were confirmed, they received, like all other confirmands, special blessings whispered into their ears by the rabbi—in this case, their own father.

Adolescents within the congregation had a choice of groups to join: Beth Sholom Temple Youth (BESHTY), a branch of the Reform movement's National Federation of Temple Youth (NFTY); the Temple Thespians, a theater group; and Young Judea. In addition, groups were introduced for adults—the Maccabees, for age thirty and older; and the Young in Hearts, for seniors.

Kronish perceived a new willingness among the congregants to study texts and introduced Torah study groups on weekly and monthly cycles. Classes covered both the weekly Torah portion and a range of topics including prayer, holidays, *tzedakah* (philanthropy), ritual, Jewish history, the Holocaust, Israel, and the American Jewish community. Additionally, classes in modern Hebrew were offered to adults.

Leading the Wave in American Reform Judaism

Expansion of Jewish education programs for adults and youth in the late 1950s and early 1960s was common practice in Reform congregations according to Max Feder, author of an UAHC report on temple programs.

> There is a growing complex of groups, programs and events which is changing the composition of the modern temple. Adult Education programming is being stressed and there is interest in Hebrew and Israel. The rabbi is being drawn more and more into the program structure.[39]

In South Florida, Rabbi Kronish was leading that wave.

Kronish never forgot Professor Alexander Dushkin's teaching that the educational process was as important to educating as the lesson's content. Think of whom you want to educate and why. Then think of what methods and which content would best serve to meet those goals. By serving on the Central Conference of American Rabbis Education Commission and the National Curriculum Committee, Kronish kept abreast of national policies. Applying Dushkin's process principles, he tailored them to match Temple Beth Sholom's particular needs.

New Horizons: Judy Drucker and Cultural Education

In addition to these innovations in substantive content, Kronish and Temple Beth Sholom were also innovators in the musical, and larger cultural aspects of Reform Jewish religious education. Kronish had long encouraged musical innovations as an important complement to his liturgical writings and collaborated with Cantor Conviser and the choir in arranging moving and sensitive compositions.

In the mid-1960s one of the choir's members, Judy Drucker, felt the time was ripe to add a more pronounced musical dimension to the synagogue-center programs and activities.[40]

Judy was born in Brooklyn and moved to Miami Beach as a young child. Her mother, Lillian Nelson, was an opera singer and concert pianist. Wanting her child to pursue music, Lillian enrolled Judy in private classes from Arturo De Filipi, founder of the Miami Opera Guild, and she performed during her college years at the Latin Quarter Club. She and Barbara Walters, the owner's daughter, did their homework together backstage.

The Nelsons attended Temple Beth Sholom and Rabbi Kronish married Judy to David Drucker. As a member, Judy was encouraged by Kronish to use her talents for the congregation. She sang in the choir, chaired programs and helped organize events. Many of the snowbirds were dear friends. By the mid-1960s, Kronish and Judy had worked on many programs together.

In early 1967, Judy suggested to Kronish that a concert be substituted for one session of the temple's lecture series. So well-received was the concert that a musical series directed by Drucker was instituted the following year as part of a cultural educational arts program. Talented Jewish American and Israeli musicians were invited to perform. These musical events quickly attracted not only Beth Sholom members and snowbirds, but also the entire greater southeast Florida community.

Drucker's background as a professional singer, and her talents and dedication to initiate, encourage and organize others, turned Temple Beth Sholom into greater Miami's foremost musical arts center. According to Drucker, this would not have been possible without Kronish's visionary leadership. "Rabbi Kronish became the catalyst in my life. He doesn't think in the present, he actually thinks in the future."[41]

For the next two decades, Beth Sholom enjoyed this distinction by providing South Florida with world-renowned instrumentalists, vocal soloists, and dancers.

In addition, an art gallery was opened adjacent to the sanctuary where the works of Israeli artists were frequently exhibited. Photographic exhibits from *Beth Hatefutsot* (Museum of the Diaspora) have been exhibited regularly at the gallery: "A Century of Zionist Immigration to *Eretz Yisrael*," "The Jews of Kaifeng, China" and "The Jews of Ethiopia." Paintings on the Holocaust, and Soviet Jewish artists have also been highlighted.

Social Action: The Prophetic Mission of Reform Judaism

At the same time Kronish was moving to revitalize both the temple in particular, and the Jewish community in general, he was also lending a powerful Jewish voice to the movements for social change then roiling the United States. He did so by integrating the ideals of Liberal Judaism with special emphasis on the obligations of prophetic covenant and mission.

Before 1940 Reform Judaism's rhetoric of mission stressed service to humanity. Its use of mission "paralleled that of the Protestant Church but with an anti-nationalist and an anti-traditionalist universalism."[42]

After World War Two, the Union of American Hebrew Congregations, the national umbrella organization for Reform Judaism, under the leadership of Maurice Eisendrath (from 1943 to 1973), redefined the meaning of mission. Mission now came to mean the application of the "precepts and practices of prophetic Jewish faith to combat all forms of injustice and bigotry." Social action was not to be abandoned, but "it was to be redefined in terms of Jewish particularism and nationalism, or Zionism."[43] Increasingly, in the 1950s, the

Reform rabbinate began to echo Eisendrath's reformulation and followed his lead by instituting social action programs and committees.

Translated into educational values and activities at Temple Beth Sholom, Jewish identity came to mean a call to social action with a Jewish voice, supported by the values of Liberal Judaism. "God's covenant with his people demanded a response to social injustices," exhorted Kronish.[44]

Throughout the 1950s and the 1960s, there was ample opportunity to test the congregants' internalization of Kronish's teachings of Liberal Judaism and their commitment to this new meaning of prophetic covenant and mission.

Separation of church and state, the question of civil rights, and nuclear disarmament were three of many emotionally charged and timely issues that demanded Kronish's attention on the American civic agenda.

Separation of Church and State

The first challenge, separation of church and state, simmered in the 1950s and came to a head in 1960. Miami public schools were reenacting the crucifixion as part of the Easter holiday programs. At one school, Jewish students requested permission to be excused from attending the sectarian observance, but they were required to be present.

The American Jewish Congress, representing the Jewish students, protested the religious practices of the public schools of Dade County. A court hearing was set. Immediately, the case gained national significance as it brought to the public's attention the sectarian practices of prayers, sermons, and religious holiday observances within public schools, *de facto* religious tests for public school teachers.

During the late 1950s, before the Miami school case, Kronish and others had worked quietly, behind the scenes, to alter the sectarian practices of the Dade County School Board. They were not successful.

As vice-president of the American Jewish Congress' South Florida chapter, Kronish threatened to prosecute, advocating "principle over considerations of public opinion."[45] In doing this he broke with many other local Jewish leaders who, remembering the overtly anti-Semitic real estate restrictions of an earlier decade, were reluctant to aggravate old wounds.

Kronish addressed the issue repeatedly from his pulpit, challenging the constitutionality of sectarian religious practices. He asked congregants to inquire about religious activities of their children in the public schools. A committee was established to process information and to flag those who wished to volunteer for a more active role.

Although the American Jewish Congress adopted a policy that was not initially popular, the Unitarian Church and the Florida Civil Liberties Union joined the effort and filed lawsuits in the spring of 1960 challenging the religious practices of the public schools of Dade County.

> The case marked the first time in American jurisprudence that a whole constellation of religious practices in the public schools has been attacked in a single suit: Bible instruction, prayers and grace, sermons, religious films, hymns, holiday observances and symbols, baccalaureate programs, census taking and tests for teachers.[46]

Kronish remained staunchly supportive and stood shoulder to shoulder with Bernard S. Mandler, chairman of the Commission on Law and Social Action for the South Florida Council of the American Jewish Congress. Kronish also openly backed Jack Gordon, a strong advocate for the separation of church and state and a vice-president of the American Jewish Congress, in the upcoming autumn 1960 election for the Dade County School Board.

The case was heard in July, October and November 1960 in Miami and attracted national press coverage. Associated Press and United Press ran the daily court proceedings on their national newswires and the *New York Times* sent a reporter to cover the story.

Catholic and Protestant press were also present, frequently in support of the plaintiffs. An editorial in *Christian Century,* an influential interdisciplinary Protestant publication, not only supported the plaintiffs but also requested its national membership to "have the grace to acknowledge that they have been in the wrong."[47]

Mr. Leo Pfeffer,[48] the Chief Counsel and a renowned constitutional lawyer, called Rabbi Kronish as a key witness and asked him to express to the court why Jews found the teachings of the divinity of Jesus, the dogma of the Trinity, the New Testament, the Resurrection, and the Cross unacceptable subjects for public education.

Kronish explained why Jews, other non-Christians, and many Christians find these beliefs inappropriate content for the public school. "The separation of church and state in our Constitution precludes such sectarian practices," asserted Kronish.[49]

Standing up for one's beliefs was the tradition of his mentors. His rabbinical training and the lessons that he had learned from Wise and Kaplan had prepared Kronish to brave the resulting storm of bad publicity.

Later that year the Dade County Circuit Court ruled that the depiction of the Crucifixion and Nativity in public schools breached the separation doctrine. Christmas and Easter programs were deemed "religious teachings." According to Mandler, the lawyer who led the battle in Dade County, the success of the case was in no small measure due to Kronish who "coordinated much of the historic effort."[50]

In June 1962 the Florida Supreme Court unanimously affirmed the Dade County Circuit Court decision. Two years later, the Supreme Court of the United States overturned another Florida Supreme Court ruling, one that allowed Bible reading in the public schools.[51]

Civil Rights

The second challenge, civil rights—the confrontation between African Americans and whites—was a litmus test for Liberal Judaism and Kronish. Kronish's attitude and behavior toward incidents of blatant racism were unequivocally critical. Social action programs in civil rights became a regular feature of temple life, and a vehicle to respond to the local situation.

At the time of the *Brown v. Board of Education* desegregation decision in 1954, Jim Crow was alive and healthy in Florida where it was part of the state's cultural and statutory tradition.

African Americans in Miami could not swim at a white beach, walk into a white movie house nor eat in a white restaurant. They had to sit in the back of the bus. There were separate drinking fountains, separate lavatories, and separate seating for public performances and special events. Residential segregation, substandard housing, job discrimination and economic marginality were the diet of black Americans in Miami.

In the 1956 Florida gubernatorial election, LeRoy Collins continued his pledge to retain segregation in the Florida public schools.[52] In Miami, only two public schools were partially desegregated by the end of the decade.[53]

While certainly not victimized to the same extent as blacks, Jews were also targeted by the forces that were leading the opposition to desegregation.

Attacks on Miami synagogues during the 1950s by the White Citizen Council, a white supremacist group, were frequent. The White Citizen Council targeted synagogues whose rabbis were particularly outspoken. Temple Israel was attacked by dynamite; Temple Beth-El was bombed; Temple Petha Tikva in Coral Gables was threatened; and Temple Beth Sholom received ominous phone calls. The Miami Police Department was advised that "more bombings would follow unless 'desegregation' or 'integration' was stopped in Miami."[54]

During one week in the late 1950s, threats were made against eleven Dade County buildings whose owners had instituted desegregation policies. Several of the targeted buildings were Jewish institutions.

In the early 1960s, school board member Jack Gordon and Dade County City Attorney Richard Gerstein were on a "hit list," scheduled to be assassinated. Between 1962 to 1964, Jews were regularly the target of violence by right-wing groups. Indeed, such threats led Miami Beach police during this period to order special protection for Temple Beth Sholom and many other Jewish institutions.[55]

Kronish often shared his concerns about black-Jewish relations with Burnett Roth, a member of Temple Beth Sholom. Roth was a founding member of Miami's Anti-Defamation League and had spoken out repeatedly on the attitudes of the Miami community towards African Americans.

At the conclusion of World War Two, Roth and other ex-servicemen organized themselves as part of the Anti-Defamation League effort to fight against restriction signs. They paid quiet house calls on the managers of hotels, motels, and apartment houses displaying or otherwise advertising a "Gentiles Only" policy. In 1947, Roth worked with Miami Beach councilman D. Lee Powell to draft a municipal anti-discriminatory sign ordinance.

Although the State legislature invalidated the ordinance on the grounds that the municipality lacked jurisdiction, by 1949 they passed new legislation that provided the municipality the legitimacy to prohibit discriminatory advertising.[56] Two years later, Roth and Powell joined forces again to foster an anti-Ku Klux Klan Act prohibiting the burning of crosses and the wearing of masks and hoods.[57]

During the 1950s when African-American entertainers were forced to find accommodation in Overtown, a black section of Miami, Roth invited them to stay as his guests at his Miami Beach home. Frequently he asked Leon and Lillian Kronish to share bread with his guests, including Lena Horne and Sidney Poitier. On these occasions they heard first-hand how blacks were organizing and reaching out for support.

Poitier, son of a Bahamian tomato farmer, was born in Miami and poignantly recalled his fear of white supremacist groups. In his autobiography, *This Life*, Poitier recalls working as a delivery man and trying to leave a package at the front door of a Miami Beach resident. Several nights later the Klansmen looked for Sidney Poitier at his brother's house. "I decided that Miami wasn't so good for me when I began to run into its not-so-subtle pattern of racism."[58]

Dinnertime at the Roth home invariably led to discussing coalitions to develop a better, peaceful America. These *tète a tète* sessions led to a number of interfaith programs cosponsored by Temple Beth Sholom and African-American churches.

The Reverend Theodore Gibson, who headed the Miami chapter of the NAACP, became Kronish's friend.[59] From time to time they would brainstorm with other Miami Jewish religious leaders.[60] In 1955 a joint program was held with the Reverend Ed Graham with a dual focus—civil rights for African Americans and freedom for the Falashas, the black Jews of Ethiopia.[61]

The by-products of these co-sponsored programs were joint efforts to introduce bills in the Florida Legislature to stop discrimination against minorities. In 1955 Florida passed an Anti-Discrimination Advertising Act.[62]

Local black activists and a handful of Jewish liberals at Temple Beth Sholom worked to desegregate hotels and restaurants. In 1956, Jewish hotels on Miami Beach accommodated fifteen hundred delegates to an African Methodist Church convention.

Ongoing dialogue between whites (including Jews) and African Americans, legal challenges by the NAACP, and militant activism by the Congress of Racial Equality (CORE) encouraged the desegregation momentum.

Local marches were joined by civil rights leaders, including such area politicians as John B. Orr, Dade County legislator.

Significant changes began occurring. Municipal and state laws were passed legitimating the desegregation of buses (1956 and 1957), beaches, parks, and hospitals (1958), and schools (1960).[63]

Rabbi Jacob Rothschild of the Hebrew Benevolent Congregation of Atlanta, and a civil rights colleague of Martin Luther King, Jr., addressed the Union of American Hebrew Congregation's (UAHC) biennial conference in Miami in 1959, speaking on"the Personal Demands of Social Justice." Rothschild challenged the Reform movement to translate its Jewish faith into prophetic mission. In his view, a rabbi's role is to teach "the ideals of his Jewish faith [and to] reaffirm his belief in the vigor of American democracy. He must do this despite the climate of opinion."[64]

Rothchild asked the audience of nationwide congregational leaders to scrutinize their reaction "when a Negro moves onto your street."[65] Those present were also challenged by Rabbi Eisendrath. He expressed to the convention delegates that the essence of religion is "man's relation to man, and is judged by actions not only words."[66] With Rothchild's challenge and Eisendrath's support, the UAHC voted to establish a Religious Social Action Center in Washington, D.C. Poverty, ignorance, and insecurity would be attacked through social commitment and political activism. The UAHC Emile and Kivie Kaplan Center for Religious Action opened its doors in 1961.

In 1960, following the UAHC decision to build a Religious Action Center in Washington, D.C., Beth Sholom established an Interfaith Institute to encourage communication between Jews and non-Jews. Ministers and priests were invited to participate in dialogues about religion, national politics, and local events.

At one of the first gatherings of the Interfaith Institute, Kronish drew upon Percival Goodman's design of Temple Beth Sholom and spoke on "Peace as Reflected in the Art and Architecture of the Synagogue." At another session, Miami Beach public schools held a workshop on interfaith education. Myra Farr, a Beth Sholom member and longtime Beach resident, whose uncle had built the Nemo, the first Beach Kosher hotel, took the lead in linking congregation activities with school board functions.

In 1963, members of the Interfaith Institute actively participated in a unity march for African Americans that was jointly sponsored by the Rabbinical Association of Greater Miami, the Catholic archdiocese, and local Protestant clergy. Through actions such as these, Temple Beth Sholom played a role in the establishment of a Metro-Dade Community Relations Board. Kronish was a charter member.

The commitment by Kronish to stop segregation had a religious as well as a political basis. The prophetic tradition criticized harshly those who did not treat other humans with honor and respect. Standing on the *bimah* (podium),

Kronish would draw on Amos, Hosea and Isaiah for his sermons to motivate his congregants to march in protest of segregation.

> The story of segregation is a sordid and sinful one. Who is there among us who, in the tangled troubled realm of race relations is so righteous that he doeth good always and sinneth not through his own prejudices and bigotry, his own acts of exclusion and segregation? We may self-righteously squirm at the spectacle of segregated buses in the South, but we are not averse to joining in keeping 'lily-white' the very neighborhoods from which we as Jews were until but recently banned. If this problem has no relevance to Judaism; if we refuse, no matter how many statements we have previously made, to continue to 'cry aloud and spare not,' if we fail to take such action as may be within our power to end every vestige of discrimination, then Judaism really has no meaning or relevance to life itself.[67]

Kronish would make personal appeals to the temple's social action committees to be more involved. He encouraged them to invite the Reverend Gibson and other NAACP leaders to speak at their meetings. Kronish spoke out when political figures like Senator George Smathers of Florida blasted black voter registration drives as a "dangerous invasion of carpetbaggers."

Not all congregants shared Kronish's civil rights ideology. Although most were second-generation Jews who held liberal political views, many opposed rapid desegregation or the methods being used to achieve it. James Wax, writing in the *Central Conference American Rabbis Journal*, has commented that these Jews have "acculturated [and] share attitudes of the South—the Negro should have the opportunity to improve himself through education but in separate schools."[68]

Intellectually, congregants could understand the parallel between the African-American's fight for civil rights and the Jew's struggle against discrimination. A handful could also remember the signs, "No Jews and No Coloreds," one decade earlier.

However for many, their view was one of gradualism. In the words of one southern rabbi, "the majority of [Southern] Jews deem it unwise to identify publicly with the struggle to eliminate segregation."[69] For them, progress towards racial equality was fine, but progress should move forward ever so cautiously. Along with many Jews in the greater Miami area, they feared a white, gentile backlash.

Kronish listened to their views and dealt with his congregants' personal struggles to come to terms with change in America. Many of Temple Beth Sholom's outspoken liberals later joined their more politically conservative co-religionists when compulsory busing was introduced in Miami Beach in the late 1960s.

Some were adamant in their loyalty to the neighborhood-school concept, especially where it concerned primary- and elementary-age children. Others, copying many northerners, were committed to moral and financial support for civil rights until those rights legislated integration in their own backyard.

The teachings of Liberal Judaism and its prophetic mission of responding to social injustices were not easily digested by many congregants when confronted by rapid social change and opposing ideological values.

Nuclear Disarmament

The third challenge for Temple Beth Sholom and Liberal Judaism, nuclear disarmament, transcended religion and race. The very nature of human existence was at stake. Kronish, remembering the Holocaust, exhorted his congregants to consider what the consequences are of creating a golem, a Frankenstein's monster that could be unleashed on the world: "Paradoxically, the H-bomb being created in the name of God could very well put an end to that which God hath created."[70]

Laboring for *sholom*, for peace, was a cornerstone of Rabbi Kronish's life teaching. From his arrival in Miami in 1944, he preached of peace. His early sermons looked toward "V.E. Day" and a "peace party" once the war ended.[71] "Pray with me," he asked his congregation when Israel was established. "Pray with me each week for peace in the Middle East, and not only for Israel."[72]

Throughout the next decade Kronish took a public stance in his opposition towards atomic weapons research, testing and deployment. In March 1950, Kronish wrote a protest letter to President Truman:

> Dear Mr. President,
>
> I am shocked that you have ordered the construction of the H-bomb.... You have chosen to disregard the voices in our Congress who plead for the exhaustion of every possibility of outlawing A-bombs and H-bombs.... I am free to write to you and to protest the building of the H-bomb while the people of the Soviet Union are not free to write to their Premier.... With our moral strength and desire for peace, strengthened by our technological superiority and our stockpile of A-bombs.... the time has come for the American Eagle and the Russian Bear, and even the British Bull, to find a way of living together....[73]

Three years later, Kronish would deliver a similar message to President Eisenhower, exhorting him as the "Chief" of the Armed Forces to reconsider nuclear testing.[74]

Kronish repeated to his congregation the warnings of the Prophets protesting against the Israelites' imitation of the Canaanite cult and applied their teachings to the contemporary threat of nuclear warfare:

> It is a lesson to us in these trying and chaotic times, in the atomic age, to be careful. It is so easy to unleash primitive instincts... to cry for atomic bombing of alien people in distant lands.[75]

Kronish urged his congregants to write letters to Congress, "even to ten of your friends," propounding peace. For Kronish there were two alternatives: humanity's self-destruction—by the "Hydrogen-Hell bomb"—or a safer, healthier earth entrusted the next generations. The choice is "co-existence or co-extinction."[76]

In his 1955 Passover sermon, "Redemption from Atomic Bondage," the rabbi pointed out, "Atomic bondage transcends all political or racial issues which work to alienate people from one another." Recalling Jewish tradition, he urged the congregation to "be of the disciples of Aaron, loving peace and pursuing peace."[77] Four years later, the Union of American Hebrew Congregations at its biennial convention in Miami, voiced its strong opposition to the testing of nuclear weapons.

Life magazine's January 12th 1962 cover story was titled "The Drive for Mass Shelters." Among the clergy whom *Life* reporters had canvassed for opinions on the subject was Rabbi Kronish: "Shelters delude people into accepting the inevitability of war... and the possibility of survival. Belief in safety is a hoax."[78]

Nuclear disarmament, in other words, was not a theoretical exercise. For Kronish, it involved praxis—and praxis was only possible if everyone joined in pursuing peace.

Later that year, in October, when the Cuban Missile Crisis brought the issue of nuclear war to Miami Beach's very own doorstep, Kronish continued to speak out for nuclear disarmament. When Vice-President Lyndon Johnson spoke at the Fontainebleau Hotel a few days before the crisis was made public, Kronish echoed the feelings of most Americans in his Friday sermon—nervousness about communism in Cuba but no commitment to begin a nuclear war with Russia over its future. "H-bombs do not settle a crisis. People pursuing peace solve crises."[79]

As a national outspoken Jewish leader on nuclear disarmament, Kronish was invited to the "Washington Conference on Disarmament and World Peace" in 1964 and to the "National Inter-Religious Conference on Peace" in 1966. The goal of both conferences was to recommend ways that organized religion could play a role in governmental decisions affecting war and peace.[80]

The Center for Religious Action of the UAHC, created in Miami in 1959, played a pivotal role in organizing the conferences. Out of the 1966 conference came a declaration to promote peace in Vietnam and to consider "an immediate halt to the bombing," which Kronish fully supported.[81]

Kronish's Rosh Hashanah messages in the late 1950s epitomized his deep personal commitment to the search for peace. Standing in Beth Sholom, the

House of Peace, ready to hear the sounds of the *shofar*, he read the words of a survivor of Hiroshima who later died of leukemia:

> Give back father, give back mother,
> Give back grandpa, give back grandma,
> Give back boys, give back girls.
> Give me back myself...
> Give back peace,
> Peace that never crumbles.[82]

Kronish's application of prophetic covenant and mission to civic issues–separation of church and state, civil rights, and nuclear disarmament–suited the rapidly changing social needs of American and Reform Jews in the late 1950s and the 1960s.

The Living Legacy of Kronish's Liberal Judaism

As a result, then, of Kronish's commitment to both the internal, cultural revitalization of the Jewish people, and his no less profound allegiance to the "prophetic mission" of Liberal Judaism, Temple Beth Sholom became one of the great synagogue-centers of American Judaism.

The unique combination of educational and cultural programs had an electrifying influence on Jews all over greater Miami, and especially on the youth. Many teenagers, both from Temple Beth Sholom and other temples, sought out the rabbi to learn the meaning of a "Liberal and Living Judaism." In the corridors outside the sanctuary or in his office, they would engage him in dialogue and ask his advice about entering a Jewish vocation. More than a handful would go on to become rabbis and cantors. These included Beth Sholom members Marty Lawson, Greg Marks, Rachelle Nelson and Steven Haas, and Temple Israel members, Stanley Ringler and Gerald Serotta.[83]

Temple Beth Sholom youth who visited Israel during the early 1960s were especially affected by Kronish in this way. One student wrote to Rabbi Kronish in June 1963, "[living in Israel] is the real Bar-mitzvah. You have enrolled me in the great Jewish debates, of why we are, what we are, and why should we be, Jews. The essence of Judaism [is] both Torah and People."[84]

Family Life

As we have seen, the life of Leon Kronish was a busy one, filled from morning until night with a myriad of activities that led him to encounter a wide range of issues and people.

Like any person, however, Kronish needed to relax. One of his favorite ways to do so was to take early morning walks around the neighborhood, or take a swim in the huge pool at the nearby Fontainebleau Hotel, where he was always a welcome guest. Swimming at the Fontainebleau, however, had its disadvantages. Snowbirds from New York and elsewhere, and others who had befriended him over the years—all tried to capture him for breakfast or dinner, whether to discuss a trip to Israel, or an upcoming Bond drive, or an editorial in the morning newspaper. Caught between jeopardizing family dinners, and disappointing a friend, Kronish occasionally ate two dinners in one evening.

By and large, however, Kronish shared dinner and the early evenings within the bosom of his family. Lillian continued to insist that her husband save his early evenings for his family. Dinner time was "sacred." "There was always a tacit agreement among us to protect father's private time," Ronald recalled.[85] Early evenings were dedicated to catching up with the children's activities, debating current events in Israel and the United States, and discussing the Torah portion of the week.

Shabbat *Shalom!*

Sabbaths were especially memorable in the Kronish home. Lillian prepared the traditional sabbath meal consisting of wine, challah, chopped liver, chicken soup, brisket or chicken, kasha and other delights. Seated at the colorfully decorated table, the family sang *zmirot*, sabbath songs, as well as modern Hebrew songs from the rabbi's Zionist youth. Frequently, out-of-town visitors including many distinguished guests from "up north" and from Israel joined the family for the sabbath meal.

After the meal the family walked to temple, only three blocks away. Lillian and the children sat on the left side of the sanctuary, closest to the rabbi's position on the podium, to pray and hear the Friday night sermon.

They would join the congregation in responsive readings from the *Union Prayer Book*, augmented by the rabbi with mimeographed additions of liturgy and compositions he wrote. At the conclusion of the service, he blessed the congregation with outstretched arms. With resonant voice his benediction echoed through the sanctuary before fading into silence.

After services, Rabbi Kronish walked to the lobby where he welcomed all those who had shared in the sabbath celebration and prayers. He greeted most by name, with a hearty handshake and, "*shabbat* shalom." Even during the peak of the winter tourist season, when the Friday night crowd resembled Rosh Hashanah with fifteen hundred worshippers, he warmly greeted any familiar face, even if the person was not a congregational member.[86]

Invited guests and "temple activists" would accompany him and his family to their home or go with them to *Juniors* for coffee and cake and a discussion of the sermon.[87] Many who participated in these post-sermon gatherings fondly remember the heat of the dialogue and his humor.

The next morning, the family would return to the temple to pray. When Kronish introduced more traditional sabbath morning services in the 1940s, they were unusual among Reform congregations in Florida. However, by the mid-1960s, most Reform congregations across the country had instituted more traditional practices.

Although the number of people attending these Saturday morning services was not as large as on Friday night, the hundreds of congregants who did attend formed a core that embraced Kronish's calling for American Jewry to enrich their understanding of Torah and *mitzvot*.

They too affirmed and embraced Polish's and Doppelt's convictions in the *Guide* that Jewish education "fulfills the spiritual destiny of the Jewish people."[88] Covenant and study of Torah are symbiotic. Rabbi Kronish gave a *d'var torah*, a timely exposition of the Torah portion of the week, also each sabbath morning.

Holidays

Members recall invitations to Rabbi Kronish's home for holidays such as *Sukkot*, Passover, and Hanukkah. The Hecht family, long-time members of Beth Sholom, who had been instrumental in securing supplies for Israel during the War of Independence, often shared the second Passover *seder* (meal) at the Kronish home.[89]

Isabelle Hecht Amdur was confirmed in the first confirmation class in the new temple sanctuary. Shortly before confirmation, she celebrated Passover at the Kronish home and used the rabbi's *Passover Supplementary Haggadah*. "These two events back to back," she recalled, "connected me in some way to the Jewish people and Israel as a teenager and this connection has lasted until today."[90] Other members who were frequent guests included Gary and Niety Gerson, James and Helen Knopke, Marvin and Betty Cooper, Dave and Phyllis Miller, Harold and Alice Vinik, and Muriel and Sol Lichter.

The Extended Family

Kronish's activities regularly took him to New York where he attended national meetings of Hebrew Union College-Jewish Institute of Religion, Israel Bonds, the Histadrut, the CCAR Commission on Jewish Education and the Hebrew University of Jerusalem.

After a business-packed day, he often met his brother Zev at a vegetarian restaurant downtown and caught up on family news. Occasionally, Leon asked a brotherly favor such as visiting his children in camp.

In the 1960s Maxine attended the Reform movement's National Federation of Temple Youth camp in Warwick, New York, and Ronald worked there as a counselor and teacher in the early 1970s. Sometimes Lillian would accompany her husband to New York where she visited her three sisters. Invariably, a trip north together also meant theater tickets for such popular shows as *Fiddler on the Roof*.

Tragedy and Transcendence

In 1959, a tragedy occurred in the usually happy home of Leon and Lillian Kronish—teenaged Jordan, their first born, died suddenly. With Jordan's passing, the Kronish family life changed.

During the 1950s, Kronish's congregational and familial responsibilities restricted him from taking advantage of many offers to travel to the beloved State of Israel he had seen only once, just after statehood in 1949.[91]

After Jordan's death, Kronish began to make annual pilgrimages to Israel for a plethora of compelling reasons. While nothing could replace a first-born child, Kronish drew spiritual sustenance from his ever-closer connection to the land and people of Israel.

A Renewed Commitment to Israel

Aside from his overall love of Zion, what drew Kronish to Israel was his ever-widening involvement with several major institutions of the developing Jewish state: Israel Bonds, the Histadrut, the Hebrew University of Jerusalem, and the emerging presence of Reform Judaism in Israel.

Connecting Reform Institutions in America and Israel

Kronish served on the Board of Governors of Hebrew Union College-Jewish Institute of Religion, the rabbinical seminary from which he was ordained, and a leading institution of Reform Judaism in America. There he had regular contact with Nelson Glueck, HUC-JIR president from 1947 to 1971, and Alfred Gottschalk, dean of the college's California campus in the 1960s and subsequently Glueck's successor as president.

In the mid-1950s, the Israeli government offered President Glueck a two-acre site for a Hebrew Union College House, a Jerusalem campus, on King David Street overlooking the Old City. The rental fee would be one Israeli pound per year, and the Israeli government would allow the use of Bonds to defray the costs of construction.[92]

Glueck sought counsel and support from his Zionist-minded American colleagues. Kronish, with his Israel Bonds activities and Zionist ideology, was a natural ally. With others he helped to arrange the purchase of the land in Jerusalem through contacts with Israeli leaders—especially veteran Mapai and Histadrut leader Pinhas Sapir, who held during his political career a number of Cabinet positions in Labor governments.[93]

In this fashion, Leon Kronish played a role in helping to establish the new Jerusalem School of Hebrew Union College-Jewish Institute of Religion in 1963.

Bonding with Israel

In 1960, Kronish accompanied Morris Sipser, director of the Miami office for Israel Bonds, on a "Bonds mission" to Israel. Immediately upon his arrival in Israel, the rabbi was astonished by the changes he noticed since his first visit in 1949. The country had modernized. Development towns were no longer fringe communities but had grown into regional economic centers. Rapid urbanization and competitive industrialization had turned Tel Aviv into a flourishing metropolis. *Ma'abarot*, tent cities, no longer existed. In their place were new neighborhoods in cities and development towns.

When visiting old friends like Yehuda Ben Chorin on Kibbutz Kfar Menachem, Leon listened to the optimism that prevailed among the first-generation pioneers. However, some Israelis Kronish met no longer seemed to share the pioneering spirit of earlier generations. They were finding Israeli life hard. Members of the mission met with Israeli leaders and heard first-hand why integration among the new immigrants was a trying experience and why Israel continued to require greater financial support, economic investments, and *aliya*.

Ronald and Maxine joined their parents in Israel for the first time in the summer of 1964 after Ronald's graduation from high school. Their father's infectious love for the country quickly captured them. As a family they visited friends and toured the nation from north to south. They prayed at Israeli synagogues, visited Hebrew Union College's year-old Biblical and Archaeological School in Jerusalem, and enjoyed the life and culture of the sabra. Ronald spent much of the summer at Kibbutz Kfar Menachem with the Ben Chorins and Maxine was billeted at Kfar HaYarok, a youth village, directed by the Histadrut outside Tel Aviv.

Upon their return to Miami Beach, Ronald left home to study at Brandeis University, and Maxine was so inspired that she sought out Shula Ben-David, an Israeli Hebrew teacher, at the temple for private Hebrew lessons.

By the mid-1960s, Temple Beth Sholom congregants began requesting that Kronish lead them on pilgrimages. Although this idea did not fully materialize until after 1967, several members met up with Lillian and Leon when they traveled to Israel.

If members were lucky enough to bump accidentally into them in Israel, they could enjoy a spontaneous private tour. Betty and Mike Cooper's introduction to the Histadrut and Kibbutz Kfar Menachem in 1964 arose from such a chance meeting.

Israel Bonds

Each time Kronish visited Israel, he returned with greater resolve to connect American Jewry with Israel. From the mid-1950s, when Sipser first arrived in Miami to head the Miami Israel Bonds office, and recruited Kronish as his captain, Israel Bonds—a means to develop the country through investment—became the flagship activity to make this link.

Sipser spent long hours with Kronish. They conferred in the Israel Bonds' office on Lincoln Road, over breakfast at hotels, and in the rabbi's study at Temple Beth Sholom. Sometimes, when the need arose, the Kronish kitchen or living room was more than adequate. They would *nosh* (snack) while developing strategies for attracting funds for investment in Israel.

Sipser asked Kronish to help organize the 1957 Inaugural Conference for Israel Bonds. The conference was held at the Fontainebleau Hotel, with former President Harry Truman as the keynote speaker, and featuring a tribute to Eddie Cantor. In 1958, Florida's Bond campaign had totalled less than $250,000. By 1961, with Kronish as its chair, the receipts were $1.5 million.[94]

In recognition of his service to the Jewish state through Israel Bonds campaigns, the State of Israel awarded Kronish the Sword of Haganah. Pinhas Sapir, Minister of Commerce and Industry, wrote Rabbi Kronish that "I am very grateful for your continuing help and cooperation."[95]

Kronish's persistent efforts strongly contributed to the remarkable increase in Bonds purchases in Florida. Each High Holy Day season, from the inception of Israel Bonds in 1951, Kronish used the pulpit to exhort his congregation to buy Bonds. It was an act of faith, linking the Jews of America—particularly the members of Temple Beth Sholom—with the people of Israel. In Kronish's view, "there was no more concrete way of demonstrating faith in Israel's future, and for that matter, in the future of the whole Jewish people."[96] Purchasing Bonds was one way to labor for messianic redemption.

The Miami Group

Kronish increasingly turned to certain individuals to buy Bonds. Samuel Friedland, Max Orovitz, Sam Blank, and Dan Ruskin—later to be known as the "Miami Group," were favorites. Orovitz had traveled to Israel in 1947 as part of a United Jewish Appeal (UJA) mission. A series of circumstances arose that led Yekutiel (Xiel) Federman, a key Haganah personality, to ask Orovitz to be his business partner.

Orovitz returned to Miami seeking partners to invest funds in Israel with the understanding that all profits would be put at the disposal of the Israeli government for borrowing on favorable terms or for reinvesting in Israeli projects. From this period to the 1960s, the "Miami Group" made large investments in Israel in oil exploration in the Negev, in construction of the Dan hotels, in the purchase of the King David Hotel in Jerusalem, and in founding service-related industries.

Requested to serve as Kronish's captains, Friedland, Orovitz, Blank, and Ruskin became role models for other Jewish community leaders and philanthropists. The "Miami Group" developed expert techniques at nudging the noncommitted donor to reconsider. The "Miami Group," in turn, chose Kronish to deliver the appeal at organized Israel Bonds functions.

In 1962, Kronish feted Friedland, Orovitz, Blank, and Ruskin at an Israel Bonds dinner that featured Ezer Weizmann as the keynote speaker.[97] One million dollars was pledged in less than one hour.[98]

Kronish Ascends the Bonds Hierarchy

Kronish was invited to serve on the Israel Bonds National Board Campaign Cabinet in 1962. Meanwhile, he continued to lead the Bonds efforts in Miami and Florida. From Central Conference of American Rabbis meetings to the board room of Hebrew Union College-Jewish Institute of Religion, Kronish solicited Israel Bonds from his Reform rabbinical colleagues.

Those involved during these formative years praise Kronish's efforts in generating support from Reform congregations throughout the United States in introducing annual Israel Bond dinners. Lillian Simonhoff, the wife of the founder of the first Zionist District in greater Miami in the 1920s, described zealously Kronish's charisma in those heady days of the mid-1960s in her book *Reminiscences*:

> He was an expert at selling Bonds. He could stir the most reluctant prospective purchaser. During the rally, he was so convincing that the women were worked up into such a degree of enthusiasm that they spontaneously rose to their feet and announced their [Israel] Bonds purchases.[99]

Kronish and the Histadrut

In addition to his involvement in Israel Bonds, Kronish continued to further his interest in socialist ideas by becoming actively involved in the Histadrut—the giant umbrella Israeli federation of organized labor.

In 1965 he founded the Histadrut Foundation of the United States and remained chair and president of the national board of directors until 1984. The Histadrut, the General Federation of Workers in Israel, was one of the principal socio-economic instruments responsible for the renascence of the modern Jewish state.

Combining secular socialist ideals with a commitment to Jewish nationalism, the Histadrut built the country's socio-economic infrastructure. In the 1960s nine out of ten Israeli workers belonged to the Histadrut.[100]

Among the many agencies and hundreds of companies under the Histadrut wing are *Kuppat Holim*, medical insurance; *Mish'an*, houses for the aged; *'Amal*, vocational trade schools; *Solel Boneh*, construction; and Zim, Egged, and El Al, transportation. Kronish's own identification with Labor Zionist ideals went back to his youth in *Hashomer Hatzair*.

Conclusion

From the consecration of the new sanctuary in 1957 to the eve of the Six Day War in 1967, Temple Beth Sholom grew from a midsize congregation of near eight hundred households to a large congregation of twelve hundred.

Under Rabbi Kronish's galvanizing leadership and guidance, the synagogue became one of the leading centers of American Jewish life. Pulsating with the best of Jewish culture and education, it served a myriad of Jewish needs for thousands of people week in and week out.

Situated on Miami Beach, it was the seasonal choice for snowbirds, who fully participated in the temple's social and political activities. As the congregants internalized more traditions, as they learned more about Jewish and Israeli current events—the bonds between themselves, *Klal Yisrael* and *Eretz Yisrael* were ever strengthened.

Indeed, in no small measure due to Kronish and Temple Beth Sholom, Miami Beach became one of the major focal points of American Jewish life during this period.

The Six Day War in 1967 brought irrevocable change to the entire Jewish world. For Kronish, the notion of "prophetic mission" would change and a determination to link Diaspora Jewry to Israel in all endeavors would become much more pronounced. Israeli-centered programs would redefine the relationship between his temple—and, indeed, Reform Judaism and all institutions of American Jewry—with the State of Israel.

Chapter Five

THE TRANSFORMATION OF MIAMI
THE GROWTH OF A TEMPLE

Introduction

The years between 1967 and 1984 marked the most fruitful period in the life of Leon Kronish.

A large proportion of his great energies were directed towards the complex process we call here the "Israelization" of American Reform Jewry in general, and the Miami Jewish community and Temple Beth Sholom in particular. Due to the extensive array of activities Kronish undertook within this rubric, the entire final chapter of his biography has been devoted to this multi-faceted endeavor—one which gave these years their great meaning and dynamism for Kronish and everyone whose life touched his.

But these seventeen years, while motivated by the calling of "Israelization," were marked simultaneously by a wide range of other activities, centered mostly around his spiritual leadership as rabbi of Temple Beth Sholom which was his primary institutional focus.

As before, Kronish spent a considerable amount of time revising and updating the liturgy—a constant preoccupation since his days as a student of Mordecai Kaplan. At the same time Kronish was continuing to follow in Kaplan's footsteps with the liturgy, he was also introducing another of his mentor's innovations—the promotion of *havurot*, small fellowship groups from within a congregation, males and females, who would come together informally to infuse their lives with Jewish content.

More formal attempts to introduce Jewish content into the lives of his congregants came with Kronish's commitment in this period to what he called "living Judaism."

The first such venture was the re-orientation of the temple's previously existing religious education program into a School for Living Judaism. For Kronish, it was crucial for Jewish youth to be aware of the Jewish opportunities available to them at every major stage in their development—from babies and infants, through the childhood years, and into the pre-teen and teenage years, when the final elements of a living Jewish identity could be fused into a dynamic adult that would be both able and willing to raise the next generation of Jews.

In tandem with this re-orientation of the school was the creation in 1969 of the Institute for Living Judaism. Just as the school opened the possibility of a vibrant Jewish existence for young people, so the Institute served to make available to adults a whole range of emotionally meaningful experiences that would provide a rich and evolving Jewish identity throughout the mature phases of the life-cycle.

The content of the Institute's activities revolved around all aspects of Judaism, and especially Reform Jewish living. Teaching about Israel and Zionism were blended into learning about Judaism. The product was the "Israelization" of Jewish life at Temple Beth Sholom and it was achieved in a multiplicity of ways, detailed extensively below.

But perhaps the most notable in the current context was the cultural programming organized by active Beth Sholom member Judy Drucker. Her successful efforts to bring world-class artists, like Leonard Bernstein and Luciano Pavarotti among others to Miami, laid the groundwork for greater Miami's evolution from a cultural backwater into a major stop on the global cultural circuit.

Not surprisingly, the expansion of Temple Beth Sholom as a significant institution during this period took place within the context of the parallel development of Miami in general, and Miami Beach in particular, into a world-class metropolis.

The population of both Dade County in particular, and South Florida (Dade, Broward and Palm Beach counties) in general exploded from the late 1960s to the mid-1980s—in Dade, from 935,047 to 1,625,500, and in the region as a whole from 1,497,099 to 3,220,600.[1]

Even more important than the sheer growth in numbers was the change in ethnic composition of Dade County overall and Miami Beach in particular. In 1960, Miami was still a Southern hinterland, just emerging from a legacy of entrenched racial segregation. By the early 1980s, the largest single ethnic group in Miami was neither blacks nor whites but Hispanics. Taken together, blacks and Hispanics comprised for the first time more than fifty per cent of the Dade County population (53%).[2]

The Jewish demography during this period tells a somewhat different story. In 1975, Dade County had a Jewish population of nearly 300,000, comprising close to twenty per cent of the total, with the largest proportion living on Miami Beach.[3] Throughout the 1970s, American Jews saw Miami, quite literally, as "New York South."

By the early 1980s, however, the Jewish population in Dade County was in evident decline (253,000 in 1982). Dade Jews began to move north in large numbers to Broward and Palm Beach counties, a trend noticed by northern Jews who likewise began to eschew Dade as a desired destination. By the end of the 1980s, in fact, more Jews lived in Broward County (262,000 in 1988).[4]

A major – although hardly the sole – reason for this trend was the general phenomenon among Anglos known as "white flight" – in the case of Miami, from both the growing Hispanic population, and a newly mobilized black population, which emerged from the civil rights movement of the 1960s and the riot of 1980 more organized and active than ever before.

In this context, the biggest flashpoint for black/Jewish relations during this period was the integration of Miami Beach Senior High School – an event that occurred, literally, in Kronish's backyard, as Beach High was the *alma mater* of his children Ronald and Maxine.

While Kronish himself, as well as two of his congregants – Sol Lichter, principal of Beach High, and Phyllis Miller, a member of the Dade County School Board – were among the leading white proponents of desegregation, many Jews, concentrated on Miami Beach, were opposed to this change, and the negative reverberations between the two communities persisted long after the formal integration in 1970.

For Leon Kronish and his family, finally, the years between 1967 and 1984 held a mixed bag of blessings and tragedies. Among the blessings was the coming to adulthood of son Ronald and daughter Maxine.

Maxine became a wife and mother, blending the traditional role embodied so gracefully by her own mother Lillian with the innovative activism of her rabbi father. Her professional life was committed to Jewish communal service, both as associate director of Hillel at Brown University and, later, as director of Jewish Campus Activities with the Jewish Federation of Washington, D.C.

Son Ronald, meanwhile, not only became a Reform rabbi, just as his father had done, but he also, in 1979, made the commitment to live in Israel – a move that brought great joy to his family, especially to a father who, in a document discussed in detail in Chapter Six, had argued that all Jewish families should have at least one child "return" to *Eretz Yisrael*, the Land of Israel.

More painful were two serious setbacks to the health of the dynamic rabbi, active locally, nationally and in Israel.

In 1978, Kronish suffered a major heart attack, from which he was able to recover, and which infused his subsequent efforts with a passion borne from his realization that even someone as energetic as himself had limits.

More tragically, in January of 1984, Kronish suffered the stroke that was to sidetrack unavoidably his wide range of activities on behalf of Israel, both in the United States and abroad. While he was able to make a partial recovery – enough, for example, to participate in synagogue services and in a *festschrift* organized by son Ronald in 1988 – there is no doubt that the 1984 stroke marked the effective end of his justly storied career.

In the remainder of the next two chapters, then, we will examine the range of Kronish's activities from the period between the Six Day War in 1967 and his tragic stroke in early 1984—focusing in Chapter Six on the many programs encompassed under the rubric of the "Israelization" of American Jewry, and in the rest of this chapter, on the many other works which so consumed his energies and, ultimately, his health.

Family Life

In contrast to the 1960s, when Ronald and Maxine, the rabbi's children, were teenagers at home and participating in the activities of Temple Beth Sholom, the 1970s saw many changes in family life. Ronald graduated from Brandeis University in 1968 and entered rabbinical school at his father's *alma mater*, the Hebrew Union College-Jewish Institute of Religion (HUC-JIR), in New York. As had his father three decades earlier, Ronald felt the need to enrich his spiritual roots. By coincidence, his father had been elected president of the HUC-JIR alumni association that same year.

In 1969, Ronald married Amy Weiss. They spent the 1970-1971 academic year in Jerusalem. Ronald and Amy both studied at the Hebrew University of Jerusalem and Ronald also took some courses at the Hebrew Union College in Jerusalem. That year the inaugural class of first-year rabbinical students seeking ordination from Hebrew Union College in the United States was also required to study in Israel as part of HUC's new curriculum. Thus, unintended, Ronald was able to exchange with his father first-person accounts of the restructured Reform Judaism's rabbinical ordination program which the senior Kronish had helped to initiate and design.

Maxine spent the following year, 1971-1972, at the Hebrew University as part of her university's undergraduate study abroad program. During these years, Avraham Avi-Hai, the director of Overseas Student Programs at the Hebrew University, and other friends in Israel whom Kronish had met over many years, kept a watchful eye over the Kronish children.

Leon and Lillian's frequent trips to Israel meant family reunions on a regular basis. Explorations of archaeological digs in the City of David and Mount Scopus—inaccessible from 1949 until the aftermath of the 1967 war—were two of the many trips they shared together.

Kronish often asked his children, Ronald and Maxine, for their thoughts regarding how their Israeli experience might lend itself to extending more "bridges" to American-Jewish college students. Watching his own children and their friends, he observed how American-Jewish youth provided with an Israeli educational experience internalized Jewish and Israeli values and felt more strongly linked to Zionism.

With each visit to Israel, Lillian and Leon sensed a strengthening bond between their children and *Eretz Yisrael*. For the first time, *aliya* was becoming a distinct possibility for them. Ronald had voiced the opinion on several occasions that his commitment as a Jew might be better fulfilled by settling in Israel. Although Ronald returned to America in June 1971 to finish rabbinical school, settling in Israel was never far from his and Amy's future plans.

In April 1973, six weeks before Ronald's ordination as a rabbi, he was invited by his father to give the sabbath sermon during Passover at Temple Beth Sholom. His topic, "College Youth–Are they Alienated?" was addressed to parents and their responsibility to provide their children with a Jewish identity. The idealism of the 1960s and the cynicism and disenchantment of the early 1970s are only historical moments, Ronald explained. College years are a time "to struggle with basic questions of personal and collective Jewish existence."[5] College youth still required parents to be Jewish role models.

In a letter to the editor of *Reform Judaism* a decade later, Ronald recalled the problem of this period as one of "familiarizing youth with some of the basic elements of traditional Jewish life, styles, and practices."[6] It echoed the spirit of his father who, a generation earlier, had voiced similar concerns, and advocated "Liberal Judaism" as a means to re-inspire the post-war baby-boomers and their parents.

Later that spring, the Kronishes traveled to New York to attend Ronald's graduation and ordination. As a former trustee of the Board of Governors of the Hebrew Union College-Jewish Institute of Religion (1965-1972) and as a past president of the alumni association, Leon was proud that his son had chosen to combine traditional Jewish education with secular American studies. As he watched Rabbi Alfred Gottschalk preside, Kronish recalled his own ordination by Rabbi Stephen Wise thirty-one years earlier.

Gottschalk had invited Kronish to be the keynote speaker for the 1973 graduation class in New York.[7] Full of hope and promise, he spoke of the Reform movement and its prophetic role in shaping the future of Judaism. He reflected on how fifty years earlier Stephen Wise inaugurated the Jewish Institute of Religion and was sympathetic to Zionism. Today's HUC-JIR graduates bear the fruit of these ideals, he preached. "Each of you are the conduits to carry the message to a future generation. Each of you are responsible to strengthen *Klal Yisrael*, to elucidate how the covenant can be made relevant to Americans and Israelis."[8]

Frequent trips to New York to attend national Board meetings of Israel Bonds, Histadrut and the Hebrew University were also an opportunity to spend time with Zev, Leon's brother, and Lillian's sisters and their respective families. Zev still played a role of counseling the Kronish children when called upon and sensitizing his brother to concerns of Orthodox Jews.

Between 1973-1978, Ronald and Amy lived in the greater Boston area, where Ronald continued his secular education and completed his doctorate at Harvard University focusing on Jewish education. Maxine, during the mid-

1970s, was a graduate student in Boston at Brandeis University in Jewish Communal Service.

In addition to exploring their Jewish identity in academic settings, Ronald and Maxine continued to deepen their spiritual roots. Both had joined local *havurot*, small fellowships, and shared their religious understanding and curiosity with like-minded contemporaries. Moreover, by choosing careers in Jewish education and communal service, Ronald and Maxine adopted a new role—serving as a "kitchen cabinet" for their father to air ideas about the future features of the American Jewish experience.

Lillian's role, as rabbi's wife, also changed when the children left home for college. Without the children, she found herself more in demand. She served on local and Israeli organizational boards, filled temple roles and welcomed new members. She also continued to manage a household and attend to the cares of her now-distant family members.

In 1982, Lillian helped to plan the wedding of Maxine to Eddie Snyder in Washington, D. C. and the subsequent celebrations in Miami Beach. In the years that followed, Maxine and Eddie have had two children, Davida and Amiel who have joined Ronald and Amy's daughters, Sari, Dahlia, and Ariella as the devoted grandchildren of the Kronish family.

Lillian continued to serve as hostess and provide home hospitality for the bevy of congregants, visitors, and Israeli dignitaries that visited the Kronish home. Over the years Israeli guests included the president and prime minister of Israel, ambassadors, diplomats, cabinet ministers, senior government advisors, Histadrut leaders and professors from the Hebrew University of Jerusalem. When Kronish was the national chairman of the Israel Histadrut Foundation and host for its annual winter convention in Miami, Lillian was the official hostess for the event both at the convention and at home.

Among the continuous and growing stream of out-of-town guests were some that became "extended" kin. Kronish used to tease the Israeli Zonik Shaham that "it doesn't matter where Zonik is going, you can be sure that he will go by way of Miami."[9] When he was in town, Zonik often joined Leon and his close friend from the temple, Mike Cooper, in a late night stroll for ice cream. Engrossed in conversation, they would return to Kronish's or Cooper's home to continue debating ways in which American Jews could be more committed to Israel.

In the late 1970s and early 1980s, Kronish's close circle, in addition to Mike Cooper, also included Milton Gaynor, James Knopke, and Harold Vinik—all former Temple presidents from that period. They acted as his sounding board for new ideas, and frequently met with him in his office and at his home.

Heart Attack and Recovery

On February 28, 1978, Leon Kronish's life abruptly changed. That evening he attended a planning meeting at Betty and Mike Cooper's home to complete plans for the temple's 35th anniversary dinner. Later, at home in bed, in the middle of the night, Kronish became deathly ill and was rushed to Mount Sinai Hospital.

Kronish later joked, "one of my arteries got older a little bit faster than some of the others."[10] According to the cardiovascular team, he suffered a heart attack and required a pacemaker.

Hundreds of letters and cards from well-wishers reached the rabbi during his convalescence. Lying in bed, Kronish pondered how he was to respond to his congregation and friends.

> I've always maintained a personalized relationship with our congregants.... We have told our children that Jewish identity can be experienced by making generous contributions... but for all their importance, these things don't define the substance and content of Jewish living.[11]

The period of convalescence allowed Kronish to reflect on his past thirty-six years in the rabbinate. Writing four days before Passover to Ephraim Shapira, one of Beth Sholom's former "Israelis-in-Residence," he wondered:

> What are my "normal activities?" Management, administration, and director of spiritual and cultural activities [at the temple. Also] activities outside the congregation in the community, in the Israel Histadrut Foundation, in the Israel Bonds organization. How can I serve my people and my family in the best possible way?[12]

Zonik Shaham visited Kronish in May 1978 and spoke to the congregation in honor of Israel's 30th anniversary. He threatened, only half in jest, "If you don't take better care of Rabbi Kronish, [my *rebbe*], we're taking him back to Israel! We need him as much as you do."[13]

The tensions between being an international figure with an incessant array of demands and that of being a rabbi serving a congregational family did not disappear after the heart attack. The period of recuperation and reflection gave way to pressures from many quarters. His family encouraged him to slow down, but their pleas fell on deaf ears.

A Debilitating Stroke Forces Retirement

The day before yet another trip to Israel for Israel Bonds, in January 1984, Kronish went to his office after sabbath services to collect some papers. When he did not return within a short time, his bookkeeper went to look for him. The rabbi was hunched on the floor, not moving. A massive stroke had left him an invalid, with only partial speech and movement.

Over the years, Kronish believed that hard work was how one lived. The family, the temple, the community, and Israel – all needed his seemingly tireless energy. Although these non-stop activities were contributing factors, his medical attention also was not sufficient to offset this tragedy.

Ironically enough, the week after Kronish's stroke, Harold Kushner, author of *When Bad Things Happen To Good People*, was scheduled to speak at Temple Beth Sholom. Standing before a packed auditorium, Kushner intoned:

> How could God let this happen to a man so giving of himself, so tireless in pursuit of the things he believed in; to someone who should have had so much to look forward to? Was this the reward for a life-time of service to the Jewish people, to Israel, to Judaism?[14]

Over the next several months, Leon Kronish and his family nurtured one another, weathering the storm. Friends, including Israelis like Yitzhak Rabin, Abba Eban and Zonik Shaham, visited his bedside and prayed. Congregants anxiously held vigil at Mount Sinai hospital. Elie Wiesel spoke to the congregation at a dinner in the rabbi's honor.

As Rosh Hashanah neared, Kronish and the temple leadership made arrangements for Rabbi Alfred Gottschalk, president of HUC-JIR and a long-time friend of Kronish, to be guest rabbi. Gottschalk graciously accepted and later commented why he felt honored:

> I was enthralled with the quality of Jewish education that he struggled to achieve, and with the high standards he set for community participation and congregation participation.[15]

By December, 1984, Kronish had made remarkable progress in his recovery, but he was confined to a wheelchair, and required constant medical attention and therapy.

That Hanukkah, the School for Living Judaism was renamed the Rabbi Leon Kronish School for Living Judaism. With his children and grandchildren by his side, he valiantly spoke with slurred speech about Jewish education as the seeds of Jewish commitment and action.

Two months later, one thousand people assembled in Miami – many traveling from distant corners of the United States and Israel – to attend a special Israel Bonds dinner to honor Leon Kronish and to be with him when he was presented Israel's Golda Meir Award. Long recognized as "Mr. Israel in Florida," the evening's tributes lauded his accomplishments and prepared for a new age without his leadership.[16]

Rabbi Joseph Glaser, executive vice-president of the Central Conference of American Rabbis, poignantly described Kronish's unique contribution to the audience assembled:

> there were other Reform rabbis whose voices were raised eloquently and powerfully on behalf of Israel, of Zionism, but it was Kronish who worked with the masses of rabbis, daily plugging away, pouring his spirit out on conventions and smaller group gatherings and, indeed, on individuals, young and old, big congregation rabbis and tiny congregation rabbis.[17]

Leon Kronish responded, "I accept this award not for myself, but only because I want to remind you that you cannot rest."[18]

Miami: Demographic Changes

By the time of Kronish's stroke in 1984, the Miami area to which he and Lillian had journeyed four decades before had become a very different place.

The resident population in Dade County underwent tremendous growth, increasing from 267,739 in 1940 to 1,625,500 in 1980.[19] And between 1960 and 1980, greater Miami's popularity among tourists doubled, rising from just under six million to twelve-and-a-half million.[20]

In 1960, although no longer a segregated city because of federal and state legislation, Miami still exhibited segregated attitudes and policies (schools). The Hispanic presence was barely visible.[21]

By 1980, Miami had become an Hispanic city. The tri-ethnic community of Anglos (including Jews), African Americans and Hispanics, in the words of a recent author, created a *City on the Edge*.[22] Minority groups, Hispanics and African Americans, comprised more than fifty percent of the population.[23]

Over this period, the Hispanic presence led American multinational corporations to locate their Latin American headquarters in Miami. A "free zone industrial park" was introduced in the early 1980s. Business opportunities that looked south and catered to Hispanics were supported. Frequently, Spanish superceded English. These developments also encouraged "white flight" from Dade to Broward and Palm Beach counties.

Jewish Demography

Between 1960 and 1972 the Jewish population in Florida grew three times faster than the general population; one hundred and forty-one percent Jewish growth to forty-one percent general growth.[24]

By the mid-1970s nearly 300,000 Jews resided permanently in Dade County (greater Miami)—twenty percent of the county in 1975—with the greatest proportion on Miami Beach.[25] With this growth, American Jewry's perception of the most southeastern state was radically altered—Miami Beach had become "New York South."

In contrast to the 1940s, when Jews were unable to live in many areas of Miami Beach north of Lincoln Road, the demographic distribution of Jews by the mid-1960s had redefined the residential map. Jewish neighborhoods were present everywhere from the tip of the island to North Miami Beach.

South of 17th Street on Miami Beach, one could re-experience New York's Lower East Side with kosher meat markets and kiosks, Jewish bakeries, and newsstands with Yiddish and Hebrew papers.

Polly Redford, a Florida author, illustrates the vibrancy of Jewish life in the area during this period:

> In Flamingo Park two rival discussion groups meet beneath different banyan trees to argue over Jewish and current events: one, the Flamingo Park Cultural Group, is Marxian socialist, doctrinaire and anti-Zionist; the other, an offshoot of the first, is made of more affluent Bonds-for-Israel types who now look down on the parent organization as 'communist.'[26]

A new phenomenon began to appear—American *landsmannschaften*, people in Miami who had come there from other American cities. Affiliation to these groups was often a combination of congregational and organizational memberships, as much as social class and provenance. These "city-clubs" provided the backbone for the flourishing national Jewish organizations that established local chapters on the Beach. Hadassah, for example, swelled from five thousand members in 1960 to nearly fifteen thousand in 1974.[27]

Jews were engaged in every type of local industry and professional undertaking—finance, (banking, investment, and retirement funds); tourism, (hotels and travel related services); real estate (development and construction and the building service trades); and retail and wholesale merchandising and manufacturing. They thrived on the high-rise condominium boom and took advantage of regional, national, and international expanding markets. Just as Eilat had blossomed into a winter tourist haven in the Negev of Israel, so had Miami Beach become the "winter capital" of American Jewry.

Committed voters and politically active, Jewish seniors favored candidates that shared their pro-Israel ideology and liberal agendas.[28] It was not uncommon on voting day to see Jewish seniors marching to the polls *en masse*, organized by voting captains in high-density Jewish condominiums. Robert Kimmel Smith, in his novel *Sadie Shapiro in Miami*, describes the Miami Beach Jewish community as a southeastern version of the Gray Panthers when it came to issues affecting seniors.[29]

This growth in political power culminated in the election in 1974 of Richard Stone of Miami Beach, the first Jew since David Levy Yulee—the father of Florida statehood in 1845—to be elected to the United States Senate from Florida.[30] Jewish state legislators dominated Miami Beach and many districts of Dade County. Since the 1950s, the mayors of Miami Beach, as well as members of the city commission, have frequently been Jewish.

By the late 1970s, however, Jewish migration to Dade County was beginning to undergo a decline. Miami Beach no longer was the major destination for Jewish tourists and retirees. As Ira Sheskin has noted in several studies of the South Florida area, by the 1980s Jews from northeastern states not only preferred Broward and Palm Beach counties, immediately north of Miami Beach, but Broward County had surpassed Dade County as the community with the most Jews in South Florida.[31] By the early 1990s, even Palm Beach County would have more Jews (209,000 in 1993) than Dade County (166,000 in 1994).[32]

Demography and Ethnicity: Jews and Cubans

The growth in the Jewish population in Dade County in the 1960s and early 1970s was overshadowed by the burgeoning visibility of a Hispanic culture. Hundreds of thousands of Cuban refugees migrated to Miami in the wake of Castro's revolution; between 1962 and 1974, more than 450,000 Cuban exiles were processed in downtown Miami's Freedom Tower. By 1975, thirty-two percent of Dade County was Latin.[33]

According to Hebrew Immigrant Aid Society (HIAS) records and Seymour Liebman's estimates, approximately thirty-five hundred of these exiles were Cuban Jews.[34]

Yet in spite of growing Hispanic and Jewish influence in greater Miami—over fifty percent of Dade County in the mid-1970s—there was little contact between Cubans and Jews. Most Cubans did not reside on the island sandbar. They lived in "Little Havana" (SW 8th Street), Coral Gables and suburban Kendall. Jews, on the other hand, lived primarily on Miami Beach and in North Miami.

Jewish Cubans who lived on the Beach had little contact with the established Jewish community. No concerted Federation effort was organized to integrate them into the community. With the exception of Rabbi Meyer Abramowitz's congregation, Temple Menorah, many synagogues—including Temple Beth Sholom—tended to open their doors to individuals, rather than extend their resources and facilities to the refugee Jewish-Cuban community as a whole.[35]

With the increased profile of Cubans, non-Floridian Jews began to look for other South Florida regions in the 1970s to establish Jewish life. Over time they were joined by Miami Jews seeking a more "comfortable" and congenial environment. Less than ten percent of the greater Miami population in 1960, the Hispanic population approached fifty percent by 1990.[36]

In 1980, for the first time, greater Miami's population was less than half Anglo, the term referring to English-speaking whites. The Jewish population—which peaked at twenty percent of Dade County in 1975—declined to eleven percent by 1990, down from 290,000 to less than 202,000. In contrast, Broward County grew from 10,053 in 1960 to 262,000 in 1988.[37] Much of Dade County's decline occurred on Miami Beach, where the Jewish population, once boasting well over 100,000 residents (1975), had fallen to less than half that amount by 1990. Moreover, nearly one in two of those Jewish residents was sixty years of age or older in the early 1980s and a significant number were poor.[38] The prognosis for the future of Miami Beach's Jewish population was bleak.

Hispanic Jews formed a significant minority on the Beach by the late 1970s. They organized a variety of congregations that catered to their Cuban and South American geographical origins and their Ashkenazic and Sephardic religious traditions.[39] Many Hispanic Jews, with the erection of these synagogues, shied away from their Anglo counterparts and their established synagogues that conducted services in English.[40]

In 1980, Citizens for Dade United led a campaign to change Miami from a bilingual city to a unilingual city and to prohibit "the promotion of any culture other than that of the United States."[41] Inspired by the growing resentment among Anglos of the growing Hispanic economic power, a poll taken at the time of the vote indicated that "among various groups, Jews gave the unilingual resolution the strongest support." Led by a Miami Beach Jewish resident, the unilingual campaign motto was, ironically, "Bring Miami back to the way it used to be."[42]

Voting to keep Miami an English-speaking city could not, however, change the increasingly Hispanic landscape of Miami Beach. From the mid-1970s, and especially after the arrival of the Marielitos (Cubans) in 1980, South Beach was characterized as a high crime, poor, urban slum. Allman in his mid-1980s book on Miami describes the disruption.

> Marielitos invaded South Miami Beach's welfare hotels, mugging its elderly Jewish retirees, robbing its delicatessens, staging cockfights in erstwhile kosher dining rooms. The [art] deco district [became] a drug peddler's paradise.[43]

Jews who lived in South Beach and were unable to afford alternative accommodations became fearful. Lincoln Road fell on hard times and no longer appealed to the seasoned tourist. The area around 41st Street, the backyard of Temple Beth Sholom, still catered to middle-class Anglos, but the Jewish population had noticeably decreased.

With little potential for new members from the immediate area, Temple Beth Sholom began experiencing the pains of contraction and displacement. Third-generation members had since moved to the suburbs and were far from the temple. For Temple Beth Sholom, dislocation from the center of its constituency and the possible reduction of its membership in the 1980s, would be a growing challenge.

Ethnicity and Civil Rights: Jews and African Americans

Miami's changing demographics in the 1960s resulted in few changes in the political power of African Americans. Cuban migration short-circuited the economic and social gains that African Americans had achieved from the civil rights movement and federal legislation in the late 1950s and 1960s.

The overwhelming numbers of Cubans seeking employment created an "enclave economy," that catered to their own ethnic group. In economic sectors where the blacks had made gains, such as the hotelier service industry, this was compounded by Miami Beach hoteliers, for example, preferring to hire Cubans to local blacks.

During the 1970s, African American resentment over Cuban success was underscored by the failure of civil rights legislation to change perceived attitudes toward them and to improve their social and economic conditions.

Kronish's reaction to these developments remained consistent with his past behavior and his charge of prophetic mission. He continued to attack segregation and support federal policies throughout this period that encouraged more equitable labor relation practices.

When Martin Luther King was assassinated in 1968, Kronish asked his congregants not to forsake their civil rights voice. He remained a strong advocate for Reform Judaism's prophetic mission platform to alleviate the plight of the disadvantaged and appealed to his members to lend a hand, create a job, give of their time.

As national vice-president of the American Jewish Congress, Kronish also addressed these same concerns. In the early 1970s, he helped to draft a policy condemning supporters of racial separation and reaffirming the American Jewish Congress' commitment to integration.[44] For Kronish, Liberal Judaism's mandate of prophetic mission never wavered.

The Showdown over Beach High

Although Kronish was a strong supporter of integration, many of the other members in his congregation did not share his liberal tendencies. In the late 1960s, a test case arose on Miami Beach that divided neighbor from neighbor, rabbi from congregant.

Miami Beach Senior High was a segregated school. Attempts to integrate the school had failed. A majority of parents of teenagers did not want their children schooled with inner-city blacks in the backyards of their white middle class neighborhood.

Sol Lichter and Phyllis Miller, co-chairs of Temple Beth Sholom's School for Living Judaism, stood apart from many of their co-religionists. Lichter had instituted the first community school in Miami in the early 1960s. In 1969 he was appointed principal of the segregated Miami Beach Senior High and charged with integrating the school, from which Ronald and Maxine Kronish had graduated in the 1960s. Its student body was ninety percent Jewish. Yet, in spite of federal legislation supporting integration, Jewish parents vetoed the integration of African-American students.

A second congregant, Phyllis Miller, served on the Dade County Public School Board and was a strong advocate of integration. As a school board member, she had taken the lead on many occasions in similar situations to motivate her board to do the right thing, and if necessary, introduce litigation to force integration.

Both Lichter and Miller looked to Kronish to help support their mission to integrate the segregated Miami Beach high school. Working together, the three along with others, mounted a campaign to canvass Beth Sholom members and develop a consensus that would bring about integration. Many who were previously active in the civil rights movement and on the temple's social action committee were opposed to the proposed integration plan, which included busing. They argued that the quality of their children's education would suffer and that their children would learn undesirable "street lessons." Many feared, moreover, that some of their children would be "displaced" and have to travel great distances from home. This was too high a price to pay for integration.

Kronish appealed to these members personally to reconsider. Supported by a 1969 Union of American Hebrew Congregations (the national organization of Reform Judaism) General Assembly resolution endorsing busing, he asked his congregants to stand behind Reform Judaism's prophetic mission which mandated integration. He solicited Jack Gordon, a veteran Temple Beth Sholom member and now a state senator from Miami Beach, to speak to his congregation and to appeal to his Beach constituency.

In the end many listened. Others remained opposed to busing and placed their children in private schools. Those who supported integration took a more active role in the PTA and in school activities.

In the fall of 1970, Beach High was integrated. Twenty-five percent of the students and teachers were bused from Overtown, a depressed black neighborhood in Miami's inner city. To overcome stereotyping and other manifestations of bigotry, Temple Beth Sholom organized a Human Relations Program to bring African Americans and Jews together. Speakers, luncheons and parent workshops were organized to promote integration. In Principal Lichter's assessment, a "symbiotic relationship developed among the temple, the rabbi, and the school."[45]

Black/Jewish Relations in the Aftermath of Beach High

Although Dade County schools were integrated in the 1970s, opportunities for African Americans to become upwardly mobile, be elected to municipal office or serve in senior government positions were few and far between. To this day, for example, no African American has served on the Miami Beach City Commission, or been appointed city manager or any other top-level senior municipal positions.

Police harassment and violence against African Americans continued. In 1980 a white policeman beat to death an African-American insurance salesman, Arthur McDuffie. A race riot exploded and the city was closed down for several days.[46]

During the racial unrest, the added presence of Marielitos, Cuban immigrants, wandering the city aimlessly—further tarnished South Florida's reputation as a tourist mecca. With civil strife, a foreign culture perceived as an invasion of Miami, and a severe economic recession, *Time* magazine labelled Miami "Paradise Lost."[47]

Kronish and Temple Beth Sholom members were outraged by the police behavior. Through Beth Sholom's social action committee, food, clothing and children's toys were collected and distributed among the innocent victims of the riots. After calm was restored, a cultural outreach program was developed for the African Americans most affected by the riot. Judy Drucker extended the Institute's Cultural Arts Series to include free performances to inner-city schools. She also arranged for black dance companies from outside Miami, such as the Alvin Ailey Dance Company and the Dance Theater of Harlem, to offer free performing arts classes to these schools.

Kronish also appealed to his congregation to make extra contributions to the Martin Luther King Foundation, established in the late 1960s after the leader's assassination.[48]

The temple, although situated on Miami Beach several miles away from the riots, was directly affected by the 1980 riot. Beth Sholom's printer was in the "combat zone," and the confirmation programs could not be delivered or picked up. The May 23rd bulletin suffered the same fate.[49]

That sabbath, Kronish recalled the black race riots in the North in the 1960s and asked his congregation to ponder not only terrorism in Israel, but the implications of "Terrorism in Florida" as well. "Can we as a people stand by idly and condemn? We must continue to reaffirm the moral law and act justly. Replace fear with helping hands."[50]

In spite of more than two decades of civil rights experience, integration of schools and programs to address disproportionate representation, Miami remained caught up in the web of racial inequities and social injustice.

Church and State Revisited

The tri-ethnic Miami community of Anglos, African Americans, and Hispanics created a social environment that lent itself to raising issues that were dormant for two decades. The increasing popularity of the Moral Majority in the late 1970s and 1980s reactivated the debate about the separation of church and state.

Neither Hispanics nor African Americans spoke with one voice. Although most African Americans and Hispanics opposed prayer in public schools and the teaching of "creationism," there were significant numbers of both groups, including a majority of Hispanics, who favored right-to-life and were anti-choice on the issue of abortion.

These "articles of faith" were most strongly advocated by Anglo-Christian fundamentalists whom Kronish often countered by regularly warning his congregation of the new battle lines that would soon be visible on the horizon. Reminding them of the ideological wars of twenty years earlier in greater Miami, Kronish described in detail the scars from the last confrontation, the fight over prayer in the public schools. Now it was not only prayer but also reproductive choice and the introduction of religion-based "creationism" into the science curriculum. For Kronish, "a church-dominated state is not healthy for freedom of thought.... A rigid separation of church and state must always be maintained."[51]

To achieve this goal, before the upcoming 1981 municipal elections Kronish mailed a personal letter to each congregant. He urged everyone to vote: "Think carefully and try to select those candidates who represent planned, pragmatic renewal of our city."[52]

Regularly he updated his congregation on the evolution/creationism battlefront. When Federal Judge William Overton declared "scientific creationism" a religion, not a science, and inappropriate for the classroom, Kronish passed it on to keep his congregation current with national policy.[53]

Kronish's stand against the Moral Majority on American domestic issues was juxtaposed by his explicit support for their position on Israel. The Moral Majority proponents were strong advocates for Israel, and they lobbied their political leaders and allies to keep Israel strong. Whenever the need arose Kronish prevailed on them to help the State of Israel receive economic aid and military commitments.

Kronish believed that building blocks of coalitions to support Israel were essential for the state's survival. Christian fundamentalists, although they may misinterpret the redemption of Israel, could speak to Congress, the President and Christian constituencies much more boldly than Jews. A political pragmatist, Kronish understood that people could agree on one agenda and be opposed on another. "Was that not the American way?" Moreover, with their strong support for Israel, the Moral Majority were potential investors in Israel and Israel Bonds.

Prophetic Mission in the 1970s and 1980s

Kronish's liberal interpretation of prophetic Judaism and social justice continued to be manifested on other sensitive topics besides civil rights and church and state issues. In the 1970s he spoke out on poverty, homelessness, and problems among the elderly. He castigated hotel speculators who would throw the poor out on the street to upgrade their hotel or to convert it into a condominium. Kronish was especially sensitive to the Jewish elderly. Many were members of the congregation or parents of members. In 1970 the average annual income of South Beach residents was under $3,000. Nearly eighty percent were over sixty-five years of age. Many had been pensioned off by their unions and were on fixed incomes.[54] Empathizing with their plight, he took it upon himself to serve as their ombudsman from the pulpit.[55]

Kronish was against the Vietnam War and repeatedly spoke out on the subject. His son, Ronald, an anti-war activist at Brandeis University in the late 1960s, encouraged his father to speak out on this issue repeatedly to his congregants and the community.

Since the mid-1960s, Kronish had been identified with the left wing of the Reform movement on United States' social and political issues as long as Israel was not the focus. As early as 1965, Kronish voted for the Union of American Hebrew Congregations (UAHC) resolution calling for the end of the Vietnam War.[56]

Even after 1967, when the Israelis supported the United States in Vietnam, Kronish continued to support the UAHC resolution opposing the war. Kronish argued that the Vietnam War was not only politically incorrect, it was morally repugnant. The war was causing widespread horrors among the Vietnamese peoples.[57]

An advocate of nuclear disarmament, Kronish could not understand why the United States did not use other political avenues to end this catastrophe. He deeply feared that the situation could escalate into a major nuclear confrontation. On several occasions Kronish drew from his past experiences when he had confronted those who were against the ban-the-bomb movement. Once again, he preached, "labor for peace, not war."

In 1968, while the Republican National Convention convened a few blocks away from the temple at the Fontainebleau Hotel, Kronish took advantage of the situation to preach a liberal position on the war. Although some in the congregation strongly disagreed, they accepted his right to speak freely from the pulpit as stated in the temple's constitution.

Affirmative action was yet another example of the liberal agenda in the 1970s that Kronish expounded for his congregants. Locally and nationally, Jews and Jewish organizations were divided over policies of affirmative action. Kronish believed in compensatory rebalancing of the historic scales in favor of American minorities. He stood squarely behind the Union of American Hebrew Congregations' position in support of affirmative action in 1969 and continued to support this position each time it was challenged.[58]

Kronish's reputation as an outspoken preacher on contemporary issues led to an invitation in the early 1970s to participate in a special television documentary hosted by Chalmers Dale, of CBS's "Look Up and Live." Also featuring other local Jewish leaders, the special half-hour show focused on the city's Jewish community.[59]

Among the many issues discussed was Israel. When Dale asked Kronish for his comments, Kronish spoke of Israel as an example for Miami of how various minority and ethnic groups can live and work side by side. He called for community relation committees to expedite dialogue among and between the different groups. Kronish also had the opportunity to describe Miami Beach's transformation from a location initially hostile to Jews to one that offered warmth and welcome, and he explained the legacy that caused many Jews to support liberal causes, such as civil rights and the anti-Vietnam War movement.

After the Camp David Accords (1979) moral issues frequently were the focus of Kronish's sermons in the pulpit and messages in the temple bulletins. Kronish opposed capital punishment, the genocide of Cambodians, an immigration policy that failed to absorb more Vietnamese refugees, the slow progress of nuclear disarmament, and the lack of American moral leadership against the blackmail of terrorism and oil.[60]

Kronish also took a leading role in opposing terrorism of another sort—that of the violent and ultra-militant Jewish Defense League (JDL). In October, 1977, members of the JDL took over Kronish's office in a protest against the cultural program of the Temple—organized by the indefatigable Judy Drucker—which was sponsoring the visit of two Soviet musicians to Miami. Despite his obvious antipathy towards the Soviet regime, Kronish forcefully rejected the tactics of the JDL protesters. "They believe they have the answer to the problem of the Jews in the Soviet Union, but they are following the tactics of the Soviet government."[61]

Jewish public policy issues, such as those of the Council of Jewish Federations, were also of vital concern to Kronish and at times also felt the bite of his tongue when defined as a moral issue. When Morton Mandel, the president of the Council of Jewish Federations, announced in 1980 that a "billion dollar level of annual campaigning was needed by the Jewish communal enterprise," Kronish wrote a letter to Mandel and published it in the weekly bulletin, venting his anger. Kronish questioned the spending of a billion dollars for a national Federation agenda that did not address our Jewish education concerns. Where, Kronish thundered, was the policy to create and develop a

> high quality of Jewish life for our children.... [our] 350,000 Jewish university students.... [our] 3,000 synagogues.... if we are to survive, with the quality of Jewish life we want for our children?... 'Jewish survival' rests both on the positive Jewish programs of our Federations– and the necessary educational and cultural activities of our synagogues.[62]

Jewish communal priorities for soliciting and allocating funds within the Jewish community were of great moral concern to Kronish.

Kronish's concern with prophetic Judaism and social justice remained resolute and resilient throughout the 1970s and 1980s. The lessons learned under his revered teacher, Stephen S. Wise, at the Jewish Institute of Religion in the 1940s served him well. With support from a congregation to speak his mind from the pulpit, Kronish tackled the moral issues of his day with dignity, determination and consistency.

Prophetic Mission and the Holocaust

For many Jews, including Kronish, the 1970s brought a concerted effort to educate the Jewish and non-Jewish community about the Holocaust. Elie Wiesel's account of the Nazi terror in his autobiographical book, *Night*, and his moral supposition about the historical uniqueness of the Holocaust, created a swell of growing concern among educators about the need for Holocaust programs and curriculum.

Unlike many congregations in North America, Temple Beth Sholom had a significant number of Holocaust survivors. Kronish's *New Haggadah in Israel*, penned in 1950, was composed with these members in mind. "Lo! Let all who have been afflicted with the scourge of Fascism and Nazism and homelessness come to share the *Seder* of Redemption in the homeland. Slaves we were to Pharaoh" was replaced by "slaves we were to Hitler."[63]

Beginning in the early 1970s, Kronish, began to seek out these members for programs for the temple's School and Institute for Living Judaism. With the encouragement and assistance of Dr. Helen Fagin, a Warsaw Ghetto survivor and Director of the Judaic Studies Program at the University of Miami, members of the temple under Kronish's guidance began to harness the resources in the community to educate and memorialize.[64]

On December 2, 1979, with Elie Wiesel as the keynote speaker, a Sanctuary Garden—with a ceramic sculpture on two of the walls entitled *From Holocaust to Homeland*—was dedicated in the temple grounds in memory of those who perished. Wiesel read from *Night* and spoke of hope. The service included poems by Hanna Sennesch, "*Blessed is the Match*" and Yitzhak Katznelson, "*The Song of the Slaughtered Jewish People*." Remembering his own family's suffering in Zborow, the small village in the Ukraine where his father had grown up, Kronish's Memorial Service included a new liturgical composition dedicated in memory of "the Heroes and Martyrs."[65]

A decade later, under the leadership of these same individuals and with Elie Wiesel, by then a Nobel Laureate, as the victims' voice, the Miami Beach Holocaust Memorial was dedicated.[66]

The Temple Beth Sholom Sanctuary Garden became a sacred location for temple members to meditate and for events commemorating those killed during the Holocaust–*Yom Hashoah* (Holocaust Memorial Day) and the Warsaw Ghetto Revolt. It also became the location to which members congregated for rallies protesting citizenship for Nazis who had gained it under false pretenses, to march for *Refuseniks* (Soviet Jewish dissidents refused emigration visas), and to show support for Israel.[67]

Sabbath sermons provided another forum to share with the congregants one of the rallies' themes–"to stand up to false accusers in the face of moral adversity"–as well as an open invitation to join him at the temple's Holocaust Memorial Wall.[68]

The moral meaning and historical uniqueness of the Holocaust weighed heavily on Kronish. The naming of his second son, Ronald–after his grandfather, Reuven, killed in the Holocaust–was a testament of rebirth and hope in humanity's future. The programs designed at Beth Sholom reinforced his efforts to learn more about his own family's martyrology and to help others in their search for threads of meaning. And his friendship with Wiesel, Fagin and other survivors, fortified his resolve to labor for peace and *Klal Yisrael*, the Jewish community.

An Auxiliary Rabbi Comes to Beth Sholom: Rabbi Harry Jolt

Temple Beth Sholom's own *Klal Yisrael* grew to embrace two individuals important in the institution's development in the post-1967 period–Rabbi Harry Jolt, who arrived from New Jersey in 1968; and Dennis Rice, who became the executive director in 1980.

Jolt was hired as auxiliary rabbi as a result of increased demands on Kronish's time by national and Israeli organizations, which necessitated frequent trips away from Miami Beach.

Harry Jolt, a first-generation American Jew, was born in Poland in 1904, and was more than a decade older than Leon Kronish, who was born in 1917. Attending the Jewish Theological Seminary (JTS) in New York in the mid-1920s, he was taught by the luminaries of the seminary in the interwar years. Jolt reveled in the *midrash* (commentary) and homiletic (preaching) classes of Mordecai Kaplan and in the Talmud classes of Louis Ginzberg and Louis Finkelstein. He and his fellow rabbinical students viewed themselves as "fugitives from Orthodoxy."[69]

During Jolt's student years, when Cyrus Adler was president of the JTS, the seminary's philosophy was one of helping the eastern-European Jewish immigrants adjust to America religiously. A new social environment did not mean that one had to discard customs and rituals and adopt Reform Judaism. Traditions could be conserved, revelation affirmed, peoplehood advocated and Zionism supported. The Zionist Organization of America (ZOA), pre-World War Two, looked upon the Conservative rabbinate "as the rabbinical bulwark of American Zionism." [70]

In 1927, Jolt's first pulpit was Tifereth Israel in Lincoln, Nebraska, which at that time had approximately the same Jewish population as Miami Beach—one thousand.[71] His colleague, Abraham Sachar, helped Jolt build an active Hillel at the local state university.

In 1944, Jolt enlisted in the Armed Forces as a chaplain and served in the Philippines and in Kyoto, Japan. Soon thereafter, in 1945, stationed outside Hiroshima, he was one of the first chaplains to enter the city after the atom bomb was dropped in August 1945. "No experience," Jolt later reflected, "did more to humanize me."[72]

Returning to the United States, he spent the next two decades at Beth Yehuda in Ventnor, near Atlantic City, New Jersey, from where he came to join Beth Sholom.

Jolt's permanent arrival on Miami Beach came after several years as a snowbird. During the 1960s he had frequently attended services at Beth Sholom and was familiar with the setting and philosophy. His brother-in-law, Jack Fink, Beth Sholom's president-elect, had invited Jolt on a number of occasions to move south after his retirement and become active in its programs.

Jolt was well suited to serve as auxiliary rabbi. His own personal journey from traditional Judaism to Reform was not unlike that of Kronish. Both Jolt and Kronish were influenced by Mordecai Kaplan in their formative years; Jolt in the 1920s, shortly after Kaplan created the Society for the Advancement of Judaism (1922), and Kronish in the 1930s, after Kaplan had published *Judaism as a Civilization* (1934). Both helped the congregants to infuse Reform practices with a strong sense of tradition. Both Jolt and Kronish shared a deep sensitivity for Israel, shaped by the American democratic experience. Each had adopted the rhetoric that the Jew in the United States lived two identities: the American and the Jewish. Even in their preaching style, they shared commonalities. Both viewed the sermon as an opportunity to bring Jewish tradition to bear upon current events. Both also used humor to make their points.

The arrival of Jolt provided the synagogue with an additional seasoned rabbi, and resulted in an enduring friend and colleague for Kronish, one he could work well with, trust implicitly, admire and respect. In return, Kronish gave the sixty-five year old Jolt a new lease on life. In addition, Jolt's presence permitted Kronish the time to meet the challenges he outlined in his articles, *Yisrael Goralenu* and *What are the 'Zionist Mitzvot'?*, concerning the struggles facing Israel in the contemporary world.

A New Administrator: Dennis Rice

Dennis Rice, a graduate of Wayne State University, was a former director of a large Conservative synagogue, Shaare Zedek, in Southfield, Michigan. He had proven managerial skills and served as a member of the board of the National Association of Temple Administrators. His hiring as the new executive director in 1980, was in large measure due to the changing demographics of Miami and the need to have an able administrator in touch with current styles of management.

Declining membership rolls were the prognosis of the decade due to out-of-county migration and deaths. Seniors were over-represented in the temple's memberships rolls. On the one hand, they were the cohort of the population that was most likely to attend services and contribute to charities, be cognizant of temple activities and follow the practices of Liberal Judaism—have a *mezuzah* on their door, light Sabbath candles, and celebrate the holidays.[73] According to Sheskin, by 1982, synagogue affiliation in greater Miami was only thirty-eight percent.[74] On the other hand, this cohort was also the group with the highest mortality rate.

Kronish's membership policy of "fair-share" did not change in the face of shrinking synagogue affiliation. It had been adopted from Wise, and although no longer able to cover the true costs of providing the range of activities supported by Temple Beth Sholom, remained firm. It was always Kronish's conviction that Beth Sholom did not need to live by the constraints imposed by lack of funds. His philosophy was to set a goal and then find the funds.[75]

Rice's arrival led to his founding the Florida Association of Synagogue and Temple Administrators (1980) which, in turn, helped Kronish keep up better with the changing conditions his temple confronted.

Liturgical Renewal

During the post-1967 period, Kronish re-evaluated his understanding of Liberal Judaism, and its component features. In 1969, he composed a collection of inspirational writings that influenced his rabbinical career. Writing in the foreword of *A Treasury of Inspiration*, he emphasized how the *shidach*, the "marriage" with his congregants had enriched his soul:

> In the quarter century that I have been privileged to serve you as your rabbi, you have encouraged me not only to teach and preach, but also to give of my strength and to lead you... for the redemption of Israel. To you—my Beth Sholom family—I am forever grateful.

In this inspirational volume, Kronish pays tribute to his mentors, Stephen Wise and Mordecai Kaplan, who set him on the course of fusing Judaism with Zionism and who infused him with the spirit of independence. It includes passages from the Torah, Ezekiel and Maimonides that promise messianic redemption and testimonies from *Psalms* and modern Israeli leaders like Ben-Gurion that speak of Israel as a "rendezvous with destiny."

Exodus 19:5-6 is quoted as God's affirmation of chosenness—"if ye keep My covenant, then ye shall be Mine own treasure from among all peoples; and ye shall be unto Me a kingdom of priests, and a holy nation." *Klal Yisrael*, the product of four thousand years of historical religious experience, "has shaped my spiritual leadership."[76]

The more Kronish felt infused with Zionism and Israel, the more he reworked his past liturgical efforts. During this period Kronish made relevant for the 1970s the *Shofar Services for Rosh Hashanah*, the *Hanukkah Candlelight Service*, and the *Passover Supplementary Haggadah*.

The Haggadah included the "Matzah of Hope" and an invocation to share in the "Seder of Redemption" in our Homeland. Also incorporated were "four modern questions," drafted by Leon Kronish, that spoke of "dipping into our strength and energy to keep the state secure and to purchase Israel Bonds," and a section on "four kinds of modern Jews"—the evil one being the one who "draws a false line between Judaism and the Jewish people, [and] between Judaism and human rights."[77]

Kronish also made changes in the sabbath service liturgy to augment the feeling of peoplehood. A modern song which emanated from the Soviet Jewry movement, entitled, "Let My People Go," was added as an opening hymn to the *kabbalat shabbat*, the sabbath service on Friday night—an expression of solidarity with Soviet Jewry. The song, *Yerushalyim Shel Zahav* (Jerusalem of Gold), originally written in 1967 during the Six Day War, was sung as the closing hymn of sabbath services to signify unity with the people of Israel.[78]

The inclusion of an Israeli-centered liturgy meant working closely with Cantor Conviser to bring contemporary Israeli musical arrangements to complement the prayers. At the same time, traditional cantillation also remained important, and additional congregational hymns were sung in Hebrew. New musical events and creative liturgies were introduced, combining a variety of Judaic and Israeli melodies, reflecting the changes and experimentation occurring in Reform Judaism in the 1960s and 1970s.

The Central Conference of American Rabbis (CCAR) strongly affirmed Zionism within the liturgy of Reform Judaism after 1967 and this position was endorsed by Kronish. A series of Reform prayer books published in the 1970s—*Gates of Prayer*, for Sabbath and festivals (1975), *Gates of the House*, for the home (1976), and *Gates of Repentance*, for the High Holidays (1978)—proudly reinforced this attitude. These liturgical changes in the prayerbooks had a profound influence on the religious school's curriculum, while further complementing Kronish's passion to synthesize Reform Judaism with Zionism and an Israel-centered curriculum in the classroom.

The Temple Beth Sholom School for Living Judaism

Israel's 1967 victory in the Six Day War also led Kronish to re-evaluate the relationship of Liberal Judaism and the educational process. The religious school – renamed the Temple Beth Sholom School for Living Judaism – became a vehicle to transmit Zionism and Israel along every axis of Jewish experience. Jewish continuity was dependent on the values internalized by youth during their formative years of Jewish education.

A new curriculum was structured that followed the pattern of a youth's religious life-cycle of events and the goals of "Israelization" – placing Israel as one of the central building blocks of the curriculum. Five sacred covenants were set forth:

- *consecration* - when a child enters religious school;
- *bar and bat mitzvah* - when, at age 13, a youth accepts a Jewish way of life;
- *b'nai Sinai* - confirmation, when, at age 15, on *Shavuot*, teenagers confirm their commitment to Judaism in celebration of the revelation at Mt. Sinai;
- *aliya le-regel* - pilgrimage to Israel undertaken the summer after confirmation; and
- *b'nai Yisrael* - continuing Jewish and Israeli studies in Judaica High School after confirmation and until the end of high school.[79]

The combination of these five covenants inspired youth to commit themselves to the covenant between the Jewish people and God, and the American Diaspora and Israel.

The restructuring of the curriculum at Temple Beth Sholom was a pedagogical translation of Kronish's framework outlined in *Yisrael Goralenu* and *The Zionist Mitzvot*. It was a contemporary hermeneutic of Liberal Judaism that placed Israel at the center of the curriculum within each subject area – basic customs and ceremonies, Bible and history, and Hebrew.

Formal education reached its climax through *aliya le-regel*, a post-confirmation pilgrimage to Israel. Only by experiencing the land and the people of the State of Israel, could the *gesher vakesher* – the living links of communication and caring – be fully realized. Jewish education in the American Diaspora, if it was to extend traditional Zionism, required the bringing of American Jews to Israel – a "hands-on," "face-to-face" experience – without the moral imperative of demanding *aliya*.

Upon their return these students were consistently attracted to the temple's school final milestone, the Judaica High School. Not suprisingly, many were active in BESHTY (Beth Sholom Temple Youth) and would participate in the Greater Miami High School in Israel program.[80] Some former participants of the confirmation class pilgrimage to Israel, such as David Lichter, returned to serve as youth leaders at the temple.

Along with the philosophical reformulation of the curriculum came structural changes. The religious school expanded its early childhood classes from half days to full days. Programs from the School of Fine Arts were integrated into the religious school offerings. Hebrew training became more intensive and complemented other activities.

In 1982 Kronish approached the temple leadership with the idea for an expanded school. They wholeheartedly supported the need but wondered if the timing was propitious. A few board members, along with Rice, the executive director, expressed concern that the temple did not have the reserves to carry a large mortgage and to extend such a financial burden into the future. Like Shepard Broad in the 1950s,[81] they argued that the majority of funds should be in hand or pledged before the building proceeded.

Board members who supported the idea pointed to the growing popularity of Reform day schools and pre-schools throughout the United States, and, the very successful day school in South Miami, under Rabbi Herbert Baumgard's direction, that had been operating for several years at Temple Beth Am. They favored more educational options for the temple's children.

There was also a general feeling that the temple was financially healthy, and that their rabbi would be able to overcome any shortfall that may develop. Past precedent had taught them not to worry. Thus, they agreed to move forward, provided they had assurances that Kronish and the building committee would be more than able to meet the building campaign's demand.[82] The board had complete confidence in Kronish's abilities to solicit funds, develop new programs, and implement them. The principle of "fair-share" membership was not abandoned, and fundraising remained the vehicle to supplement membership revenue shortfalls.[83]

The Temple Beth Sholom School for Living Judaism touched thousands of youth in the post-Six Day War era. All experienced Israel vicariously. Most joined a temple mission, a summer camp experience, or a Zionist program and visited Israel while still a teenager. All could read Hebrew and some were quite competent in speaking. The Zionization and "Israelization" of the temple's youth, which developed into their commitment to a partnership between Israel and the Diaspora, may be Kronish's most enduring legacy.

Havurot

During the 1970s, Kronish followed the lead of other Reform rabbis that began to introduce *havurot* as a means to co-opt disenchanted youth. *Havurot* was a new way to recharge Liberal Judaism. *Havurot* are small groups of congregants who worship, study, and celebrate Judaism together, independent of the larger congregation.[84] They provided an innovative response to meaningful worship.

These small fellowships were first established by Mordecai Kaplan in the 1940s as a way to convey and participate in Reconstructionist thinking.[85] Reform Judaism adopted the *havurot* for baby-boomers and it attracted many who sought more creative expressions of being Jewish.[86] At Temple Beth Sholom, *havurot* were "open-ended 'fellowships of faith,' a rediscovery of congregational camaraderie and support."[87]

In time, *havurot* also came to serve another purpose. They became seed beds to nurture the ideas of Liberal Judaism and "Israelization" which Kronish was preaching and teaching to his congregants.

Temple Beth Sholom *havurot* consisted of several families who met on a regular basis outside of the synagogue in the congregants' homes. They shared with one other what it meant to be an American Jew and how to become more connected to Israel. Each *havura* was a renewal of the covenant between God and *Klal Yisrael*. For some members, the *havura* became an extended family. One *havura* that began in 1976, has continued to meet for fellowship for the last two decades.[88]

Another *havura* organized in the 1970s met every sabbath to study the weekly Torah portion. In the *havura's* view, the deeper one understands Torah, the greater the commitment to Judaism and Zionism.[89] Kronish led this sabbath morning study session—which took place from 9:00-10:30, before the regular 10:45 *Shabbat* morning service—for several years before transferring its leadership to Levy Soshuk, an educator, biblical scholar and Hebraist.

On many sabbaths, Kronish and Soshuk argued over points of *midrash* and modern interpretation. An intellectually demanding group of thirty to forty people, the Saturday morning *havura* also drew inspiration from visiting scholars, among whom were Harry Orlinsky, Nahum Sarna and Elie Wiesel. In the early 1980s Dr. Yehuda Shamir replaced Soshuk.

The institution of *havurot* at Temple Beth Sholom was not unique, nor was their longevity. What made the *havurot* stand apart was the commitment of its members to turn their attention to Kronish's passion—the "Israelization" of their lives—a process we will address fully in the next chapter.

The Leon Kronish Institute for Living Judaism

In the years immediately following the Six Day War, Kronish experimented with new ideas and programs regarding how to transform the temple into a center of Israeli life and culture. Speakers, adult education, youth activities, as well as other programs, were a regular feature of temple life. But, for the most part, these events were neither organized with an unifying central theme nor coordinated or housed under the auspices of a central arm of the temple. Kronish voiced concern that the temple was not reaching its full potential and that educational opportunities and community efforts that could profile Israel were being squandered.

In response to this concern, in 1969, Temple Beth Sholom's board dedicated the Leon Kronish Institute of Living Judaism. Conceived as an institute for Jewish formal and informal education and culture in the broadest sense, it presented a wide spectrum of Jewish civilization activities and programs. Adult education programs, youth groups, *havurot*, performing and visual arts, and the Israelis-in-Residence program came under its wing. Zionism, with a prominent Israeli focus, was integrated with Americanism in the programming. The Institute of Living Judaism was a celebration and promoted in Kronish's words, "the heritage of Israel and the spiritual destiny of the Jewish people."[90]

Bible and Talmud classes were offered by the institute for adults every Tuesday morning. Frequently attended by couples, and often led by Rabbi Jolt after 1971, a particular theme would be discussed each session. These themes reinforced the concepts of covenant and the land of Israel.

For example, one of the topics concerned Job. "What was the meaning of Job's suffering? Did he serve God from love or from fear?" Challenged by Jolt to reconcile faith with reason, class members vacillated between dogma and human experience as he or she tried to open the gate to God's moral law.[91]

Other adult educational programs available on a regular basis included: a Book Review Series and the Great Books Series (often with Israeli topics) organized by Lillian Kronish through the sisterhood; a Sunday morning culture club, "Culture, Coffee and Conversation," moderated by Jolt; and an *ulpan*, modern Hebrew class, offered by Shula Ben-David.

An evening adult studies program was introduced and drew national figures who had retired to Miami Beach—first as participants and later as teachers. Dr. Isaac Fein, a former professor at Baltimore Hebrew College, taught a course. So did Dr. Joseph Diamond, the former director of Jewish Education of Toronto.[92]

The reputations of Fein and Diamond preceded their tenure at Temple Beth Sholom. Many "northern" congregational members knew them personally in Baltimore and Toronto as their own teachers or teachers of their children. These educators also served as consultants to the teachers in Beth Sholom's religious school and were advocates of Kronish's educational mandate of integrating Israel and Zionism within Reform Judaism.

The institute established a distinguished lecture series which encouraged affiliated and non-affiliated Jews to come together under Beth Sholom's canopy. Organized around a thematic format, often with an Israeli accent, the series sponsored a parade of notables over the years. Isaac Bashevis Singer, Amos Oz, Martin Gilbert, Howard Sachar, Lucy Davidowicz, Jacob Timmerman, Max Dimont, Herman Wouk, Emil Fackenheim, Elie Wiesel, Yosef Yerushalmi, Haim Herzog, Yitzhak Rabin, Golda Meir, Shlomo Avineri and

Pinhas Sapir were just some of the personalities who spoke before hundreds and sometimes thousands of eager listeners at Temple Beth Sholom.

Many of these speakers were friends as well as colleagues of Kronish who long had been associated with his activities, frequently concerning Israel. These engagements were opportunities to re-acquaint, share memories and discuss upcoming agendas of mutual concern.

The Institute's Jo-Ellen Levinson Youth Center served the needs of temple youth with organized activities and programs. BESHTY (Beth Sholom Temple Youth), SEFTY (Southeast Federation of Temple Youth) and NFTY (National Federation of Temple Youth) all came under the institute's wing. Children attending UAHC (Union of American Hebrew Congregations) summer camps were also coordinated by the Institute.

Kronish took special interest in college students. With his own children at college age, Kronish viewed their cohorts' experiences as a window into the psyche of the 1960s and 1970s generation. He worked closely with Hillel rabbis in Miami, the state of Florida, and nationally in understanding the currents of the time.

One of the former youths who had participated in Temple Beth Sholom programs was Stanley Ringler, who returned to Miami in the 1970s as a Reform rabbi and Executive Director of Hillel Jewish Student Centers of South Florida. Ringler and Kronish, together with the educational directors of Temple Beth Sholom, Joel Finer and Stanley Liedeker, planned activities to enrich the Jewish identity of college youth and to navigate their interests toward Israel and Zionism. On many weekends, Hillel and Temple Beth Sholom held joint programs for Miami Jewish college students.

In addition, Kronish regularly invited college youth to his home during the winter break to listen to their experiences and concerns, and encourage them to visit Israel during the summer. Gerald Serotta, who grew up on Miami Beach and was a close friend of Ronald, the rabbi's son, later became a Reform rabbi and served as president of the International Association of Hillel Directors. He recalled that "few rabbis have maintained Rabbi Kronish's inherent patience and enthusiasm in supporting the efforts of Hillel to challenge the Jewish student within the rapidly changing milieu of the campus."[93]

Special institute activities were complemented by Friday night sermons that highlighted the program's theme and by missions to Israel that dovetailed with Israel Bonds, Histadrut, and the temple. The Leon Kronish Institute for Living Judaism became a central address in the Jewish community of greater Miami.

The Institute's Cultural Virtuoso: Judy Drucker

The Leon Kronish Institute for Living Judaism's mandate was also to promote a program for the performing and visual arts. Judy Drucker's success in galvanizing attention to classical music led to popular demand by members for the temple's institute to host more concerts. Encouraged by Kronish, Drucker expanded her city-wide culture and fine arts series, Miami's Great Artist Series—later expanded to include a Great Performance and Israel Showcase Series.[94] These series attracted young undiscovered talents—Pinchas Zuckerman, played to a Beth Sholom audience during his first United States tour in 1969—as well as international celebrities, many Israeli.

In the 1970s, Miami audiences witnessed performances by Vladimir Ashkenazi, Leonard Bernstein, Zubin Mehta, Yehudi Menuhin, Luciano Pavarotti, Yo-Yo Ma, Vladimir Rostropovich, Itzhak Perlman, Richard Tucker, Marilyn Horne, the Israeli Philharmonic Orchestra, and leading chamber-music ensembles from London, Paris and Montreal. In addition, through Drucker's efforts, Miamians were introduced to renowned opera and ballet such as the Metropolitan Opera and the American Ballet Theater with Mikhail Baryshnikov.

By the mid-1970s, the Great Artist Series was so popular, subscriptions were sold out before the season began and the temple could no longer accommodate the crowds.[95] To provide equal opportunity for all members, tickets for the elderly were discounted by eighty percent and for students by forty percent.

Until Judy Drucker introduced classical music, as well as theater, opera, and ballet, to greater Miami, the city was considered a cultural backwater. Entertainers who made the hotel rounds every season viewed Miami Beach as an all-expense-paid two weeks in the sun. Drucker's efforts, therefore, were all the more remarkable. With the constant encouragement and leadership of Kronish, she enhanced the cultural image of Miami and, at the same time, provided a special forum for Israeli artists. In 1994, *The Miami Herald* still described Drucker's organization as "South Florida's premier presenter of classical music and dance."[96]

Participating in Jewish cultural arts, punctuated by Israelis, was another tie to bind the congregants to *Klal Yisrael*, take pride in their heritage and strengthen the partnership between the American Diaspora and Israel.

Drucker's enthusiasm with the institute's cultural undertakings was also extended to the children of Beth Sholom. A School of Fine Arts was inaugurated in 1969. Under Drucker's direction, the curriculum provided "the opportunity [for the child] to express himself [or herself] Jewishly and artistically."[97] Students could study piano, pottery, drama, dancing, art and music. The school introduced a Music Workshop for Tots, and another for very young children. Theater productions, such as *The Diary of Anne Frank* and *Fiddler on the Roof*, piano recitals, and children's art exhibits were regular features. Rachelle Nelson, later trained as a cantor at Hebrew Union College and currently cantor at Temple Beth Am, Miami, taught music classes and frequently performed for the School of Fine Arts.

For Drucker, the word "arts" stood for a distinctive body of expression, for a quality of existence that could and would strengthen each participant's

Jewish identity. Exposing a Jewish dimension through the arts was as important to Kronish as teaching children and adults to learn Hebrew.

One activity organized by the School of Fine Arts arose from a temple mission to Jewish Spain led by Kronish in the mid-1970s. Inspired by their trip, mission participants asked Drucker to initiate an art project that used the medium of ceramics to integrate the American Bicentennial within American Judaism. Under the guidance of Henry Small, the temple ceramic art teacher, Shula Ben-David, educator and Hebrew teacher, and Dorothy Knopke, a lay leader, more than one hundred children participated in the creation of a ceramic wall in the temple.

Started in an old trailer borrowed for the year, the project led to the submission of a National Endowment of the Arts proposal. Uriah P. Levy, Isaac Leeser, Emma Lazarus, and Stephen Wise shared space with other prominent American Jews on the wall. Titled *L'Chayim Ul 'Sholom* (The Way of Life and Peace), the 9-by-16-foot mural was labelled by one local newspaper, a "one-ton clay creation in which Lincoln is parallel to Moses."[98]

Jewish visual arts and film were also promoted within the institute and served to complement Drucker's musical, opera, ballet and theater programs. Exhibitions were housed in the Lowe-Levinson Gallery, and Israeli artists especially were solicited. Amos Amit's batiks, Leonard Baskin's *Haggadah* paintings, Henry Gramson's sculpture, and Zvi Raphaely's murals were exhibited in the 1970s.

Frequently the exhibits were combined with social action programs. The 1970 photographic exhibition, "Art in a Concentration Camp—Drawings from Terezin," was advertised as a program to help Soviet Jews. The art "contain[s] a message for Christians and Jews alike about the real meaning of Passover and the *Exodus* today," Kronish explained to a *Miami Herald* interviewer. "'Let My People Go' is a Soviet Jew calling as much as it is a Holocaust survivor or even Moses in the time of Pharaoh."[99] Liberating Soviet Jewry would also strengthen Israel demographically. For Kronish, Jewish education was to be carried out through every available cultural form, including the media.

The Leon Kronish Institute for Living Judaism was a dynamic pulsating center of Jewish and Israeli activity which served as an institutional model for the greater Miami Jewish community. In many ways, the institute paralleled other leading synagogue-center developments in the United States in the post-1967 period. However, Miami Beach did not have what most other communities could boast—generations of Jewish pioneers who had laid foundations, established standards, and endowed programs to benefit later generations. What it lacked was compensated for by Kronish's passion to deepen the Jewish education of his congregants and by pioneering "Israelization" programs which brought them into contact with the central issues and personalities of the times.

Concerns for the Younger Generation

By the mid-1970s, Temple Beth Sholom functioned as a "home base" for Kronish's far-flung and ever-expanding national and international activities. Kronish was involved with, among others, the following Jewish institutions: the Hebrew University, Brandeis University, Hebrew Union College-Jewish Institute of Religion, Jewish Federation, Central Conference of American Rabbis, American Jewish Congress, the Histadrut and Israel Bonds.

Planning sessions followed committee cycles, with meetings in New York and elsewhere across the nation. When a gala fundraising event occurred, it was not uncommon for Kronish to deliver a keynote address at the function. Frequently this meant trips far from Miami Beach: Los Angeles, Chicago, Washington, New York, Tel Aviv and Jerusalem.

The professional and educational staff carried the ball, and programming was not disrupted during his absences. Nevertheless, a handful of members wanted his presence more frequently. On the one hand, they, like other congregants, were proud of the national reputation of the congregation and their rabbi. They understood that much of his success was due to Beth Sholom members serving as his grass roots "control group," assuming responsibility for a "pilot test" on local terrain, and undertaking advocacy roles. On the other hand, they wanted their senior rabbi to respond to unscheduled needs whenever and wherever.

Rabbi Kronish was successful in retaining veteran members as well as bringing in new ones into his 1200-member congregation throughout the 1970s and into the 1980s. His charismatic leadership, multi-faceted programs and national reputation were all drawing cards.

Yet some, members, and especially third-generation American Jews, were less responsive to the Kronish Israel agenda. Born after the birth of Israel, and in many cases too young to be significantly affected by the Six Day War, they viewed Israel as the strongman of the Middle East. Less trustful of politicians in the wake of Vietnam and Watergate, they supported airing opinions, even if publically critical of Israel.

Third-generation temple members were American Jews who came to adulthood in the 1970s and 1980s. Many of this generation had sensitized their parents to the political issues of the 1960s. Although they strongly identified themselves as American Jews, some were receptive to Palestinian refugee demands for dialogue as a prelude to peace, a stance which Kronish claimed would lead to their being co-opted in the propaganda war.[100]

Conversely, most members of the second generation, who had shared the aftermath of the Six Day War (1967) with Kronish glowed in his comprehensive linkage of Israel to their temple and vice versa. Indeed, they revelled in Kronish's ability to capture the pulse and politics of Israel and integrate it in a meaningful way into their lives in "The Negev of America."

They accepted his interpretation of events and applauded his policy of one-hundred-percent public support of Israel, while keeping criticism private "within the family."

Second-generation congregation members, who had grown up during the Depression and World War Two, saw Israel as a symbol of redemption. They accepted Kronish's perspective that "the Jewish state is a religious ideal in a political form.... Israel represents redemption."[101] And they also shared Kronish's viewpoint that support for Israel's policies, regardless of which political party was elected, was essential.

Nearly one in every two of these temple members either had visited Israel on a mission or as a tourist, or had sent their children as a confirmand. Zonik Shaham, who was in contact with Temple Beth Sholom's youth in the 1970s and 1980s more than any other Israeli, commented that "a higher percentage of the young people have taken part in educational programs in Israel than in other congregations that I have known."[102]

For members of this group, Israel became a home away from home, where the highs and lows of Israeli life – and Israeli friendship – were shared with near equal intensity to their counterparts in the United States. The translations from Hebrew to English of the testaments in memory of Eyal Shaham, Zonik's son who died in the Yom Kippur War, and in memory of Amram and Yohanan Ben Chorin, sons of Yehuda who died in the Six Day War (1967), remained potent for these members.

It was as though *Yisrael Goralenu* and *What are the 'Zionist Mitzvot'?* had different meanings to each generation. Each voiced opinions based on its own value-generating experiences.

Many Reform congregations in the United States were experiencing difficulties with their rabbis during this period. Nearly three out of four rabbis perceived a "distance" between themselves and their congregation in the 1970s.[103] Rabbi Arthur Hertzberg, responding to this gap in 1975, wrote that today's rabbi "feels terribly cold and terribly alone and he would like to say like Moses.... 'Go send somebody else.' But here we are. We are sent. We cannot avoid it."[104] This was not the case at Temple Beth Sholom.

Kronish was sensitive to concerns and needs of the younger generation. He heard their yearnings and, in typical Kronish style, he challenged them to work with him in defining the future contours of leadership for Temple Beth Sholom and Reform Judaism.

> Thirty-six years ago most of our "pioneers" and "founders" and "builders" were young men and women – young parents – who wanted to develop a Liberal Jewish life-style for themselves and their children – within the framework of a congregation that was prepared to search for new ways of perceiving an ancient tradition.... Who will be our future leaders when the older ones are gone?[105]

Kronish welcomed young families, especially young parents, to be active in the many educational and cultural programs of the synagogue at the same time that he urged them to develop and strengthen their commitment to Israel. He invited them to show their support by becoming active in current Israeli-Diaspora joint projects, such as Project Renewal.[106] Only by committing themselves to *Klal Yisrael* was it possible to bring American Jewry to *Hazon Geulah M'sheechee*, to the vision of messianic redemption.

All of this was suddenly brought to an end on sabbath morning, January 14, 1984, when Leon Kronish suffered a severe stroke which forced him to retire from the active rabbinate. This abruptly ended his role as a leader at Temple Beth Sholom and in the greater Miami Jewish community and in North American Jewry. One of the great ironies is that the stroke occurred just after he had completed conducting services for his congregation and on the eve of a planned trip to Israel as one of the leaders of the annual Israel Bonds Prime Minister's Mission to Israel.

(Above) Bar Mitzvah of Harvey Farr, 1950s. (Left to right) Leon Ell, president, Temple Beth Sholom, Harvey, Ambassador James McDonald, Rabbi Leon Kronish.

(Below, left to right) Leonard Ratner, Vice-President Hubert Humphrey, Leon Kronish, 1968.

(Above) Frank Sinatra (bow tie) and Leon Kronish, 1964.

(Below left, left to right) Leon Kronish, Ralph Renick, Judy Drucker, Richard Tucker, early 1970s.

(Below right) Jackie Gleason and Leon Kronish, 1964.

(Above, left to right) unkown, Presidential Candidate George McGovern, Leon Kronish, Congressman Claude Pepper, 1972.

(Above) President Gerald Ford and Leon Kronish, 1978.

(Below, left to right) Gary Gerson, Leon Kronish, Governor Bob Graham, 1982.

Elie Wiesel and Leon Kronish, 1979.

Chapter Six

THE "ISRAELIZATION" OF REFORM JUDAISM AND THE "RE-FORMING" OF ISRAEL

Introduction

For Leon Kronish, as for so many American Jews of his generation, the Six Day War of June 1967 marked a watershed in his identity as a Jew. Until that point, Kronish had maintained a careful balance between the universal social mission of Reform Judaism, and the more exclusively Jewish concerns of Labor Zionism—a synthesis Kronish called Liberal Judaism.

After the June 1967 war, however, there was a definite, albeit subtle shift in the dynamic relationship of the elements comprising Liberal Judaism. For Kronish, as for Diaspora Jewry more generally, the possibility of Israel's destruction in the run-up to the war—and the generally "hands-off" attitude towards that possibility evinced by the United Nations and the Great Powers—was shockingly traumatic. Even though Israel ended up winning the war—in a stunning fashion that became a landmark in modern military history—Kronish and others could not forget what they saw as the world's pre-victory indifference to Israel's fate.

As a result, Kronish's focus—previously balanced between the universal social mission of Reform Judaism and the particular concerns of Zionism—now moved decisively in the direction of the centrality of Israel in contemporary Jewish life. This did not mean that Kronish repudiated any of his previous positions. But it did mean that in the aftermath of the 1967 war, Kronish's energies would become much more consumed by his mission of building *gesher vakesher*—bridges and bonds—between the State of Israel and the affluent, increasingly self-confident Jewish communities of Miami Beach in particular, and North America in general.

The incredible range of Israeli-centered programmatic activities that Kronish initiated in the post-1967 period will be described in significant detail below. Here it is crucial to point out the unusual nature of this complex of initiatives—what we call the "Israelization" of Reform Judaism and Jewry in America, a term we introduce in this chapter to indicate both the intimate relationship with—and significant differences from—the range of pre-1967 Zionist activities in the United States.

First, we examine briefly the catalytic Middle Eastern historical events that shaped the thinking of Kronish and so many others on the course of Jewish history in the last third of the twentieth century—the Six Day War (1967), the October War (1973) and the Sadat initiative leading to the Camp David Accords and peace with Egypt (1979).

Next, we explore in some detail Kronish's ideological and practical response to these events—expressed in two significant articles. *Yisrael Goralenu* (Israel Is Our Destiny) in 1968, and *What Are the 'Zionist Mitzvot'*? in 1977. These lay out the framework of ideological assumptions that guided Kronish during the period from the end of the 1967 war until his untimely stroke in January 1984.

At that point, we then introduce our concept of "Israelization"—the extension, expansion and modernization of traditional Zionist ideology and activities undertaken by Kronish during this period. The basis of "Israelization" in traditional Zionism is described, as well as the ways in which Kronish's activities moved beyond that framework along a variety of dimensions.

This conceptual framework is then followed by a systematic examination of the ways in which Kronish brought to fruition this notion of "Israelization" in each of the significant settings of his life: first and foremost, at Temple Beth Sholom; then, the metropolitan Miami area; at the national level in the United States; and, finally, in Israel.

Once this tour of Kronish's manifold activities has been completed, we conclude the chapter with an analysis of his impact on life in the State of Israel—as a pioneer in the Reform movement there, and finally, through his unparalleled success with Israel Bonds.

The Six Day War

On the eve of June 5, 1967, hours before the outbreak of the Six Day War, Leon Kronish and David Polish, his veteran rabbinic colleague and friend from Chicago, walked the streets of Cincinnati, where they were attending a Central Conference of American Rabbis convention. They shared their anxieties about Israel's future, both fearing it was perilously close to annihilation.

Kronish, once the optimist, who for two decades had preached *sholom* to his congregation and to his rabbinical colleagues, now voiced deep fears for Israel if the state did not take immediate action.

Three weeks earlier, the United Nations Emergency Force withdrew from the Middle East at the request of Egypt. On May 23rd, Egypt's President Nassar barred Israeli shipping from the Straits of Tiran, denying ships access to the Gulf of Aqaba and Eilat. The next week, Jordan's King Hussein had placed his forces under Egyptian control.

"How could *Eretz Yisrael*, the State of Israel, be the destiny of the Jewish people if it did not exist? What more can we do to animate Diaspora Jews to declare their solidarity with the people of Israel?" anguished Kronish. Four months earlier, with the winds of storm brewing, Rabbi Polish had joined Rabbi Kronish on the pulpit for a sabbath service at Temple Beth Sholom. Polish echoed his friend's prophetic message that American Jewry had to be more concerned about Israel.[1]

With the war raging, Kronish returned to Miami. That sabbath, Kronish spoke to his congregation's soul. Temple Beth Sholom was filled to capacity. Kronish talked of Zionist *mitzvot* (commandments) in broad brush strokes—to uphold the moral right of Israel's birth and to fully embrace *Klal Yisrael*. He quoted Abraham Isaac Kook, an Orthodox Jew, a Zionist, and Israel's first Chief Rabbi, who had beseeched Jews time and again that Jewish sovereignty is the only nonnegotiable aspect of Israeli redemption. The covenant of redemption involved belonging. "Fate may have had a role in the beginning of the Six Day War but choice will determine its outcome," proclaimed Kronish. "Who is with me?"[2]

During those six long days, June 5th through the 10th, Kronish, like other American Jewish leaders, was called by Prime Minister Eshkol and given the mission of collecting funds for Israel.

Together with the Greater Miami Jewish Federation, on behalf of the Israel Emergency Fund of the United Jewish Appeal (UJA), and the Israel Bonds Organization, Kronish led appeals on the radio, in board rooms, on hotel auditorium stages and on street corners.

On June 8th he flew to Washington to join hundreds of Jewish leaders from across the nation to express solidarity with Israel. On June 10th he flew to New York to confer with his Reform colleagues and the Israel Bonds office about how best to serve Israel's needs. While in New York, he paused to receive an honorary Doctor of Divinity degree from his *alma mater*, Hebrew Union College-Jewish Institute of Religion (HUC-JIR).

Back on Miami Beach several nights later, he hosted Golda Meir, introducing her to more than a thousand attendees at an Israel Bonds dinner at the Fontainebleau Hotel. Reports later circulated that Kronish's passionate vision of messianic redemption, expressed that evening, was as responsible for the millions of dollars raised as was Golda's presence and appeals.[3] A quarter of a century later, Ronald, the rabbi's son, still refers to the event as transformative—"it was one of the most emotional and electrifying evenings of my life."[4]

Miami's response to the Six Day War was similar to the response of other cities across North America. The fate of Israelis dominated the thoughts and emotions of American Jews to the near exclusion of everything else. Support for Israel was spontaneous. Children who had grown up in post-Holocaust America, and their parents who recalled their inability to save

European Jews during World War Two, now gave money, volunteered to go to Israel, and offered to serve on local committees. Reared with Zionist values in congregations like Beth Sholom, several of these American Jews would later decide to make *aliya*. About forty thousand American Jews made *aliya* to Israel in the late 1960s and early 1970s as part of the post Six Day War exhilaration.[5]

The Six Day War also drew out a large number of unaffiliated Jews who were not participants in organized Jewish life. *Klal Yisrael*, one people, was awakened in crisis. As the month of June ended, over $100 million had been realized and the UJA/Israel Emergency Fund Drive that year peaked at more than $225 million.[6]

Soon after the war, Kronish was invited to participate in a national United Jewish Appeal mission to Israel. Defense Minister Moshe Dayan and Chief of Staff Yitzhak Rabin were on the mission's debriefing team. From the Sinai to the Golan Heights, from the Jordan River to East Jerusalem, Kronish saw many of the biblical foundations of Zionism which he had not seen on previous visits to Israel. He walked through the Jewish quarter of the Ottoman walled city and saw the *kotel*, the western wall of the Second Temple, destroyed by the Romans nineteen hundred years earlier.

The war also exhibited another, ugly face. While in Israel, Kronish went to see his friends Yehuda and Tikva Ben Chorin and found them devastated. They had lost both their sons to the war: Amram perished in Gaza, and Yohanan, in Umm Kathef in Sinai.

After returning, he expressed to his congregants that he felt different, that "there was a sense that we [on the mission] were sharing in *tikun olam*, in repairing the world."[7]

The Yom Kippur War: Another Turning Point

On October 6, 1973, while Jews around the world were praying for atonement on Yom Kippur, Egypt and Syria stormed across the borders that had been established as a result of the Six Day war.

Like Jews throughout the nation, Rabbi Kronish and the seventeen hundred and fifty Temple Beth Sholom members present that October 6th morning, were ignorant of events transpiring six thousand miles away. Consumed by their petitions to God seeking forgiveness and peace, war was the farthest thought from their consciousness.

That Yom Kippur morning, Kronish's sermon beseeched them to *tshuvah* (repentance), to return and realize their congregational responsibility, their linkage to the Jewish people, *Klal Yisrael*. "Who will say, *Hinneni*, 'Here I am,' when asked by Israel?" He called on them to further their understanding of messianic redemption both as a personal goal and as a collective undertaking. "For what is redemption without peace; and who but God can bring *sholom*?"[8]

Shortly after the sermon, someone inconspicuously whispered into Kronish's ear: "Israel is at war." Benjie Nemser, a teenager who had been manning the ham radio hook-up in the temple's youth center with the High School in Israel program in Beit Berl, Israel, had innocently turned the dial to catch Israeli news. Much to his surprise, rather than hearing prayers for peace – he was listening first-hand to a broadcast informing Israelis that war had broken out!

At once Kronish initiated a spontaneous appeal for funds, supplies and volunteers to help the Israeli war effort. "*Hinneni*" meant now. Kronish, like rabbis throughout the nation, appealed to his congregants to write letters to Congress and the President in support of Israel – "to preserve Israel's moral right of legitimacy." In contrast to the behind-the-scenes approach of Jewish leaders in the generation of Stephen Wise and President Roosevelt, the Jewish leadership of the 1970s did not hesitate to call upon President Nixon for help, and to use the media to address the plight of Israel.

Within days Kronish spoke with Prime Minister Golda Meir, who inspired him with the following message: "the word *lochem*, to fight, and the word *cholem*, to dream, have the same letters. Dreams are realized by fighting for them."[9]

As chairman of the national Rabbinic Cabinet for Israel Bonds, Kronish's pressing task was to direct and coordinate donations from congregations across the United States. Together with Morris Sipser, national executive vice-president, Sam Rothberg, general chairman, and Ira Guilden, president, and other devoted Israel Bonds committee members, a strategy was developed to assist Israel in this time of crisis. The postwar National Emergency Bonds Drive set its goal at $650 million.[10]

Forty-eight hours after the Yom Kippur War began, Kronish and Milton Parsons, greater Miami's director of Israel Bonds, convened a meeting at the temple to solicit volunteers to help congregations throughout the United States as well as in Miami to meet the target goals proposed by Israel Bonds. Immediately, teams of workers left the temple with address lists, going from door to door soliciting aid for Israel. Gary Gerson, Jack Chester, Marvin (Mike) Cooper, Michael Goldstein and Marvin Stonberg were among dozens of those who spearheaded activities catalyzed by the rabbi. Over $8 million dollars was raised over the next several months.[11]

In addition to his Bonds role, Kronish also served as associate general chairman of the 1973-1974 United Jewish Appeal/Israel Emergency Fund campaign of the Greater Miami Jewish Federation. Under his leadership twenty million dollars was raised, ten times more than a decade earlier.[12]

The Tragedy of War

The Yom Kippur War brought personal tragedy to Leon, Lillian and many members of Temple Beth Sholom. Eyal Shaham, the son of their good friends Zonik and Gila, was killed. Richard and Susan Cooper Zinn, Beth Sholom congregants, had been the last civilians to see, and photograph Eyal. A letter from Eyal's widow, Mickey, was forwarded to the Zinns while the war was still raging.

> October 20, 1973
>
> Dear Susan and Richard:
>
> The worst thing that could happen to us did happen. Eyal got killed during this horrible war. His tank got hit on the 7th. We got the bad news only on the 17th.
>
> Today, the 20th, is exactly five months after [our] marriage and I really don't know from where I have the strength to write you a letter.
>
> There is one thing we all would like very much to get from you: the pictures you took when you were on the Golan Heights with Eyal. Please, do anything you can in order to help our country finish this awful war of survival.[13]

Betty and Mike Cooper, stopping in Teheran on their return from a trip to the Far East, learned of Eyal's death and immediately caught the next plane to Israel. Arriving at 3 a.m., November 5th, they went straight from the hotel to Zonik's home. That morning was Eyal's funeral. Only two years earlier, Zonik and Gila Shaham, while on a visit to Temple Beth Sholom, had sat in the Coopers' living room and read a letter from Eyal informing his parents that he had chosen the military as his vocation.

Temple Beth Sholom responded as a community. Believing "history should not be limited to the Hebrew-reading public of Israel," they published an English translation of the Hebrew memorial testament for Eyal (*As the Hart Panteth/Keayal Ta'arog*). In the foreword to the testament, Kronish voiced the anguish of his congregation:

> We want this story to live as a continuing inspiration...against hostile forces that would deny the Jewish people their legitimate right to rebirth in their ancestral homeland. We believe that those who read about Eyal will develop a greater sensibility to Israel and a deeper understanding of the people of Israel.[14]

Less than thirty days after the Yom Kippur War ended, David Ben-Gurion, Israel's first Prime Minister, died. That sabbath, Kronish spoke of the father of Israel's rebirth as a modern day prophet, as a social idealist, and as a man who "has always understood that the 'Vision of Messianic Redemption' would have to be defended against those who are hostile."[15]

Israel, Egypt and the Peace Process

The threats to Israel's very existence in 1967 and 1973, in part, were responsible for the diametrically opposite position taken by President Anwar Sadat of Egypt and Prime Minister Menachem Begin of Israel in 1977. In November, Sadat set foot in Jerusalem and commenced the peace initiative. Eighteen months later, with President Carter serving as mediator, Egypt and Israel announced a stunning breakthrough: an agreement for an enduring peace.

Leon Kronish was personally invited to witness the peace signing ceremony at the White House between Begin and Sadat in April 1979. One of the several hundred American Jewish leaders representing the Diaspora partnership, Kronish shared in the exhilaration of observing the signatories as they sealed their promise for peace. For Kronish, this was a most significant step towards messianic redemption and reaffirmed the potent links between Israel and the Diaspora.

Returning to Miami Beach later that week, Kronish conveyed to his congregants his feelings in the temple's bulletin:

> Dear Friends,
>
> I was on the North Lawn of the White House when the historic peace pact between Egypt and Israel was signed...[and the leaders quoted] Isaiah's prophecy, 'And it shall come to pass in the end of the days that Nation shall not lift up sword against nation; neither shall they learn war any more.'[16]

That sabbath, the sabbath before Passover, he preached for an everlasting peace: "may the hearts of all people be turned to each other in love, understanding, and peace."[17] The signing of the Camp David Accords was an important symbol and lesson of how a united Jewish community, *Klal Yisrael*, could realize its dreams.

Soon after, Kronish was enlisted by Israeli leaders to help move the peace process forward. Although he was not aligned with Likud nor intimate with the new leadership that had come to power in March, 1977, Kronish quickly was taken into their confidence. His efforts to link Reform Judaism to Zionism had not gone unnoticed, even by those Israelis opposed to Kronish's traditional allegiance to Labor Zionism.

The Impact of History

The Six Day War (1967), the Yom Kippur War (1973) and the Camp David Accords (1979) had a profound effect upon Kronish, as they did on so many other American Jewish leaders of the period. All were challenged by the need to understand and integrate what had transpired—survival, expanded borders, land for peace. After the initial jubilation, political reality demanded resolutions to a variety of issues that inevitably surfaced in the wake of these events—Jewish settlements, refugees, massive infrastructure development and religious revival. Jewish Americans began to become polarized over which policy would be in the best interests of Israel and the Diaspora.

Throughout the period from 1967, the Six Day War, to his dehabilitating stroke in 1984, Kronish's viewpoint did not change—Israel was the central focus in the self-understanding of American Jewry. Israeli-Diaspora relations depended on *Klal Yisrael*, the Jewish people, being united. Moreover, it was the responsibility of Jewish leaders to refrain from public criticism of the government of Israel, regardless of its actions.

Kronish did not share the opinion of a vocal minority of American Jewish leadership which posited that American Jews had the right to determine what foreign policy Israel should adopt. "Advice, yes; decision-making, no." Israeli-Diaspora relations depended on *Klal Yisrael* speaking with one voice, and unified public support for Israel by American Jews was a prerequisite. Criticism of Israel, if it was to be responsible and effective, should be done "within the family" and not through the pages of the *New York Times* or the *Village Voice*.

From the inception of the State of Israel in 1948 to the Six Day War in 1967, Kronish gradually had moved to an agenda where Zionism took firmer hold and had a greater influence on his ideology and programming. Always a strong advocate of the position of his mentors, Mordecai Kaplan and Stephen Wise, that American loyalties were not put at risk when one supported Zionism, Kronish began to redefine the nature of Reform Judaism's link to Zionism via the central institution of the synagogue.

The Six Day War compelled Kronish to recast his understanding of how the temple and American Jews could become more Israel-centered. In 1968 he published *Yisrael Goralenu* as a manifesto that affirmed the symbiotic relationship—the *gesher vakesher*, between Israel and the Diaspora. The Yom Kippur War intensified his passion that this relationship had to be deeper and more vigorous. In 1977, on the eve of President Sadat's historic visit to Jerusalem, he published *What are the 'Zionist Mitzvot'*?, a working manual on how temples and communities could be agents in the process of bringing Israel to their members and their members to Israel, thus ensuring individual Jewish identity and collective Jewish solidarity.

In part, the catalyst for Kronish's personal transition to a more intensive Zionist involvement was not just the Six Day War, but the response by his non-Jewish colleagues whom he had joined on other liberal causes. Kronish, like many of his colleagues, was deeply and personally disappointed by the Christian response to the Six Day War. Leading figures such as Reinhold

Niebuhr and Martin Luther King, Jr. supported Israel but the formal establishments of both the Protestant and Catholic churches were silent. Their silence in the face of deathly peril made Kronish more skeptical of ecumenical agendas for Israel. During the postwar rejoicing, the same Christian elements who had joined together to fight for civil rights for African Americans, to resist nuclear testing, and rally against involvement in Vietnam, now tilted towards the Palestinian refugees. Israel was denounced as the aggressor. Black radicals and the "New Left" sided with the Arabs. "Israel was more important to Jews than the concerns for racial justice and peace," was Arthur Hertzberg's summation of the period.[18]

In part, it was also a reaction to what Kronish observed and absorbed as he traveled across the country and to Israel, speaking out for Zionist causes: Israel Bonds, The Hebrew University of Jerusalem, the Histadrut. Kronish's activities and ideology in the synagogue and the community had become more intertwined than ever with Israel's significance and survival.

Yisrael Goralenu—Israel Is Our Destiny: 1968

Kronish's vision of the synthesis of Reform Judaism and Zionism, with its foundation blocks of covenant, peoplehood and Israel, received national attention when *Yisrael Goralenu* appeared in the June 1968 issue of the *Central Conference of American Rabbis Journal*. He exclaimed in the opening paragraph:

> The destiny of *Am Yisrael*, the Jewish people, was inseparable from the destiny of *Medinat Yisrael*, the state of Israel.... We declare our solidarity with the State of Israel and the people of Israel. Their fate is our fate.[19]

In the pages that followed, Kronish challenged American Jews "to convert the crisis reaction into a permanent partnership"[20]—what we call the "Israelization" of Reform Judaism and American Jewry. For Kronish, each Jew should consider personally the following possibilities:

(1) *aliya*, every Jewish family should have one of its children living in Israel
(2) visiting Israel
(3) sending one's children to visit Israel
(4) sending one's rabbis on sabbaticals to Israel
(5) establishing Israel committees in local congregations.[21]

Yisrael Goralenu, was not only a challenge for American Jews to build links of communication and caring—*gesher vakesher*—between the Diaspora and

Israel, but of equal importance, it was imperative for the Reform movement to design institutions in Israel.

In Kronish's view, Reform Judaism needed to translate the concept of covenant into support for Progressive Judaism, enabling American Reform Jews who decide to live in Israel to exercise their religious beliefs in accordance with their conscience.

Calling for dialogue with "our liturgical brothers and sisters in the [Israel] Progressive Congregations," he prescribed that the Union of American Hebrew Congregations (UAHC) and the Central Conference of American Rabbis (CCAR) expand and publicize National Federation of Temple Youth (NFTY) pilgrimages and that congregations offer scholarships and subsidies for study and work programs.[22] *Yisrael Goralenu* also argued that the Reform movement should declare Israel Independence Day an official holiday.[23]

Some members of the Central Conference of American Rabbis commented that Kronish was advocating nothing less than the "exporting" of Reform Judaism to Israel as a way of stimulating the search for new, non-Orthodox ways of expressing Liberal Judaism, and that the training of American Reform rabbis was to be in the vanguard of the Israel-centered metamorphosis of American Jewry.

The response to Kronish's *Yisrael Goralenu* manifesto was enthusiastic. Individual congregations across the nation followed Kronish's lead and introduced programs that encouraged members and their children to visit Israel as well as create opportunities for rabbis to spend significant time there. Organizationally, the Central Conference of American Rabbis and the Union of American Hebrew Congregations implemented many of Kronish's innovative and inspiring recommendations.

The Yom Kippur War in October, 1973 motivated Kronish to revise his thinking regarding the links between the Diaspora and Israel. He became more outspoken and increasingly identified with the more centrist elements of the Reform movement and the Israeli Labor Party regarding Israel. He was critical of the dovish Jewish "New Left" in America and Israel, who considered the exchange of land without absolute international guarantees of peace, and of the right-wing Jewish Defense League (JDL)—"the JDL does not speak for the Jewish people"—because of its advocacy of violence.[24]

Once again, a Middle East war had divided some liberal Christian clergy from their Jewish counterparts. Father Daniel Berrigan, the American anti-Vietnam crusade hero, attacked Israel in the heat of the Yom Kippur War for being "skilled in the fashioning of violence." Kronish was pained by Berrigan's reading of the situation and immediately shot back, "Has the organ of the clergy, *American Report*, the publication of rabbis, priests, and ministers with an anti-Vietnam platform, now adopted an anti-Israel policy?"[25] He also joined his colleague of the American Jewish Congress and the outstanding spokesman among the rabbinate, Arthur Hertzberg, in defense of Israel against the "New Left" attacks.

The Central Conference of American Rabbis' 1976 San Francisco Platform of Reform Judaism also served as a catalyst in Kronish's reformulation of connecting Israel to the Diaspora. Its stronger emphasis on the role Israel should play in congregational life stimulated Kronish to contemplate his revision in terms of a practical guide that could reach out to American Jews every day and in a natural way.

Zionist Mitzvot—A Working Manual: 1977

By 1977, Kronish's thought crystallized around a working manual for American Jews entitled *What are the 'Zionist Mitzvot'*?, a practicum to help American Jews bond with Israel. Published in the *Jewish Frontier*, the National Journal of American Labor Zionism, the essence of Kronish's message was a more potent dose of the "Israelization" of American Jewry and Reform Judaism. *Gesher vakesher*, the bridge and bonds between the Diaspora and Israel, were outlined as ten practical objectives or *Zionist Mitzvot* (obligations):

(1) visit Israel
(2) send children to Israel
(3) read Zionist literature
(4) study Hebrew
(5) join a branch of the Zionist movement
(6) participate in Israeli fundraising programs
(7) respond politically when Israel is in need
(8) uphold "the moral right" of Israel's rebirth
(9) share in Israel's culture (food, songs, art, etc.)
(10) link with an Israeli family through letters and telephone[26]

The Zionist Mitzvot was a succinct statement of what was achievable after 1967, elucidated over nearly a decade of Zionist programming.

Kronish's reformulation of *Yisrael Goralenu* into *The Zionist Mitzvot* was an acknowledgement of how much had changed in the decade following the 1967 war. On the one hand, congregations and many American Jews now viewed Israel as a "personal" concern and were becoming increasingly Israel-centered in their programming. But on the other hand, the rate of those unaffiliated with congregations was growing substantially and it appeared that for many the absorption of Zionistic values appeared superficial. *The Zionist Mitzvot*, which emphasized the centrality of Israel in contemporary Jewish life, was Kronish's remedy for the future solidarity of *Klal Yisrael*.

The "Israelization" of American Jewry

These two documents, *Yisrael Goralenu* and *What are the 'Zionist Mitzvot'?,* written ten years apart, reveal the core dynamics of Kronish's ideology and program in the post-1967 era. They serve as the indispensable framework of assumptions that guided Kronish's manifold activities in the seventeen years between the end of the Six Day War and his stroke in 1984.

In certain ways, *Yisrael Goralenu* and *The Zionist Mitzvot* represent the powerful revival of traditional Zionism, infused with new vigor in the unexpected and unprecedented conditions of the post-Six Day War period. But in many other ways, the sentiments expressed by Kronish in *Yisrael Goralenu* and *The Zionist Mitzvot* represent a major extension of the tenets of traditional Zionism—what we will call, for reasons to be discussed shortly, the "Israelization" of American Jewish life.

In keeping with the spirit of traditional Zionism, Kronish placed renewed emphasis on the option of every Zionist to make *aliya* to Israel—long a de-emphasized strain in the American Zionist thinking articulated by his mentors, Stephen Wise and Mordecai Kaplan. In this context, Kronish not only re-examined his own commitment to living as a Jew in America, he quite literally practiced what he preached by encouraging his only adult son, Ronald, and daughter-in-law Amy, to pick up stakes and leave the New Jerusalem of America, "Miami Beach," for the Old Jerusalem—a decision Ronald and Amy made final in 1979, just before the signing of the Camp David Accords. In this sense, of course, Kronish espoused a profound re-commitment to the traditional Zionist goal of the "in-gathering of the Exiles," one of the fundamental doctrines of modern Zionism.

While crucial and fundamental, however, this return to traditional Zionist values was only a small part of the range of the multifaceted pro-Israeli programs and activities on which Kronish embarked in the post-1967 era. It is this expansion and, in a certain sense, modernization of traditional Zionist thinking that leads us to characterize Kronish's mission in this period as the "Israelization" of Reform Judaism in America—and, conversely, for reasons discussed in the last part of the chapter, his mission in Israel itself as the "Re-Forming" of Israel.

What, then, constitutes the "Israelization" of Reform Judaism and American Jewry—and what distinguishes it from traditional American Zionism?

As noted above, the key element of traditional Zionism is the personal commitment to leave the Diaspora and move to the Land of Israel (*Eretz Yisrael*). While Kronish himself decided not to make this change, he called on every Jewish family to have at least one member undertake *aliya*—a pledge his own family redeemed with son Ronald's *aliya* in 1979.

Beyond this, however, Kronish initiated a whole range of programs and activities whose purpose was not to motivate American Jews to move to

Israel – although certainly none discouraged them from so acting – but to build living links between the State and people of Israel within both the American Jewish community and the United States itself.

Kronish's mission from 1967 to 1984, therefore, is most accurately understood as the "Israelization" of first Reform Jewry, then American Jewry, and, in its broadest sense, a whole web of political/social/economic relations between the United States and the small Middle Eastern democracy of Israel.

The remainder of the chapter will examine these wide-ranging activities in detail. Here, however, the aim is to lay out briefly the dimensions that distinguished Kronish's mission of "Israelization" with traditional American Zionism. Broadly speaking, there are five aspects of "Israelization."

The first might be called "bringing Israel to America." Starting with a small program at Temple Beth Sholom in the immediate aftermath of the Six Day War, Kronish began the practice of inviting Israelis from all walks of life to come and live with members of his congregation in Miami Beach for several weeks at a time. In this way, Kronish felt, both Israeli and American Jews could get a personal sense of how their brethren experienced the world. American Jews could be exposed to the sensibilities of Israelis, and Israelis could see, through their own direct experience, what life was like for Jews living in America.

At the same time, Kronish also felt it was crucial to achieve the same goal – better personal understanding between Israeli and American Jews – by "bringing American Jews to Israel." The purpose was not necessarily to convince those American Jews that they should immediately move to Israel – the traditional goal of Zionist travels – although any who felt so inclined to make *aliya* after a trip to Israel would certainly be encouraged to do so. Nevertheless, the purpose was more to help American Jews receive for themselves a real sense of Israelis as part of the Jewish people, and of the manifold ways in which life in Israel differed from life in the United States. In this way, Kronish reasoned, American Jews would become ever more committed to working in whatever way they could to advance in America the cause of Israel, a commitment given passion and purpose by direct contact with the land and people themselves.

The third aspect of "Israelization" developed by Kronish was to make American synagogues and temples – in addition to their more strictly spiritual ends – into visible centers for the promotion of Israeli life and culture. Temples and synagogues were encouraged to include festivals celebrating Israeli music, cuisine, arts and crafts, and all kinds of forums, symposia, and special seminars featuring major Israeli personalities from politics, the arts, archeology, the military and religion.

At the same time, Kronish also took a leading role in catalyzing the major Jewish organizations in America – especially, but not exclusively, those in the Reform movement – to develop a significant and systematic relationship with Israel, including growing links with Israeli institutions of similar orientations. For example, Kronish helped to establish the Israel Committee of the Central Conference of American Rabbis (CCAR) in 1967, and was, indeed, the founding chairman of that committee, a position he held for more than a decade. He was also one of the charter founders of ARZA, the Association of Reform Zionists of America.

These institutional initiatives in the United States were complemented by similar moves in Israel. Kronish played a major role, for example, in helping to establish Reform *kibbutzim* in Israel in the 1970s. In this sense, the "Re-Forming" of Israel was as important for Kronish as the "Israelization" of Reform Jewry in America.

The fifth and final aspect of what we call "Israelization" revolves around the establishment of permanent links between political, social and economic institutions in both Israel and the United States – institutions not linked solely to American Jewry, that is, but to United States as a country.

Perhaps the best example of this was the significant role played by Kronish in helping the State of Israel establish a consulate in Miami, a goal finally achieved in 1982. Even before that, however, Kronish had been instrumental in helping to organize the Miami-Israel Chamber of Commerce in the mid-1970s, a group whose membership was by no means restricted to Jews, and in paving the way for direct flights between Miami and Tel Aviv on El Al.

In this way, Kronish moved along five very different dimensions to expand and extend the relations between the State of Israel and both Jews and non-Jews in the United States. They all represented an Israel-centered focus for Jewish life in America. But they all went far beyond the traditional Zionist goal of bringing Jews to live in Israel. The purpose was to develop a wide array of interrelations between Israeli and American institutions – a web that, in Kronish's view, would redound to the benefit of not just Israeli and American Jews, but to the benefit of both Israel and the United States as interdependent, cooperating democratic nation-states.

Kronish did not abandon his belief that one can live fully as a Jew in two civilizations – American and Israeli – but he reformulated its foundation to suit the needs of post-1967 Jewish Americans.

Thus, unlike most Diaspora leaders who shied away from advocating *aliya*, Kronish adopted it as a necessary ideological principle, while at the same time preaching "Israelization." Moreover, he advocated that American Reform rabbis live in Israel from time to time,[27] that future American Reform rabbis be trained in part in Israel, and that American Reform institutions be established in Israel to cater to American Reform Jews making *aliya*.

For Kronish, *gesher vakesher* came from a deep personal commitment to Zionism and Israel: "We will develop the meaning of Jewish peoplehood only as we establish living links between us and the people of Israel."[28]

Kronish's challenge was to plant the seeds, water and fertilize the concept of "the centrality of Israel," an emphasis shared by other Jewish-American leaders, which by the 1970s became the *leitmotif* for the Jewish community. This meant developing strategies, creating programs, organizing the community and bringing people to Israel. It meant having national organizations—the Israel Histadrut Foundation, the American Jewish Congress, Jewish Federations—adopt policies that made Israel a central focus. And it meant bringing Israelis and their institutions—the Histadrut, Israel Bonds, the Hebrew University of Jerusalem—to American Jews, as well as creating, in Israel, structures for American and Reform Jews who would visit, spend a period of time, and, perhaps, even make *aliya*.

Zonik Shaham: Kronish's Personal Gesher-*Bridge*

A month before the *Yisrael Goralenu* article appeared in the *Central Conference of American Rabbis Journal* in June 1968, Ze'ev Shaham, known affectionately as Zonik, arrived in Miami.

Zonik Shaham was a member of a delegation of senior Israeli Defense Force officers who traveled to the United States on behalf of Israel Bonds in 1968. Volunteering to go to South Florida to assist Temple Beth Sholom in celebrating its 25th anniversary, Shaham's only knowledge of "America's Negev" was from a Frank Sinatra movie (*Hole in the Head*) that he had seen a week earlier, featuring scenes of Miami Beach.

When Shaham descended the stairs of the aircraft, he had never met his official greeters, Leon Kronish and Mike Cooper. "I got off the plane and started to make my way to the gate," he recalled. "Then I saw two tall gentlemen come towards me. One was huskier, with graying hair and a mustache. I asked them [years later] how they knew I was the one." Kronish replied: "Of everyone getting off that particular plane, we figured you were either an Israeli or a Cuban refugee!"[29]

During his first visit to Miami, Shaham followed the trail of Frank Sinatra and stayed at the Fontainebleau Hotel. He shared the sabbath with the Kronish and Cooper families. As a guest speaker he spoke of Israel's security needs. A former member of the Palmach, the crack force of the Haganah, the precursor of Israel's Defense Forces, a company commander in the War of Independence, and a Brigade Commander in the Six Day War, Shaham still hoped for peace. Before departing, he invited the members of Temple Beth Sholom to visit Israel and to call on him.[30]

The following month, July 1968, Kronish led a Temple Beth Sholom mission to Israel. Part of the itinerary was a sabbath party with Zonik, his wife Gila, and some of his officers at his home in Tzahala, a suburb of Tel Aviv. The Kronishes had flown to Israel a few days before the mission, and joined the Shahams early Friday evening. The bus with the rest of the Miami contingent never arrived. A delay at JFK Airport resulted in a schedule change. That evening the Kronishes and the Shahams shared life experiences, aspirations and Israeli songs.

Later that week, Shaham invited the Temple Beth Sholom pilgrimage on a tour of the West Bank. As military commander of a sector there, Shaham served as their personal guide, pointing out the ancient sites of Biblical Israel. While stopped near the Damia bridge, Shaham learned that his second in command, Colonel Regev, had been killed in a terrorist attack close by. Kronish flew to Israel the following year, 1969, to be present at the unveiling of Regev's tombstone.

In the short time that Kronish and Shaham were together, a deep friendship developed. Leon Kronish became Zonik's rabbi and Zonik, Kronish's Israeli emissary. Shaham was the ideal role model for connecting Israel with the Diaspora and the temple.

Many years later Shaham would write of Rabbi Kronish that he intuitively felt when he met him in Miami in 1968 that he was "a man with whom I share the same Zionist vision and the notion that commitment to Zionism is rooted in a commitment to Judaism."[31]

Israelis-in-Residence at Temple Beth Sholom

Shaham's friendship, and intense dialogue between Kronish and congregants, led in 1969 to the establishment of the Temple Beth Sholom Israel Committee as a means to implement Kronish's "Israelization" mandate for Reform Jews. A new program entitled "Israelis-in-Residence" was one of the committee's planks.

The idea of American synagogues sponsoring Israelis-in-Residence was raised in Kronish's article, *Yisrael Goralenu*, as a vehicle to bring the reality of Israeli life into the homes and hearts of American Jews living in the Diaspora of Miami Beach. The nuts and bolts of who these "para-ambassadors" would be, and how they would be integrated into congregational life, remained to be worked out.

When Kronish wrote *Yisrael Goralenu* he perceived it as more than an appeal for American Jews to bring Israel into their minds and feel a kinship. Kronish understood that a bridge's strength depended upon trusses and girders for support. The Israel Committee created by Temple Beth Sholom in 1969 was to support the American side of the Diaspora-Israel linkage. "It was a congregational project, not in the framework of fundraising, but in the frame-of-reference of rediscovering the spiritual and cultural ethnic links that bind us together in a common destiny."[32]

The chance arrival of Shaham, a year earlier in 1968, gave it form. Zonik Shaham represented an example of how Israeli life could be integrated into the "Negev of America," Miami Beach.

The Israelis-in-Residence program was organized around the concept that each year the temple would invite an Israeli to come and live as a guest of the congregation at a member's home. In the context of an informal educational program, the Israeli would spend several weeks in the community speaking to confirmands, adult classes, the Sunday Breakfast Club, and other temple-related gatherings. When Temple Beth Sholom pilgrimages ventured forth to Israel, the Israelis-in-Residence would serve as contacts and assist those on the mission to experience Israel.

The Israelis-in-Residence program thus served a dual purpose. Not only was it important for American Jews to internalize the values and be informed of the reality of the State of Israel, but it was incumbent upon Israelis to understand American Jews and acquire knowledge of their perceptions of Israel. The "Israelization" of the temple worked both sides of the street.

When Kronish suggested to the temple's Israel Committee, in 1969, that they invite Yehuda and Tikva Ben Chorin to serve as their first Israelis-in-Residence, they immediately agreed. Many members knew of the rabbi's friendship with Yehuda over the past thirty years since his *aliya* to be a pioneer on the kibbutz, Kfar Menachem, in 1939. They appreciated the role the Ben Chorins played in the life of the rabbi's son, Ronald, during his first summer in Israel in 1964 as their guest on the kibbutz.

Moreover, they were acutely aware of the tragic death of the Ben Chorins' oldest sons, Amram and Yohanan, during the Six Day War. A few of the members of Temple Beth Sholom who had visited the kibbutz on their pilgrimage to Israel with the Kronishes in 1968 had kept in touch.

Yehuda and Tikva Ben Chorin spent one month in 1969 at Temple Beth Sholom. They lived at a member's house and participated in temple life. They shared their experience as grieving Israeli parents who had lost two sons. In response, members of the congregation helped finance a cultural center, *Heikhal HaTarbut*, at the Ben Chorins' kibbutz, Kfar Menachem, and expedited publication of the memorial volume, *B'nai Chorin* (*Children of Freedom*), in remembrance of Amram and Yohanan.

Over the next decade, Beth Sholom's Israelis came from all walks of life. In 1970 Zonik Shaham was the congregation's second Israeli-in-Residence. Zvi Krauthammer, Beth Sholom's fifth Israeli-in-Residence, in 1973, came directly from Schonau, Austria, immediately after the Austrian government had closed the Soviet Jewry transit center. As the deputy director of the center between 1971 and 1973, Krauthammer had assisted thousands of Soviet Jews emigrating from the Soviet Union to Israel.

Just a few months earlier, Kronish had met Krauthammer on a Beth Sholom mission to Schonau. On learning that the transit center was to close, Kronish recommended to the temple Israel Committee that they invite Krauthammer to continue his Soviet Jewry consciousness-raising efforts in

Miami at Temple Beth Sholom. Kronish's understanding and implementation of prophetic mission applied equally to Soviet Jews as to African Americans.

Ephraim Shapira, a teacher of bible, Judaism, and philosophy, and a physical education instructor, was the 1974 Israeli-in-Residence. Shapira taught Temple Beth Sholom members about the biblical roots of the Jewish experience and the importance of understanding the present in terms of Jewish history from its earliest beginnings.

In 1977 the Israeli-in-Residence was Avraham Avi-Hai, author of *Ben-Gurion: State Builder* and a member of the executive of the World Zionist Organization and the Jewish Agency for Israel. Previously, he had worked closely with Teddy Kollek, Mayor of Jerusalem, and had served under Prime Minister Levi Eshkol.

Avi-Hai had been a friend of Kronish since the latter's visit to Israel in 1960. In the early 1970s, when Ronald and Maxine were students at the Hebrew University of Jerusalem, Avi-Hai was the university's director of Overseas Student Programs.

The Israeli-in-Residence program in the late 1970s and into the 1980s continued to bring new faces. As they opened their homes to their guests, members listened to first-hand accounts of Israel's changes in the wake of a severe economic recession, kibbutz redevelopments that proposed new living arrangements and the return of Sinai to the Egyptians, a condition of the Camp David Accords.

Israel Missions

In addition to the establishment of Israel committees in local congregations, another objective of *Yisrael Goralenu* was sending children to visit Israel. "Bringing Israel to America" and "bringing American Jews to Israel" were complementary features of the "Israelization" process.

To meet the goal of sending children to Israel, Kronish instituted in 1970 the annual confirmation class pilgrimage. Appealing to his congregants to open themselves to the experiences of their children, Kronish challenged parents to remember how meaningful early adolescent experiences were. "Imagine," he said, "if instead of American images filling their hearts and minds, there were Israeli and Jewish images. Such an experience would make them more committed Jewishly than anything we do here."[33] Visiting Israel would not only further their Jewish education, but would challenge them to clarify for themselves what being Jewish means.

Although confirmation parents were reticent, twelve confirmands ventured forth that first year. For eight weeks they toured the country. They visited Jerusalem, Lake Kinneret, and Tel Aviv. They met Zonik and Gila Shaham, and Yehuda and Tikva Ben Chorin, the Israelis-in-Residence in 1969 and 1970. They visited the HUC Jerusalem campus, were introduced to

Progressive Judaism, Reform Judaism's Israeli complement, and prayed at the Western Wall of the Second Temple, built more than 2000 years ago.

Several returned to Israel as confirmand youth-group leaders three and four years later. Asked why go through it again, one youth leader replied, "Because I learned to be Jewish and want to pass it on."[34]

Throughout the 1970s and 1980s, the Beth Sholom youth who joined the confirmation class pilgrimages to Israel did so as a culmination of years of formal and informal Jewish education. They followed a comprehensive path—minimum of three years of Hebrew School, a bar or bat mitzvah, weekend conclaves at Camp Sholom, first in Ocala and later at West Palm Beach, a summer at a National Federation of Temple Youth (NFTY) camp, and finally confirmation.

Subsidized by temple men's club scholarships, Kronish personally led many of the confirmands on visits to places and with people in Israel—opportunities that few would have otherwise experienced. Former Israelis-in-Residence, leaders of Progressive Judaism and other friends and politicians made themselves available to Kronish, and gladly gave of their time to engage in dialogues with Beth Sholom's youth.

Upon returning from the pilgrimage, these students were emotionally charged; they identified with Israel and their own Jewish identities. This "Israelization" of temple youth is the reason so many of them gave when asked why they remained actively involved in the temple youth group (BESHTY: Beth Sholom Temple Youth) during their high school years.

Back in Florida, the first stop for the Israeli touring confirmands was a temple activity, often a men's club Sunday morning breakfast, where they reported on their experiences. There, they would publicly acknowledge their inner feelings.

One of the unexpected results was that many children of first- and second-generation temple members reawakened their parents' ties to Reform Judaism and Israel. These trips generated such excitement that parents of confirmands followed their children to Israel on missions sponsored by the temple, the Greater Miami Jewish Federation, United Jewish Appeal, Israel Bonds, and Histadrut—often led by the rabbi. This also was a fulfillment of the goals of *Yisrael Goralenu*—for adults to visit Israel.

In response to growing requests by parents to visit Israel, Kronish began to experiment with other ways to deepen their Jewish identity and expand his temple missions. In 1973 he added a Holocaust dimension to the parent mission, with an itinerary that included stops in Vienna, Bucharest, and Matthausen, the slave labor camp in northern Austria. The mission also included Soviet Jewry consciousness raising, with a stop to see the Schonau (Austria) railroad station through which the Soviet Jews passed on their way to Israel. In 1975, the Beth Sholom parent mission toured Spain, and sought *conversos*, descendants of the Spanish Jews who were forced to convert in the fifteenth century, and the synagogues where they once prayed in Cordoba, Seville, and Toledo.

In 1976, Kronish organized an inter-generational family mission in conjunction with the Institute for Leadership Development of the Jewish Agency under the directorship of his close friend, Zonik Shaham.

Congregants who joined Kronish on these missions to Europe and Israel tell of special moments, of how he brought them closer to the people of Israel and to their own Jewish identities in unique ways.

One illustration typifies how Kronish grasped the moment. While conducting a Beth Sholom tour in Jerusalem, Kronish learned that Soviet Jews were soon expected to land at Ben-Gurion Airport. Instantly he revised the tour itinerary and told everyone to get onto their waiting bus. When they neared the airport, the bus was stopped by a roadblock. The police reported that the airport had been closed because of terrorists in the area. Kronish got off the bus and went to make a telephone call. Soon after he returned to the bus, the police allowed them to proceed to the terminal—under escort. Beth Sholom congregants welcomed the Soviet Jews as they arrived as new immigrants. Together, the Americans and Soviets experienced the meaning of *Klal Yisrael*, Jewish peoplehood in *Medinat Yisrael*, the State of Israel.

Years later, those who were present during this experience point to it as the catalyst in raising their consciousness about Judaism's prophetic mission, the *raison d'être* of the State of Israel, and the need for American Jews to be concerned with her survival. For these pilgrims, the congregation and Israel were inextricably interwoven.

Shuk Hasholom

The Temple Beth Sholom Israel Committee and Kronish also explored other ideas that could realize the goals of *Yisrael Goralenu*, Israel is Our Destiny. It was not enough to strengthen the bonds linking the Diaspora to Israel through missions and residence programs. Few congregants understood Hebrew, more stayed home than joined missions, and Israelis-in-Residence were not effective in reaching the masses. To have a wider impact, Israel Committee members embarked on developing programs and events that turned the temple into a center for the promotion of Israeli life and culture—the third feature of "Israelization." Through the Leon Kronish Institute for Living Judaism, Israeli music, art and speakers were a regular diet.[35]

One of the most significant events organized by the Israel Committee that illustrated this collective experience, while pulsating with Israeli spirit, was the 1975 *Shuk Hasholom*, "Peace Fair." Designed as a six-day Israeli cultural and trade fair, an Israeli environment was created—with clothing, housewares, art, folklore objects, and religious artifacts among the many items exhibited. Israelis marketed their goods as if they were on Dizengoff Street in Tel Aviv.

Marcie Lefton, chairperson of the *Shuk Hasholom*, visited Israel to scout for talent and invited artists to take part. Kronish arranged for introductions and guided her to former Israelis-in-Residence and friends who served as sounding boards. Israelis participating in Miami Beach were paired with congregation members, thus experiencing *gesher vakesher* first hand.

Over forty thousand people attended the *shuk* in December 1975. They purchased Israeli-manufactured products, art and handmade crafts, tasted Israeli food, listened to Israeli music and observed the diversity of Israeli sub-cultural communities. Of the many artists who came, one silversmith and sculptor of Judaica ritual art, Michael Ende, returned to the temple to participate in later exhibits under the auspices of Judy Drucker and the Leon Kronish Institute for Living Judaism.

The "Israelization" of the temple resulted in Temple Beth Sholom becoming identified as a "congregation that lives and breathes Israel and Zionism, and [an] Israeli cultural center of activity for all age groups."[36]

Ronald Kronish's Aliya

The most demanding proposition outlined by Kronish in *Yisrael Goralenu* was *aliya*, that "every family should have one of its children living in Israel."[37]

As a young man Kronish had flirted with the idea of emigrating to Palestine but had never considered it seriously after his marriage. His calling was to bring a renewed emphasis of traditional Zionism and to "Israelize" the American Diaspora, rather than to make *aliya* himself.

Leon and Lillian had strong, decades-long relationships with Israelis–Zonik and Gila Shaham, Yehuda and Tikva Ben Chorin, and many others. However, immediate kin in Israel was the one stream of life still outside their experience.

The year 1979, therefore, was a watershed year for the Kronish family. Ronald, the rabbi's son, and his wife, Amy, decided to make *aliya* and moved to Jerusalem with their two children, Sari, age three-and-one-half and Dahlia, age eighteen months. Ronald had considered the possibility since his student rabbinical year in Israel in 1970-1971 and had aired the idea repeatedly over the decade. His decision, after much ambivalence on his part, fulfilled *The Zionist Mitzvot*. It also illustrated to Temple Beth Sholom members in the most significant way possible that the inculcation of Zionist values begins at home.

The following year, 1980, Leon and Lillian became the proud grandparents of a sabra, Ronald's and Amy's third daughter, Ariella Orit, named after the city of Jerusalem and the holiday of Hanukkah.

Ronald's *aliya* prompted Kronish to ask his friend, Zonik, one evening while relaxing in Miami a short time later, "What kind of man am I that I can emphasize and preach *Zionist Mitzvot* yet not make *aliya* myself?" Without hesitation Zonik replied, "Your work outweighs a thousand times any *aliya*.

Zionism has many faces. Do not feel incomplete. Israel needs more people like you in the Diaspora."[38]

Institutional Developments: Bringing Israel to the Wider Miami Community

Side by side with the tremendous energies Kronish invested in implementing the principles of *Yisrael Goralenu* and *The Zionist Mitzvot* in the temple, he was also known as "Mr. Israel" in Miami, a result of his non-stop efforts to bring concern for Israel into the life of the community at large.[39]

When Kronish wrote *Yisrael Goralenu* (1968) and *What are the 'Zionist Mitzvot'?* (1977), his immediate audience was Reform American Jews within a congregational framework. But his message implicitly had wider implications and was targeted more generally to the whole Jewish community and the numerous organizations that were instrumental in maintaining Jewish continuity. Moreover, from Kronish's perspective, one did not have to be affiliated with a Jewish institution to visit Israel or become involved with Israel. With baby boomers less willing to follow their parents' example and become synagogue members, and with intermarriage on the increase, Kronish explored other avenues to bond South Floridian Jews to Israel and "Israelize" the community. Through these efforts he helped to establish permanent links between political, social and economic institutions in Israel and the United States.

The first step was to bring a *schaliach*, an Israeli emissary without portfolio, to the greater Miami Jewish community. Israeli policy post-1967 was to build on the momentum of its "heroic" victory and focus especially on youth programs, an investment that had the potential of nurturing future Jewish American leaders.

Kronish, along with others, readily adopted this strategy. Together with the Israel Embassy in Washington and with representatives of the Greater Miami Jewish Federation, a youth *schaliach* was sent to Miami in 1969, a year after *Yisrael Goralenu* appeared in print. Leaders like Kronish were instrumental in mediating Israel's needs because of their grassroots constituencies and Zionist youth programs.

The *schaliach's* function was to expose American Jewish youth to Israel and to develop resources that would sponsor youth to visit Israel—the explicit goals of *Yisrael Goralenu*. Housed in community centers across the nation, the *schlichim* (emissaries) soon were catering not only to youth but also to the wider community as well.

The overwhelming response for information, local programming and personal visitations led the Israeli government in the early 1970s to change the job description of the *schaliach*. *Schlichim* would appeal to all age groups, not just youth, and their residency would be a location within Jewish Federations, rather than a community center. With the position's expansion, the *schaliach's* office became the central clearing house in Miami for all Israeli programs.

Over the next decade, Kronish worked closely with the various *schlichim* in developing Israeli programs for the Miami Jewish community.

Kronish also helped to expedite the establishment of the Greater Miami-Israel Chamber of Commerce and the Consultants for Israeli Industry in the 1970s. The Chamber of Commerce served not only as a booster club for Israel, but also played an important role in seeking out investment opportunities, frequently linked to Israel Bonds strategies. The Consultants were professionals who could secure volunteer experts to help the *kibbutzim* expand economically.

An Israeli Consulate Comes to Miami

Cooperation between members of different organizations within the Jewish community was strengthened by the *schaliach's* presence. Communication between Miami and Israel, the *gesher vakesher* of association, were fortified by the Miami-Israel Chamber of Commerce and the Consultants for Israeli Industry.

Thus, by the late 1970s, a number of Miami Jewish leaders began to question "why Atlanta, a smaller Jewish community and more off the beaten path, was assigned a Consul-General and not Miami?"[40] For Kronish, the "Israelization" of the community demanded the presence of a permanent consulate in south Florida.

Kronish and Mike Brodie, the executive director of the Greater Miami Jewish Federation, had established warm personal bonds with Yoel Arnon, Consul General of Israel's Atlanta office, when he represented Israel's interests in the southeastern United States. They consulted with Arnon, then stationed in Boston, on how best to proceed to establish a consulate.

By the late 1970s South Florida's Jewish population exceeded one-half million and was rapidly growing.[41] In the view of Kronish and Brodie, an Israeli address was necessary as a sign of support to the community and as a motivating force to encourage economic and political succor. It would complement the Miami-Israel Chamber of Commerce, serve as catalyst for trade and investment, encourage *aliya* and elevate Israel's profile within the Jewish and non-Jewish community. Complimenting the effort, was the decision by El Al, the Israeli airlines, to begin flights to Miami in 1979.

Arnon suggested that the Greater Miami Jewish Federation petition Israel to establish a Miami consulate. To the surprise of everyone, the reply they received was "insufficient funds." Kronish thereupon took it upon himself to lead the effort to have an Israel address in Miami. With support of the Greater Miami Jewish Federation, he resolved to solicit funds from Miami donors to establish a consulate in Miami with Arnon as Israel's representative. Not surprisingly, Kronish looked to his temple membership for endorsement.[42] In the 1982 the office opened.

The inauguration of an Israeli Consulate in Miami was the culmination of more than a decade of building strong community bonds with Israel. It reflected a perceptual change on the part of the Israeli Foreign Ministry of Miami's role as a player in American Jewish life, and it implicitly recognized the national and international significance of Miami's Jewish leadership in establishing connections between political, social and economic institutions in Israel and the United States.[43]

High School in Israel

One of the most innovative and successful national programs that was launched from Temple Beth Sholom and targeted at "Israelizing" youth was the High School in Israel Program. It combined "bringing American Jews to Israel" with the creation of a new organizational structure that encouraged permanent links and even *aliya*.

Designed as an Israeli experience for American students, the High School in Israel program had many of the same features as the Israelis-in-Residence program: the internalization of Zionistic values and exposure to Israeli experiences. However, rather than have the temple as center stage, the location of the campus became Israeli educational settings, the country and her people.

The program was born under Kronish's inspiration and influence. The presence of the Temple Beth Sholom's Israel Committee, Israelis-in-Residence and ongoing missions to Israel, motivated congregants to be on the lookout for ideas and programs that could be modified to enhance the momentum of the "Israelization" process.

In 1971 Phyllis Miller, a Dade County School Board member and a congregant of Temple Beth Sholom, was introduced to the idea of American schools abroad. She approached Kronish and Sol Lichter, principal of Miami Beach Senior High, for help in developing an Israeli model of the study abroad program as a vehicle to implement the principles of *Yisrael Goralenu*. As co-chair with Sol Lichter of Beth Sholom's Education Committee, Miller hypothesized that Beth Sholom confirmands, as well as others, might seek out this educational option.

Working with the Dade County School Board, Miller laid the groundwork for Dade students to study abroad in Israel for a semester as a pilot experiment and earn equivalent credit. In the spring semester 1972, the pilot program was inaugurated, targeted solely for greater Miami senior high school students. It was advertised as an American high school study abroad program. Five students from Miami Beach Senior High (among them, three members of Temple Beth Sholom) were billeted in Israeli homes in Michmoret, an Israeli seaside town near Netanya. Half the day they studied at Kfar Shmaryahu, the prestigious international English language high school, while the other half day was dedicated to town life.

The fostering of Jewish identity and commitment to Israel by High School in Israel participants did not go unnoticed by Israeli and American Jewish educators. The combination of formal and informal educational experiences in a communal setting profoundly influenced the youngsters' perceptions and attitudes towards Israelis. To this day, Ellen Cooper Channing, one of the original five participants, maintains contact with her Israeli family and returns regularly to visit them.[44]

The success of the pilot project led to a second group from Miami Beach Senior High that same year, again with several students from Beth Sholom. Upon their return, Rabbi Morris Kipper invited Phyllis Miller to lunch at *Juniors*, a notable Miami Beach restaurant. He requested that she consider recommending to the Dade County School Board the permanent establishment of an Israel high school experience. Shortly afterwards, the school board adopted a resolution to endorse the program.[45]

With the sanction of the Dade County School Board, the nature of the program changed from an American study abroad experience to an Israeli experience for American students. As a result, the program shifted to Beit Berl the following year to accommodate more students and the change of the curriculum. By the end of the decade the program was renamed (Alexander Muss High School in Israel) and there was another location change.

The success of the program in Miami led to its adoption by school boards across the nation. Today, more than twenty years since its inception, the curriculum includes a variety of subjects (Archaeology, Bible, Hebrew and History) and is enriched by field trips, all for high school credit. High school students from Baltimore to Los Angeles, from Rochester to Phoenix, have participated in the program, all coordinated from Miami.[46]

Throughout the 1970s and 1980s, Temple Beth Sholom sent scores of students to Israel to participate in the High School in Israel program. Many were graduates of Kronish's post-confirmation missions to Israel. Parents of Beth Sholom children attending the program were able to speak to them via a ham radio that Kronish had set up in Israel at Beit Berl and at the temple's youth center. Parents of some of the youth were motivated by their children's experiences and enthusiasm later to join one of Kronish's missions to Israel for the United Jewish Appeal, Israel Bonds, Histadrut and Temple Beth Sholom.

The High School in Israel program fulfilled many of the objectives of *Yisrael Goralenu* and *The Zionist Mitzvot*. It enhanced Zionist values, encouraged American teenagers to visit Israel, provided opportunities for the youth to experience first-hand Israeli culture and germinated seeds of contacts between the American youth and Israeli families and friends. By 1984, over a thousand youth around the country per year were undergoing a deep and meaningful "Israelization" experience. A significant number who later made *aliya,* credit this program as responsible for introducing them to the idea.

The Hebrew University of Jerusalem

Youth who participated in the High School in Israel Program frequently sought out university junior year study abroad programs a few years later. More often than not, this would mean a year of study in Israel at the Hebrew University of Jerusalem. Kronish's son, Ronald, spent his rabbinical junior year, 1970-1971, at the Hebrew University as did his daughter, Maxine, in her university junior year, in 1971-1972.

Similar to the High School in Israel Program, university study abroad programs brought youth to Israel, exposed them to Israeli life and introduced them to the concept of *aliya*. It paved the way for social bonding and strengthened institutional links between Israel and the United States. Individually and organizationally, it enhanced the "Israelization" experience.

For Kronish, this continuation was a natural outgrowth of his own decades-long connection to the Hebrew University. Active in South Florida for the Hebrew University as a fundraiser and spokesperson from the 1950s, he was appointed to its International Board of Governors after the Six Day War and in 1970 was invested as an Honorary Fellow. Kronish was the only American Reform rabbi to serve in this capacity during this period.

Kronish felt a special relationship to the Hebrew University that dated back to the late 1930s when he met Alexander Dushkin. Dushkin, the founder of Hebrew University's School of Education, argued that the process of learning was as important as the content. Three decades later, in the early 1960s, Kronish had worked closely with Avraham Harman, Israel's Ambassador to the United States before his appointment as President of the Hebrew University of Jerusalem. It was Harman who had recommended that Kronish be appointed to the international board.

Kronish maintained that college students were the most open to "Israelization" experiences. Living in Israel, exposed to its culture and language, history and religion, the probability of long-lasting friendships and shared memories enduring, was very promising for them. Flashpoints of confrontation for American Jewry—assimilation and intermarriage—were negligible. An Israeli year abroad safeguarded Jewish continuity.

Kronish worked diligently after the Six Day War to inspire Temple Beth Sholom members to send their university-age children to the Hebrew University as part of their college experience. He invited college-age students to his home regularly, especially during semester breaks, to expose them to the offerings of Hebrew University. He jointly programmed with the University of Miami's Jewish student association, Hillel, and served on Hillel's national board to further encourage university students to consider Hebrew University's study abroad program.

Kronish often asked his children for their thoughts regarding how their Israeli experiences might lend itself to extending more "bridges" to Jewish-

American college students. Watching his own children and their friends, he observed how American-Jewish youth provided with an Israel educational experience internalized Zionist values and felt more strongly linked to Israel. In Kronish's view, without his son's Hebrew University experience, *aliya* may never have become a reality.

Histadrut

Leon Kronish's leanings towards Labor Zionism were a product of his upbringing and socialization. He experienced first-hand his father's union struggles, learned the humanitarian values of utopian socialism from his teachers, especially Stephen Wise, and observed with his own eyes the significance of its application in the formation and development of Israel. The adoption of the Histadrut as his self-imposed mission in the United States therefore flowed naturally.

In *The Zionist Mitzvot*, Kronish appealed for American Jews to join some branch of the Zionist movement. Although many opportunities were possible, for Kronish the Histadrut stood out as the most attractive vehicle. By sustaining the Histadrut one supported the state and its workers, the people that built the country, manned its industries and defended its territory. From Kronish's perspective, the objectives of Labor Zionism were a natural complement to the prophetic ideals of Reform Judaism.

In the early 1960s Kronish founded and chaired the Israel Histadrut Foundation. In February 1966, and every year thereafter until his stroke in 1984, he helped organize its mid-winter Miami Beach conference. Throughout these years Kronish worked closely with Sol Stein, Histadrut's national executive director, and in the 1960s with Arthur J. Goldberg—labor attorney, former U.S. Secretary of Labor, Ambassador to the United Nations, and U.S. Supreme Court Justice—in promoting Histadrut policies in the United States.

Linking the Histadrut in Israel with the United States through the Histadrut Foundation amplified the economic and labor links between the two countries. It became a significant feature of the "Israelization" process.

Temple Beth Sholom's Israel Committee also played a key role at these February conferences. Inculcated with Zionist values, the members viewed the conference as a golden opportunity to intensify Kronish's mandate of Zionizing Reform Jews and a practical way to extend the *Yisrael Goralenu* objectives of "Israelizing" the temple. To achieve this goal, they paired each attending Israeli with a temple member, and conference delegates were invited to the temple to participate in events, services and fellowship.

In 1975 and 1976, Kronish and Stein organized international Histadrut Solidarity Conferences in Israel to buttress support among American Jews for the Labor government's policies. These conferences were strongly supported by the government and provided Labor leaders a chance to "market" their ideas and hear Diaspora concerns.

The 1976 conference reveals how significant a player Kronish was in linking American Jewry to the Histadrut and the Labor government. The morning before the Histadrut Solidarity Conference convened, Kronish learned that half of the American delegates were stranded in New York due to fog. Golda Meir, the immediate past Prime Minister of Israel, as opening conference speaker, would be speaking to a half empty hall. Kronish, Stein and Yehoram Meschel, secretary general of the Histadrut, discussed how to resolve the crisis over breakfast. Their recommendation was to tell Golda that unforeseen circumstances had changed the schedule and that her role would have to be downgraded. Kronish was delegated to go to tell Golda.

Kronish, accompanied by Sol Stein, took a taxi to Golda's office in Ramat Aviv. When the two arrived without appointment, Golda asked them in Yiddish, "Is there something wrong?" Kronish explained the problem and suggested how the situation could best be resolved. Over tea and biscuits, the schedule was rearranged once again to accommodate Golda. She and Yitzhak Rabin, the Prime Minister of Israel, would share the podium together.[47]

Kronish brought many of the creative strategies he developed for Israel Bonds in the United States to the Histadrut in Israel. For example, learning of the need for soldiers to have a fund to draw mortgage dollars, he assisted in the establishment of the Histadrut Mortgage Fund to help discharged soldiers buy apartments and homes.[48]

He also introduced new approaches. In the spring of 1977, six months before President Anwar Sadat made his historic visit to Jerusalem, Kronish sent a plan for an Israel-Egypt Development Bank to foster joint economic development to Prime Minister Begin via U.S. Senator and Miami Beach resident Richard Stone, and Yehuda Avner, Begin's Diaspora advisor. The plan included support for railroad lines between the two countries, joint explorations for oil, and cooperative agricultural and industrial projects. For peace and economic development in the Middle East, Kronish advocated the replacement of "desultory diplomatic debate by bold new economic development ideas...[and] *real proposals*."[49] Although this plan was not adopted, it reflected the political climate of the period among liberal-leaning Labor Zionists who viewed the peace process as one further extension of their socialist principles.

Socialism for Kronish was not just political rhetoric, but a requisite for the fulfillment of Zionism. Histadrut leaders praised his efforts in "Israelizing" American Jewry and in drawing others towards Labor Zionism. Hebrew University professor and a former director-general of the Ministry of Foreign Affairs, Shlomo Avineri, who worked closely with the rabbi in the 1970s and early 1980s, wrote that Kronish "lead[s] people towards goals transcending their immediate interests."[50]

Kronish the "Liberal": America and Israel Compared

Kronish's socio-economic liberal orientation in America paralleled his orientation in Israel. In America, he concentrated on minority rights and individual freedoms. In Israel, he supported the socialist undertakings of Histadrut, the Israel Labor Federation, which supported worker's rights. Both American and Israeli socio-economic agendas were rooted in his youth socialization experiences with his father, school and youth movements, and remained part of his social philosophy: Democrat and liberal in the United States; Labor and socialist in Israel.

Political orientations between the two countries, America and Israel, however, were not always compatible. In the United States, Kronish leaned towards being dovish on issues like Vietnam, and critical of any American policy that was not supportive of Israel. With regard to Israel, Kronish took the position that it was the responsibility of Jewish leaders to support and work with the leadership of the democratically elected government of Israel, whether Golda Meir, Yitzhak Rabin or Menachem Begin. One's role was not to be publicly critical, but to be a staunch supporter of the State of Israel.

The adoption of this position over time evolved into supporting Israeli policies unpopular with some American Jews, such as the invasion of Lebanon. Thus, Kronish frequently spoke out against those who publicly criticized Israel—such as Breira and the Jewish New Left—who were an anathema to his vision of *Klal Yisrael*, a united peoplehood, and who, intentionally or not, weakened Israel's public profile in the United States.

Leon Kronish also took the attitude that Yasir Arafat and the Palestinian Liberation Organization (PLO) were as much against American interests as they were against Israel's. In a letter to Yehuda Avner, Prime Minister Begin's Diaspora advisor in the late 1970s, Kronish suggested that "the USA demand the extradition of Arafat not because it's likely to happen, [but because] it's important to label Arafat the Genocidal War Criminal he and the PLO are."[51]

Reform Judaism and Israel: New Horizons

As a Zionist rabbi who preached Liberal Judaism, Kronish steered a path that inspired congregants to internalize Zionist values, and simultaneously uphold religious practices that would support a more traditional Judaism.

Between 1948 and 1967, Kronish viewed his performance of this role more in terms of bringing Zionism to American Jewry than in bringing Liberal (Reform) Judaism to Zionism. After the Six Day War in 1967, an equilibrium began to appear. Kronish viewed his mission not only in terms of "Israelizing" American Jewry, but also as advocating an increasingly visible profile of Reform Judaism in Israel.

Between 1967 and 1984, when a stroke silenced him, Kronish unceasingly encouraged his colleagues to adopt the view that Israel must be the central component in the self-understanding of Reform Judaism. Both his articles, *Yisrael Goralenu* and *What are the 'Zionist Mitzvot'*?, adopt this position unequivocally. Consequently, it was no surprise that many perceived him as one of the handful of leaders within the Zionist movement concerned with the "Re-Forming" of Israel as much as with "Israelizing" Reform Judaism.

To be effective, argued Kronish, *Yisrael Goralenu* (and later *The Zionist Mitzvot*), had to be internalized by Reform rabbis, and the new generation of Reform American rabbis currently being trained must be in the vanguard. Towards this cause, Kronish worked vigorously with the Central Conference of American Rabbis (CCAR) and the Hebrew Union College-Jewish Institute of Religion (HUC-JIR) leadership in the late 1960s to endorse a policy that required entering rabbinical students to spend their first year at the Hebrew Union College (HUC) Jerusalem campus. Moreover, in Kronish's opinion, such a policy would not be successful unless those presently ordained within the American Reform rabbinate made a commitment to spend a considerable amount of time in Israel themselves.

In Boston, at the 1968 CCAR meetings, Kronish succinctly voiced this goal—"to develop an address in Israel to which Reform rabbis could come again and again to learn from Israeli experts and not merely to engage in superficial 'touring.'"[52] He asked his colleagues to consider joint pilgrimages in Israel, programs to encourage *aliya* for rabbis, and projects leading to the establishment of more institutions for American Jews to experience Reform Judaism in Israel.

In 1970, the Hebrew Union College-Jewish Institute of Religion instituted the first-year-in-Israel policy for entering rabbinical students. The rabbinical year-in-Israel program was inaugurated under the CCAR presidency of Roland Gittelsohn and the HUC-JIR presidency of Nelson Glueck.[53]

That same year, in the summer of 1970, the CCAR hosted its annual meetings for the first time in Israel. Kronish was given the honor of introducing Gershom Scholem, his former teacher at the Jewish Institute of Religion, who delivered a paper on "Who is a Jew."[54]

In large measure, the idea for a convention in Israel was conceived during CCAR meetings in Los Angeles convened shortly after the Six Day War in 1967. In a special session on Israel, Kronish introduced a motion that the Union of American Hebrew Congregations and the Central Conference of American Rabbis establish permanent committees on Israel.[55] The motion passed and Kronish was appointed the committee (CCAR) chairperson.

Kronish's definition of its mandate was to deepen "the significance of Israel in our lives individually and congregationally" and to preserve "the sense of interlocking destiny between Israel and United States Jewry in *Klal Yisrael*."[56] The *Yisrael Goralenu* goal of encouraging rabbis to visit and spend sabbaticals in Israel was in the forefront of Kronish's efforts to have the CCAR host its annual convention in Israel.[57]

For Kronish, *gesher vakesher* was not limited to his congregation or his local community – it was a principle to be applied to all aspects of Jewish life. Synthesizing Reform Judaism with Zionism was a national effort.

The advance into Israeli territory by Reform Judaism was viewed by some sectors of the Orthodox Israeli religious establishment with hostility. These fears were compounded when Rabbi Roland Gittelsohn, president of the CCAR, proclaimed in his opening address at the Jerusalem convention in Israel in 1970 that Reform Judaism had adopted at its convention in 1969 that it would observe Israel Independence Day and a special liturgy would be written – a significant step in legitimizing the movement's struggle for acceptance by Israelis.[58] Traditional Israeli Jews were even more wary that the impact of Reform Judaism's forthcoming transformative theological changes would further exacerbate the growing tension between themselves and their American co-religionists.

Reform Judaism and Israel: Halacha *and Modernization*

The first of many theological changes promulgated by Reform Judaism after the 1970 Central Conference of American Rabbis conference in Israel was the 1972 ordination of Sally Priesand, a woman rabbi. Immediately, the debate challenging the legitimate authority of Reform Judaism sprang up once again.

Kronish accepted that the demands of the Reform movement were considered contrary to *halacha* by Orthodox Jews, but he also could not ignore the feminist movement's cogent arguments for equality. Adopting the position of theological pragmatism, he tried throughout the 1970s to bridge the gap between the tendencies of the Reform movement towards the religious left and the Government of Israel's inclinations that were increasingly moving towards the right.

In Kronish's view, if male Reform rabbis were not viewed as legitimate by the Orthodox establishment, the same standard would apply to female Reform rabbis. Kronish firmly believed that the Reform rabbinate should be open to all Jews, regardless of gender. Active female members of Temple Beth Sholom had found it problematic reconciling their equal status in public life with their unequal status in Judaism.

Kronish knew all too well that the Reform movement's ideology professing the equality of women did not go much beyond bat mitzvah and, sometimes, lay leadership. Extending the covenant of *Klal Yisrael* to meet the needs and social agenda of the late twentieth century meant opening the rabbinate, the cantorate, and the movement's leadership to all Reform members, women as well as men.[59]

For a number of years, Kronish had expressed these opinions to his colleague, David Polish. As president of the Central Conference of American Rabbis in the early 1970s, Polish respected his colleague's comments regarding the spiritual and organizational ramifications of opening up the rabbinate to women. Polish often confided in him and valued Kronish's innovations regarding the involvement of women in Temple Beth Sholom.[60] Kronish reported continually that his congregation—male and female—was overwhelmingly supportive of the innovation of equal opportunities for women in Judaism.

In contrast to his support of the feminist movement over the issue of equality in the rabbinate, Kronish was much more cautious when it came to supporting Reform Judaism's conversion practices. Orthodox Judaism in no uncertain terms delegitimized Reform Judaism's conversion of non-Jews and Reform Judaism's serving of a *get* (divorce contract).

In 1975 Rabbi Joseph Glaser, executive vice-president of the CCAR, forwarded to Kronish copies of his correspondence with Yitzhak Raphael, Minister of Religion in Israel, regarding a recent Reform conversion. The Israeli ministry had refused to accept an affidavit of Rabbi Arthur Lelyveld, president of the CCAR, testifying to the Jewish lineage of one of his students. Glaser's reply included the threat that such a position could hinder Reform Judaism's "efforts to promote *aliya*."[61]

Kronish believed that both American Jews and Israel would suffer by this repressive policy. Nonetheless, in a revealing letter to Glaser, Kronish wrote, "We should do both—get the appropriate validation of the Jewishness of any one of our congregants—even as we make an issue in principle."[62] For Kronish, *halacha* still stood firm ground in conversion practices until—and only until—there was a new principle of validation established. The principles of Liberal Judaism remained resolute for Kronish. Support for Israel was essential. But Reform Jews should not be discriminated against. *Yisrael Goralenu's* binding message was to encourage links with Israel, not to diminish them.

Opposing Patrilineal Descent

Another controversial development within Reform Judaism in the early 1980s threatened to thwart, rather than foster, the bridge-building between American Jewry and Israelis. The Central Conference of American Rabbis and the Union of American Hebrew Congregations decided in 1983 to adopt patrilineal descent in Judaism—to identify children of Jewish fathers and non-Jewish mothers as Jews.

This rocked Jewish tradition, and in Kronish's opinion, was premature. Coming on the heels of the ordination of women rabbis and challenges to the legitimacy of Reform conversions the previous decade, the patrilineal issue divided American and Israeli Jewry on core theology. One stream of the

Orthodox element within Israel responded by branding these new "patrilineal Jews" as "non-Jews."

Kronish was adamantly against patrilineal descent. Not only did the patrilineal resolution stand against his personal belief, but he shared Polish's fear that it also was a public acknowledgment that "Reform Judaism had abandoned hope of reconciliation with Orthodoxy."[63] Moreover, in his reply to Rabbi Joseph Glaser nearly a decade earlier regarding conversions, Kronish had forthrightly stated conformity to *halacha*, "even as we make an issue in principle."[64] Moreover, *Klal Yisrael* could ill-afford divisiveness at a time when Israel had fewer and fewer friends.

Emphasizing patrilineal descent, in Kronish's view, would not strengthen the pulse of a Jewish rhythm or Liberal Judaism. Nor was it a viable strategy to break the monopolistic control of the Orthodox establishment in Israel. Kronish continued to believe and preach that a pluralistic Jewish society demanded pluralistic alternatives. But, in his opinion, patrilineal descent not only broke with *halacha*, it would weaken *Klal Yisrael*.

To buttress his position, Kronish sought out his friends like Richard Hirsch, executive director of the World Union for Progressive Judaism, to preach from his Temple Beth Sholom pulpit in support of this sentiment.[65] In due course, Rabbi Hirsch was able to lead the Israel Progressive Judaism-Reform rabbinate to side with those in the American Reform rabbinate who opposed patrilineal descent. Progressive Judaism in Israel rejected the legitimacy of patrilineal descent.

ARZA: The Bonding of Reform Judaism and Zionism

Kronish's renewed vocation to deepen the roots of American Jewry in Israel through Reform Judaism passionately consumed his thinking at formal and informal gatherings where Reform Jews congregated. As chairman of the Central Conference of American Rabbis Committee on Israel from 1967 and the Central Conference of American Rabbis-Union of American Hebrew Congregations Joint Commission on Israel from 1972, Kronish steered a course accentuating common ground with Israel while simultaneously advocating that the Reform movement create a Zionist political organization to present its positions and lobby the Israeli government.

Between the writing of *Yisrael Goralenu* in 1968 and *The Zionist Mitzvot* in 1977, Kronish had come to the realization, like many of his colleagues, that the "Re-Forming" of Israel would be impossible without a political Zionist movement that spoke for American Reform Judaism. One needed a viable, legitimate entity that would focus on the interests of Reform Zionists and have as its mandate bringing Reform concerns and institutions to Israel.

In 1977, ARZA (Association of Reform Zionists of America) was founded to achieve this goal. Kronish was a founding member.

Historian Michael Meyer, among others, has argued that ARZA was Reform Judaism's response to the growing political power of Orthodoxy, as manifested in the increasing parochialism of Israel.[66] It advocated liberal religious policies that acknowledged the validity and legitimacy of Reform Judaism, and religious equality for men and women in Israel. Reform Jews found distasteful the aggressive interference of religion in state matters. They believed that Israel should maintain a pluralistic environment that required a definitive separation between the state and religion as found in the United States. Israel's official religious position–that women rabbis were without legitimacy and that conversions by all Reform rabbis were invalid–exacerbated the situation.

In Israel, not only did the Orthodox have monopolistic power to define "who is a Jew," "who is divorced," and "who may be a rabbi," but the partnership that unfolded between the ultra-Orthodox religious parties with the Likud government, post-1977, was viewed by many Reform Jews as further threatening the fragile secular landscape that had evolved in Israel over the past three decades. "How could American Reform Jews be called upon to support Israel," Kronish asked, "if they are perceived to be second-class Jews?"[67]

The institutionalization within the Reform movement of a new political organization, ARZA, that had broad appeal and strongly supported Zionism, provided a forum for American Jews to speak out on issues that affected their religious liberty in Israel. With the establishment of ARZA, the majority of the work of the CCAR Israel Committee was assumed under its auspices.

In temple bulletins from 1977, Kronish encouraged his congregants to become members of ARZA, and lobby Israel to assert their rights.[68] In February 1978, Reform Zionists representing ARZA took their place for the first time at the World Zionist Organization meetings in Jerusalem.

Reform Kibbutzim

One of the ways in which Reform Judaism and its counterpart in Israel, Progressive Judaism, reached out to Israelis and American Reform Jews was by advocating the establishment of Reform *kibbutzim* in Israel.

The idea for a Reform kibbutz, according to Saadia Gelb, originated when Leon and Lillian Kronish, along with David and Aviva Polish, visited Gelb at Kibbutz Kfar Blum in the early 1970s. Gelb had attended the Jewish Institute of Religion (JIR) with Kronish in the 1940s and later made *aliya*. The discussion turned to the inadequate status of the Reform movement in Israel, and the fact that "*kibbutzim* were not being sufficiently helpful in advancing its growth."[69] Kronish, in his capacity as chair of the UAHC-CCAR Commission on Israel, with Saadia Gelb, Sheldon Lilker, Richard Hirsch, and other leaders of the World Union for Progressive Judaism, helped bring together representatives of the Kibbutz movements and a delegation of Reform rabbis and leaders at the seminar center in Oranim (near Haifa) in July 1973 to discuss the possibilities.[70]

In 1976, a Reform kibbutz, Kibbutz Yahel, was dedicated north of Eilat, and officially recognized by the Union of American Hebrew Congregations.[71] By 1986, a second Reform kibbutz, Lotar, was also functioning in the Arava.

One of the immediate spinoffs of Reform *kibbutzim* was the establishment of National Federation of Temple Youth (NFTY) summer camping experiences in Israel. Summer camping became another option to confirmation "youth missions," an expansion of the programs Kronish and others had instituted in their temples, and a means for Jewish-American youth to experience first-hand collective life. Youth from Temple Beth Sholom were again in the forefront in volunteering to attend the Reform kibbutz summer camp.

The establishment of these Reform communities, Gelb, Polish, Kronish and others believed, would serve as a prelude to meeting the demands of younger Israelis for a more flexible Judaism and serve as a foothold in Israel within the socialist Zionist tradition.[72] Reform *kibbutzim* were a way of "Re-Forming" Israel that harked back to traditional Zionist values. They also served as another illustration of how Reform Judaism and Zionism could be integrated and of the dual commitment to Jewish survival in America and in Israel.

Israel Bonds

Of all the organizations outside the temple in which Kronish immersed himself, Israel Bonds was by far the most important. It was "an extension of his religious dream, the redemption of Israel."[73]

Israel Bonds, for Kronish, were the ideal link, the *gesher vakesher*, between American Jewry and the temple to Israel. They represented a commitment to Israel's future, an investment in her people, and a conviction that peace was possible. Reaching out to the average American Jew, Israel Bonds did not discriminate by gender and were affordable. Bonds were not fettered by hierarchy arising from allegiance to Israeli political parties and American Jewish organizational life, and in particular, the Jewish Federations.

Most importantly, Israel Bonds triggered the essence of *Klal Yisrael*–identifying with Jewish peoplehood, even if not affiliated with any aspect of Jewish communal life. Israel Bonds nourished Jewish identity, community continuity and Israeli stability.

In *Yisrael Goralenu* and *What are the 'Zionist Mitzvot'?*, Kronish illustrated the principle of *gesher vakesher* with reference to Israel Bonds. When he composed new liturgy for the temple, such as the *Passover Supplementary Haggadah*, Israel Bonds were firmly imbedded in the text–"keep the state secure and purchase Israel Bonds."[74] When invited to speak at conventions and conferences all over North America, Israel Bonds were never far from his thoughts.

Kronish's intense commitment to Israel Bonds stretched from its inception in 1951 until his stroke in 1984. He held leadership positions locally and regionally in the 1950s and 1960s, and nationally in the 1970s and 1980s, including chair of the Rabbinical Cabinet and National Chairman of Israel Bonds. His performance of these duties were not at the expense of his other organizational endeavors nor his responsibilities to the Greater Miami Jewish Federation. He viewed Bonds as a bridge-maker.

Kronish's personal pledge to support Israel Bonds in 1951 had matured and grown through the 1950s and 1960s. With increased knowledge of Israel's financial and economic goals and first-hand observations of Israel's changing urban landscape, Kronish became acutely aware of how badly Israel needed the loyalty of American Jews.

Until the late 1960s, the campaigns for Israel Bonds and the United Jewish Appeal (UJA) were highly competitive in Miami. Arthur Rosichan, executive director, Greater Miami Jewish Federation, challenged Kronish after the Six Day War to become an assertive leader in the community and to ameliorate the sources of tension between Israel Bonds and the UJA. In Rosichan's report to the executive committee of Federation in 1968, he commented that the Federation "did not possess leadership for aggressive fundraising; and there is little concern and little time for planning.... We are regarded as the poorest fundraising community among the large communities in the United States."[75]

Kronish heeded Rosichan's call and worked closely with Bob Russel, president of the Greater Miami Jewish Federation in the early 1970s. Russel, like Kronish, was a graduate of Brooklyn College. A healthy relationship developed between the Miami Israel Bonds Office and the Federation. In 1972, heeding Russel's request, Kronish flew home from a Chicago vacation especially to vote for Myron "Mike" Brodie to be the new executive director of the Federation.

In 1972, as president of the Rabbinical Association of the Greater Miami Jewish Federation, Kronish deepened his friendship with Brodie, and a strong and warm working relationship materialized. On Thursday mornings throughout the following year, a select group of Federation leaders, including Brodie and Kronish, met to review pledge cards, take assignments, and set priorities.

In his capacity as chairman of the Rabbinical Cabinet in the 1970s, and as National Chairman in the 1980s of Israel Bonds, Kronish joined forces with Mike Brodie, Norman Lipoff and the Greater Miami Jewish Federation time and time again to bring Israeli programs to Miami and to further the Israel Bonds campaigns.[76] Similarly, Kronish worked closely with Shragai Cohen, national Bonds director of congregational and rabbinic activities, and volunteers around the country. Congregations looked to him to set goals for the Israel Bonds High Holy Day appeal and to conduct leadership conferences.[77]

Under Kronish's direction, over 1,200 congregations in the United States participated in the High Holy Day appeal by the late 1970s. Each synagogue would receive a High Holy Day kit that included a step-by-step outline for a successful appeal, sample synagogue tab- and non-tab cards with Responsive Reading selections on the reverse side, and releases for synagogue bulletins, brochures and the general media. Linked to the New York Israel Bonds headquarters by a special red phone in his office, Kronish was able to maintain daily contact on the progress of the national campaign. By the end of the decade, Kronish was leading Bond campaigns that raised $50 million dollars during the High Holy Days.[78]

Kronish also appealed to the membership of the Central Conference of American Rabbis more directly to purchase Israel Bonds. He introduced in 1971 (and re-introduced it for many years thereafter) a resolution at the CCAR annual convention, urging all members to enroll as active participants in the National Rabbinic Cabinet of the Israel Bonds Organization and to encourage their congregation and congregants to purchase Israel Bonds annually.[79] This formal resolution was complemented yearly by a reception he hosted on behalf of Israel Bonds, with a leading Israeli personality present to address those assembled at the convention.[80]

The campaigns Kronish led for Israel Bonds from 1967 to 1984 demonstrated a keen sensitivity not only to the various religious denominations within American Judaism and especially Reform Judaism, but also to the local demographic and cultural mosaic of South Florida. For example, Kronish targeted the snowbird constituency as an untapped resource. Special Israel Bonds programs were introduced for the condominium owners that matched insurance agents, bankers, and lawyers with their accounts. Appeals were conducted that urged seniors to assign their life insurance policies to Israel.

These different strategies peaked at the temple's annual congregational Bonds dinner in December, an initiative introduced by Kronish to create a sense of solidarity, *Klal Yisrael*, between the various individuals and groups that bought Bonds that year. In due course, these annual Bonds dinners spread to many congregations throughout the United States.

Kronish canvassed non-Jews as well as Jews to purchase Bonds. He appealed to their religious convictions and economic common-sense: "If Israel can be redeemed—the land itself, from desert to farms, and the people, from the persecuted victims of Nazism—then the whole world can be redeemed."[81]

By buying Bonds, Kronish argued, they would be assisting in maintaining the "only democracy in the Middle East" and simultaneously helping in the improvement of America's economy by expanding Israeli purchases of United States-produced machinery, equipment and raw materials. Carlos Arboleya, for example, president of Republic Bank, the Cuban bank in Miami, bought Bonds regularly from Kronish, and introduced him to his Cuban entrepreneurial friends and business associates.

Kronish also took the lead nationally when international current events dictated new strategies. In the aftermath of the Camp David Accords between Egypt and Israel in 1979, Kronish joined with veteran Bond leaders to develop policies to increase foreign investment in Israel in order to offset the costs associated with surrendering the Sinai for peace. The policy involved expanding the pool of corporations, unions, banks, and pension funds (including the State of Florida's) that bought Israel Bonds, and, in the process, providing information to potential brokers for exports from Israel.[82]

Although Kronish was a national and international figure in the Bonds world, Temple Beth Sholom firmly remained his homestead to test ideas, begin campaigns and invite friends and guests to join him on an Israeli Bonds mission. Experience Israel, "Bonds style," Kronish exulted. In addition to visiting religious places and historic sites, a Bonds mission would focus on economic projects financed by Bonds money—a Negev industrial factory, the port of Eilat, a pipeline from Aqaba to the Mediterranean, the Arad petrochemical complex, military locations, and new housing developments. Mission members could see where their investments were being spent and suggest new projects.

Temple Beth Sholom members were proud of Kronish's "Bonds" persona and supported his weekly "pitch," issue after issue, in the temple bulletin. They listened attentively to his sermons, many of which were Bonds appeals. Invariably, he would ask his congregants, as part of his Bonds exhortation, if they wanted "to be the savior of the Jewish people."

Kronish's indebtedness to his congregation for supporting Israel Bonds was steadfast throughout the years. Whenever possible, he went the last mile to create situations to honor his congregants. For example, in 1982 Kronish arranged for the Israel Bonds Organization and Temple Beth Sholom to be "the first Jewish group to welcome officially Israel's new Ambassador to the United States, Moshe Arens."[83] On March 29, 1982, at a special Tribute Dinner for Israel Bonds, Ambassador Moshe Arens was introduced to the American Jewish community. That evening, Kronish, as master of ceremonies, led a solicitation which produced several millions of dollars, much of which was donated by Temple Beth Sholom members.

A commitment to Bonds, in Kronish's view, was a commitment to Zionism. Through the framework of the synagogue, Israel was strengthened.

Israeli politicians, cognizant of Kronish's fundraising abilities, viewed Miami in the 1970s as the "winter campaign capital of American Jewry,"[84] and constantly sought out Kronish. In May 1973, at the Silver Anniversary Dinner of the State of Israel, at the Fontainebleau Hotel, Leon Kronish was presented the Prime Minister's Anniversary Medal by Abba Eban, Israel's Foreign Minister, for his service to Israel. He was one of twenty-five individuals from across the world who were selected personally by Prime Minister Golda Meir.

Often, a visiting Israeli politician passed an afternoon or evening sitting in the Kronish living room discussing Israel's current agenda and future Bond campaign activities.

Yitzhak Rabin and Leon Kronish, for example, had developed a warm relationship while Rabin was Ambassador to the United States in the late 1960s and early 1970s. When Rabin was recalled, Kronish was one of a handful of national Jewish American leaders invited to his farewell party.[85]

A few years later, after Rabin had been elected Prime Minister, he visited Miami and sought out Kronish. They spent the afternoon relaxing in Kronish's living room and discussing Israel's concerns. In due course, the conversation turned to sightseeing. Kronish mentioned that a friend had an airplane that might be available. Soon afterwards, with security man in tow, Prime Minister Rabin was flying over Miami Beach taking in the sights. Several hours later Kronish introduced the Prime Minister to a packed house at the Israel State Bonds dinner.[86]

On another occasion, Israel's Prime Minister, Menachem Begin, sent his advisor on Diaspora Affairs, Yehuda Avner, to the temple in 1978 "to bring to our [Miami] leaders a special off-the-cuff report on what is developing."[87] After the presentation, Avner, Kronish and other community leaders retired to Kronish's house to confer regarding future economic investments in Israel and Bonds strategy.

On several occasions, Meir Rosenne, Israel's representative to the Israel-Egypt peace talks–and later Israel's ambassador to the United States (mid-1980s) and chairman of Israel Bonds (early 1990s)–had requested Kronish's assistance, and had shown his appreciation by flying to Miami himself or by sending emissaries on his behalf. Frequently, before he (or his colleagues) addressed the greater Miami Jewish community on the status of the negotiations, Rosenne would meet with Kronish in his home to be briefed for the upcoming event. Sometimes these community gatherings were organized at Temple Beth Sholom in gratitude for Kronish's endeavors.

Israeli leaders would also show their appreciation by attending Temple Beth Sholom sabbath services when in Miami. In 1975, Ephraim Katzir, President of Israel, was the congregation's guest.

In 1979, Kronish was appointed National Chairman of Israel Bonds. His meetings with Israeli leaders became more frequent and their long range policy plans more challenging. Meetings in New York and Miami Beach were scheduled at regular intervals under the coordinating arm of Morris Sipser to review Israel's needs. These meetings also set the agenda for Bonds' missions to Israel and laid the groundwork for meetings with Israeli public and private sector officials.

In the 1982 sessions, the Israel Bonds national executive set a campaign goal of $550 million and organized "Operation Welcome," a U.S. tour for

Prime Minister Menachem Begin, which raised $100 million to help offset the costs of Israel's military intervention in Lebanon.[88]

Kronish's fundraising style was novel, humorous and full of warmth. It was not uncommon for Kronish, at an Israel Bonds dinner, to turn off the air conditioning and invite the guests to tell him when they began to feel uncomfortable. After several minutes of rising temperatures he would thunder that it was always hotter in Israel and that it was their responsibility "to cool Israel off."

Those who encountered Kronish with rolled up sleeves confronting them over their pledges, remember not their level of giving but his affection and tenaciousness. For Kronish, the purchase of the State of Israel Bonds was the strongest, and the most direct, link with Israel, its people, and their future. "He had," as a rival fundraiser commented after seeing Kronish at work, "a third dimension of giving."[89]

Kronish observed the growth in Jewish identity of his congregants. Youth who had grown up during the 1940s and 1950s, remained active in temple life with their families and were inclined to take leadership roles, were singled out by Kronish for Bonds activities. In due course, it was not uncommon for these individuals to volunteer for added responsibilities in Bonds campaigns. Several achieved positions of local and national prominence.

Jules Arkin received the "Israel Masada Award" from the Israel Bonds Organization for his distinguished service. A president of the Greater Miami Jewish Federation and the Miami Beach Chamber of Commerce in the late 1970s, Arkin worked hard to build a strong Israel Bonds infrastructure.

Gary Gerson, later president of Mount Sinai Hospital and vice-president of the Greater Miami Jewish Federation, became Greater Miami Israel Bonds General Campaign Chairman in the late 1970s. Gerson had been one of the first bar mitzvahs in Temple Beth Sholom during Kronish's first year (1944-1945), and devoted his philanthropic efforts after becoming an accountant to supporting Kronish's initiatives in Bonds. As General Campaign chairman, Gerson met with Kronish regularly to develop Bonds strategy. At their working sessions they identified new leads, organized committees to follow up pledges, and selected individuals to be honored at the Beth Sholom annual dinner.

Meetings with Jules Arkin and Gary Gerson and others who shared leadership positions in the community and the Federation invariably were an opportunity to discuss Jewish agenda events. The close working relationship between Israel Bonds and the Federation was enhanced by this networking. The problems identified by former Federation executive vice-president, Arthur Rosichan, in the late 1960s had disappeared. Both organizations now worked in close concert in a symbiotic relationship in Miami – in no small measure due to Kronish's personality and mediating influence.

Kronish's ability to target future leaders from within the temple and his emphasis on their "Israelization" development contributed to a significant number of Beth Sholom's board members in the 1970s and early 1980s serving in prominent positions in the Greater Miami Jewish Federation. Three were elected President of the Greater Miami Jewish Federation: Jules Arkin, Harry Smith and Donald Lefton. Many others became active on a national level in Jewish organizational life – Norman Braman, Myra Farr, Bruce Menin, Arthur Courshon, Phyllis Miller and Nan Rich.

The Kronish approach to generating support for Israel Bonds became legendary. *Florida Trend* magazine wrote that "it was not unusual to hear individuals engaged in selling Israel Bonds call Miami 'Israel's second most important city in America.'"[90] And Adon Taft of *The Miami Herald* described Kronish's skill as one of "changing fundraising for Israel from a distasteful necessity into an act of worshipful duty in synagogues throughout the United States of America."[91]

The unparalleled success of Leon Kronish in stimulating pro-Israeli sentiment in America is symbolized above all by his achievements with Israel Bonds. For Kronish, Bonds combined in one concrete activity his overriding mission – to "Israelize" the temple, his community, Reform Judaism and American Jews.

(Above, left to right) Leon Kronish, Prime Minister David Ben-Gurion, Paula Ben-Gurion, Jerusalem, 1964.

(Below, left to right) Burnett Roth, Abba Eban, Israel's Ambassador to the United States, Leon Kronish, Morris Goodman, Zionist Organization of America, Miami Beach, 1951.

(Above, left to right) Leon Kronish, Lenny Miller, Prime Minister Golda Meir, Miami Beach, 1973.

(Below, left to right) Yehuda Avner, Prime Minister Menachem Begin, Leon Kronish, Yehuda HaLevi, Jerusalem, 1983.

(Above, left to right) Prime Minister Yitzhak Rabin, Bill Sylk, Leon Kronish, Yehoram Meschel, secretary general of the Histadrut, Tel Aviv, 1975.

(Left, left to right) Ira Gilden, Sam Rothberg, International chairman, Israel Bonds, Yitzhak Navon, President of Israel, Colonel Yehuda HaLevi, Leon Kronish, Jerusalem, 1982.

(Above, left to right) Leon Kronish, Maurice Eisendrath, president UAHC and Herb Friedman, Jerusalem, 1970.

(Below, left to right) Ephraim Shapira, Zonik Shaham, Gila Shaham, Tikva Ben Chorin, Yehuda Ben Chorin; (sitting) Leon Kronish and his graddaughter, Dahlia Kronish, at Dahlia's Bat Mitzvah, Jerusalem, 1989.

Chapter Seven

Leon Kronish and the Dialectics of Liberal Judaism

One Life: Four Stories

The life of Leon Kronish can best be understood as four stories in one: a generation, a place, an institution and an individual.

Born in 1917, Kronish is part of a fascinating generation of Jewish Americans that came of age during the Depression and New Deal, World War Two and the Holocaust, witnessing the birth of Israel and the Cold War, civil rights and Vietnam as adults.

The place was Miami—the greater Miami area in general, and Miami Beach in particular. When Kronish came to Miami Beach in 1944, Miami was a humid, Southern backwater in the process of becoming one of the most diverse and dynamic metropolitan areas in the entire United States.

From the moment Kronish arrived in that steamy setting, his energies were devoted to the Miami Jewish community at large, and especially his own sanctuary, Temple Beth Sholom. Under Kronish's leadership, the congregation grew from a score of families to one of 1500 members and one of the most active and influential in the nation—paralleling the emergence of Miami as one of the most important Jewish cities in America.

And last but not least, the life of Leon Kronish is the story of an individual of unique talents: a man of inexhaustible energy and passionate commitment to the causes he embraced; a riveting speaker and programmatic innovator; and most of all, a person of unmistakable warmth, able to make the people he met feel both comfortable and enlivened.

Liberal Judaism

The framework of beliefs and practices that has sustained Kronish throughout a life of ceaseless activity in the public eye was Liberal Judaism.

Liberal Judaism is a uniquely American variant of the Jewish experience —one whose flowering in the period after World War Two precisely matched the course of Kronish's growth and development. It synthesized three elements into a religious/social/political movement that had considerable impact in both the United States of America and Israel: prophetic mission, renewal of tradition, and Zionism.

Throughout his life, Kronish has pursued a myriad of activities in all three areas, a reflection of the fact that he is one of the most able and charismatic disciples of two highly influential rabbis and teachers in American Jewish life.

The first was Rabbi Stephen Wise (1874-1949), the great prophetic voice of American Jewish life in the first half of the twentieth century – a social reformer, a religious iconoclast, and an apostle of ecumenicism widely known and revered by both Jews and Christians.

The second was Mordecai Kaplan (1881-1983), the founder of Reconstructionist Judaism, who saw Jewish history as a fundamentally cultural phenomenon, the product of a uniquely Jewish civilization, rooted in the constant evolution of the Jewish people as a living organism – a man who saw the continual renewal and revitalizing of ritual as the living link between a rich past and an open future.

From Wise, Kronish took the profound commitment to the prophetic mission of social justice, principles he would apply in the context of the civil rights and peace/disarmament movements of the 1950s and 1960s. From Wise too, he took the ecumenical notion of *Klal Yisrael*, the Jewish people as a whole – whose collective well-being was more important than the interests or concerns of any particular denomination within.

From Kaplan, he took the idea of a vibrant Jewish people, whose identity was constantly evolving, and could be authentically expressed by a living liturgy, and a commitment to intensive Jewish education, Hebraically based.

Finally, he inherited from both Wise and Kaplan, the idea of a politically active, spiritually-infused Zionism – one that could be practiced as legitimately in America as in Israel, as long as the ties that bound the communities were nourished by constant care and communication.

The Six Day War and the Transformation of Liberal Judaism

Until the Six Day War in June, 1967, Leon Kronish divided his energies more or less equally between the universal concerns of Reform Judaism and the more particular concerns of Labor Zionism. The war, which threatened the very existence of Israel, coupled with the apparent indifference of the United Nations and the great powers to that eventuality, was traumatic for Kronish, as it was for virtually all of Diaspora Jewry.

Even though Israel was victorious, the taste of its vulnerability remained in Kronish's mouth, and he began to shift his emphasis solidly in the direction of Israel. He didn't repudiate the liberal positions he held – though many of his generation did, but after the 1967 war, his energies were almost totally consumed by his attempts to build *gesher vakesher*, bridges and bonds, between the affluent Jewish community of Miami, and of America as a whole, and the State of Israel. In his view, the very survival of Israel, and the continued existence—physical and spiritual—of Diaspora Jewry depended on their mutual support and interlocking destiny.

The "Israelization" of Reform Judaism in America

For Kronish, the period between the June, 1967 war and his tragic and untimely stroke in January, 1984 is best characterized, we have argued, by the term "Israelization."

In our view, Kronish pursued the "Israelization" of Reform Judaism in America along five very different dimensions, but all moving towards the end of consolidating, expanding and extending relations between the State of Israel and both Jews and non-Jews in the United States.

1) Bringing Israelis to America.
2) Bringing American Jews to Israel.
3) Making American synagogues and temples into visible centers for the promotion of Israeli life and culture.
4) Prodding major Jewish institutions in America—especially, but not exclusively, those in the Reform movement—to recognize the centrality of Israel for Jewish survival and to develop a prominent pro-Israel program, including growing links with Israeli institutions of similar orientations.
5) Establishing permanent links between political, social and economic institutions in Israel and the U.S.—secular and non-denominational.

All represented an Israel-centered focus for Jewish life in America. They also represented a major step beyond the traditional Zionist goal of bringing Jews to live in Israel—a web of inter-connection between Israeli and American institutions that would redound to the benefit of not just Israeli and American Jews, but to Israel and the United States as interdependent, co-operating democratic states.

Israel Bonds—the Bridge That Binds

While Kronish pursued "Israelization" through a variety of means, his extraordinarily successful achievement in the Israel Bonds program is the most richly emblematic of his calling.

For Kronish, Bonds were the real tangible link, the *gesher vakesher*, between American Jewry and Israel. They represented a commitment to Israel's future, an investment in her people and a conviction that peace was possible.

Reaching out to the average American Jew—the bedrock of the Kronish constituency—Bonds were an affordable connection that did not discriminate by gender or income. They were outside the conflicting allegiances of Israeli political parties and American Jewish organizations, embodying an investment in a whole people.

In that sense, Bonds represented for Kronish the essence of *Klal Yisrael*, the collectivity of the Jewish people, the willingness of Jews everywhere in the world to recognize the inter-connection of their fates, and act to preserve the priceless continuity of the Jewish experience. Thus, through Bonds, Kronish was able to persuade thousands upon thousands of North American Jews that tangible support of Israel was a meaningful and relevant expression of their individual Jewish identity.

The Legacy of Leon Kronish: the Interlocking Destiny Between Synagogue and State

> We need a network of community institutions—federations, UJA, Israel Bonds, etc., etc. The synagogue has been central to this whole network.... If we want to recharge our spiritual batteries and if we mean to raise up a generation that knows what it means to be Jewish, then we have to be certain that our synagogue is stronger than ever.[1]

> More than Israel sustained the synagogue, the synagogue sustained Israel.[2]

In this way, Leon Kronish pithily summed up the umbilical connection between the Beth Sholom community—and, by extension, all Reform Jewry in America—and the State of Israel. For Kronish, the main responsibility of all Diaspora Jews—and American Jews in particular—was to preserve *Klal Yisrael*. While this was to be done in many ways, by far the most important was to deepen the *gesher vakesher* between themselves and the people and State of Israel, what we have termed "Israelization."

Leon Kronish was a pioneer in arguing that Zionism and Israel should be neither perceived nor experienced as separate from more strictly religious concerns. In his view, the agenda of Diaspora Jewry necessitated pilgrimages to Israel as an important religious-cultural experience in the identity-formation of American Jewry in general, and of youth in particular.

In this regard, his ultimate legacy is the inheritance of the generation of congregants and leaders who have come of age under his tutelage during the last half-century. It is they who continue into the present day the spirit, values and commitments that marked the life and passion of Rabbi Leon Kronish.

EPILOGUE

by
Rabbi Gary A. Glickstein

From the Yemenite community of Jews comes the proverb, "Every change is chancy, *Kol Shinui Shanui*." Nevertheless, change is inevitable. It comes to every human being and to every institution. When it arrives it is fought with anxiety and tension. Moments of change are critical to life. How the transition occurs determines to a large measure the future health and direction of an individual's or institution's life.

January 1984 looms as a crucial period for Rabbi Leon Kronish and for Temple Beth Sholom. No change in the overall structure of the congregation and its leadership had been anticipated by anyone. No plans had been formulated for transitions. The membership had declined over the previous decade. The Foundation School and the younger grades of the School for Living Judaism were shrinking in size. Many generous supporters of the past had died or moved to Boca Raton and Palm Beach. The new building was progressing, enormous debts were being amassed. Months of continued decline and confusion stretched into a year.

In fact, Rabbi Kronish and the leadership of Temple Beth Sholom had embarked beginning in 1982 upon an optimistic building program to prepare for future growth in the School of Living Judaism and for administrative and cultural needs in the present. In 1984, few people were predicting the comeback of Miami Beach. Most were wringing their hands at the exodus of Jews to North Miami Beach, Broward County and Palm Beach County. The consensus in the press was of an aging, dying Jewish population in the midst of a decaying, crime-filled city. Rabbi Leon Kronish and a majority of the leadership of Temple Beth Sholom were of another opinion. They believed in the future of Miami Beach. They foresaw young Jews moving in with children. They knew that if Temple Beth Sholom were to remain vital, it had to re-emerge from its own period of aging and diminishing membership. This congregation needed a facility which addressed young families' needs. The new building was carefully planned: a modern school wing with classrooms for early childhood on the first floor and rooms for older Hebrew and Judaic students on the second floor. The building was reinforced for a possible third floor addition if growth was greater than anticipated. A library and computer room along with an extensive ceramics room and a music suite of three rooms were included on the second floor. The first floor also had school offices, administrative offices, offices for cultural programming, work rooms and an arts and crafts room. All of these facilities on the first floor were connected by the Art Gallery.

Groundbreaking for the new building took place on June 5, 1983, and the major challenge remaining was the raising of needed revenues to cover the costs of building. This task was taken over enthusiastically by the Rabbi. Rabbi Kronish was known as a powerful fund raiser. His work in Israel Bonds is legendary. His ability to tap the generosity of Jews for Jewish causes was the envy of his peers. At Temple Beth Sholom he was the central source of fundraising. Over the years, Jewish professional fundraisers had been hired to help at various times. Their chief contribution was to nudge the Rabbi to see the appropriate people. They also helped him hone his skills of ascertaining the appropriate amount to ask, but funds came to Temple Beth Sholom largely as a result of meetings and phone calls initiated and conducted by Rabbi Leon Kronish. Most of the Board of Directors were convinced that once again the Rabbi would come through. Not all the Directors supported the new building. Some saw it as premature. Some believed that the rebirth of Miami Beach was too far off in the distance and some doubted it would ever occur. In spite of some opposition and doubts, the project proceeded, largely on the energy and drive of the Rabbi.

Suddenly, in January 1984 everything changed. Rabbi Leon Kronish suffered a massive stroke. For some time his life hung in the balance. For weeks stretching into months of agony, his condition following recovery and therapy was uncertain. The Rabbi, ever an optimist, believed he would be back with his abilities and energies intact. His future and the future of Temple Beth Sholom were, for the first time since his arrival, a question mark.

A group of younger leaders stepped forward into the void. Under the presidency of Neal Amdur, they began to evaluate the situation. They remained constantly in contact with Rabbi Kronish as they attempted to form a transition process that would tide the Temple over until it was clear whether the Rabbi could return to his duties. All of the vital services of Temple Beth Sholom continued: worship, education, culture. Loans were secured and monies raised to meet the mounting bills. Rabbis Harry Jolt, the Auxiliary Rabbi, and Rabbi Paul Kaplan, the Assistant Rabbi, performed yeoman's work in facilitating these programs. Cantor David Conviser maintained the vibrancy of the worship and life-cycle occasions. Judy Drucker tirelessly produced quality culture throughout the community and in the Temple. Shula Ben-David, Gary Eisenberg, Anita Koppelle and Ally Sheer kept the youth and education departments creative. And Dennis Rice worked closely with great determination and energy with the Board and with Neal Amdur and his officers to achieve a level of stability.

When it became clear that Rabbi Kronish would not recover entirely and congregants were expressing their deep concern for the future of the congregation, Rabbi Kronish, Neal Amdur and the leadership agreed to search for a new senior rabbi.

Following a national search that lasted a year, I was chosen to become the Senior Rabbi of Temple Beth Sholom. In November 1985, twenty-two months after Rabbi Kronish's stroke, I assumed my role as Rabbi of Temple Beth Sholom.

I was frightened and overwhelmed. This esteemed congregation had only been led by one Rabbi since 1944. This Rabbi was an internationally known Jewish leader of stellar reputation. The challenges presented by the crisis left in the wake of his illness were daunting. I was convinced my tenure at Temple Beth Sholom would be brief. I would fill the role of *Korban* - a Sacrificial Rabbi. I thought I would fill the transition period and make way for the true and deserving successor of Rabbi Leon Kronish.

The membership of the Temple, the citizens of Miami Beach, and God had other plans. As I write these words I am in my tenth year as Senior Rabbi. In large part I remain the Senior Rabbi because I was encouraged and supported by Rabbi Leon Kronish himself, his wife Lillian and his family, the leadership of this congregation and the Miami Jewish community.

As in 1944, when Miami Beach Jewry opened its arms to Rabbi Leon Kronish and his family, so in 1985 the Miami Jewish community welcomed me, my wife Joanie and our children, Avi, Sarah and Jesse. Our children attended Nautilus Middle School and Miami Beach Senior High School as did the Kronish children. Joanie became active in the National Council of Jewish Women and Federation as Lillian had displayed leadership in many Jewish organizations. And I was brought into the leadership of Federation, Israel Bonds, UJA Rabbinic Cabinet and many civic organizations, as Rabbi Kronish had served before me.

Temple Beth Sholom was unprepared for the sudden change. As they say in Yemen, "All change is chancy." Yet when this moment occurred, a transition emerged out of the intense loyalties built over the years by Rabbi Kronish and the leadership of the congregation.

Today we are a new congregation. Over 60% of our present membership has joined in the past seven years. The new school wing is bursting. Hebrew and *Shabbat* School and youth programs flourish including yearly pilgrimages to Israel, a tradition begun in 1970 by Rabbi Leon Kronish. In addition, the congregation now leads two to three adult and family missions to Israel yearly facilitated and given spirit by our cantor Steven Haas. Our continuing education courses are growing and expanding. They meet at all times throughout the community. Rabbi Harry Jolt, 91 years of age, *Ad Meah V'esrim*, anchors much of this work. Our Holy Days Services and Festivals are joyous, meaningful and well-attended. Our *Shabbat* worship continues to inspire all who attend. We are embarking on new directions, including the establishment of a Jewish Center for Healing and Spirituality, experimental worship opportunities and the renewal of life-long learning and observance among more of our congregants. Recently, we completed a five-year long-range plan which includes the following Mission Statement, adopted by our Board and congregation:

OUR MISSION STATEMENT

Temple Beth Sholom will affect Jewish lives in a positive way.

- We will foster and promote Jewish continuity through our spiritual, religious, and textual value system.
- We will create a sense of community among our members.
- We will achieve the highest quality, in all we do, while focusing on the lives of our members and their families.

Much of the work begun by Rabbi Kronish continues. We build on his foundations. We are actively in the process of retooling our synagogue to meet the needs of the new, diverse Jewish community of Miami Beach. We will accomplish this task in the rich traditions of Temple Beth Sholom – innovation, bold optimism, warmth and openness. Israel remains our family and our partner. We work to build bridges and bonds with her following Rabbi Kronish's blueprint, as we reach out to all Jewish institutions, synagogues and committed individuals to meet the emerging challenges before us.

World Jewry stands in the midst of our greatest Golden Age. Temple Beth Sholom remains a jewel in the Jewish crown. Fifty two years after its founding and fifty years after Rabbi Leon Kronish assumed rabbinic leadership, Temple Beth Sholom grows from generation to generation, from strength to strength, from *gesher* to *kesher*.

AFTERWORD

Some Personal Memories and Reflections

by
Dr. Ronald Kronish, Rabbi

I would like to begin these reflections with a few words of gratitude. Firstly, I would like to thank Rabbi Gary Glickstein—a friend and colleague of many years, from our days as young rabbis nearly twenty years ago in Worcester, Massachusetts to the past ten years that he has served as successor to my father as spiritual leader of Temple Beth Sholom in Miami Beach, Florida—for agreeing to support and help carry through to fulfillment this project. When I initiated the idea of producing a biography on the life and rabbinic career of my father, I was met with enthusiasm and encouragement. Without his understanding and support, this idea would have never been brought from concept to reality.

Secondly, I want to express my deepest and sincerest thanks to Dr. Sol Lichter, my teacher and my father's co-worker for so many years at Temple Beth Sholom and in the greater Miami Beach community, for his loving and time-consuming efforts at organizing my father's papers and photos since his illness. Sol's archival efforts provide the essential ingredients without which this book could not have been written.

Thirdly, I want to thank Professor Henry Green, Director of the Judaic Studies Program of the University of Miami, who approached this task with unusual commitment, devotion, and dedication. I know that he put many years of research and writing and rewriting into this book, and I feel that his investment of time, energy and thought has turned out to be very worthwhile. He has succeeded in documenting the life and times of my father in a substantive and sophisticated fashion, which offers the reader—and Jewish history—an inside look at the issues of this last century which my father has admirably tackled and the vibrant family, educational, religious and cultural background which gave him the necessary tools to do so.

I offer these personal reflections on behalf of the Kronish family—my mother, my sister, Maxine, my wife, Amy, my brother-in-law, Eddie, and all five Kronish grandchildren—Sari, Dahlia, Ariella, Davida, and Ami. We all share in the memories which go along with my father's long association with Temple Beth Sholom and the Greater Miami Jewish Community. As members of the extended Kronish family, we have always felt the congregational family atmosphere, which my father and mother labored so hard to build for so many years, as part and parcel of the sense of community which is so intrinsic to the temple and the larger community which he served.

I first sat down to write these reflections the day after *Shabbat Zachor*, the Sabbath of Remembrance, before *Purim*. Remembering is a good thing for Jews to do, on a collective and personal basis. Our collective memory, as a people, is undoubtedly one of the things that has kept us going for so many thousands of years. The Bible, the Mishnah, the Talmud, and other sacred books, are the record of our people's keen and penetrating memory. At the same time, collective memory is not enough. It is vital to personalize our collective memory, as we learn from the *Pesach Haggadah* when it instructs us to view ourselves as if we personally went out of Egypt.

I hope that this book will serve to refresh many people's memories about the greatness that my father has brought to his service to the Jewish community in Greater Miami, primarily through Temple Beth Sholom, and to World Jewry through his multitudinous active involvements in so many causes and concerns.

This is my contribution towards personalizing our collective memory, in celebration of my father's 50th year as a rabbi and his half-century of service to Temple Beth Sholom and the Jewish People all over the world. As recorded in this biography, my father has served this congregation—as well as the South Florida Jewish Community, the North American Jewish community and World Jewry—with wholehearted dedication and commitment for these past five decades. His life has been so intertwined with the life and dynamics of Temple Beth Sholom—and with the life and times of the Jewish People everywhere during this century, and especially in the State of Israel—that the two are virtually inseparable.

When I was a child growing up, the temple was very much part of my life, as I suppose it is of many other R.K.'s (Rabbis' Kids). I went to Temple every Friday night with my family, as was customary and expected. As many of the readers of this book will recall, the Kronish family always sat on the left side of the sanctuary ("the Rabbi's side," because it was directly opposite the lectern from which he delivered his sermons), along with many of the veteran leaders of the congregation. I suppose this enabled us to have good eye contact with "the rabbi" and vice versa. We in the family always knew when he was looking at us, although he always had excellent eye contact with everyone in the congregation.

Listening to the sermon, especially as I grew older and wiser, was always the high point of the evening. It was dynamic, relevant and interesting (and we frequently found ourselves discussing the content of the sermon after the services, over coffee in our home, or at a local restaurant with a group of friends). My father was unquestionably one of the great orators in the American rabbinate, and listening to him for so many years, week in and week out, was certainly much more beneficial than anything I ever learned about homiletics (the art of sermonizing) in rabbinical school!

All of the sermons used to be audiotaped by a young man named Steve Krams, who grew up in the temple and was for many years my father's audio-visual assistant. I remember that Steve sat in a little audio studio off to the left of the stage in the social hall. These taped sermons are a unique treasure of Jewish oral history from the days before video—the 1950s and 1960s. I used to join him for long *shmoozes* during the services whenever I could. But I was always back inside the sanctuary, to stand at the back of the center aisle during the benediction—to receive my father's blessing which I and everyone else in the congregation was sure came straight from God because of the stately and spiritual way in which he delivered it—and to greet him as he came off the pulpit, as he marched down the long aisle on his way to the lobby to greet all the congregants with his traditional warm and personal "*Shabbat Shalom*." I was always amazed that he knew each and every person and gave each person a sense of caring and concern by welcoming them into his midst.

In addition to regular Friday night and Saturday morning services, I remember vividly and fondly many life-cycle events at which my father officiated, and I am sure that many hundreds, and even thousands, of Beth Sholom members—and people from all over the community and the country—remember similar occasions in their lives and the life of the Temple. My father's and mother's role in my Bar Mitzvah and Confirmation ceremonies—as well as those of my brother, Jordan, and my sister, Maxine—will remain indelibly etched on my mind and heart.

I remember, especially warmly, my father's role in officiating at my wedding twenty-five years ago, and at my sister's wedding twelve years ago. It is a special joy and privilege to be married by one's father, and in my case, and the case of my sister, my father's warmth and wit and Jewish sensitivity on those days will stay with us and our spouses forever (my sister was luckier because she was able to preserve it on videotape). Naturally, many of the members of the greater Beth Sholom family joined with us in celebrating these *simchahs*, and therefore share these memories with us.

One more life-cycle event stands out in my memory. This was the day that my father was the main speaker at my ordination from rabbinical school, in June 1973, at Temple Emanuel in New York. I remember that he was particularly brilliant on that day, and, as proud as he and my mother must have been of me, I think that I was even prouder of him. When he ascended the majestic pulpit of Temple Emanuel, and delivered his address with his characteristic poise and preciseness, his inspiring presence and message filled the sanctuary with sunshine and hope for the future.

In my college years, and as I grew older, I returned home to Temple Beth Sholom often. Every time that I come back, I am impressed with the dynamism of this institution which my father has nurtured and built over the years, with so much love and devotion. It often struck me that here was a unique community institution, through whose doors hundreds (and sometimes thousands) of people would pass in a given week. In the turbulent decades of the 1960s and 1970s, in addition to the regular features of worship services and religious school, this Temple was without doubt one of the most thriving and lively synagogue-centers in the country, sponsoring a myriad of cultural events, probably unparalleled for a single synagogue in North America. I am sure that it is no exaggeration to say that the synagogue pulsated and hopped because its rabbi was a mover and a shaker. He made things happen. His energy was boundless, and there was no limit to the amount of creative ideas that he could come up with in a day or a week. If you don't believe me, just ask some of the Temple staff, who had trouble keeping up the pace. In short, this has been a dynamic synagogue because its rabbi has been a dynamic leader.

To me, my father's activism and dynamism was symbolized by the fact that he never had time to clean up his desk in his study. His desk was always cluttered, and he had to install a sliding door between his desk and the rest of his study, so that guests in his office would not see the papers. He simply never had time for straightening up things, and besides, it was too mundane an activity anyway! He kept a very quick pace, and he accomplished quite a lot in one day. He was always a big user of the telephone (and he still is, thank God), and he kept in touch with the world – in North America, and in Israel – through his many telephones. He even had a special "Hot Line," a red phone, which for many years was his direct link to the Israel Bonds office in New York.

He was, and he remains, a great communicator with people, not only from the pulpit but also in face-to-face interaction and via the telephone. He is very much a people person – this has been, and continues to be one of his great strengths of character. As inspiring and impressive a rabbi as he is, he has the unique ability to be with people, to share in their joys and sorrows, and to just be with them. His sense of humor, his intellect, and his communicative clarity all transmit the message that he is not a faraway, distant rabbi, but rather a near and caring one, a fact of his rabbinic personality which has made all the difference in his relationships with his congregants over this past half-century.

Although he was always primarily involved with his synagogue, my father's years in the active rabbinate took him beyond the synagogue into the wider local, national, and international Jewish community. He has been a great believer in *Klal Yisrael*, Jewish Peoplehood, and this is certainly one of the greatest treasures that I have inherited from him. Not only has he been a great ideologue and builder of the synagogue, but he has lent his strength and support to many vital Jewish institutions and organizations. Foremost among his many commitments has always been and devotion to the State of Israel.

Often, when I am asked why I decided to live in Israel, I answer that I took Ben-Gurion's speeches and my father's sermons seriously! My parents took my sister and me to Israel for the first time in 1964, the summer after I finished high school in Miami Beach. And I fell in love with Israel on that first visit because my father's love for Israel was infectious and overwhelming. Since then, many congregants and friends have shared his love and commitment to Israel over the years, whether by making pilgrimages to Israel with the rabbi, or by feeling the spirit and the culture of Israel in the synagogue. After all, how many synagogues in North America sang *Yerushalayim Shel Zahav* for years and years on Friday nights as the concluding hymn! And how many synagogues in America have established living links with real people in Israel by building the kind of relationships with Israelis—the kind of *gesher vakesher*, links of caring and communication—that my father has been able to build over these fifty years that he has served his people as a rabbi. It is no wonder that Professor Green chose this theme as his title for the book and as the main contribution of my father's activism on behalf of American Jewry and Israel.

My father has been a great teacher of the concept that both Israel and the Diaspora are vital for the continuity of Judaism and the Jewish People. Not one or the other, but both are crucial and are inextricably intertwined—this has been his greatest message. It is certainly a message that I learned from him and cherish deeply until this very day. And, it is the sort of concept that I believe we still need to strengthen and develop, as we work towards the future of both the local community and the State of Israel with a growing realization of the fact of our interlocking destiny as a people, which binds us together in common concern, caring and commitment.

Concern for the future is very much on my father's mind these days. Those of us who are in regular communication with him know this. He is worried about the threat of nuclear holocaust and the potential destruction of the world, about the rampant assimilation of American Jewry, about the continuing precarious survival of the State of Israel, about the future of the synagogue which he built and developed for so many years. Yet, despite his worries concerning the future, I believe that he remains an optimist and even a messianist.

He continues to believe and work for a better tomorrow, as he always taught. The Biblical vision of *Hazon Geulah Meshichit,* of Messianic Redemption, is very much a part of his life and of his consciousness, as it has always been. It informs his theology as well as his day-to-day life.

The most amazing feature about my father, especially in the eleven years since his stroke, is that he does not give up, and he does not let us—his family, friends and disciples—fall prey to the disease of despair of despondency. He discovered the meaning of the popular term "Jewish Continuity" decades before it became popular in the 1990s in Federation/UJA circles. And he practices what he preaches, to this very day. He continues to participate in worship services at his synagogue every Friday night and every *Shabbat* morning, and to grace the pulpit on major holidays. He continues to study Bible with the Bible study group, now taught by Professor Yehuda Shamir, every *Shabbat* morning. He continues to remain in contact and communication with family, friends, and congregants. He continues to visit his children and grandchildren in Washington, D.C. and in Jerusalem every year. And he continues to maintain an acute interest in the fate of the people and the State of Israel, in its good times and its bad ones, as it enters an era of peaceful relations with its neighbors at the same time that it is beset with ongoing violence and terror. Throughout it all, he remains the inveterate optimist, the persistent messianist, the believer in a better future for Israel and for all humankind.

Jewish continuity is the name of the game—personal, congregational, communal, national, international continuity. Most important, his continued presence is a source of blessing to all of us who have been privileged to come under the shadow of his abiding influence, and we pray that his future, and that of his wife, Lillian, will be a future of *shalom*, a future of peace and well-being, to be shared with cherished friends and loving family who, together with them, will continue to dream and build for a better tomorrow.

Since I mentioned my mother, Lillian, I want to add a few words about her. She really deserves to have a book written about her as well. The public would learn a lot about a great Jewish woman whom they do not know and do not sufficiently appreciate. Every honor that my father has ever been given has been jointly shared by her, and rightly so because she has always been there with him, at every sad and joyous occasion in their life together.

On my last visit to Miami Beach, I found an article in an album on my father's desk in his study at the temple about the "woman of the week" in *The Jewish Floridian* of April 28, 1961. In it, the writer captured the essence of my mother when she wrote: "Lillian's devotion to her family is paramount in her life. She is not a matriarch, but a bulwark of strength against which all lean." If this was true 34 years ago, how much the more so during the past eleven years, since my father's debilitating stroke in 1984.

To use Biblical imagery, she has literally been Aaron to Moses, helping him during this difficult period with every step and every thought. She has been an unbelievable tower of strength and support, even while fighting off a multiplicity of problems, including many medical ones. She is genuinely an unsung hero, and if I were an opera singer, I would be the first one to sing her praises with as loud a baritone voice as I could muster. In so doing, I would praise her unusual warmth and sensitivity, her deep and abiding dedication to her husband and her family, including and especially, of course, her children and grandchildren as well as her three sisters. I would also acknowledge without hesitation her intelligence and inquisitiveness and her thirst for knowledge, her charm and conversational conviviality, and most of all her caring and compassionate charisma, which has often bordered on selflessness, whereby she has so passionately devoted herself to her husband's welfare. She has been my father's "life partner" (his term) and the world should know that he could never have been the great rabbi and communal leader that he has been for these past fifty years without her at his side, every day, in every way.

Jerusalem
December, 1994
Tevet 5755

ESSAYS by RABBI LEON KRONISH

The essays in this section illustrate a selection of Leon Kronish's writings regarding "Israelization" (*Yisrael Goralenu, What are the 'Zionist Mitzvot?'*), liturgy (*Passover Supplementary Haggadah, Service of Memorial for the Heroes and the Martyrs of the Warsaw Ghetto,* and *Chanukah Cantata*) and education (*A Treasury of Inspiration*). They reflect his constant commitment to *Klal Yisrael*, the State of Israel and Liberal Judaism.

Yisrael Goralenu*

Hakdamah

"We declare our solidarity with the State and the people of Israel. Their triumphs are our triumphs. Their ordeal is our ordeal. Their fate is our fate."

These are the closing words of Daniel Silver's statement on Israel which was adopted by the CCAR on June 21, 1967, just after the "Six Days That Shook the World"—six days that shook the Jewish world so much so that it can never be the same again—and it should never be the same again.

These words must be our guidelines! Never before in the history of our movement has the oneness, the unity, the interlocking destiny of the Jewish people been so sharply and simply stated. If this be considered an exaggeration, then let the statement serve as an exclamation point to previous pronouncements and platforms on the peoplehood of Israel—but remember that these were always voiced in the shadow of a struggle to "harmonize opposing viewpoints" reconciling Zionism and non-Zionism and anti-Zionism (as Arthur Lelyveld points up in his critique of the CCAR view of the "position of the Jew in the modern world"—*Retrospect and Prospect*, CCAR, 1965, p.129). The time for harmonizing opposing viewpoints ended last June. We had come face to face with one of those historic moments of truth. The politicide and genocide proclaimed by the Arab world against the State and the people of Israel had no geographical limitation. As Richard Hirsch has phrased it: "In June, 1967, it became clear that the destiny of *Am Yisrael* was inseparable from the destiny of *Medinat Yisrael*."

One hundred and fifty years after the assembly of Jewish notables convened by Napoleon and 82 years after the Pittsburgh Platform, we have come full-cycle. "Their ordeal is our ordeal, their fate is our fate"—we are one people without equivocation, without apologies, explanations, rationalizations, ideologies, etc., etc. No responsible Jewish group got involved last June in drawing lines of distinction between *Eretz* and *Chutz L'Aretz*. The entire Jewish people was simply not going to countenance another Holocaust—(although that may not be the full explanation of what happened last June, we have come full-cycle).

The French assembly of Jewish notables attempted an historic diversion from the mainstream of Jewish continuity. In the wake of the new emancipation that granted equal rights to individual Jews, the assembly rewrote Jewish destiny and Jews ceased to be a "peculiar people" or a "holy people" clinging to a centuries-old vision of "return-to-Zion" and "Jerusalem redeemed." The eternal ethnic element of Jewishness was suppressed; emancipated Jews were to enjoy freedom of religion as full-fledged citizens. A certain Samuel Levy wrote at the end of the eighteenth century in a Paris journal: "France, which has been first to remove from us the shame of Judea, is our land of Israel; here is our Zion; here is our Jordan." This denial of Zion in the new delineation of Jews as a religious grouping only was crystallized in the fifth article of the Pittsburgh Platform (1885) which declared that "Jews are no longer a nation but a religious community; they do not desire to return to Palestine, establish a Jewish State or restore themselves as an official cult."

The 50th Anniversary of the Pittsburgh Platform in 1935, saw a majority of the CCAR searching for a new set of guiding principles for Reform Judaism. It was now nearly

*Reprinted from the *CCAR Journal* 16 (June, 1968), 31-37.

20 years after the historic Balfour Declaration; it was twenty years after the Russian Revolution and its strangulation of the most creative Jewish community in the history of Diaspora—the community that produced rebirth, renaissance, redemption. Already a sizable and creative and progressive Yishuv existed in Palestine. The dichotomy between the ethnic and religious launched by the assembly of notables and crystallized in the Pittsburgh Platform had begun to appear less real or relevant in the face of the kinship and concern which Jews sensed for Jews and for Jerusalem. The Columbus Platform made an attempt to bring the ethnic and religious together again within the mainstream of Jewish continuity:

> Judaism is the soul of which Israel is the body. Living in all parts of the world, Israel has been held together by the ties of a common history, and above all, by the heritage of faith. Though we recognize in the group-loyalty of Jews who have become estranged from our religious tradition a bond which still unites them with us, we maintain that it is by its religion and for its religion that the Jewish people has lived. The non-Jew who accepts our faith is welcomed as a full member of the Jewish community.
>
> In all lands where our people live, they assume and seek to share loyally the full duties and responsibilities of citizenship and to create seats of Jewish knowledge and religion. In the rehabilitation of Palestine, the land hallowed by memories and hopes, we behold the promise of renewed life for many of our brethren. We affirm the obligation of all Jewry to aid in its upbuilding as a Jewish home-land by endeavoring to make it not only a haven of refuge for the oppressed but also a center of Jewish culture and spiritual life.

We were obviously still equivocating; we were caught in the sociological semantics of an America which underscored religious pluralism though ethnic or cultural pluralism was not the dominant fact of the American scene. We affirmed our historic sense of mutual responsibility but not quite a clear cut interlocking destiny—yet Hitler had been in power for five years. We were not quite ready to return to the historic concept of peoplehood. We underscored the fact that we were primarily a "religious tradition."

When the State of Israel began its fifteenth year (1962) the CCAR felt the need for a new statement. We now came much closer to the reality of historic Jewish existence:

I. We affirm our faith in the one living God, creator and governor of the universe. Our fathers pledged eternal loyalty to Him and He, we believe, accepted them as a people consecrated to His service. It is this covenant between God and Israel that gives historic Jewish existence its distinctive character.

II. Changes of time, place and circumstances have evoked divergent views among Jews as to the nature of Israel's covenant with God and its implications for our time. Some give primary emphasis to Jewish nationhood. Some limit their interest to the maintenance of ethnic and cultural continuity. For us, Jewish religious faith is indispensable to the Jewish way of life. Yet we Jews are one people the world over, with a common historic background and a distinct consciousness of Jewish brotherhood. The familiar classifications of race, nationality, and church do not properly describe us. We are a unique community.

III. Jewish religious duty and Jewish historical experience both demand of us constant concern with all that Jews do and all that happens to them wherever they may live.

"All Jews are responsible for one another" does not mean for us that we must approve and defend the words and actions of all Jews. It means that we are obligated to provide help for the people of the State of Israel. We note with deep gratification the establishment of Liberal Jewish Congregations in the land of Israel. This new religious movement now requires our wholehearted encouragement and support. We pledge ourselves to continued effort toward fuller understanding between the Jews who live in the land of Israel and those who live elsewhere. We have no right to speak for each other; but it is our duty to speak to each other continually in mutual concern and genuine love. Our lives as Jews in America are enriched by the creative development of Jewish life in the State of Israel. The lives of our brothers in the State of Israel are, in turn, enriched by the distinctive and creative Jewish experience in America. Jewish creativity knows no geographical boundaries.

There will be disagreements between us, and even criticism of each other. American Jews should not give the impression that they are trying to direct the affairs of the State of Israel and the leaders of the State of Israel should avoid giving the impression that they speak for American Jewry. Yet the bridge of communication and help, built with knowledge and love, must stand firm and unshaken.

IV. The distinctive character of historic Jewish existence rooted in our covenant with the one living God, affirmed in each generation and in every place and circumstance by the noblest teachers of Judaism, imposed upon us all the unceasing striving for the implementation of the Jewish prophetic vision.

This divine mission again unites and challenges our brothers in the State of Israel, in America, and everywhere on earth.

It was a long step forward considering that the 70th anniversary volume of the Hebrew Union College (1949) still contained a Zionist and a non-Zionist interpretation of Reform Judaism and Zionism. Even the 1962 Statement was characterized by Arthur Lelyveld as a "non-definition" (*Retrospect and Prospect, p. 171*). We were still engaged in a struggle to reconcile two imperatives: "One flowed from the role of the people of Israel and the history of mankind; and the other had its origin in the demands of those realities of Jewish life which culminated in the establishment of a portion of that people as an independent nation-state on its ancient soil." The 1962 statement came close to reconciliation in speaking of our striving for the implementation of the Jewish prophetic vision and in underscoring the divine mission that unites and challenges our brothers in the State of Israel, in America and everywhere on earth.

But the expression of this divine mission was much more a prayerful hope than actuality. The 1962 Statement speaks of support of Progressive Congregations in Israel which we have yet to give. It speaks of a bridge of communication that we have hardly begun to build. We have been far more concerned with statements and resolutions than with the reality of our growing more and more apart. More and more of the young Jews of Israel are rooted in the land and the language and in the literature of Israel reborn. Outside of Israel our young people know little Hebrew, near zero of the literature and not much more of Torah.

Then came June 5th, and Jewish people were suddenly united as never before. The ultra-Liberal and the ultra-Orthodox were caught up in a common concern for Jewish survival. They were joined by those who had no religious association whatsoever—nor many of them secular Jewish association for that matter either. They were moved by what Al Vorspan has called a "primal visceral gut" reaction. The united response of American Jews was a miracle that was second only to the miracle of Israel itself. Never in history—not even during the Hitler Holocaust or Israel's War of Independence or the Sinai Campaign were the

Jewish people so united and so responsive both politically (not that it helped Israel) and financially. Never was so much money given by so many different people in so short a period of time.

Perhaps the most dramatic element of all was the outpouring of teenagers and college students—many of the "lost generation"—ready to go as volunteers to be used in any way that Israel deemed necessary—to pick the fruit and vegetables or to pick up the wounded.

It was an outpouring of spiritual sentimental sensitivity—a sense of belonging to that world-wide Jewish people which defies description! Without debate, without picayune semantics, secularists and atheists and religionists felt part of this world-wide Jewish people, with Israel as the spiritual center and Jerusalem as the spiritual capital and the Western Wall as the spiritual symbol.

We came by thousands from every corner of America on Thursday, June 8, the fourth day of the war; and directly across the street from the White House we declared out loud, unabashed, our complete identification with the State and the people of Israel. The issue of dual loyalties did not concern us. Whether we were American Jews or Jewish Americans was an academic question! The only real and relevant fact was our Jewishness.

TACHLIT

Will the miracle now fade away because Israel has passed from "serious danger to successful resistance" (to borrow a phrase from Abba Eban)? Are we so crisis-conditioned that Jewish sentiment, courage, sacrifice and commitment can be evoked only by the threat of genocide and the memory of the Holocaust?

Or can we convert the crisis reaction into a permanent partnership—a permanent peoplehood? Can we continue the search for a definition of Jewishness within a framework of unqualified peoplehood made possible by some kind of mystical common denominator embracing ultra-orthodox, ultra-liberals, Diaspora and *Eretz*—and also those with no ideological Jewish commitment, no real sense of being Jewish, except the vague awareness that they were born Jews—the thousands who came "crawling out of the woodwork." What brought all these diverse elements together? Was it only the sensitive antennae of a people who had been through the Hitler Holocaust and was therefore especially sensitive to the genocide, clearly proclaimed by the Arab world: and who were determined that never again would Jews submit like sheep to the slaughter? Or was there something deeper, some sense of history, some awareness of Jewish destiny, a feeling that this was a rendezvous with destiny.

There are no easy answers but it is clear that explanations will not be found if we limit ourselves to academic discussions or sterile attempts to define our unity and our destiny in the old ideological formulas. We will develop the meaning and the feeling of Jewish peoplehood only as we establish living links between us and the people of Israel, if we build a "bridge of communication."

Here then are some challenges:

I. Are we prepared to confront the question of *Aliyah*? If we are partners in the preservation of peoplehood, and we believe the State and the land of Israel to be essential to our existence, and if we accept as a premise that no part of Israel is really part of the Jewish State unless it has Jewish settlers—East Jerusalem will not really be Jewish unless large numbers of Jews settle there—are we prepared to sponsor the proposition that every Jewish family should have at least one of its children living in Israel?

II. Can we establish as a *mitzvah* the sacred obligation incumbent on every family to make at least one pilgrimage to Israel? These pilgrimages should not just be sightseeing tours.

These are some of the possibilities:

a. One month study seminars in cooperation with the HUC in Jerusalem or the Jewish Agency or some other Israeli institution or some Kibbutz or Progressive Congregation and/or the Leo Baeck School in Haifa.

b. The creation of a resort village where Israeli and American Jews would spend a month together in organized dialogues and discussions:
   (1) What was the miracle of June 5th?
   (2) What is the mystique of Jewish unity?
   (3) What is the vision of Messianic redemption?

c. A six month sabbatical for the entire family with the parents attending an Ulpan while the children go to school.

d. Dialogues with our liturgical brothers and sisters in the Progressive Congregations; what can we do to strengthen them?

III. If such a pilgrimage can not be made a *mitzvah* for the entire family, can we make it one for our young people?

a. Will UAHC and CCAR expand and publicize the NFTY Pilgrimages, the EIE and all the other pilgrimages, study programs, work opportunities, i.e. *Sherut La-Am* sponsored by the Jewish Agency, the study programs of the Hebrew University, Brandeis-Hiatt, etc.

b. Will we encourage congregational scholarships and subsidies for these study and work programs?

IV. Can we develop special seminars and sabbaticals for the re-orientation of Rabbis in order to "inspire" our spiritual leaders to build these living links between Israel and American Jewry?

a. Will congregations subsidize their Rabbi's participation once in five years at a summer seminar at HUC in Jerusalem?

b. Will congregations finance suggested seminars and sabbaticals in Israel?

c. Will our Regional and Annual CCAR meetings set aside time to discuss these challenges? The Israel Embassy is prepared to send competent staff.

V. Will each congregation organize an Israel Committee for the above and also examine what we do on the homefront?

a. About conducting campaigns for UJA and Israel Bonds—as congregational commitments.

b. About "political" activity in support of Israel.

c. Concerning the intensification of the study of Hebrew at NFTY camp, Torah Corps and at special programs in Israel.

d. To provide financial support of Progressive Judaism in Israel.

e. To bring an "Israeli-in-Residence" to larger congregations to teach on every level.

If we make even a humble beginning in this direction, we would begin to measure the intensification of our congregational and communal life that will follow. We would really experience what Israel has done for American Jewry.

I. Israel is the counterpoint to the humiliation and the horror of the Holocaust. The morale of ordinary Jews everywhere has been heightened–
  a. Twenty years ago by the miracle of Israel reborn.
  b. On June 5th, by the miracle of Israel's remarkable resistance against genocide. "Their triumph is our triumph" to quote again from the closing sentences of the CCAR Resolution of last June. "Jews could look Hannah Arendt and Bruno Bettelheim squarely in the eye" (*Reconstructionist,* November 3, 1967).

II. Israel, in general, and June 5th, specifically, put an end to the ideological gap between Zionist and non-Zionist. Every Jew and every Jewish group is pro-Israel (with the exception of a few extremists in the American Council for Judaism).

III. The very existence of Israel has saved many an alienated Jew. Israel has served as a magnet drawing thousands from near assimilation. Or as David Polish put it, "Israel has made inroads among the unconcerned."

IV. Israel has made the Bible come alive again. It is a living literature for the school age generation and it is a living land with real people who are farming and building and defending the land of Abraham and Isaiah.

V. Israel has made the vision of Messianic redemption come alive again:
  a. The ingathering of the exiles.
  b. A light unto central African and Central American nations.

VI. The many miracles of Israel: survival, redemption of Jerusalem and the Western Wall, the stirring of American and world Jewry (like nothing else), the resurrection of Hebrew as a living language.

VII. The meaning of "Miracle and Providence." Did God save Israel? Or did Israel save God?

It will also stimulate a reevaluation of what we think we have done for Israel.

1. Philanthropy.
2. Investments.
3. Sending young people for study or service.
4. Encouragement of tourism and pilgrimages.
5. "Exporting" Reform–not for the purpose of creating an exact pattern but to stimulate the search for new, non-Orthodox ways of expressing our faith.
6. Building a Progressive Rabbinical School in Jerusalem.

If we begin to forge these living links, if we begin to build a "bridge of communication," then our rediscovered peoplehood and the sense of interlocking destiny which gripped us last June will not fade away.

We may even be moved to add a second Shema to our services:

"Shema Yisrael, Yisrael Goralenu, Yisrael echod!"

"Hear O Israel, Israel is our destiny, Israel is one!"

WHAT ARE THE 'ZIONIST MITZVOT'?*

It is a Mitzvah:

1. *To visit Israel as often as possible*. Every Jewish family should make a pilgrimage to Jerusalem at least once every seven years, if possible in connection with some family celebration, such as Bar or Bat Mitzvah. This is the minimal fulfillment of the Mitzvah of "*Aliyat Regel*"—the traditional pilgrimage to the land of Israel, whereby the Jew renews his ties with the homeland.

2. *To encourage our children to participate in the various study and work programs in Israel designed for teenage and college students*. There is a variety of programs involving study at one of Israel's universities or work on a Kibbutz. Of particular importance is the year-long program of "*Sherut La'am*." Families should plan for this as part of their children's Zionist education by setting aside special funds beforehand.

3. *To read the classic literature of the Zionist Renaissance and to know the Biblical roots of Zionism*—especially the Biblical passages that deal with the promise of redemption—the *Hazon Geulah M'Sheechee*—the Vision of Messianic Redemption—"The Bible and the Promised Land."

4. *To study Hebrew* and minimally to be familiar with Hebraic terms and phrases which represent the philosophical and ideological premises that are basic to Judaism and Zionism. No single English word is an adequate translation for *geulah* or *shevat Tziyon*, or *galut*, or *eretz*, or *oleh regel*, or *binyan ha-aretz*. Maximally, it is desirable to learn enough Hebrew to read the classic Biblical passages or to follow an easy Hebrew newspaper or to carry on a simple Hebrew conversation. It is imperative for every American Jew to join a local Ulpan.

5. *To join some branch of the Zionist movement* and/or participate in a congregational Israel Committee or sub-committee.

6. *To make a contribution* to the United Jewish Appeal, to buy Israel Bonds and to participate in selected fund-raising programs on behalf of Israel (Hadassah, Hebrew University, Histadrut, etc.).

7. *To be politically sensitive* to the situation in which we find ourselves and to be ready to participate in community action or to use our telephones to telegraph or write our Senators and Congressmen, the State Department or the President—to take whatever steps are essential to guarantee the necessary diplomatic, military and financial support requisite for the safe existence and survival of Israel.

8. *To uphold the moral right of Israel's rebirth* as an independent state on its ancestral soil—and also to constantly remind America and the western countries of this moral right.

*Reprinted from *Jewish Frontier* 44/1 (January, 1977), 15.

9. *To share the cultural life of Israel* to the degree to which one is capable, thereby strengthening the spiritual bonds linking Israel and the Jewish people. This includes Hebrew literature, celebrating Israeli holidays and functions and learning and singing the songs of Israel's rebirth and hopes.

10. *To maintain warm relationships* with some family in *Eretz Yisrael* and so establish strong friendships.

*THE NEW HAGGADAH IN ISRAEL**
Passover Supplementary Haggadah

The *Exodus* from Egypt has been one of the continuing experiences of the Jewish people since the time of that first *Exodus* from ancient Egypt. In our time, the *Exodus* continues from the Soviet Satellites and from Egypt, from North Africa and from other Arab Lands.

*Invocation (*Ha Lachna Anya*)*

Lo! Let all who have been afflicted with the scourge of Fascism, Communism and Nasserism come to share the Seder of Redemption in the Homeland! Let all those who are hungry, enter and eat with us; let those who are homeless come and celebrate next Passover. This year still finds some of our brothers in the lands of exile. May next year find them safely in the land of Israel. This year some Jews are still enslaved by insecurity, threatened by pogroms and engulfed by homelessness. Next year may all of them be free in Israel at peace with historic Jerusalem reunited and redeemed.

*Four Modern Questions (*Mah Nishtanah*)*

Why is Passover different now from previous Passovers "Since the State of Israel was reborn on *Iyar* 5, 5708, May 14, 1948."

ONE: Every other Passover some of our people have been enslaved and some of our people have tasted the fruits of freedom. Now all who are still enslaved can be redeemed by coming to the Land of Israel.

TWO: Every other Passover a free Israel has not been included among the variegated family of nations. This Passover there is included among free peoples of the world a representative of that people whose lot has been the bitterest of all.

THREE: Every other Passover we have hardly dipped into our resources. On this Passover we are dipping into all our strength and energy to keep our newborn state secure and we expect our American brothers and sisters to dip into their resources as they have never dipped before, to contribute to the Israel Emergency Fund of the United Jewish Appeal and to purchase Bonds of the Israel government.

FOUR: On all other Passovers, and this Passover, too, in the Jewish communities of the Diaspora, some have been enthroned as kings; others beg for freedom. This Passover, all who can come to the Land of Israel will find there no kings and no beggars; for all are equally enthroned with the crown of Freedom.

*Slaves Were We (*Avadim Hayeenu*)*

Slaves were we unto Hitler in Naziland, and unto Nasser in Egypt, and unto the Kremlin in Sovietland, but God has redeemed us and continued to redeem us with strong

*(Miami Beach, 1974).

hands and the outstretched arms of Israel's people. Had this not happened, we and our children and our children's children might still be enslaved under Fascism and as millions are still enslaved under Communism. Therefore, even though we are now wiser men, because of our enslavement under twentieth century tyranny and even though the memory is still fresh in our minds, it behooves us each year to dwell upon the story of our *Exodus* and the drama of our redemption from Naziland and Egyptland and Sovietland, and to recall our bitter struggle to defeat the enemy and to zealously guard our independence. Thus, by dint of our continued retelling of this glorious epic, the meaning and value of freedom will be indelibly impressed on our minds and hearts and we shall strengthen our determination to keep its blessings for ourselves and our children.

And more, we shall not rest until yet another chapter has been added to the Haggadah when those enslaved behind the Iron Curtain and those in exile in North Africa or on any continent have been redeemed.

The Four Kinds of Modern Jews

The story of the *Exodus* was told and retold from generation to generation. It was especially a delight for children. But children are not all alike, as the Rabbis discovered many centuries ago. In fact, they divided all children into four groups. There are some who do not have any questions to ask. There are some who are indifferent. There are some who are downright wicked and disrespectful, and there are those who are curious and interested and truly wise.

An so, today, we say there are four kinds of modern Jews—those who are evil, those who are indifferent and whose lives are too simple—and those so far removed from Jewish realities, they don't even know that Jews have problems.

There's the ONE WHO "DOESN'T KNOW ENOUGH TO ASK"—the one who is so far removed from Jewish life that he is unaware of the festivals of our faith or the problems of our people—this one will be lost to us if we don't wake him up. He doesn't belong to a synagogue; he doesn't buy Israel Bonds; he doesn't identify himself clearly with anything Jewish. He doesn't deny that he a Jew; in fact, he considers himself a good Jew "at heart." He must be awakened from this kind of passive Jewishness if he is not to be "lost." And it may be that he was stirred by the "Six Days That Shook The World."

THERE IS ANOTHER—THE "SIMPLE ONE," THE INDIFFERENT ONE. His desires and needs are small. He earns a good living, goes to the movies, watches T.V., takes a trip overseas. Jewish life doesn't touch him because he is busy in his small tasks, and because he rarely thinks. He does not concern himself with anything Jewish, except when a baby is born, or his son is Bar Mitzvah, or his daughter is Confirmed, or someone is getting married, or when the inevitable end comes. Such a man can be roused from his indifference.

AND THE EVIL ONE—"HE IS THE SMART ONE." He is the one who is always worried about a "back-lash" that will affect his own security in these United States. If the Conference of Presidents of National Jewish Organizations speaks out on behalf of Israel, he feels his loyalty to America is undermined. When Jewish religious leaders and all major national Jewish bodies participate in the struggle for human rights for every American citizen regardless of creed or color, he is concerned that his position is endangered. He draws a false line between Judaism and the Jewish people—between Judaism and human rights. And we wonder whether the drama of Israel's redemption from bondage can rouse him to an understanding that REDEMPTION is our real religious heritage. We wonder whether he was stirred by the "Six Days That Shook The World."

THE WISE ONE—HE KNOWS THE LESSONS AND THE MORALS OF JEWISH HISTORY. He has great pride in his people and their accomplishments. He does not think it's unsophisticated to be reared in Jewish tradition, to respect it and love it. He does not sneer at the Hebrew language. He teaches his children the spirit of Judaism and the language of our faith. He understands our problems and is loyal to our needs. He is a Builder of the synagogue; and the State of Israel for he knows that in America, survival is spelled S-Y-N-A-G-O-G-U-E; and for the Jews of the Soviet Satellites and of North Africa and of Egypt, survival is spelled S-T-A-T-E!

WITH SUCH WISE JEWS WE SHALL SOME DAY CELEBRATE A *SEDER* OF UNIVERSAL FREEDOM FOR ISRAEL AND ALL MANKIND.

READER: You haven't fully celebrated Passover unless you have actually tasted the bitterness of bondage and resolved never to inflict it upon another person's spirit or will.

CONG: You haven't fully celebrated Passover until you have felt the anguish of those whose daily fare is not much more ample than unleavened bread and have resolved to help alleviate their plight.

READER: You haven't fully celebrated Passover unless you have taken fresh delight in the glories of the nascent Spring Season.

CONG: You haven't fully celebrated Passover unless you have truly said DAYENU: "Thank you, O lord, for the blessings which are mine. Even a fraction of them would excite my gratitude!"

READER: You haven't fully celebrated Passover unless you have acquired renewed appreciation of a house-wife's toil and talent.

CONG: You haven't fully celebrated Passover unless, like Moses, you realize that you are obligated to resist evil that threatens not yourself, but others.

READER: You haven't fully celebrated Passover until you have realized that Judaism summons you to sing as well as to sigh, to feast as well as fast, play as well as pray.

CONG: You haven't fully celebrated Passover unless you have decided to prove yourself worthy of the suffering, the sacrifice, and the courage of your more farseeing predecessors.

READER: You haven't fully celebrated Passover until you have sensed again that Judaism is a faith which likes to be explained.

CONG: You haven't fully celebrated Passover unless you have understood that the opinions and the ideas of children deserve to be honored.

READER: You haven't fully celebrated Passover until you have sharpened your appetite for freedom... for yourself and the other fellow.

SERVICE OF MEMORIAL FOR THE HEROES AND THE MARTYRS OF THE WARSAW GHETTO*

The Anniversary of the Warsaw Ghetto Revolt

The memory of the WARSAW GHETTO REVOLT becomes more luminous with the passing of the years and it has now become a historic custom for the Jewish people to commemorate the uprising of the Ghetto Jews against their Nazi tormentors and murderers during Passover 1943. Thousands of desperate, sick, tired Jews, young and old, rose against the modern Pharaoh in Warsaw and died for the honor of their people and for the cause of human freedom.

The events which led up to and culminated in the Ghetto uprising continue to live in the collective memory of the Jewish people. There has arisen, in Ludwig Lewisohn's phrase, "A new literature of martyrdom." But the Warsaw Ghetto Jews are being remembered in other ways as well. In Israel, Kibbutz Yad Mordecai exists as a living memorial to Mordecai Anielwicz, leader of the uprising; and in Jewish communities throughout the world the revolt's significance is recalled in concrete ways, just as we set aside the Day of Memorial in remembrance of these heroic martyrs.

Understanding the Holocaust

In different parts of the world—and on sites of the various concentration camps: Buchenwald, Bergen-Belsen, Auschwitz and Dachau—Jews will gather to recite the Prayer of Remembrance along with the Kaddish.

We dare not forget! Six million cannot become "a rapidly fading moment in history," as one columnist recently wrote.

In April, exactly twenty-nine years ago, the first Allied Forces (from the West) liberated Bergen-Belsen and Buchenwald. We must never forget how "they were staggered by what they saw, heard and smelled."

Arthur Friedlander reminds us in the introduction to "Out of the Whirlwind": "Darkness pervaded every street of every town, city and country occupied by Nazi Germany. The innermost circle of this geography of hell was the concentration camp. Once inside this circle, humanity moved from the light of day to the valley of the shadow of death. Yet, life did go on. And the testimony of survivors of that life reaches out to us, demanding our concern, our attention, our anguish, and our dedication for tasks left undone, for the expansion of our own experience which must come to encompass those six million lives and bring them back into a world which must not and dares not forget all that took place."

And so we must enter the past. Somehow, we must enter the Holocaust and its geography in this two-fold way: with a clear mind and with the humility and openness linked in the Bible with the contrite soul. Only then will we see, and seeing, understand.

*(Miami Beach, 1974).

Service for the Six Million Who Died During the Shoah

RABBI: Remember, O Lord, the decimation of Thy people, be mindful of our woeful bereavement.

CONG: No generation in Israel's long and sorrowful chronicle has known a destruction as immense as we have witnessed in this age.

RABBI: We have seen the design of the ancient tyrant well nigh accomplished in our day: "to destroy, to slay, and exterminate all Jews, both young and old, little children and women."

CONG: The household of Israel was devastated, its sanctuaries were desecrated, its houses of learning razed, its treasures looted; its elders and sages and guardians and people were slain.

RABBI: With wanton cruelty and consummate craft, strange lethal devices were wielded against us to destroy us utterly.

CONG: We were accounted as sheep for slaughter. We were crushed into the dust and covered with the shadow of death.

RABBI: Smitten, impaled and suffocated, burned, poisoned and buried alive, the hosts of Israel, perished in daylight and in darkness, in camps, in sealed box cars, in open fields, in murky forests, in foul tunnels.

CONG: Taken from the pursuit of their labors, from the study of Thy law, from their homes, from their hiding places and while fleeing from the relentless sword.

RABBI: Remember, O Lord, the decimation of Thy people, be mindful of our vast bereavement.

Chanukah Cantata*

The light that is never extinguished
A chanukah candlelight service

RABBI:

Almighty god!
Thou, who are the source of all our inspiration
Thou, who didst inspire Herzl and Weitzman and
Ben-Gurion and Menachem Begin
To recreate the Jewish Nation
On this Chanukah Festival we turn to Thee
As we kindle again the flame of liberty.

O Protector of mankind's sacred rights,
Thou who dost bid us kindle the lights
Of Freedom; for these candles aflame
Israel's ancient blessings we now proclaim.

CANTOR
AND CHOIR:

Kindling of chanukah lights - *Brachot*

RABBI:

Wonders and miracles Thou didst perform,
In those days when Antiochus didst storm
Against our fathers in Israel's ancient land,
But Thou didst save us through the Maccabean band!

Once there were miracles that took place in Israel's land
Miracles of which we're told.
But miracles are something we moderns have difficulty
Trying to understand,
What miracles do we ever behold?

CANTOR:

Oh, come my dear child, a tale I will tell you,
A tale full of miracles grand
The older you'll grow and the more you will ponder,
The more you will then understand.

We once had a Temple in ages of yore,
Magnificent, passing all measure,

*(Miami Beach, 1977).

And 'mongst all its implements, many and rare
A lamp was, a wonderful treasure.

For ages this lamp, it has burned and warmed
With radiance kindly and human
Its rays that have shone on the forebears of yore
Did later their grandsons illumine.

Since then many years, many ages have passed.
From its homeland our people was driven,
The Temple lies waste, all its implements gone,
But left is the light that's God-given!

RABBI: Those are beautiful words, but we remain in the dark,
What have these miracles to do with this lamp?
We know of this lamp that ever burns before the Ark
First kindled in Israel's desert camp.
But what is the miracle—where is the wonder?
We find it very, very hard
To believe in these wonders of which you thunder –
Miracles performed by God!

And yet of that very lamp the miracle's to be found.
For it's a lamp that's ever aflame!
It's a beacon to all who are imprisoned and bound,
Silently it will ever proclaim!

CHOIR: Give me your tired, your poor
Your huddled masses yearning to breathe free,
The wretched refuse of your teeming shore,
Send these the homeless, tempest tost to me,
I lift my lamp beside the golden door!

RABBI: Thus, Emma Lazarus forged another link in the chain
Between the Lamp and the Torch of Liberty's hand!
That's the miracle, so hard to explain.
Now, do you begin to understand?

Into the darkness of exile from Zion of old
Came faith's everlasting light
This is the miracle of which we are told.
This lamp which burns so bright!

Across the seas of America's shore
Came the Lamp of Liberty.
Against tyrants 200 years ago, O how this lamp did score
Making men yearn to breathe free!

We built synagogues in this free and blessed land
We re-kindled the *Ner Tamid* of old.
This is the miracle perhaps we sometimes don't understand
Of a faith that never grew cold!

35 years ago we began to build Beth Sholom
While the entire world was at war.
The theme of the Founders of our Spiritual Home
Was, there shall be war no more!

But it was also that we rekindled the *Ner Tamid* –
The Eternal Light.
In the midst of the blackout of World War II
We sensed that part of the determination of the Jewish people
To fight for the Right
To live – was sustaining the Will to Survive!
In the Heart of Every Jew.

At Chanukah time 35 years ago we already knew
That the Nazis had the Synagogues and Schools destroyed
Even as the Nazis were determined to slaughter every Jew.
They burnt the synagogues–hoping that thus Jewish
Resistance would be destroyed!

In the Town of Zborow, where my father had studied and prayed
His synagogue and School, we knew 35 years ago, was no more,
So here in this corner of America the foundation was laid
For our Beth Sholom was created to even the score!

We built here a New House of Prayer.
A New Center of Learning.
To replace at least one of the Synagogues that
The Nazis had burnt.

We have succeeded–the Eternal Light of Faith is Still
Burning–Recharging our Spiritual Batteries–and
The Timeless Tradition is still learned!

And on this Chanukah–our 35 Anniversary Chanukah –
For this House of Peace.

On this Chanukah when the Miracle of the Jewish people
Is once again validated.

On this Chanukah when we pray
That the momentum for peace will increase.

We affirm our faith with prayer–Our God is One –
Our faith is never dated.

CANTOR AND CHOIR: Chanukah songs

RABBI: Even our century began with pogroms in a Czarist city.
Kishinev was the city of slaughter.
Pogroms became crematoria—the world had no pity.
Even Europe became a continent of slaughter.
Kishinev is replaced by the General Assembly of the United Nations.
Zionism is the new object of international scorn.
It's the old racism in new anti-Semitic variations—
The old sacrificial scapegoat is reborn.

The hatred has not ceased; in 1977 it's very much alive.
The Red tyranny, the communist conspiracy from behind
A border that is still an Iron Curtain
The Third World and the Arab Bloc don't want to see
Judaism or Western civilization survive
And the future—all that we cherish—
Remains so terribly uncertain.

Then what good is it to kindle this lamp, so different
And odd,
Even though we believe that eternal is its flame!
For what seems to be eternal—for the chosen of God—
Is that the world stands by when Terrorists try
To put the Jews to shame!

That's what the hi-jackers thought at Entebbe last July
When they held our people hostage in a strange land.
They sent word to Jerusalem the hostages would die
Unless Israel met their demands.
More than this, there was once again a separation—
Jews to the left—non-Jews to the right
Spoken by terrorists with a German accent—
And to Idi Amin's delight
Paris and Washington and London—silent!—
No hope for these Jewish hostages it seemed
But in Jerusalem—our people felt differently—
The hostages had to be redeemed.

We Jews cannot be shamed any more—And the impossible
Achieved realization that gave new faith to the Jewish people
And was also an example for all of Western civilization
Believing in peace, we Jews had too long forgotten
The art of battle
And sometimes Jews were merely to be slaughtered like cattle
So it had been during the Holocaust—But never again —

No more can Jews be the victims of those who believe
That terror can settle some imaginary score!

We Jews still want to be considered soldiers of the Lord
But we no longer are going to be the easiest victims
Of the sword!
Because we will not forget how Bialik,
The poet laureate did sarcastically condemn
His people—seventy years ago—who did not
Know how to fight like men.
Kishinev pogrom they simply ran to the synagogue to pray
And Bialik felt that he had to arouse his people
In another way
And the words of Bialik impressed themselves
On many a Jewish heart.
Bialik's sarcasm moved young Jews to a new Maccabean star.

"Look at these Maccabean descendants—
Died like dogs—they and their dependents.
Look how they sanctify the name of the Lord—
They perish in pits—slain by the sword
Sons of the lion-hearted heroes of old,
Dying like dogs—yes, they're bold!
On the morrow they go to the synagogue to pray
They cry out to God aloud, and say:
'Almighty God, we have sinned' This is their cry,
But don't think of vengeance. Don't even try!"

After Bialik these bitter words had spoken,
The prison spell of exile was finally broken.
This is the miracle—that Jews never lost faith,
Despite their constant pain and sorrow—
Because they believe that oil for one day
Lasted through the eighth
They continued to believe in tomorrow!
That light kept alive courage and hope
Until the time came again for modern Maccabees to show it
In Jerusalem high on Mount Scopus slope
This is the miracle of faith captured by the poet.

CANTOR: Laugh at all my dreams, my dearest;
Laugh, and I repeat anew
That I still believe in man—
As I still believe in you.

For my soul is not yet sold
To the golden calf of scorn
And I still believe in man
And the spirit in him born.

RABBI: Tchernichovsky spoke and Bialik spoke and David Frishman spoke
And they began to lift from the people – persecution's yoke
Bialik's City of Slaughter, his people did condemn
Because they had forgotten how to fight like men.
Frishman's Messiah – locked up in chains
Unable to relieve the people's aches and pains
And the people crying, when will the Messiah come?
When will he begin to redeem?
When will he fulfill the hope and the dream?
And a voice was heard answering:

"Until a new generation arises,
A generation that will understand redemption,
A generation that will desire to be redeemed,
Whose soul will be prepared to be redeemed!
Then wilt thou, too, achieve thy destiny and be redeemed:
Then wilt thou, too, achieve thy destiny and redeem!"

That generation has risen
The light which had smoldered became a torch of resistance,
No longer did Israel depend on God alone for assistance.
The smoldering candle became a heroic, glorious flame.
Jews fought back proudly, no longer dying in shame!

Once again like Maccabees, Jews fought back
When the Cossacks in Russia launched an attack.
Chalutzim through *Hashomer* fought back
When against their colonies Arabs launched an attack.
Jewish partisans in Europe against Nazis fought back
Whenever they had arms with which to attack.

Jews had become again the hammer of Maccabean glory,
Hammering, they have hammered out a new Jewish State.
Hammering, they have hammered out something
That will continue to shape their fate.

A third Jewish Commonwealth has come to stay,
No powers on earth will say our people nay!
And the lights of Chanukah were not kindled in vain,
Jews have become brave heroes once again,
No longer just looking dreamily into the lights of chanukah
Jews everywhere cry out – I am a Zionist –
That is the miracle of Haganah!

CANTOR: (solo) Haganah Song *(Shir Ha Hagana)*

RABBI: Because of Haganah, we have celebrated the tenth year
Since the Six Days that shook the world,
When Israel's Haganah

Demonstrated that Jews have overcome their fear
And they drove the Arab aggressors out of Sinai
And the West Bank and out of the Golan Heights.

The Jews demonstrated to the world
That we have the right to elementary human rights.

An now Jews have settled on the Golan–
And they till the soil–and they build industry–
And they want to live in peace.
We reach out our hands and hearts to them,
For they will stay in the Golan
Til Arab aggression will cease.

CANTOR: (solo) Mountains of Golan Song (*Shir Haray Golan)*

RABBI: We have also celebrated the tenth anniversary
Of Jerusalem redeemed and reunited.

An historic distortion at long last has been righted
And Jews are free–so also Moslems and Christians–
Free to go to all the holy places.
In David's City of Peace–
One does indeed see many different faces.

In fact, the entire world did indeed see a strange face
In Jerusalem–the face of Anwar Sadat–Egypt's President!
And with the protection of the Israel Defense Forces,
He was safe in prayer at the Al'Aksa Mosque–
It was quite evident!
On the Eve of Israel Reborn's 30th Anniversary–
Miracle of Miracles!–
From the land of the Pharaohs came a
Courageous Arab leader to *Yerushalayim*
And he was received with outstretched arms–
Everyone had flags of Welcome in their hands–
In their *yadayim*!
A sight never to be forgotten–
the President and the Prime Minister of Israel
Saying to Sadat: "*Shalom*."
He responding, "No more war!"

We can together make of the Middle East
A Sanctuary of *Shalom*!

Is it all a dream?
Is Jerusalem forever redeemed?

Can we believe that it is forever redeemed
Because it is the prelude to the great dream
That we Jews have dreamed?

For this is where the prophets were inspired by our Lord
To dream of that day when no nation
Would ever lift up the sword!

No more war!
Sadat spoke these words in reunited, redeemed Jerusalem.

No more war
He proclaimed in Israel's Parliamentary Home!

No more war!
Between Egypt and Israel!

No more war!
Some day not only Egypt and Israel–
Not only Jews and Arabs,
But we dare to believe some day all peoples
Will coexist in *Shalom*!

*A TREASURY OF INSPIRATION**

Dedicated to my
beloved Congregation

Foreword

These are (some of) the texts that have influenced my rabbinical career. Even before I studied these texts I was nurtured by the warm, vibrant folk-faith that permeated the family life of my parents and grandparents. I am native to this land; yet I am also a child of Jerusalem as well as Zborow and Most and Raveruska, where my parents and grandparents were born. They brought with them from Eastern Europe a respect for and a love of learning, a very deep sense of kinship with the Jewish people, the dream of Messianic redemption and a moral and ethical outlook that was transmitted from generation to generation—flowed out of their saturation with the spirit of these sacred scriptural sections that have shaped my spiritual leadership.

The Volume Contains Selections from:

Torah
Mordecai M. Kaplan
Milton Steinberg
A.D. Gordon
Isaiah
Maimonides
Columbus Platform
Joshua Liebman
Psalms
Theodor Herzl
Maurice Sandmel
Ezekiel
Stephen S. Wise
Legends of the Bible
David Ben-Gurion
Ahad Ha'am
Amos

*Composed on the 25th anniversary of Rabbi Leon Kronish's tenure at Temple Beth Sholom (December, 1969).

Table One

TEMPLE BETH SHOLOM PRESIDENTS

	1.	Alfred Rosenstein	July 1942
	2.	Abraham Frankel	1943
	3.	Morris Berick	1944-45-46
	4.	Harry A. Cornblum	1947-48
	5.	Sam Lachman	1948-49
	6.	Shepard Broad	1950-51-52
*	7.	Leon Ell	1952-53-54
*	8.	Ralph Spero	1954-55-56
*	9.	John Serbin	1957-58
*	10.	Harry Arthur Greenberg	1959-60
*	11.	James Albert	1961-62-63
*	12.	Louis Snetman	1964-65-66
*	13.	Jack Fink	1967-68-69
*	14.	Eli Katzen	1970-71-72
	15.	James Knopke	1973-74-75-76
	16.	Milton Gaynor	1977-78-79
	17.	Harold Vinik	1980-81-82-83
	18.	Neal Amdur	1984-85-86-87
	19.	Helen Kotler	1988-89-90
	20.	Marvin Stonberg	1991-92-93
	21.	Michael Dribin	1994-

*Deceased

END NOTES

Chapter One

1. Erik Erikson, *Young Man Luther* (New York, 1962).
2. For writings and biographies of Stephen Wise, see Stephen S. Wise, *Challenging Years: the Autobiography of Stephen Wise* (New York, 1949), Melvin Urofsky, *A Voice that Spoke for Justice: the Life and Times of Stephen S. Wise* (Albany, 1982) and Robert Shapiro, *A Reform Rabbi in the Progressive Era: the Early Career of Stephen S. Wise* (New York, 1988). For writings and biographies of Mordecai Kaplan, see Mordecai Kaplan, *Judaism as a Civilization* (New York, 1967), Mordecai Kaplan, *Dynamic Judaism,* ed. E. S. Goldsmith and Mel Scult (New York, 1985), Richard Libowitz, *Mordecai Kaplan and the Development of Reconstructionism (New* York, 1983) and Mel Scult, *Judaism Faces the Twentieth Century:* A *Biography of Mordecai M. Kaplan* (Detroit, 1993).
3. See Michael Meyer, *The Origins of the Modern Jew* (Detroit, 1967) and *Response to Modernity* (Oxford, 1988), 1-223; Gunther Plaut, *The Rise of Reform Judaism* (New York, 1963); and Steven Lowenstein, "The 1840s and the Creation of the German Jewish Reform Movement," in W. Mosse, A. Paucker, R. Rurup, eds., *Revolution and Evolution: 1848 in German-Jewish History* (Tübingen, 1981), 255-297.
4. See Arnold Eisen, *The Chosen People in America:* A *Study of Religious Ideology* (Bloomington, 1983), and Marshall Sklare, ed., *The Jews: Social Patterns of an American Group* (New York, 1958) for both ideological and sociological developments of American Jewry in the decades immediately following World War Two.
5. Michael Meyer, "Reform Judaism" in R. Seltzer, ed., *Judaism: A People and its History* (New York, 1987), 307.
6. Stephen Wise's role in American Zionism has been well-documented. See, among others, Yonathan Shapiro, *Leadership of the American Zionist Organization, 1897-1930* (Urbana, 1971) and Melvin Urofsky, *American Zionism: From Herzl to Holocaust* (New York, 1975).
7. Stephen Wise, *JIR Annual,* 1926.
8. See Samuel Karff, ed., *Hebrew Union College-Jewish Institute of Religion at One Hundred Years* (Cincinnati, 1976), 137-169.
9. The Reconstructionist Rabbinical College was inaugurated in October, 1968 in Philadelphia.
10. Harold Schulweis, "Reconstructionist Judaism," in Seltzer, ed., *Judaism: A People and its History,* 301-302.

11. Mordecai Kaplan, E. Kohn and I. Eisenstein, eds. *The New Haggadah for the Pesah Seder* (New York, 1941) and Mordecai Kaplan, *Reconstructionist Sabbath Prayer Book* (New York, 1945).
12. For example, Kronish's activities with Theodore Gibson of the Miami Chapter of the NAACP, and "ban the bomb" movement, most poignantly expressed in his letters to Presidents Truman and Eisenhower. See Chapter Four, 106-112.
13. See for example, Kronish's *Explanatory Notes to Shofar Services for Rosh Hashanah* (Miami Beach, 1970) and *The New Haggadah in Israel: Passover Supplementary Haggadah* (Miami Beach, 1974).
14. Kronish expressed these ties best in his article, "What are the 'Zionist *Mitzvot'?,* " *Jewish Frontier* 44/1 (January, 1977), 15.
15. Stephen Wise's organ to speak out for a Palestinian homeland and against oppression was the American Jewish Congress' publication, *Congress Weekly*.
16. Stephen Wise played an active role in American unionization. He advocated the right of labor to organize, helped the American Federation of Labor to unionize workers of the steel industry, and supported women's suffrage and union membership.
17. A.D. Gordon typifies this position. See his Collected Works (Tel Aviv, 1930), in Hebrew.
18. See H.Y. Roth, ed., *Ahad Ha'am: Collected Works* (Tel Aviv, 1976), in Hebrew.
19. *"Yisrael Goralenu, " CCAR Journal 16* (June, 1968), 31-37 and "What are the 'Zionist *Mitzvot'?"*.
20. Kronish, "*Yisrael Goralenu*," 31.
21. Polly Redford, *Billion-Dollar Sandbar: A Biography of Miami Beach* (New York, 1970), especially, 204-286 and H.A. Green, "The New Establishment: Miami's Jewry Post World War II," (Miami, 1990), paper presented at the Ethnic Minorities and Multi-cultural Conference.
22. *Miami Vice* was a television show that aired between 1984-1989.
23. Beth Jacob still serves the community as an Orthodox congregation. One of its buildings, a Henry Hohauser Art Deco masterpiece designed in 1936, will be reopened as the Jewish Museum of Florida in 1995.
24. The conversion of tourist facilities to wartime needs on Miami Beach led to the training of one-fourth of the Army Air Force officers, and one-fifth of the enlisted men on Miami Beach. Charlton Tebeau, A *History of Florida* (Coral Gables, 1971), 417.
25. Raymond Arsenault, "The End of the Long Hot Summer: The Air Conditioner and Southern Culture," in Ray Mohl, ed., *Searching for the Sunbelt* (Knoxville, 1990), 176-211.
26. Sermon, May 10, 1957.
27. Letter to President Truman, March 15, 1950.
28. *Life* magazine, January 12, 1962, 36.
29. *Chamberlain v. Dade County School Board,* 17 Florida Supp. 196, 1961 and 142 So. 2d, 21; *American Jewish Yearbook,* 62 (1961), 89-90; 63 (1962), 184-185; 64 (1963), 123 - 124.
30. For example, three members of his congregation in the 1970s and 1980s became president of the Greater Miami Jewish Federation (Jules Arkin, Harry Smith and Donald

Lefton); several took leading roles in Israel Bonds (Gary Gerson, Marvin Cooper, Milton Gaynor and James Knopke); some became cantors (Rachelle Nelson and Stephen Haas); a handful chose rabbinical careers—Marty Lawson (San Diego), Ronald Kronish (Jerusalem), Gregory Marks (Wynnwood, Pennsylvania) and Gerald Serotta (Washington); while others rose to leadership positions in national organizations such as the National Council of Jewish Women (Nan Herman Rich, Myra Farr).

31. Maxine Kronish Snyder, "My Father and My family: Growing Up Jewish" in Ronald Kronish, ed., *Towards the Twenty-First Century: Judaism and the Jewish People in Israel and America* (Hoboken, 1988), 334-335.

Chapter Two

1. See *Encyclopedia Judaica* 16 (Jerusalem, 1971), 945 for a description of Zborow. Zborow, currently in the Ukraine, was part of eastern Galicia in the early part of the twentieth century. For a history of the town see also the *Yizkor Buch* (memorial book) published by its *landmannschaften* in Israel in 1982. Yehuda Shamir informed me of this memorial volume.
2. There are many vivid descriptions of the migration process to the United States. See, for example, Irving Howe, *World of Our Fathers* (New York, 1976) and Ronald Sanders, *The Downtown Jews: Portrait of an Immigrant Generation* (New York, 1970).
3. By the early 1900s United States policy mandated that steamship companies return rejected immigrants to Europe at the shipping company's own expense. To offset any economic setback, immigrants were screened more carefully for diseases, lack of funds and invalid passports. The Kronish children, Zev and Leon, cannot remember the specific health problem, but they do recall hearing that it was a health problem that caused their father to be rejected by American immigration authorities. Interview with Leon Kronish, July 1988 and Zev Kronish, July 1988.
4. Howe, *World,* 33.
5. Interviews with Zev and Leon Kronish, July 1988.
6. See Stephen Speisman, *The Jews of Toronto* (Toronto, 1976), 71, 74, 76.
7. Interviews with Zev and Leon Kronish, July 1988.
8. See Speisman, *Jews of Toronto,* especially Part II, 79-208 for immigrant Jews in Toronto in the early twentieth century. For Cabbagetown and the Kensington Market area, the Greenbaum oral histories (Shooky and Pearl) provide first-person accounts. Interview with Murray Sidney Green, August 1988 and Pearl Greenbaum, August 1988.
9. The McCaul synagogue amalgamated with the University Avenue synagogue to form Beth Zedek in the 1950s and affiliated with the Conservative movement.
10. Interviews with Zev and Leon Kronish, July 1988.
11. *Ibid.* See Chapter Three, 71-72.
12. Interviews with Zev and Leon Kronish, July 1988.
13. Ewa Morawska, "The Sociology and Historiography of Immigration" in Virginia Yans-McLaughlin, ed., *Immigration Reconsidered* (Oxford, 1990), 203.
14. Albert Rees, *Real Wages in Manufacturing, 1890-1914* (Princeton, NJ., 1961), 3-16.
15. Lena Seligman was born in Most, Lithuania.

16. Interview with Leon Kronish, July 1988.
17. *Ibid.*
18. Zev was one of twins. His brother, Milton, died at four weeks old. Interview with Zev Kronish, July 1988.
19. Interview with Zev Kronish, July 1988.
20. After 1929 the socialist *Forward* supported Zionism.
21. Interviews with Zev and Leon Kronish, July 1988.
22. Howe, *World,* 163.
23. Interview with Leon Kronish, August 1989.
24. Interview with Leon Kronish, July 1988.
25. Louis Brandeis, *The Jewish Problem—How to Solve It* (New York, 1917), 12. In 1916 Brandeis was elected chairman of the Provisional Executive Committee for General Zionist Affairs. That year he was also appointed to the Supreme Court of the United States. Brandeis was the first Jew to serve on the highest court.
26. Lee O'Brien, *American Jewish Organizations and Israel* (Washington, 1986), 38.
27. Many years later Kronish recalled how important songs such as *Me-al Pisgat Har Hatzofim* ("from high on the hill of Mt. Scopus") played in awakening his Zionist feelings. See *Temple Beth Sholom Bulletin,* June 3, 1977. Interviews with Leon Kronish, July 1988 and Yehuda Ben Chorin (formerly Julius Freeman), August 1988.
28. *The Protocols of the Elders of Zion* was an anti-Semitic literary hoax written by an agent of the Russian secret police in the late nineteenth century. It was popularized in the United States by Henry Ford in his *Dearborn Independent* under the title, "The Jewish Peril." See Robert Singerman, "The American Career of *The Protocols of the Elders of Zion*," *American Jewish History* 71/1 (September, 1981), 48-78.
29. Quoted in *Congress Weekly* 16/12 (March 21, 1949), 5.
30. Sermon, April 23, 1959.
31. Kronish's first Hebrew teacher had been one of the Jewish legionnaires who helped free Jerusalem from the Turks during World War One.
32. Rabbi Kronish's interpretation of his bar mitzvah *sedrah* to the Temple Beth Sholom Saturday morning *havura*. Professor Yehuda Shamir, who has led a Torah and Prophet class to this *havura* for more than a decade, has passed it on to me.
33. The Kronishes lived on 385 Second Street South; the Austins, at 365 Second Street South.
34. Interview with Lillian Kronish, July 1988.
35. *Ibid*.
36. Deborah Dash Moore, At *Home in America: Second Generation New York Jews* (New York, 1981) is an illuminating history of Kronish's generation and the push and pull of assimilation/survival influences.
37. In 1939, the British government issued the MacDonald White Paper on Palestine limiting the number of Jewish immigrants over the next five years. Only two years earlier, the Peel Commission had recommended the partition of Palestine into a Jewish state and an Arab state without Jewish immigration quotas.
38 Herbert Lehman, a German Jew, was elected governor of New York in 1932, and about a dozen more Jews were elected to the state legislature.

39 Lawrence Fuchs, "American Jews and the Presidential Vote," in Lawrence Fuchs, ed., *American Ethnic Politics* (New York, 1968), 52-53, for the pre-1932 period.

40 These advisors included Benjamin V. Cohen, Samuel Rosenman, Henry Morgenthau, Jr. and Felix Frankfurter.

41. B'nai B'rith (1843), the American Jewish Committee (1906), the Anti-Defamation League (1913) and the American Joint Distribution Committee (1914) were established before Kronish's birth and also played a role in helping Jews to maintain their Jewish identity while guarding against anti-Semitism. B'nai B'rith was the most prominent Jewish national organization between World Wars One and Two. Interviews with Leon Kronish, August 1989, Zev Kronish, July 1988 and Yehuda Ben Chorin, August 1988.

42. Henry Feingold, A *Time for Searching: Entering the Mainstream 1920-1945* (Baltimore 1992), 192-193.

43. Interview with Zev Kronish, July 1988.

44. Eisen in his book, *The Chosen People,* 31, notes that many of the rabbis ordained in the 1930s and 1940s studied psychology and had relatives in Europe.

45. The Hebrew University of Jerusalem was founded in 1925.

46. The Menorah Society at Brooklyn College was part of the Intercollegiate Menorah Association. Its mandate was "to work for Jewish knowledge and morals among students in colleges and universities." The society had a strong Zionist following at Brooklyn College.

47. Quoted in Howe, *World,* 76.

48. See Harold S. Wechsler, *The Qualified Student: A History of Selective College Admission in America* (New York, 1977) and Stephen Steinberg, "How Jewish Quotas Began," *Commentary 52* (September, 1971), 67-76.

49. Interview with Leon Kronish, August 1989.

50. Marc Raphael, *Profiles in American Judaism* (San Francisco, 1984), 181.

51. Mordecai Kaplan, *Reconstructionist* 2/15 (November 27, 1936), 3-4.

52. Raphael, *Profiles, 185.*

53. Dushkin lectured at the Teacher's Institute during summers and early fall. Interview with Avima (Dushkin) Lombard, July 1991.

54. Interview with Avima (Dushkin) Lombard, July 1991.

55. Feingold, *Time for Searching,* 115.

56. Raphael, *Profiles,* 183-188, and especially 184.

57. Dushkin had obligations in Palestine. Trips to America provided the income necessary to survive in Palestine. Interview with Avima (Dushkin) Lombard, July 1991. Kaplan's ongoing battle with Adler and Ginzberg is well-documented. See, for example Feingold, *Time for Searching,* 112-117.

58. Quoted in *Congress Weekly* 16/16 (May 2, 1949), 8.

59. Although Zionist rabbis represented a minority within the Reform rabbinate, some of Wise's colleagues and contemporaries also attained prominence in the Zionist movement. Among the Reform rabbis who were outspoken Zionists prior to the establishment of the State of Israel were Abba Hillel Silver, Judah Magnes, Barnett Brickner, Louis Newman and Felix Levy.

60. See Wise, *Challenging Years* and his articles in *Congress Weekly.*

61. David Stein, "East Side Chronicle," *Jewish Life* (January-February, 1966), 32.
62. Karff, *Hebrew Union College,* 150.
63. John Tepfer's great-grandfather was the Belzer Rebbe. For the importance of Tepfer and Kisch on their students see Karff, *Hebrew Union College,* 447-450.
64. Interview with Leon Kronish, July 1988.
65. Interviews with Leon Kronish, July 1988 and August 1989.
66. Interview with Leon Kronish, July 1988.
67. Karff, *Hebrew Union College,* 151.
68. Interview with Leon Kronish, August 1989. For the content of the cable, Carl Voss, ed., *Stephen S. Wise: Servant of the People. Selected Letters* (Philadelphia, 1970), 230.
69. Ezra Pound mentions Slonimsky's name in canto 77 and again in an article for T.S. Eliot's *Criterion.* See Max Gellman, "Literary Defamation," *The American Zionist* 69/1 (September-October, 1978), 18-19.
70. Tchernowitz's publications on the historical, sociological, ideological and political development of the *halacha* are still widely used by students of the history of Jewish Law. See *Toledot ha-Halakhah* (New York, 1935-1950), 4 volumes and *Toledot ha-Posekim* (New York, 1946-1947), 3 volumes. See also *Bitzaron* (May, 1949), memorial issue.
71. *Historia Judaica* amalgamated in 1962 with the *Révue des Études Juives*.
72. Professor Guido Kisch's comments on Leon Kronish's paper "Herzl and Palestine," May 31, 1942.
73. Amos Elon, *The Israelis: Founders and Sons* (New York, 1971), 154-155.
74. Gershom Scholem, *Major Trends in Jewish Mysticism* (New York, 1941), ix.
75. Interview with Leon Kronish, October 1993.
76. Voss, ed., *Stephen S. Wise*, 249.
77. Steven M. Cohen, *American Modernity and Jewish Identity* (New York, 1983), 45.
78. Leon Kronish, *Educating Children and Young People for Jewish Public Worship* (New York, 1942) 33 and 35, MHL thesis, unpublished.
79. See Chapter Three, 66 and 71, and n.80 and Chapter Four, 98-99.
80. Israel Bonds would become Kronish's vehicle to express the hope for messianic redemption. See Chapters Three, 76-77, Four, 117-118, and Six, 193-199.
81. For the influence of Wise and Kaplan on their students, see Judah Cahn, "Mordecai Kaplan and Stephen S. Wise as Teachers," *Reconstructionist* 47/5 (July-August, 1981), 32-35.

Chapter Three

1. Adrienne Millon, *The Changing Size and Spatial Distribution of the Jewish Population of South Florida* (University of Miami, Coral Gables, 1989), 53, M.A. thesis, unpublished, and *Florida Jewish Demography* 4/1 (December, 1990).
2. Miami Beach was originally a peninsula joined to the mainland at its northern tip but impassable. The peninsula was cut and a long narrow island was formed in 1923. The streets are numbered from the south to the north.

3. For the development of Miami Beach, see Redford, *Billion-Dollar Sandbar*, Harold Mehling, *The Most of Everything: The Story of Miami Beach* (New York, 1960) and Howard Kleinberg, *Miami Beach* (Miami Beach, 1994).
4. Redford, *Billion-Dollar Sandbar*, 95. See also the Carl Fisher Collection, Historical Museum of Southern Florida (Miami).
5. As quoted in Paul George in reference to a piece of communication between Fisher and one of his salesmen. See Henry A. Green and Paul George, *Miami Beach Jewish Walking Tour* (Miami, 1990), mimeo. See also the Carl Fisher Collection, Historical Museum of Southern Florida.
6. Redford, *Billion-Dollar Sandbar*, 141.
7. Interview with JoAnn (Weiss) Bass, January 1993.
8. Interview with Seymour Liebman, November 1986. See also Malvina and Seymour Liebman, *Jewish Frontiersmen* (Miami Beach, 1980), 41-42.
9. Interview with Myra Farr, October 1983. The interview was conducted by the American Jewish Committee and is archived at the Historical Museum of Southern Florida. See also, Henry A. Green, "The Farr-Goodkowsky-Magid Family," *Miami Jewish Tribune* (Miami, November 22-29, 1990), 8B and *Jewish Welfare Bureau of Miami Yearbook* (Miami, 1936-1937).
10. Justine Wise Polier and James Westerman Wise, eds., *The Personal Letters of Stephen Wise* (Boston, 1956), 184.
11. See Paul George, "Brokers, Binders and Builders: Greater Miami's Boom of the Mid 1920s," *Florida Historical Quarterly* 65/1 (July, 1986), 27-51.
12. Interview with Ruth Gudis, secretary Beth Jacob, December 1992 and Beth Jacob Congregation membership records.
13. The Jewish Museum of Florida is currently restoring Beth Jacob's 1936 building and plans to reopen it as a museum in 1995.
14. Nicholas Gage, *New York Times*, quoted in Dan Rottenberg, "Israel vs Meyer Lansky: A Talmudic Problem," *Expo* (Winter, 1979), 67. During its capital campaign to restore Beth Jacob, Marcia Zerivitz of the Jewish Museum of Florida offered Thomas Kramer, a non-Jewish German developer, the opportunity to rededicate one of Beth Jacob's stained glass windows for $50,000. Ironically, Kramer selected Meyer Lansky's window.
15. For a history of Temple Emanu-El see Paul George, *Event of the Decade: Temple Emanu-El of Greater Miami, 1938-1988* (Miami Beach, 1988).
16. For the impact of the International Style of Architecture/Art Deco see the forthcoming proceedings to the UNESCO International Style Architecture Conference (Tel Aviv, 1994) and Keith Root, *Miami Beach Art Deco Guide* (Miami Beach, 1987).
17. Green, "The New Establishment."
18. The University of Miami, founded in 1925, was severely damaged in the hurricane of 1926 and did not recover until after World War Two. A segregated private university, fees were relatively high and its admission policies mirrored those of the northeastern schools. Desegregation occurred in 1961.
19. Mehling, *The Most of Everything*, 134.
20. David Levy Yulee, a Sephardic Jew, played a significant role in having Florida join the Union in 1845. Elected to the United States Senate that year, Yulee was the nation's first

Jewish Senator. He preceded Judah P. Benjamin to the Senate by six years. Benjamin is often erroneously identified as the nation's first Jewish senator. See Henry A. Green and Marcia Zerivitz, *MOSAIC: Jewish Life in Florida* (Miami, 1991), 10-11 and especially notes 50 and 51. Earlier, in 1819, Yulee's father, Moses Levy, bought 50,000 acres in Central Florida to establish a "homeland" for the Jewish people. See Leon Huhner, "Moses Elias Levy," *Florida Historical Quarterly* 19 (1941), 319-345. For the David Levy Yulee Voter's League origins see the *New Jewish Unity* 6/38 (April 29, 1932).

21. Baron de Hirsch Meyer, in addition to his civic activities, was an early Zionist. He attended the 1923 Zionist Convention in Czechoslovakia.
22. *Miami Daily News*, April 24, 1927.
23. Letter of Cyrus Adler to Isidor Cohen, May 5, 1932. Stephen Wise's letter to Isidor Cohen, dated May 2, 1932, reads "[Jews ought not to] link the Jewish name with partisan political organizations."
24. Wolfson received the highest number of votes of all candidates in the 1943 election, 3,290. *Jewish Floridian*, June 4, 1943. He resigned in August 1943 and was commissioned as a major in the Army Specialist Reserve. His replacement was Maurice Leiberman.
25. *Jewish Floridian*, February 8, 1935.
26. M. J. Kopelowitz, *Population Survey of the Jewish Community of Greater Miami* (Miami, 1944), Census Sub-Committee Report, Greater Miami Jewish Federation.
27. Beth Sholom Center Minutes, First General Meeting, April 6, 1942.
28. Beth Sholom Center Minutes, Second General Meeting, April 9, 1942. Several weeks later women were given voting rights. Beth Sholom Center Minutes, July 14, 1942.
29. Beth Sholom Center Minutes, Seventh General Meeting, June 3, 1942.
30. Beth Sholom Center Minutes, Seventh General Meeting, June 3, 1942.
31. By the time the charter was issued membership had doubled and included Sam Lobel, Jacob Slaff, Gus Trau, David Leibman, David Moscovitz, Herman Basch, Robert Nordau, Alfred Rosenstein, Harry Klausner, Raymond Rubin, Charles Tobin, Benjamin Meyers, David Rappenport, Julius Pearson and S. Geringer.
32. Beth Sholom Center Minutes, Thirteenth General Meeting, July 14, 1942.
33. Beth Sholom Center Minutes, Installation of Officers, July 23, 1942.
34. Letter from Morris Perrell to Beth Sholom Center, August 12, 1942.
35. Contract between Lewis Green and the Beth Sholom Center, August 15, 1942, Temple Beth Sholom records.
36. *Beth Sholom Center News*, April 30, 1943.
37. *Beth Sholom Center News*, June 4, 1943.
38. Beth Sholom Center, Board of Directors Meeting, April 29, 1944.
39. Interview with Lillian Kronish, July 1988, describing her husband's visit.
40. In addition to Rabbi Irving Lehrman, other JIR graduates in Miami were Rabbi Colman Zwitman of Reform Temple Israel (1936-1949) and Rabbi Albert Michaels, Director of the Hillel Foundation at the University of Miami in the late 1940s. Interview with Rabbi Lehrman, June 1989.

41. Interview with Kronish, July 1988 and Beth Sholom Center, Board of Directors Meeting, August 9, 1944.
42. Beth Sholom Center, Board of Directors Meeting, August 9, 1944.
43. Interview with Lillian Kronish, July 1988.
44. *Ibid.*
45. Resignation letter to Huntington Jewish Center, August 28, 1944.
46. *Population Survey* (1944), 6, 9, 12; Redford, *Billion Dollar Sandbar*, 221.
47. Tebeau, *History of Florida*, 417.
48. Sermon, September 26, 1944.
49. *Ibid.*
50. *Beth Sholom Center News,* October 6, 1944.
51. Beth Sholom Center Minutes, First General Meeting 1944-1945 season, November 8, 1944.
52. When Kronish arrived at the Beth Sholom Center in 1944 there were over one hundred and fifty graduates from the Jewish Institute of Religion serving in pulpits or as chaplains in the Army and Navy. *Congress Weekly* 11/11 (March 17, 1944), 22.
53. Temple Beth Sholom, Board of Directors' Meeting, October 1, 1945.
54. *Temple Beth Sholom Bulletin*, September 17, 1948. In 1950, a study of two hundred and seventy Reform congregations noted that 90% conducted the bar mitzvah ceremony, 25% the bat mitzvah ceremony, 40% allowed the bar/bat mitzvah to wear a *tallit*, and 33% approved the wearing of a *kippa*. See *Congress Weekly* 17/33 (December 11, 1950), 6. Kronish's early commitment to renew Reform Judaism with tradition is revealing in the light of these statistics.
55. For example, his appeal to parents on Passover, *Beth Sholom Center News*, March 30, 1945.
56. Before World War Two, Hebrew was regarded by many Reform congregations as non-essential. Zionism, a repudiation of universalism, a basic tenet of Reform Judaism, was considered antithetical.
57. Kronish, *Educating Children*, 1, 36.
58. For the school statistics, see the *Temple Beth Sholom Bulletin*, May 11, 1945.
59. *Temple Beth Sholom Bulletin*, May 18, 1945.
60. *Beth Sholom Center News*, December 15, 1944.
61. According to Beth Sholom records only fifty percent of member families had paid their dues. There are no explanations in the records why such a high proportion of memberships were unpaid. Kronish has suggested that these unpaid members may have been military personnel temporarily stationed on Miami Beach. The center's membership policy was fair share.
62. Interview with Max Gratz, June 1989.
63. Interview with Stanley Arkin, July 1988.
64. Report of Leon Ell, membership committee, Beth Sholom Center, Board of Directors Meeting, April 24, 1945.
65. For the range of topics in 1944 see *Beth Sholom Center News*, October 6, 1944 to December 15, 1944.
66. *Beth Sholom Center News*, February 16, 1945.

67. Stephen S. Wise's words were:

> I could not speak of myself as an American who is a Jew. I am an American Jew. I have been a Jew for four thousand years. I have been an American for sixty-four years.

See Voss, ed., *Stephen S. Wise*, 231-232 and *Opinion* 12/9 (July, 1942), 5.

68. *Service of Installation*, March 9, 1945 and *Beth Sholom Center News*, March 9, 1945.

69. Interviews with Max Gratz, June 1989 and Shepard Broad, July 1988 and June 1989. Father Barry was also against the building of Mount Sinai Hospital, a Jewish hospital directly across 41st Street, later that decade and the rezoning of land near St. Patrick's for a Jewish day school (Hebrew Academy) in the following decade. The hospital proceeded; the school was blocked. For the hospital, see Paul George, *Visions, Accomplishments, Challenges: Mount Sinai Medical Center of Greater Miami 1949-1984* (Miami Beach, 1985), interview with Paul George, April 1989, and interview with James Orovitz, Chairman of the Board, Mount Sinai Hospital, December 1990. For the school, interview with Rabbi Haber, Principal, Hebrew Academy, April 1989, and Burnett Roth, July 1988. The controversy surrounding the Jewish day school is also noted in Irving Lehrman's unpublished manuscript about Miami and in Roth's autobiography, also unpublished. See also Miami Beach City Council zoning ordinances and Planning Board Minutes in the 1950s.

70. Several months later Stephen Wise commented on the board's decision to choose a new site in a letter to Leon Kronish (November 23, 1945):

> I am glad you succeeded in getting an adequate Temple near the public school building in which I spoke last March. You are wise to put off building a new Temple.

71. Interview with Shepard Broad, July 1988 and June 1989.

72. For example, Rabbi Irving Lehrman of Temple Emanu-El, Miami Beach.

73. For a history of Temple Israel see Charlton Tebeau, *Synagogue in the Central City: Temple Israel of Greater Miami* (Coral Gables, 1972). Zwitman, while serving as chaplain during World War Two, contracted a terminal disease and died shortly after returning to Miami.

74. Tebeau, *Temple Israel*, 99-113 and Joseph Narot, *Sermons* (Miami, 1978). Narot had also been influenced by Stephen S. Wise but more by his "oratorical prowess" than his social activism and passion for Liberal Judaism. See Joseph Narot, "First Teachers in Last Resorts," *CCAR Journal* 25/1 (Winter, 1978), 47.

75. Temple Beth Sholom joined the UAHC in 1948. See *Temple Beth Sholom Bulletin,* December 10, 1948.

76. Constitution, Temple Beth Sholom, April 24, 1945.

77. Although Kronish and Lehrman were JIR graduates in 1942 and have spent the next five decades of their life together on Miami Beach, Temple Beth Sholom and Rabbi Leon Kronish are not mentioned in Paul George's commissioned history of Temple Emanu-El. See *Event of the Decade*.

78. For example, the loss of board members Evelyn and Harry Kohn's son, Staff Sgt. Albert Kohn. See *Beth Sholom Center News*, October 20, 1944.

79. The first listing is in *Beth Sholom Center News*, October 6, 1944 and continues every week until May 8, 1945.

80. *Purim* Song (March 5, 1947):

Come, O *Purim* Day at last
Another evil threat has past
Mankind's year of victory
Repeats our Jewish history.

Welcome, welcome *Purim*
Day of joy!

From the *Megillah* we are told
Of Queen Esther brave and bold,
And her uncle, Mordecai
Who, the villain, did defy.

Welcome, welcome *Purim*
Day of Joy!

Laugh and sing, no need to cry
Jews laugh last while Hamans die
Tyrants plot to kill the Jews
In the end their heads they lose.

Welcome, welcome *Purim*
Day of Joy!

Hymn in honor of Dr. Wise's Birthday (March 5, 1947):

Bless thou, dear God, Stephen Wise
Beloved leader of our folk
Grant him the strength to remove
The weight of persecution's yoke!

Thou who art the source of life and death
We turn our hearts in prayer to Thee
Accept our hymn of gratitude
For Rabbi Wise's Seventy-Three!

Soldier Thine, Almighty God, who fights
For freedom and dignity
Veteran of the Zionist fray
He will not rest – Zion must be free!

81. *Miami Beach Sun-Tropics*, November 30, 1945.
82. See Chapter Two, n.1, 249.
83. Millon, "Changing Size and Spatial Distribution," 53, 81. Approximately 25% of the Jewish residents lived north of 41st Street. *Jewish Floridian*, March 25, 1949, 18.
84. Kopelowitz, *Population Survey* (1944) and M. J. Kopelowitz, *Population Survey of the Jewish Community of Greater Miami* (Miami, 1949), Census Sub-Committee Report, Greater Miami Jewish Federation. See also *Jewish Floridian*, March 25, 1949, April 1, 1949 and April 8, 1949.
85. Ira Sheskin's estimate based on 1950 and 1960 data. See *Florida Jewish Demography* 4/1 (December 1990).
86. For an in-depth analysis of the transformation of Miami Beach as the "Winter Catskills" see Deborah Dash Moore, *To the Golden Cities: Pursuing the American Jewish Dream in Miami and L.A.* (New York, 1994).
87. *Miami: Going Places in Business and Industry* (City of Miami, Department of Publicity, 1948), 5 and *Metropolitan Miami Florida: City of Miami's Golden Anniversary* (Miami, 1946).
88. Between the end of World War Two and the mid 1950s the number of hotels on Miami Beach increased by 20% (317 to 382). Raymond Mohl, "Changing Economic Patterns in the Miami Metropolitan Area, 1940-1950," *Tequesta* 42 (1982), 63-73.
89. Sermon, April 21, 1949.
90. *Ibid*.
91. Kronish was named the godfather of Rosebelle and Burnett Roth's son, Shlomo Zalman Shiye, on November 26, 1950.
92. The ordinance was tabled on June 15, 1949 and adopted in November, 1949.
93. *Jewish Floridian*, January 5, 19 and June 1, 1951; Redford, *Billion Dollar Sandbar*, 222; and interview with Burnett Roth, June 1988.
94. At the time David Ben-Gurion was the head of the Jewish Agency. In 1948 he became Israel's first Prime Minister.
95. The first Zionist chapter founded was by Harry Simonhoff in 1926 in Miami.
96. Harry Simonhoff, *Under Strange Skies* (New York, 1953), 318.
97. In addition to his Zionist activities, Shepard Broad was president of Temple Beth Sholom (1949-1952) and the developer and mayor of Bay Harbor Islands (1947-1973).
98. Moore, *Golden Cities*, 159.
99. *Jewish Floridian*, September 7, 1945.
100. Interview with Burnett Roth, June 1989. See also Lehrman's manuscript on Jewish Miami and Roth's autobiography, both unpublished.
101. The Haganah was Israel's army before 1948.
102. *Hatikvah* is the Israeli national anthem.
103. For example, Gabriel Seidman, a graduating Senior from Miami Senior High, applied to Congressman Pepper for a visa to visit France in June 1948. Letter of Gabriel Seidman to Congressman Claude Pepper, June 1, 1948.
104. See Moore, *Golden Cities*, 159-163 and Henry A. Green, "The Untold Story: Zionism, Miami and the Birth of Israel" (Ramat Gan, 1991), paper presented at the Third Canada Israel Conference on Social Scientific Approaches to the Study of Judaism. Interviews

with Shepard Broad, June 1989 and March 1991, Burnett Roth, June 1989 and March 1991 and Leon and Lillian Kronish, July 1988 and August 1989.

105. See *Temple Beth Sholom Bulletin*, September 21, 1951.
106. *Jewish Floridian*, May 21, 1948.
107. Others included Rabbi Nathan, director of the Tourist office in Jerusalem, Judith Beilin, United Jewish Appeal representative in Tel Aviv, and Eliezer Kaplan, Minister of Finance. Leon Kronish memo to Sam Blank on his trip to Israel, July 14, 1949.
108. McDonald first came to the Beth Sholom Center on January 24, 1945.
109. Another picture taken by Kronish of McDonald was published as part of the jacket to James McDonald's book, *My Mission to Israel 1948-1951* (New York, 1951).
110. Quoted in *Congress Weekly* 16/20 (May 30, 1949), 19 with reference to a speech Wise made in Chicago on November 30, 1947, the day after the United Nations Assembly confirmed the Palestinian Partition Plan.
111. Israel's first election occurred on January 25, 1949 while Kronish was in Israel.
112. Interview with Kronish, August 1989. Notes to himself February 17, 1949 and April 13, 1978 and letter to Ephraim Shapira, April 17, 1978.
113. *Temple Beth Sholom Bulletin*, May 4, 1951.
114. *Temple Beth Sholom Bulletin*, November 23, 1951.
115. *Jewish Floridian*, January 5, 1951.
116. *Council News*, American Council for Judaism, April 1952, 12.
117. Maxine was named after Leon Kronish's father, who died in 1949.
118. *Temple Beth Sholom Bulletin*, September 16, 1955.
119. Temple Beth Sholom brochure for new members, September 1955.
120. Her uncle, Pincus, ran a one-person welfare organization, The United Jewish Aid Committee, in the 1920s and 1930s in Miami.
121. *Temple Beth Sholom Bulletin*, January 5, 1951 and *The Miami Herald*, January 8, 1951.
122. *The Miami Herald*, February 25, 1953.
123. *Temple Beth Sholom Annual Reports*, 1950 and 1955.
124. Interview with Robert Rubin, May 1995. Immediately after Rubin was nomitated by President Clinton as Secretary of the Treasury, *The Miami Herald's* front page story also paid tribute to Temple Beth Sholom's role in his education.
125. Greenberg was appointed Educational Director in 1952.
126. Sermon, February 16, 1951.
127. *The Miami Sunday News Magazine*, July 2, 1950, 17.
128. *Temple Beth Sholom Bulletin*, March 26, 1954.
129. Raphael, *Profiles,* 71 and 197-198.
130. Meyer, *Response to Modernity*, 359.
131. Sermon, January 28, 1955.

Chapter Four

1. *Temple Beth Sholom Bulletins*, September 16, 1955 and September 29, 1967.
2. Millon, *Changing Size and Spacial Distribution*, 53, 82 and 83.
3. See Moore, *To the Golden Cities*.

4. Chapter Three, 76-77.
5. *Temple Beth Sholom Bulletins* and other promotional pieces proudly characterized the congregation with this title.
6. *Temple Beth Sholom Bulletin*, April 29, 1955.
7. Synagogues Goodman designed include, among others: B'nai Israel, Bridgeport, Connecticut; Temple B'nai Aaron, St. Paul; Temple Israel, Tulsa; Baltimore Hebrew Congregation, Baltimore; North Suburban Synagogue Beth El, Highland Park, Illinois; and Shaarey Zedek, Southfield, Michigan.
8. Percival and Paul Goodman, *Communitas: Means of Livelihood and Ways of Life* (Chicago, 1947).
9. Interview with Leon Kronish, July 1988.
10. Arthur Hertzberg, *The Jews in America* (New York, 1989), 321.
11. Shepard Broad, a past president of Temple Beth Sholom, was so incensed that the congregation began construction before the money was in hand, he sued the board of directors for breach of contract. An earlier board had executed an instrument entitled "Restriction and Against Alienation and Encumbrance" prohibiting future boards from encumbering Temple Beth Sholom in any manner, including a mortgage (Resolution of Board, June 25, 1951). Eventually, Broad dropped the suit.
12. *Temple Beth Sholom Bulletin*, November 29, 1957.
13. *Service of Dedication*, November 29, 1957.
14. "Stampede to the Sun," *Business Week*, March 9, 1963, 108-112.
15. Jacob Rudin was a former assistant to Rabbi Stephen S. Wise and in the late 1960s became President of the Central Conference of American Rabbis. Richard Hirsch was appointed Director of UAHC's Religious Action Center in Washington, D.C. in 1962 and since 1973 lives in Jerusalem and serves as Executive Director of the World Union for Progressive Judaism. Alexander Schindler succeeded Maurice Eisendrath as the President of the Union of American Hebrew Congregations in 1973.
16. The causeway opened in 1959. See City of Miami Beach Commission Minutes for the debate in the mid-1950s and Chapter One, 14 and Chapter Three, 256, n.69.
17. Deborah Dash Moore, "Jewish Migration in Postwar America: The Case of Miami and Los Angeles" in Peter Y. Medding, ed., *A New Jewry? America Since the Second World War*, Studies in Contemporary Jewry VIII (Oxford, 1992), 108.
18. *Temple Beth Sholom Bulletin*, February 19, 1960.
19. Max Feder, *The Senior Citizen Programs in Our Temples*, Synagogue Survey Research #8, UAHC (New York, 1966), 11-12.
20. Redford, *Billion Dollar Sandbar*, 263; Ira Sheskin, "The Migration of Jews to Sunbelt Cities" (Miami, 1985), paper presented at the Sunbelt Conference and Deborah Dash Moore, "Jewish Migration to the Sunbelt," in R. Miller and G. Pozzetta, eds., *Essays on Ethnicity, Race and the Urban South* (Boca Raton, 1989), 46-47.
21. Frederick A. Doppelt and David Polish, *A Guide for Reform Jews* (New York, 1957), 27.
22. David Polish, "Opportunities for Reform Judaism," *Central Conference American Rabbis Journal* 5/3 (October, 1957), 15.
23. Polish chaired the Central Conference of American Rabbis Liturgy Committee for a

number of years. He often advocated a revision of Reform prayer books and liturgy. See for example, David Polish, "A Critique on Some Ceremonies," *Central Conference American Rabbis Journal* 2/1 (April, 1954), 43-46 and "Revision of the Prayer Book," *Central Conference American Rabbis Journal* 9 (January, 1961), 11-15.

24. Leon Kronish, *Shofar Services for Rosh Hashanah* (Miami Beach, 1955, 1970), introductory explanatory notes.
25. See Ronald Kronish, ed., *Towards the Twenty-First Century* for excerpts from *Explanatory Notes to Shofar Services for Rosh Hashanah*, 319-322, and for excerpts from a *Passover Supplementary Haggadah*, 323-326.
26. Frederick Doppelt and David Polish, "A Guide for Reform Jewish Practice," *Central Conference American Rabbis Journal*, 4/2 (June, 1956), 13.
27. Many Reform rabbis during this period grappled philosophically and theologically with the concepts of covenant, God, peoplehood, messianism and the State of Israel. See Arnold Eisen, "American Judaism: Changing Patterns in Denominational Self-Definition," in Medding, ed., *A New Jewry?*, 22-30, for a succinct overview.
28. Millon, *Changing Size and Spacial Distribution*, 81-83.
29. Beth Sholom formally affiliated with the Miami Bureau of Jewish Education in the fall of 1944.
30. Uriah Zvi Engelman, *Jewish Education in Miami, Florida, 1956*, Preliminary and Partial Report, Commission for the Study of Jewish Education in the United States (Summer, 1957).
31. Temple Beth Sholom annual reports, 1946 and 1956.
32. Sol Lichter was also Principal of Ada Meritt Junior High (1957-1961) and Ida Fisher Junior High (1961-1966), both Dade County Public Schools situated on Miami Beach, during this period.
33. Doppelt and Polish, "A Guide for Reform Jewish Practice," 10-17.
34. For the pervasiveness of these questions in Reform Judaism during the post-World War Two period, see Eisen, *The Chosen People*, 148, and articles in the *Central Conference American Rabbis Journal* in the 1950s and 1960s.
35. Cantor David Conviser replaced Cantor Samuel Kelemer when the latter was forced to leave for personal reasons. Kronish played a significant role in the dismissal of Kelemer and the hiring of Conviser. See *Temple Beth Sholom Bulletin*, November 8, 1957 where John Serbin, president, introduced Conviser to the congregation.
36. Beginning in the late 1950s and continuing into the early 1980s, it was common for Reform and Conservative congregations to have two *b'nai mitzvah* during the same sabbath service because of the large numbers of youth coming of age.
37. *Numbers* 6:24-26.
38. In the late 1950s one quarter of Reform congregations in North America still did not perform a bar mitzvah. Max Feder, *Temple Facilities and their Uses*, Synagogue Research Survey #4, UAHC (New York, 1958), 13.
39. Max Feder, *The Temple Program and the Temple Auxiliaries*, Synagogue Research Survey #7, UAHC (New York, 1964), 19-20.
40. A choir was introduced for Rosh Hashanah services in 1957. It became a regular feature of Temple Beth Sholom services on sabbaths, holidays and special occasions.

41. *The Sun Reporter*, Sunday, October 15, 1972.
42. Eisen, *The Chosen People*, 69.
43. Raphael, *Profiles*, 73.
44. Sermon notes of Kronish, 1957.
45. *Jewish Floridian*, September 23, 1960.
46. *The Miami Story*, American Jewish Congress, n.d., 4-5.
47. *Ibid.*, 12.
48. Leo Pfeffer was national director of the Commission on Law and Social Action of the American Jewish Congress.
49. Proceedings of Miami's Dade County Circuit Court, November 1, 1960, and personal papers of Leon Kronish.
50. Interview with Bernard Mandler as quoted by Yehuda Shamir, n.d.
51. *Chamberlain v. Dade County School Board*, 17 Florida Supp. 196, 1961 and 142 So. 2d, 21; *American Jewish Year Book*, 62 (1961), 89-90; 63 (1962), 184-185; 64 (1963), 123-124 documented this case. Interview with Jack Gordon, June 1989. See also *Temple Beth Sholom Bulletins* during 1960.
52. In 1957 Rabbi Yaakov Rosenberg of Congregation Beth David, Miami, was refused accommodation in Pompano Beach hotels. When brought to Governor Collins's attention, he commented, "such abuses of this right are among the prices we pay for a free society." *Jewish Floridian,* July 12, 1957. Seven years later, Collins had moderated his views considerably regarding African Americans and Jews and was chosen by President Lyndon Johnson to be his civil rights ambassador with a mission to defuse the 1964 Selma, Alabama confrontation.
53. *New York Times*, August 16, 1959; see also "A Background Report on School Desegregation for 1959-1960" (1959), 36-37, in Leroy Collins Papers, University of South Florida Library, Tampa.
54. Nathan Perlmutter, "Bombing in Miami," *Commentary* 25/1 (January, 1958), 498.
55. See Henry A. Green, "Rabbi Kronish of Miami and Civil Rights" (Atlanta, 1993), paper presented to the Southern Jewish Historical Society. See also *American Jewish Year Book*, for example, 60 (1959), 45 and 61 (1960), 44, which documents several of the right-wing groups.
56. *Jewish Floridian*, June 24, 1949. Cf. 258, n.92
57. See Chapter Three, 73 and n.93.
58. Sidney Poitier, *This Life* (New York, 1980), 42-43.
59. In 1959, the Reverend Gibson spent six months in jail for refusing to release names of his NAACP members. In 1963, Justice Arthur Goldberg helped write the opinion that the NAACP was not subversive. In 1970, Gibson was elected to Miami's City Council.
60. Rabbi Herbert Baumgard of Reform Temple Beth Am played a leading role during this period.
61. *Temple Beth Sholom Bulletin*, March 23, 1955 and *Dedication Exercises for the "Leon Kronish Library of Human Relations,"* March 23, 1955. The Reverend Ed Graham had been offered the position as head of the Miami NAACP in 1954 but turned it down because of pressure from his congregation.
62. An Anti-Defamation League Miami survey in 1953 reported that the municipal sign ordinance had little impact. At the 809 resort hotels and agencies surveyed, Jewish

applicants were accepted only 28 percent of the time while non-Jews had an acceptance rate of 62 percent.

63. For a brief account of black-Jewish relations in Miami see J.D. Zbar, "Jews and Blacks Together," *Miami Jewish Tribune*, March 11, 1988. For a more general overview see Ray Mohl, "The Pattern of Race Relations in Miami since 1940" (Miami, 1990), paper presented at the Ethnic Minorities and Multiculturalism Conference.
64. Perry Nussbaum, Charles Mantinband and Jacob Rothchild, "The Southern Rabbi Faces the Problem of Desegregation," *Central Conference American Rabbis Journal* 4/2 (June, 1956), 1.
65. Rothschild, *One Voice*, 123.
66. Raphael, *Profiles*, 73.
67. Sermon, May 10, 1957.
68. James Wax, "The Attitude of the Jews in the South Toward Integration," *Central Conference American Rabbis Journal* 7/2 (June, 1959), 17.
69. Charles Mantinband, "Integration and the Southern Jew," *Congress Weekly* 25/11 (June 16, 1958), 10. According to Mantinband, "gradualism has been defined as 'building a Negro school house one brick at a time,'" 11.
70. Sermon, February 17, 1950.
71. See *Beth Sholom Center News* and *Temple Beth Sholom Bulletins*, 1944-1945.
72. *Temple Beth Sholom Bulletin*, May 20, 1948.
73. Letter to President Truman, March 15, 1950.
74. Letter to President Eisenhower, December 11, 1953; sermon, December 11, 1953.
75. Sermon, Rosh Hashanah, September 4, 1958.
76. Sermon, September 9, 1953.
77. Sermon, April 8, 1955.
78. *Life* magazine, January 12, 1962, 36.
79. Sermon, October 19, 1962.
80. See *Washington Conference on Disarmament and World Peace*, Summary of Proceedings, UAHC (Washington, 1964) and Homer A. Jack, ed., *Religion and Peace* (New York, 1966).
81. Jack, *Religion and Peace*, 5.
82. Sermon, September 4, 1958.
83. Marty Lawson became a Reform rabbi and has a congregation in San Diego. Greg Marks became a Reform rabbi and has a congregation in Pennsylvania. Rachelle Nelson became one of Reform Judaism's first woman cantors in the United States. She is cantor at Temple Beth Am in Miami. Stephen Haas became a Reform cantor and, in 1989, returned to Temple Beth Sholom as the congregation's cantor. Although Stanley Ringler was not a member of Temple Beth Sholom, he especially sought out Rabbi Kronish for guidance and participated in congregational activities. After his university education, he became a Reform rabbi, then director of Hillel centers in Miami, and, rising through the ranks, became the director, in Washington, D.C., of all B'nai B'rith's university programs. In the mid-1980s, Ringler and his family made *aliya*. Gerald Serotta, a childhood friend of Ronald Kronish, was greatly influenced by Ronald's father and was ordained a Reform rabbi. He is director of Hillel at George Washington University. There were also many youth members that would later dedicate their energies to national

Jewish organizations. For example, Nan Herman Rich is the national president-elect of the National Council of Jewish Women.

84. Letter to Rabbi Kronish, June 26, 1963.
85. Interview with Ronald Kronish, August 1989.
86. The temple holds 750 in its sanctuary and 1,050 more when the social hall is adjoined.
87. *Juniors* was a restaurant at Collins and 30th Street, owned by Arthur Horowitz, a veteran Temple Beth Sholom member.
88. Doppelt and Polish, "A Guide for Reform Jewish Practice," 13.
89. The first *seder* was a community *seder* held at Temple Beth Sholom.
90. Isabelle Hecht Amdur interview, July 1989.
91. In August 1958, Leon and Lillian were waiting at the New York airport to depart for Israel to attend the first International Bonds Conference. Just before boarding the airplane, they received the news that Lillian's father, Adolph, had died.
92. See Karff, *Hebrew Union College*, 209.
93. Leon Kronish interview, August 1989.
94. Israel Bonds, New York office, Florida records, 1961.
95. Letter to Rabbi Kronish from Pinhas Sapir, November 20, 1961.
96. *Temple Beth Sholom Bulletin,* October 19, 1951.
97. Ezer Weizman is currently the President of Israel.
98. Max Orovitz interview and Orovitz family scrapbooks. The interview with Max Orovitz was conducted in the 1960s by Temple Israel. For Orovitz's and the "Miami Group's" role in Zionism, see Green, "The Untold Story: Zionism, Miami, and the Birth of Israel."
99. Lillian Simonhoff, *Reminiscences* (Miami Beach, 1976), 27.
100. *Israel Magazine* 2/6 (March, 1970), 34.

Chapter Five

1. Millon, *Changing Size and Spatial Distribution,* 53 and 67.
2. Ira Sheskin, *Population Study of the Greater Miami Jewish Community* (Miami, 1982), 33. Report for the Greater Miami Jewish Federation.
3. Ira Sheskin, A *Summary Report-Demographic Study of the Greater Miami Jewish Community* (Miami, 1984), 4.
4. Sheskin, *Population Study (1982), 27* and *Florida Jewish Demography* 2/1 (December, 1988), 2.
5. *Temple Beth Sholom Bulletin,* April 1973. Ronald's senior thesis which was composed during this period at the HUC-JIR also addresses this subject. See the *Problems of the Uprooted in the Stories of Micah Yosef Bedichevsky (N*ew York, 1973), 110-111, MHL thesis, unpublished.
6. Ronald Kronish, "Letter to the Editor," *Reform Judaism* (Fall, 1983), 66.
7. Kronish served on the presidential selection committee that nominated Gottschalk for president of HUC-JIR.
8. Address to the graduating class of HUC-JIR, New York, June 3, 1973.

9. Ze'ev Shaham, "Zionism and Personal Commitment," in Kronish, ed., *Towards the Twenty-First Century,* 106. See also Amos Ettinger, *My Country—Laughing Between Tears* (Tel Aviv, 1991), 317-322, in Hebrew.
10. Interview with Leon Kronish, August 1989.
11. Personal memo to himself, April 13, 1978.
12. Letter to Ephraim Shapira, April 17, 1978.
13. Dialogue with Zonik Shaham, May 13, 1978. The dialogue between Kronish and Shaham took the place of the Friday night sermon at Temple Beth Sholom. See also Ettinger, *My Country, 317-322.* For Shaham's reference to Kronish as "his *rebbe"* see Ze'ev Shaham, "Zionism," in Kronish ed., *Towards the Twenty-First Century,* 106.
14. Harold S. Kushner, "Can Liberal Jews Believe in an All Powerful God?," in Kronish, ed., *Towards the Twenty-First Century,* 213.
15. Rabbi Gottschalk again served Beth Sholom as guest rabbi for Rosh Hashanah in 1985. Alfred Gottschalk, "The American Reform Rabbinate: Retrospect and Prospect: A Personal View," in Kronish, ed., *Towards the Twenty-First Century*, 169.
16. For "Mr. Israel in Florida" see the *Miami Beach Sun*, December 4, 1979, 6 and *The Miami Herald,* December 4, 1970, 12D. For the Bonds dinner, see Kronish, ed., *Towards the Twenty-First Century*, 2-3.
17. Interview with Rabbi Joseph Glaser, April 1989.
18. Ronald Kronish, "Introduction," in Kronish, ed., *Towards the Twenty-First Century,* 3.
19. Millon, *Changing Size and Spatial Distribution, 53.*
20. *Miami News,* March 17, 1981.
21. Hispanics comprised less than 10% of Dade County's population.
22. Alejandro Portes and Alex Stepick, *City on the Edge: The Transformation of Miami* (Berkeley CA, 1993).
23. Sheskin, *Population Study (1982), 33.*
24. Ira Sheskin, "The Migration of Jews to Sunbelt Cities" (Miami, 1985), paper presented at the Sunbelt Conference.
25. Sheskin, *Population Study* (1982), 59.
26. Redford, *Billion-Dollar Sandbar, 264.*
27. Arthur Rosichan, "Report of Dade County's Progression from 1960-1974" to the Greater Miami Jewish Federation (Miami, June, 1974), 1.
28. Cohen, *American Modernity,* 134-170.
29. The Gray Panthers are senior citizen activists. Much of the social activism on behalf of the elderly that developed in the United States since the 1960s evolved from their initial efforts.
30. See Chapter Three, 58 and n.20.
31. *Florida Jewish Demography 4/1* (December, 1990); 3/1 (December, 1989); Sheskin, "The Migration of Jews to Sunbelt Cities."
32. *Florida Jewish Demography* 6/1 (March, 1993), 1 for Palm Beach. Ira Sheskin, *Jewish Demographic Study of Dade County* (Miami, 1994) for Miami.
33. For a brief overview of the Cubans in Miami with a comprehensive bibliography, see Raymond Mohl, "Miami, New Immigrant City" in *Searching for the Sunbelt,* ed., Raymond Mohl (Knoxville, 1990), 157-163; and Oliver Kerr, *Population Projections: Race and Hispanic Origin, Dade County, Florida, 1980-2000* (Miami, 1987).

34. Seymour Liebman, "Cuban Jewish Community in South Florida," *American Jewish Year Book* 70 (1969), 243.
35. Interviews with Meyer Abramowitz, May 1989; Seymour Liebman, January 1985; Sender Kaplan, December 1987; Arthur Rosichan, May 1986. HIAS (Hebrew Immigrant Aid Society) and the NCJW (National Council of Jewish Women) played significant roles in the immigration and absorption of these Jewish exiles.
36. Dade's population was 49% Hispanic in 1990 according to the U.S. Census.
37. *Florida Jewish Demography* 7 (May, 1994), 1.
38. Ira Sheskin, "The Miami Ethnic Archipelago" (December, 1990), paper presented at the Ethnic Minorities and Multiculturalism Conference: Dade County's Tomorrow, and Pnina Zadka, Ira Sheskin, and Henry A. Green, "A Comparative Profile of Jewish Elderly in South Florida and Israel," *Contemporary Jewry* 11/4 (Fall, 1990), 93-119.
39. Temple Moses, The Sephardic Congregation of South Florida, caters to Sephardic Cuban Jews; the Cuban Hebrew Congregation serves Ashkenazic Cuban Jews. In the 1980s a Hebraica was organized but proved financially unsuccessful. For an overview of Hispanic Jews in Florida from 1763 see Henry A. Green, "Sefardies en la Florida," *Magen* 81/2, (October-December, 1991), 29-35.
40. Interviews with Solomon Garazi, December 1987; Sender Kaplan, December 1987; Meyer Abramowitz, May 1989.
41. Dade County resolution, November 1980.
42. Ronald Bayor, "Models of Ethnic and Racial Politics in the Urban Sunbelt South," in Raymond Mohl, ed., *Searching for the Sunbelt* (Knoxville, 1990), 110-111.
43. T.D. Allman, *Miami: City of the Future* (New York, 1987), 28. *Marielitos* refer to Cubans who left Cuba from the port of Mariel in 1980. Between April and October, more than 120,000 Cubans sailed north to Miami.
44. See American Jewish Congress, press release, 1973.
45. Interview with Sol Lichter, June 1988.
46. Raymond Mohl, "The Pattern of Race Relations in Miami Since 1940" (December, 1990), paper presented to the Ethnic Minorities and Multiculturalism Conference: Dade County's Tomorrow.
47. *Time,* May 23, 1980.
48. *Temple Beth Sholom Bulletin,* January 25, 1980 is an example of Kronish's request for funds before the May riots.
49. *Temple Beth Sholom Bulletin,* May 30, 1980.
50. *Temple Beth Sholom Bulletin,* May 30, 1980; Sermon May 23, 1980.
51. *Temple Beth Sholom Bulletin,* October 10, 1980.
52. Letter to Temple Beth Sholom members, November 1, 1981.
53. *Temple Beth Sholom Bulletin,* January 22, 1982.
54. Redford, *Billion-Dollar Sandbar,* 263-264, and Sheskin, *Population Study* (1982).
55. See for example, *Temple Beth Sholom Bulletin,* April 9, 1982.
56. Meyer, *Response to Modernity,* 366.
57. *Temple Beth Sholom Bulletin,* April 2, 1971.
58. For example, see *Temple Beth Sholom Bulletin,* May 10, 1974 in reference to the *De Funis versus Odegaard* case.
59. *The Miami Herald,* March 16, 1973.

60. For capital punishment see, *Temple Beth Sholom Bulletin,* May 25, 1979; for Cambodians, see *Temple Beth Sholom Bulletin,* November 30, 1979; for the Vietnamese immigration policy, see *Temple Beth Sholom Bulletin,* January 12, 1979; for nuclear disarmament, see *Temple Beth Sholom Bulletin,* April 2, 1982; and for terrorism and oil, see *Temple Beth Sholom Bulletin,* November 9, 1979.
61. *The Miami News,* October 26, 1977, 5A. After nine hours of deliberation Kronish called in the police.
62. *Temple Beth Sholom Bulletin,* December 12, 1980.
63. Leon Kronish, *The New Haggadah in Israel: Passover Supplementary Haggadah* (Miami Beach, March, 1950).
64. *Temple Beth Sholom Bulletin,* March 21, 1975 and below, *Essays* by Leon Kronish, 233f.
65. *Temple Beth Sholom Bulletin,* December 2, 1979 and Leon Kronish, *Service for the Six Million who died during Shoah* (Miami Beach, December 2, 1979).
66. Kenneth Triester, *A Sculpture of Love and Anguish* (New York, 1993).
67. For example, see *Temple Beth Sholom Bulletin,* April 4, 1980.
68. Sermon, April 3, 1980.
69. Interview with Harry Jolt, July 1988.
70. Raphael, *Profiles,* 107.
71. *American Jewish Yearbook* 31 (1929-1930), 308.
72. Interview with Harry Jolt, July 1988.
73. Sheskin, *Population Study* (1982); and Zadka, Sheskin, and Green, "Comparative Profile of Jewish Elderly"; For similar data in other Jewish population centers see Cohen, *American Modernity.*
74. Ira Sheskin, *Population Study,* (1982).
75. For an example of the "fair-share" philosophy in the late 1970s see *Temple Beth Sholom Bulletin, July* 1977; for the early 1980s, see June 1980.
76. Leon Kronish, A *Treasury of Inspiration* (Miami Beach, 1969).
77. *Passover Supplementary Haggadah* (Miami Beach, 1970), 2-5. Kronish conducted a congregational *seder* with his "congregational family" on the first night of Passover and held a *seder* at home for family and friends on the second night.
78. *Yerushalayim shel Zahav* was sung in Israel for the first time three weeks before the outbreak of the Six Day War. Originally, it was a song of nostalgia, expressing longings to visit the Temple Mount in Jerusalem. On June 7, 1967, after Jerusalem was recaptured, Naomi Shemer rewrote the song expressing optimism for a new future.
79. The Judaica high school courses were under the auspices of the Central Agency for Jewish Education of the Greater Miami Jewish Federation. Several were offered for community college credit.
80. See Chapter Six, 182-183.
81. See Chapter Four, 93 and n.11.
82. Interviews with Dennis Rice, June 1990; Susan Miller, June 1990; David Miller, July 1990; Harold Vinik, July 1990; Temple Beth Sholom Minutes, 1981-1984.
83. See *Temple Beth Sholom Bulletin,* February 26, 1982 for an example of the "fair-share" policy during this debate.
84. Linguistically, *havura,* the singular, is modern Hebrew for *chevra,* meaning a group that may gather for any purpose. To this day, many Reconstructionist congregations still refer

to themselves as *havurot* and their congregational association is called the Federation of Reconstructionist Congregations and Havurot.

85. See Nathan Barack, "The Role of Religious Fellowship," *Reconstructionist* 11/11 (October 19, 1945), 8-12.
86. See Raphael, *Profiles,* 64, 190-191.
87. *Temple Beth Sholom Bulletin,* January 10, 1975.
88. The Chester, Kovler, Nixon, Goldstein, and Gettis families are members of this *havura.*
89. Interview with Yehuda Shamir, March 1989.
90. Kronish, *Yisreal Goralenu,* 32.
91. Interview with Harry Jolt, July 1988.
92. Dr. Isaac Fein was the father of Leonard Fine, the founder and former publisher of *Moment* magazine and founder of *Mazon,* a program to alleviate hunger in America.
93. Gerald Serotta, "Activism on the College Campus: Retrospect and Prospects," in Kronish, ed., *Towards the Twenty-First Century,* 271. In the 1970s, Kronish served on the National Hillel Commission.
94. The Great Artist Series was organized initially for temple members for the 1967-1968 season. It was incorporated into the institute's programming in 1969 and opened to the public. The Great Performance Series began in the mid-1970s; the Israeli Showcase Series in 1981.
95. The series moved to the Miami Beach Theater for Performing Arts.
96. *The Miami Herald,* July 17, 1994, 6I.
97. Temple Beth Sholom School of Fine Arts Brochure, 1974.
98. *Jewish Floridian,* July 1976.
99. *The Miami Herald,* April 17, 1970.
100. For example, see *Temple Beth Sholom Bulletin,* November 28, 1980 where Kronish lambasts *The Miami Herald* for its "exaggerated headlines."
101. *The Miami Herald,* December 3, 1970, 4B.
102. Shaham, "Zionism" in Kronish, ed., *Towards the Twenty-First Century, 106.*
103. Meyer, *Response to Modernity,* 370, and Theodore Lenn et. al., *Rabbi and Synagogue in Reform Judaism* (West Hartford, Conn., 1979).
104. Leon Kronish's files, personal notes, n.d.
105. *Temple Beth Sholom Bulletin,* April 18, 1980.
106. Project Renewal, an urban development project, was initiated by Prime Minister Begin in 1979. Communities in Israel were twinned with Jewish communities around the world. Miami's twin was Or Akiva.

Chapter Six

1. Interviews with Leon Kronish, August 1989 and David Polish, August 1989. See also *Temple Beth Sholom Bulletin,* February 17, 1967.
2. Sermon, June 9, 1967.
3. Under Kronish's leadership, Miami purchased $6.3 million worth of Israel Bonds in 1967. See *Encyclopedia Judaica* 11, 1479.
4. Correspondence from Ronald Kronish to Henry Green, August 12, 1992.
5. Interview with Ronald Kronish, July 1991.

6. Hertzberg, *Jews in America,* 372.
7. Interview with Marvin Cooper, May 1989.
8. Sermon, October 6, 1973.
9. Interview with Leon Kronish, August 1989.
10. The Emergency Bonds Drive raised $692 million.
11. Interview with Morris Sipser, August 1989.
12. Arthur Rosichan, "Report on Dade County Jewish Progression from 1960-1974," 2.
13. Letter from Mickey Shaham to Richard and Susan Cooper Zinn, October 20, 1973. Reprinted in *Temple Beth Sholom Bulletin,* November 9, 1973.
14. As *the Hart Panteth* (Tel Aviv, 1977), ix.
15. *Temple Beth Sholom Bulletin,* December 14, 1973.
16. *Temple Beth Sholom Bulletin,* April 6, 1979.
17. *Temple Beth Sholom Bulletin,* April 6, 1979 and sermon, April 5, 1979.
18. Hertzberg, *Jews in America,* 375.
19. Kronish, *Yisrael Goralenu,* 31.
20. *Ibid.,* 35.
21. *Ibid.,* 35-36.
22. *Ibid.,* 36-37. Kronish's emphasis on the importance of what has come to be called "The Israel Experience" as a central building block in American Jewish identity is today, one generation later, a foundational feature of the organized American Jewish community.
23. In 1969 the CCAR passed such a resolution. See *CCAR Yearbook* 79 (1969), 141-142. It was formally announced in Israel at the CCAR convention in 1970.
24. Sermon, December 10, 1971.
25. *Temple Beth Sholom Bulletin,* January 11, 1974.
26. Kronish, Zionist *Mitzvot,* 15.
27. This has come to be called "partial *aliya.*"
28. Kronish, *Yisrael Goralenu,* 37.
29. Shaham, "Zionism" in Kronish, ed., *Towards the Twenty-First Century,* 105. See also Ettinger, *My Country,* 317-322.
30. Interview with Ze'ev Shaham, August 1989 and *Temple Beth Sholom Bulletin,* May 10, 1968.
31. Ze'ev Shaham, "Zionism" in Kronish, ed., *Towards the Twenty-First Century,* 106.
32. *Temple Beth Sholom Bulletin,* December 14, 1973.
33. Interview with Sol Lichter, June 1988.
34. Interview with Ellen Cooper Channing, June 1990.
35. See Chapter Five, 146-150.
36. Shaham, "Zionism" in Kronish, ed., *Towards the Twenty-First Century,* 106.
37. Kronish, *Yisrael Goralenu,* 35.
38. Shaham, "Zionism" in Kronish, ed., *Towards the Twenty-First Century,* 107; Interview with Ze'ev Shaham, August 1989; Ettinger, *My Country*, 317-318.
39. For "Mr. Israel," see *The Miami Herald,* December 4, 1970, 12D and the *Miami Beach Sun,* December 4, 1970, 6.
40. Interview with Myron Brodie, April 1988.
41. Sheskin, *Population Study* (1982).

42. Jack Chester of Temple Beth Sholom played a significant role in bringing the consulate to Miami.
43. Norman Lipoff, a former president of the Greater Miami Jewish Federation and a former chairman of the Israel United Appeal, has been especially helpful in describing the consulate's origin. Interview with Norman Lipoff, May 1989.
44. Interview with Ellen Cooper Channing, June 1990. The other students who participated in the inaugural pilot program were Dawn Neville, Jim Pomerantz, Michael Player, and Nan Sugerman.
45. Interviews with Phyllis Miller, July 1989; Sol Lichter, June 1988; and Morris Kipper, July 1989. For Kronish's role, see *The Miami Herald,* November 10, 1972.
46. In 1979, the program received the highest achievement award from the Council of Jewish Federations.
47. Interview with Sol Stein, August 1988.
48. The Fund was established by charging participants to the 1975 Histadrut Solidarity Conference $300 per person (flight, hotel and three meals a day) on condition of investing a sum of $2,500 in an annuity giving a life income of nine and one-half percent.
49. Mailgram from Leon Kronish to Yehuda Avner, March 20, 1977, 2.
50. Shlomo Avineri, "Ideology and Pragmatism in Ben-Gurion's Leadership: Lessons for the Future" in Kronish, ed., *Towards the Twenty-First Century,* 26.
51. Mailgram from Leon Kronish to Yehuda Avner, March 20, 1977, 1.
52. *CCAR Yearbook* 78 (1968), 80.
53. David Polish, "A Dissent on Patrilineal Descent," in Kronish, ed., *Towards the Twenty-First Century,* 224; Karff, ed., *Hebrew Union College, 214;* and Meyer, *Response to Modernity*, 371.
54. *CCAR Yearbook* 80 (1970), xix.
55. *CCAR Yearbook* 77 (1967), 110 and 112.
56. *CCAR Yearbook* 78 (1968), 79-80.
57. Roland Gittelsohn, president of the CCAR, in his opening remarks at the Jerusalem convention in 1970, acknowledges Kronish's efforts in bringing the CCAR to Israel and Zionizing Reform Judaism. *CCAR Yearbook* 80 (1970), 4.
58. David Polish, *Renew Our Days* (Jerusalem, 1976), 245-246 and *CCAR Yearbook* 80 (1970), 4-5.
59. In 1922 the CCAR passed a resolution affirming the complete equality of women and accepting, in principle, women as rabbis. It took fifty years for that principle to become a reality.
60. *The Miami Herald* acknowledged Temple Beth Sholom's role in initiating the equality of women in Jewish worship in Miami in an article by Adon Taft, September 16, 1977.
61. Letter from Joseph Glaser to Yitzhak Raphael, July 29, 1975.
62. Letter from Leon Kronish to Joseph Glaser, August 13, 1975.
63. David Polish, "A Dissent on Patrilineal Descent," in Kronish, ed., *Towards the Twenty-First Century,* 234.
64. Letter from Leon Kronish to Joseph Glaser, August 13, 1975.
65. *Temple Beth Sholom Bulletin,* January 4, 1980. See also Richard Hirsch, "Jewish Peoplehood – Implications for Reform Judaism," *CCAR Yearbook 89* (1979), 164-173.

66. Meyer, *Response to Modernity,* 363.
67. Sermon, November 13, 1977.
68. For example, see *Temple Beth Sholom Bulletins,* July 1977; May 30, 1980.
69. Saadia Gelb, "The Kibbutz and Kibbutz Judaism: Reflections for the Future," in Kronish, ed., *Towards the Twenty-First Century,* 37.
70. Oranim is a kibbutz near Haifa.
71. Meyer, *Response to Modernity,* 351 and 383. See also *Davar*, November 13, 1976.
72. Gelb, "The Kibbutz and Kibbutz Judaism," in Kronish, ed., *Towards the Twenty-First Century,* 37-50; *Davar,* November 13, 1976; and interview with David Polish, August *1989.*
73. Adon Taft, *The Miami Herald,* December 4, 1970.
74. *Passover Supplementary Haggadah* (Miami Beach, 1968), 3.
75. Arthur Rosichan, "Report to the Executive Committee" to the Greater Miami Jewish Federation (Miami, June, 1968), 1 and 3.
76. See Chapter Six, 180-182.
77. Kronish initiated special workshops for High Holy Day appeals as part of the Israel Bonds national and international leadership conferences.
78. National Rabbinic Cabinet Bulletin, State of Israel Bonds (New York, October, 1978), 2. In 1970 Kronish generated more than $2 million worth of Bonds from Temple Beth Sholom alone. See *Miami News,* December 3, 1970.
79. *CCAR Yearbook,* 81 (1971), 39.
80. For example, *CCAR Yearbook* 83 (1973), xxii. The Israel guest was Simcha Dinitz.
81. *The Miami Herald,* December 4, 1970, 12D.
82. Exports offered included agricultural products, polished diamonds, textiles, machinery, electronics, and a range of defense items. For the State of Florida purchasing Israel Bonds, interview with Elaine Bloom, January 1988.
83. Kronish forwarded a letter to Temple Beth Sholom members on March 18, 1982, personally inviting them to the event on March 29th.
84. *Encyclopedia Judaica* 11, 1480.
85. Interview with Ruhama Hermon, August 14, 1994, who invited Kronish to the party. When Ambassador Rabin first had arrived in the United States in 1968, Kronish dedicated his sabbath sermon in his honor. *Temple Beth Sholom Bulletin*, March 1, 1968.
86. Interview with Leon Kronish, July 1988.
87. Mailgram to Leon Kronish September 6, 1978 from Michael Arnon, president, State of Israel Bonds, informing Kronish of Avner's upcoming special visit.
88. The amount was raised by September, 1982.
89. Interview with Sol Stein, national executive director of the Histadrut, August 1989.
90. *Florida Trend*, September, 1977, 18.
91. *The Miami Herald*, December 4, 1970, 12D.

Chapter 7

1. *Temple Beth Sholom Bulletin,* July 1982.
2. Interview with Leon Kronish, July 1988.

GLOSSARY

Aliya - honor of being called up to the reading of the Torah; act of emigrating to Israel.

Aliya le-regel - pilgrimage to Israel.

Am Yisrael - people of Israel.

Anti-Defamation League - arm of B'nai B'rith that focuses on anti-Semitism.

ARZA - Association of Reform Zionists of America.

Bar mitzvah - religious ceremony at which thirteen-year-old boy becomes adult member of Jewish community; lit., "Son of the Commandment;" plural *b'nai mitzvah.*

Bat mitzvah - religious ceremony at which thirteen-year-old girl becomes adult member of Jewish community; practiced only by non-orthodox Jews; lit., "Daughter of the Commandment;" plural *b'not mitzvah.*

Bimah - podium; pulpit or reader's platform in the synagogue.

Berith milah - covenant of circumcision.

Central Conference of American Rabbis (CCAR) - association of Reform rabbis.

Conversos - Jews who converted to Christianity to save their life under threat of death in the face of the Inquisition and its aftermath.

Dor l'dor - generation to generation.

Diaspora - global dispersion of the Jews from Israel since biblical times.

Eretz Yisrael - land of Israel.

Festschrift - commemorative publication in honor of a person/event.

Gesher vakesher - bridges and bonds.

Habonim - Zionist labor youth movement.

Hadassah - a women's Zionist organization.

Hadoar Lanoar - Hebrew newspaper for youth.

Haftorah - Prophetic portion read after the Torah reading.

Haggadah - the oral law.

Halacha - the written law.

Halutzim - Zionist pioneers.

Hanukkah - Feast of Lights festival celebrating the liberation of Judaea from the Hellenists and the rededication of the Temple.

Hashomer Hatzair - Zionist youth movement.

Hashomer Hadati - Zionist Orthodox youth movement.

Hatikvah - Israel's national anthem.

Havdalah - ceremony marking the conclusion of the sabbath.

Havura - group; plural *havurot.*

Hebrew Union College (HUC) - seminary that trains and ordains Reform rabbis.

Hebrew Immigrant Aid Society - society that helps Jewish immigrants and refugees settle in the United States.

Histadruth Ivrith - organization of American Hebraists.

Jewish Defense League (JDL) - organization founded in 1968 by Rabbi Meir Kahane.

Kabbalat shabbat - religious ritual and prayers that welcome the sabbath.
Kibbutz - collective settlement in the State of Israel where property is held in common.
Kinder - children.
Kippa - skullcap; plural *kippot*.
Klal Yisrael - people of Israel, community of Israel.
Kol Nidre - vows; prayer opening Yom Kippur eve service.
Kotel - western wall of Second Temple built by King Herod, two thousand years ago.
Landsleit - people who originate from the same town, city and now live somewhere else.
Landsmannschaften - association of people who originate from the same area.
Ma'abarot - tent cities to house immigrants in Israel in the late 1940s and 1950s.
Medinat Yisrael - State of Israel.
Megillah - scroll; frequently associated with the Scroll of Esther, read at *Purim*.
Mezuzah - parchment containing passages from the Torah, rolled tightly and placed in a case, which is attached to doorposts of home.
Minhag - daily prayer book.
Mishnah - commentary on the Torah produced in rabbinical academics in the first and second centuries.
Mitzvah - commandment; technical sense, scriptural or rabbinic injunctions; also used in the sense of good deed; plural *Mitzvot*.
National Federation of Temple Youth (NFTY) - Association of Reform Temple Youth.
Nosh - to snack.
Ohel mo'ed - tent where the Ten Commandments were housed during the time of Moses.
Oleh regel - pilgrimage to Israel.
Passover (Pesach) - festival commemorating the exodus from Egypt.
Pirke Avot - "Ethics of the Fathers," a tractate of the Mishnah.
Purim - festival commemorating deliverance of Persian Jews from extermination in fifth century B.C.E.; story recounted in the Scroll of Esther.
Refuseniks - Jews who challenged the Soviet Union authorities to immigrate to Israel.
Rosh Hashanah - New Year.
Schaliach - emissary from Israel to promote its social, economic and cultural life; plural *schlichim*.
Seder - order; Passover meal and home service; plural *sedorim*.
Sedrah - Torah portion of the week.
Shavuot - Feast of Weeks; Pentecost; commemorates giving of Torah at Mt. Sinai.
Sholom - peace.
Shtetls - small villages in Eastern Europe pre-World War Two.
Sukkot - autumn harvest festival ending High Holy Day season.
Tallit - fringed prayer shawl used in morning Jewish worship and worn by adult males.
Talmud - Mishnah, plus commentary on the Mishnah, produced in rabbinical academies from the third to sixth centuries.
The Jewish Institute of Religion (JIR) - seminary founded by Rabbi Stephen Wise in 1922 to ordain rabbis; formally affiliated with Hebrew Union College and the Reform movement in 1950.
The Forward - Yiddish newspaper.
Tikun olam - to bring a just society; lit., "to repair the world."
Tisha be-Av - festival commemorating the destruction of the First and Second Temples held during the summer.
Torah - revelation; The Five Books of Moses. More broadly, the corpus of revelation, both

written and oral. Torah also denotes "study," the act of learning.

Tshuvah - to return to Judaism; to repent for sins.

Tsukunft - Yiddish newspaper.

Tu'B'shvat - Arbor Day.

Ulpan - intensive Hebrew course.

Union of American Hebrew Congregations (UAHC) - umbrella organization for Reform congregations.

Vad hakashrut - board that reviews the acceptability of food products as kosher.

Workmen's Circle - socialist Jewish worker's association.

Yeshivah - seminary; plural *yeshivoth*.

Yiddisher Kemfer - Yiddish newspaper.

Yiddishkeit - sharing Jewish culture.

Yizkor Buch - memorial book, often composed in memory of Holocaust survivors.

Yom Kippur - Day of Atonement.

Young Judea - Zionist youth movement.

Zmirot - sabbath songs.

Selected Bibliography

Major Archival Sources

American Jewish Archives
American Jewish Historical Society
Dade County Public Library
Hebrew Union College - Jewish Institution of Religion
Historical Association of South Florida
University of Florida
University of Miami

Books, Monographs, Pamphlets

Allman, T.D., *Miami: City of the Future* (New York, 1987).
_____, *As the Hart Panteth* (Tel Aviv, 1977).
Brandeis, Louis, *The Jewish Problem–How to Solve It* (New York, 1917).
Cohen, Steven M., *American Modernity and Jewish Identity* (New York, 1983).
Doppelt, Frederick A., and Polish, David, *A Guide for Reform Jews* (New York, 1957).
Eisen, Arnold, *The Chosen People in America: A Study of Religious Ideology* (Bloomington, 1983).
Elon, Amos, *The Israelis: Founders and Sons* (New York, 1971).
Engelman, Uriah Zvi, *Jewish Education in Miami, Florida, 1956,* Preliminary and Partial Report, Commission for the Study of Jewish Education in the United States (Summer 1957).
Erikson, Erik, *Young Man Luther* (New York, 1962).
Ettinger, Amos, *My Country–Laughing Between Tears* (Tel Aviv, 1991), in Hebrew.
Feder, Max, *The Senior Citizen Programs in Our Temples*, Synagogue Research Survey #8, UAHC (New York, 1966).
Feder, Max, *The Temple Program and the Temple Auxiliaries*, Synagogue Research Survey #7, UAHC (New York, 1964).
Feder, Max, *Temple Facilities and their Uses*, Synagogue Research Survey #4, UAHC (New York, 1958).
Feingold, Henry, *A Time for Searching: Entering the Mainstream 1920-1945* (Baltimore, 1992).
George, Paul, *The Event of the Decade: Temple Emanu-El of Greater Miami, 1938-1988* (Miami Beach, 1988).
George, Paul, *Visions, Accomplishments, Challenges: Mount Sinai Medical Center of Greater Miami 1949-1984* (Miami Beach, 1985).

Goodman, Percival and Paul, *Communitas: Means of Livelihood and Ways of Life* (Chicago, 1947).

Green, Henry A., and Zerivitz, Marcia, *MOSAIC: Jewish Life in Florida* (Miami, 1991).

Green, Henry A., and George, Paul, *Downtown, Shenanadoah, Miami Beach, Jewish Walking Tours* (Miami, 1990, mimeo).

Hertzberg, Arthur, *The Jews in America* (New York, 1989).

Howe, Irving, *World of Our Fathers* (New York, 1976).

Jack, Homer A., ed., *Religion and Peace* (New York, 1966).

_____, *Jewish Welfare Bureau of Miami YearBook* (Miami, 1936-1937).

Kaplan, Mordecai, Goldsmith, E. S., and Scult, Mel, eds., *Dynamic Judaism* (New York, 1985).

Kaplan, Mordecai, *Judaism as a Civilization* (New York, 1967).

Kaplan, Mordecai, *Reconstructionist Sabbath Prayer Book* (New York, 1945).

Kaplan, Mordecai, Kohn, E., and Eisenstein, I., eds., *The New Haggadah for the Pesah Seder* (New York, 1941).

Karff, Samuel, ed., *Hebrew Union College—Jewish Institute of Religion at One Hundred Years* (Cincinnati, 1976).

Kerr, Oliver, *Population Projections: Race and Hispanic Origin, Dade County, Florida, 1980-2000* (Miami, 1987).

Kleinberg, Howard, *Miami Beach* (Miami Beach, 1994).

Kopelowitz, M. J., *Population Survey of the Jewish Community of Greater Miami*, Census Sub-Committee Report, Greater Miami Jewish Federation (Miami, 1949).

Kopelowitz, M. J., *Population Survey of the Jewish Community of Greater Miami* Census Sub-Committee Report, Greater Miami Jewish Federation (Miami, 1944).

Kronish, Leon, *Service of Memorial for the Heroes and the Martyrs of the Warsaw Ghetto* (Miami Beach, 1974).

Kronish, Leon, *Chanukah Cantata* (Miami Beach, 1977).

Kronish, Leon, *The New Haggadah in Israel: Passover Supplementary Haggadah* (Miami Beach, 1950, 1958, 1970 and 1974).

Kronish, Leon, *Shofar Services for Rosh Hashanah* (Miami Beach, 1955 and 1970).

Kronish, Leon, *A Treasury of Inspiration* (Miami Beach, 1969).

Kronish, Leon, *Educating Children and Young People for Jewish Public Worship*, MHL thesis (JIR, New York, 1942).

Kronish, Ronald, ed., *Towards the Twenty-First Century: Judaism and the Jewish People in Israel and America* (Hoboken, 1988).

Kronish, Ronald, *Problems of the Uprooted in the Stories of Micah Yosef Bedichevsky*, MHL thesis (HUC-JIR, New York, 1973).

Lenn, Theodore, et. al., *Rabbi and Synagogue in Reform Judaism* (West Hartford, Conn., 1972).

Libowitz, Richard, *Mordecai Kaplan and the Development of Reconstructionism* (New York, 1983).

Liebman, Malvina and Seymour, *Jewish Frontiersmen* (Miami Beach, 1980).

McDonald, James, *My Mission to Israel 1948-1951* (New York, 1951).

Mehling, Harold, *The Most of Everything: The Story of Miami Beach* (New York, 1960).

_____, *Metropolitan Miami Florida: City of Miami's Golden Anniversary* (Miami, 1946).

Meyer, Michael, *Response to Modernity* (Oxford, 1988).

Meyer, Michael, *The Origins of the Modern Jew* (Detroit, 1967).

_____, *Miami: Going Places in Business and Industry* (City of Miami, Department of Publicity, 1948).

Millon, Adrienne, *The Changing Size and Spatial Distribution of the Jewish Population of South Florida*, M.A. thesis (University of Miami, Coral Gables, 1989).

Moore, Deborah Dash, *To the Golden Cities: Pursuing the American Jewish Dream in Miami and L.A.* (New York, 1994).

Moore, Deborah Dash, *At Home in America: Second Generation New York Jews* (New York, 1981).

Narot, Joseph, *Sermons* (Miami, 1978).

O'Brien, Lee, *American Jewish Organizations and Israel* (Washington, 1986).

Plaut, Gunther, *The Rise of Reform Judaism* (New York, 1963).

Poitier, Sidney, *This Life* (New York, 1980).

Polier, Justine Wise, and Wise, James Westerman, eds., *The Personal Letters of Stephen Wise* (Boston, 1956).

Polish, David, *Renew Our Days* (Jerusalem, 1976).

Portes, Alejandro, and Stepick, Alex, *City on the Edge: The Transformation of Miami* (Berkeley, CA., 1993).

Raphael, Marc, *Profiles in American Judaism* (San Francisco, 1984).

Redford, Polly, *Billion-Dollar Sandbar: A Biography of Miami Beach* (New York, 1970).

Rees, Albert, *Real Wages in Manufacturing, 1890-1914* (Princeton, N.J., 1961).

Root, Keith, *Miami Beach Art Deco Guide* (Miami Beach, 1987).

Sanders, Ronald, *The Downtown Jews: Portrait of an Immigrant Generation* (New York, 1970).

Scholem, Gershom, *Major Trends in Jewish Mysticism* (New York, 1941).

Scult, Mel, *Judaism Faces the Twentieth Century: A Biography of Mordecai M. Kaplan* (Detroit, 1993).

Seltzer, R., ed., *Judaism: A People and its History* (New York, 1987).

Shapiro, Robert D., *A Reform Rabbi in the Progressive Era: the Early Career of Stephen S. Wise* (New York, 1988).

Shapiro, Yonathan, *Leadership of the American Zionist Organization, 1897-1930* (Urbana, 1971).

Sheskin, Ira, *Demographic Study of the Greater Miami Jewish Community*, Summary Report, Report for the Greater Miami Jewish Federation (Miami, 1984).

Sheskin, Ira, *Population Study of the Greater Miami Jewish Community*, Report for the Greater Miami Jewish Federation (Miami, 1982).

Simonhoff, Harry, *Under Strange Skies* (New York, 1953).

Simonhoff, Lillian, *Reminiscences* (Miami Beach, 1976).

Sklare, Marshall, ed., *The Jews: Social Patterns of an American Group* (New York, 1958).

Speisman, Stephen, *The Jews of Toronto* (Toronto, 1976).

Tebeau, Charlton, *Synagogue in the Central City: Temple Israel of Greater Miami* (Coral Gables, 1972).

Tebeau, Charlton, *A History of Florida* (Coral Gables, 1971).

_____, *The Miami Story*, American Jewish Congress, n.d.

Triester, Kenneth, *A Sculpture of Love and Anguish* (New York, 1993).

Urofsky, Melvin, *A Voice that Spoke for Justice: the Life and Times of Stephen S. Wise* (Albany, 1982).

Urofsky, Melvin, *American Zionism: From Herzl to Holocaust* (New York, 1975).

Voss, Carl, ed., *Stephen S. Wise: Servant of the People. Selected Letters* (Philadelphia, 1970).

_____, *Washington Conference on Disarmament and World Peace*, Summary of Proceedings, UAHC (Washington, 1964).

Wechsler, Harold S., *The Qualified Student: A History of Selective College Admission in America* (New York, 1977).
Wise, Stephen S., *Challenging Years: the Autobiography of Stephen Wise* (New York, 1949).
Yans-McLaughlin, Virginia, ed., *Immigration Reconsidered* (Oxford, 1990).

ARTICLES/PAPERS

Arsenault, Raymond, "The End of the Long Hot Summer: The Air Conditioner and Southern Culture," in Raymond Mohl, ed., *Searching for the Sunbelt* (Knoxville, 1990), 176-211.
Barsack, Nathan, "The Role of Religious Fellowship," *Reconstructionist* 11/11 (October 19, 1945), 8-12.
Bayor, Ronald, "Models of Ethnic and Racial Politics in the Urban Sunbelt South," in Raymond Mohl, ed., *Searching for the Sunbelt* (Knoxville, 1990), 105-123.
Cahn, Judah, "Mordecai Kaplan and Stephen S. Wise as Teachers," *Reconstructionist* 47/5 (July-August, 1981), 32-35.
Doppelt, Frederick, and Polish, David, "A Guide for Reform Jewish Practice," *CCAR Journal* 4 (June, 1956), 10-17.
Eisen, Arnold, "American Judaism: Changing Patterns in Denominational Self-definition," in Peter Y. Medding, ed., *A New Jewry? America Since the Second World War*, Studies in Contemporary Jewry VIII (Oxford, 1992), 22-30.
Gellman, Max, "Literary Defamation," *The American Zionist* 69/1 (September-October, 1978), 18-19.
George, Paul, "Brokers, Binders and Builders: Greater Miami's Boom of the Mid 1920s," *Florida Historical Quarterly* 65/1 (July, 1986), 27-51.
Green, Henry A., "Tropical Paradise and the New Diaspora" (Jerusalem, 1993). Paper presented at the Eleventh World Congress of Jewish Studies.
Green, Henry A., "Rabbi Kronish of Miami and Civil Rights" (Atlanta, 1993). Paper presented at the 18th Annual Meeting of the Southern Jewish Historical Society.
Green, Henry A., "Sefardies en la Florida," *Magen* 81/2 (October-December, 1991), 29-35.
Green, Henry A., "The Untold Story: Zionism, Miami, and the Birth of Israel" (Ramat Gan, Israel, 1991). Paper presented at the Third Canada Israel Conference on Social Scientific Approaches to the Study of Judaism.
Green, Henry A., "The Farr-Goodkowsky-Magid Family," *Miami Jewish Tribune* (Miami, November 22-29, 1990), 8B.
Green, Henry A., "The New Establishment: Miami's Jewry Post World War II," (Miami, 1990). Paper presented at the Ethnic Minorities and Multicultural Conference.
Hirsch, Richard, "Jewish Peoplehood—Implications for Reform Judaism," *CCAR Yearbook* 89 (1979), 164-173.
Huhner, Leon, "Moses Elias Levy," *Florida Historical Quarterly* 19 (1941), 319-345.
Kaplan, Mordecai, *Reconstructionist* 2/15 (November 27, 1936), 1-8.
Kronish, Leon, "What are the *'Zionist Mitzvot'?*," *Jewish Frontier* 44/1 (January, 1977), 15.
Kronish, Leon, "*Yisrael Goralenu*," *CCAR Journal* 16 (June, 1968), 31-37.
Kronish, Ronald, "Letter to the Editor," *Reform Judaism* (Fall, 1983), 66.
Lawson, Steven F., "The Florida Legislative Investigation Committee and the Constitutional Readjustment of Race Relations, 1956-1963," in *An Uncertain Tradition: Constitutionalism and the History of the South,* ed. Kermit L. Hall and James W. Ely (Athens, Ga., 1989), 296-325.

Liebman, Seymour, "Cuban Jewish Community in South Florida," *American Jewish Year Book* 70 (1969), 238-246.

Lowenstein, Steven, "The 1840s and the Creation of the German Jewish Reform Movement," in W. Mosse, A. Paucker, R. Rurup, eds., *Revolution and Evolution: 1848 in German History* (Tübingen, 1981), 255-297.

Mohl, Raymond, "The Pattern of Race Relations in Miami Since 1940" (Miami, 1990). Paper presented at the Ethnic Minorities and Multiculturalism Conference.

Mohl, Raymond, "Miami, New Immigrant City" in Raymond Mohl, ed., *Searching for the Sunbelt* (Knoxville, 1990), 149-175.

Mohl, Raymond, "Changing Economic Patterns in the Miami Metropolitan Area, 1940-1980," *Tequesta* 42 (1982), 63-73.

Moore, Deborah Dash, "Jewish Migration in Postwar America: The Case of Miami and Los Angeles" in Peter Y. Medding, ed., *A New Jewry? America Since the Second World War*, Studies in Contemporary Jewry VIII (Oxford, 1992), 102-117.

Moore, Deborah Dash, "Jewish Migration to the Sunbelt," in R. Miller and G. Pozzetta, eds., *Essays on Ethnicity, Race and the Urban South* (Boca Raton, 1989), 42-52.

Narot, Joseph, "First Teachers in Last Resorts," *CCAR Journal* 25/1 (Winter, 1978), 45-51.

Nussbaum, Perry, Mantinband, Charles, and Rothchild, Jacob, "The Southern Rabbi Faces the Problem of Desegregation," *CCAR Journal* 4/2 (June, 1956), 1-6.

Perlmutter, Nathan, "Bombing in Miami," *Commentary* 25/1 (January, 1958), 498-503.

Polish, David, "Revision of the Prayer Book," *CCAR Journal* 8/4 (January, 1961), 11-15.

Polish, David, "Opportunities for Reform Judaism," *CCAR Journal* 5/3 (October, 1957), 13-18.

Polish, David, "A Critique on Some Ceremonies," *CCAR Journal* 2/1 (April, 1954), 43-46.

Rosichan, Arthur, "Report of Dade County's Progression from 1960-1974" to the Greater Miami Jewish Federation (Miami, June, 1974).

Rottenberg, Dan, "Israel vs Meyer Lansky: A Talmudic Problem," *Expo* (Winter, 1979), 67.

_____, "Stampede to the Sun," *Business Week*, March 9, 1963, 108-112.

Shafter, Toby, "Miami: 1948," *Jewish Frontier* 15 (January, 1948), 18-20.

Sheskin, Ira, "The Miami Ethnic Archipelago" (Miami, 1990). Paper presented at the Ethnic Minorities and Multiculturalism Conference.

Sheskin, Ira, "The Migration of Jews to Sunbelt Cities" (Miami, 1985). Paper presented at the Sunbelt Conference.

Singer, Isaac Bashevis, "My Love Affair with Miami Beach," in Richard Nagler, ed., *My Love Affair with Miami Beach* (New York, 1991).

Singerman, Robert, "The American Career of the Protocols of the Elders of Zion," *American Jewish History* 71/1 (September 1981), 49-78.

Stein, David, "East Side Chronicle," *Jewish Life* (January-February, 1966), 32.

Steinberg, Stephen, "How Jewish Quotas Began," *Commentary* 52 (September, 1971), 67-76.

Wax, James, "The Attitude of the Jews in the South Toward Integration," *CCAR Journal* 7/2 (June, 1959), 14-20.

Zadka, Pnina, Sheskin, Ira, and Green, Henry A., "A Comparative Profile of Jewish Elderly in South Florida and Israel," *Contemporary Jewry* 11/4 (Fall, 1990), 93-119.

INDEX

South Florida Studies in the History of Judaism

240001	Lectures on Judaism in the Academy and in the Humanities	Neusner
240002	Lectures on Judaism in the History of Religion	Neusner
240003	Self-Fulfilling Prophecy: Exile and Return in the History of Judaism	Neusner
240004	The Canonical History of Ideas: The Place of the So-called Tannaite Midrashim, Mekhilta Attributed to R. Ishmael, Sifra, Sifré to Numbers, and Sifré to Deuteronomy	Neusner
240005	Ancient Judaism: Debates and Disputes, Second Series	Neusner
240006	The Hasmoneans and Their Supporters: From Mattathias to the Death of John Hyrcanus I	Sievers
240007	Approaches to Ancient Judaism: New Series, Volume One	Neusner
240008	Judaism in the Matrix of Christianity	Neusner
240009	Tradition as Selectivity: Scripture, Mishnah, Tosefta, and Midrash in the Talmud of Babylonia	Neusner
240010	The Tosefta: Translated from the Hebrew: Sixth Division Tohorot	Neusner
240011	In the Margins of the Midrash: Sifre Ha'azinu Texts, Commentaries and Reflections	Basser
240012	Language as Taxonomy: The Rules for Using Hebrew and Aramaic in the Babylonia Talmud	Neusner
240013	The Rules of Composition of the Talmud of Babylonia: The Cogency of the Bavli's Composite	Neusner
240014	Understanding the Rabbinic Mind: Essays on the Hermeneutic of Max Kadushin	Ochs
240015	Essays in Jewish Historiography	Rapoport-Albert
240016	The Golden Calf and the Origins of the Jewish Controversy	Bori/Ward
240017	Approaches to Ancient Judaism: New Series, Volume Two	Neusner
240018	The Bavli That Might Have Been: The Tosefta's Theory of Mishnah Commentary Compared With the Bavli's	Neusner
240019	The Formation of Judaism: In Retrospect and Prospect	Neusner
240020	Judaism in Society: The Evidence of the Yerushalmi,Toward the Natural History of a Religion	Neusner
240021	The Enchantments of Judaism: Rites of Transformation from Birth Through Death	Neusner
240022	Åbo Addresses	Neusner
240023	The City of God in Judaism and Other Comparative and Methodological Studies	Neusner
240024	The Bavli's One Voice: Types and Forms of Analytical Discourse and their Fixed Order of Appearance	Neusner
240025	The Dura-Europos Synagogue: A Re-evaluation (1932-1992)	Gutmann
240026	Precedent and Judicial Discretion: The Case of Joseph ibn Lev	Morell
240027	Max Weinreich *Geschichte der jiddischen Sprachforschung*	Frakes
240028	Israel: Its Life and Culture, Volume I	Pedersen
240029	Israel: Its Life and Culture, Volume II	Pedersen
240030	The Bavli's One Statement: The Metapropositional Program of Babylonian Talmud Tractate Zebahim Chapters One and Five	Neusner

240031	The Oral Torah: The Sacred Books of Judaism: An Introduction: Second Printing	Neusner
240032	The Twentieth Century Construction of "Judaism:" Essays on the Religion of Torah in the History of Religion	Neusner
240033	How the Talmud Shaped Rabbinic Discourse	Neusner
240034	The Discourse of the Bavli: Language, Literature, and Symbolism: Five Recent Findings	Neusner
240035	The Law Behind the Laws: The Bavli's Essential Discourse	Neusner
240036	Sources and Traditions: Types of Compositions in the Talmud of Babylonia	Neusner
240037	How to Study the Bavli: The Languages, Literatures, and Lessons of the Talmud of Babylonia	Neusner
240038	The Bavli's Primary Discourse: Mishnah Commentary: Its Rhetorical Paradigms and their Theological Implications	Neusner
240039	Midrash Aleph Beth	Sawyer
240040	Jewish Thought in the 20th Century: An Introduction in the Talmud of Babylonia Tractate Moed Qatan	Schweid
240041	Diaspora Jews and Judaism: Essays in Honor of, and in Dialogue with, A. Thomas Kraabel	Overman/MacLennan
240042	The Bavli: An Introduction	Neusner
240043	The Bavli's Massive Miscellanies: The Problem of Agglutinative Discourse in the Talmud of Babylonia	Neusner
240044	The Foundations of the Theology of Judaism: An Anthology Part II: Torah	Neusner
240045	Form-Analytical Comparison in Rabbinic Judaism: Structure and Form in *The Fathers* and *The Fathers According to Rabbi Nathan*	Neusner
240046	Essays on Hebrew	Weinberg
240047	The Tosefta: An Introduction	Neusner
240048	The Foundations of the Theology of Judaism: An Anthology Part III: Israel	Neusner
240049	The Study of Ancient Judaism, Volume I: Mishnah, Midrash, Siddur	Neusner
240050	The Study of Ancient Judaism, Volume II: The Palestinian and Babylonian Talmuds	Neusner
240051	Take Judaism, for Example: Studies toward the Comparison of Religions	Neusner
240052	From Eden to Golgotha: Essays in Biblical Theology	Moberly
240053	The Principal Parts of the Bavli's Discourse: A Preliminary Taxonomy: Mishnah Commentary, Sources, Traditions and Agglutinative Miscellanies	Neusner
240054	Barabbas and Esther and Other Studies in the Judaic Illumination of Earliest Christianity	Aus
240055	Targum Studies, Volume I: Textual and Contextual Studies in the Pentateuchal Targums	Flesher
240056	Approaches to Ancient Judaism: New Series, Volume Three, Historical and Literary Studies	Neusner
240057	The Motherhood of God and Other Studies	Gruber
240058	The Analytic Movement: Hayyim Soloveitchik and his Circle	Solomon

240059 Recovering the Role of Women: Power and Authority in Rabbinic Jewish Society — Haas

240060 The Relation between Herodotus' *History* and Primary History — Mandell/Freedman

240061 The First Seven Days: A Philosophical Commentary on the Creation of Genesis — Samuelson

240062 The Bavli's Intellectual Character: The Generative Problematic: In Bavli Baba Qamma Chapter One And Bavli Shabbat Chapter One — Neusner

240063 The Incarnation of God: The Character of Divinity in Formative Judaism: Second Printing — Neusner

240064 Moses Kimhi: Commentary on the Book of Job — Basser/Walfish

240066 Death and Birth of Judaism: Second Printing — Neusner

240067 Decoding the Talmud's Exegetical Program — Neusner

240068 Sources of the Transformation of Judaism — Neusner

240069 The Torah in the Talmud: A Taxonomy of the Uses of Scripture in the Talmud, Volume I — Neusner

240070 The Torah in the Talmud: A Taxonomy of the Uses of Scripture in the Talmud, Volume II — Neusner

240071 The Bavli's Unique Voice: A Systematic Comparison of the Talmud of Babylonia and the Talmud of the Land of Israel, Volume One — Neusner

240072 The Bavli's Unique Voice: A Systematic Comparison of the Talmud of Babylonia and the Talmud of the Land of Israel, Volume Two — Neusner

240073 The Bavli's Unique Voice: A Systematic Comparison of the Talmud of Babylonia and the Talmud of the Land of Israel, Volume Three — Neusner

240074 Bits of Honey: Essays for Samson H. Levey — Chyet/Ellenson

240075 The Mystical Study of Ruth: *Midrash HaNe'elam* of the Zohar to the Book of Ruth — Englander

240076 The Bavli's Unique Voice: A Systematic Comparison of the Talmud of Babylonia and the Talmud of the Land of Israel, Volume Four — Neusner

240077 The Bavli's Unique Voice: A Systematic Comparison of the Talmud of Babylonia and the Talmud of the Land of Israel, Volume Five — Neusner

240078 The Bavli's Unique Voice: A Systematic Comparison of the Talmud of Babylonia and the Talmud of the Land of Israel, Volume Six — Neusner

240079 The Bavli's Unique Voice: A Systematic Comparison of the Talmud of Babylonia and the Talmud of the Land of Israel, Volume Seven — Neusner

240080 Are There Really Tannaitic Parallels to the Gospels? — Neusner

240081 Approaches to Ancient Judaism: New Series, Volume Four, Religious and Theological Studies — Neusner

240082 Approaches to Ancient Judaism: New Series, Volume Five, Historical, Literary, and Religious Studies — Basser/Fishbane

240083 Ancient Judaism: Debates and Disputes, Third Series — Neusner

240084	Judaic Law from Jesus to the Mishnah	Neusner
240085	Writing with Scripture: Second Printing	Neusner/Green
240086	Foundations of Judaism: Second Printing	Neusner
240087	Judaism and Zoroastrianism at the Dusk of Late Antiquity	Neusner
240088	Judaism States Its Theology	Neusner
240089	The Judaism behind the Texts I.A	Neusner
240090	The Judaism behind the Texts I.B	Neusner
240091	Stranger at Home	Neusner
240092	Pseudo-Rabad: Commentary to Sifre Deuteronomy	Basser
240093	FromText to Historical Context in Rabbinic Judaism	Neusner
240094	Formative Judaism	Neusner
240095	Purity in Rabbinic Judaism	Neusner
240096	Was Jesus of Nazareth the Messiah?	McMichael
240097	The Judaism behind the Texts I.C	Neusner
240098	The Judaism behind the Texts II	Neusner
240099	The Judaism behind the Texts III	Neusner
240100	The Judaism behind the Texts IV	Neusner
240101	The Judaism behind the Texts V	Neusner
240102	The Judaism the Rabbis Take for Granted	Neusner
240103	From Text to Historical Context in Rabbinic Judaism V. II	Neusner
240104	From Text to Historical Context in Rabbinic Judaism V. III	Neusner
240105	Samuel, Saul, and Jesus: Three Early Palestinian Jewish Christian Gospel Haggadoth	Aus
240106	What is Midrash? And a Midrash Reader	Neusner
240107	Rabbinic Judaism: Disputes and Debates	Neusner
240108	Why There Never Was a "Talmud of Caesarea"	Neusner
240109	Judaism after the Death of "The Death of God"	Neusner
240110	Approaches to Ancient Judaism	Neusner
240111	Ecology of Religion	Neusner
240112	The Judaic Law of Baptism	Neusner
240113	The Documentary Foundation of Rabbinic Culture	Neusner
240114	Understanding Seeking Faith, Volume Four	Neusner
240115	Paul and Judaism: An Anthropological Approach	Laato
240116	Approaches to Ancient Judaism, New Series, Volume Eight	Neusner
240117	The Talmud of the Land of Israel, A Complete Outline of the Second, Third, and Fourth Divisions, II. A	Neusner
240118	The Talmud of the Land of Israel, A Complete Outline of the Second, Third, and Fourth Divisions, II. B	Neusner
240119	Theme and Context in Biblical Lists	Scolnic

South Florida Academic Commentary Series

The Talmud of Babylonia, An Academic Commentary

243001	Bavli, Volume XI, Tractate Moed Qatan	Neusner
243002	Bavli, Volume XXXIV, Tractate Keritot	Neusner
243003	Bavli, Volume XVII, Tractate Sotah	Neusner
243004	Bavli, Volume XXIV, Tractate Makkot	Neusner

243005	Bavli, Volume XXXII, Tractate Arakhin	Neusner
243006	Bavli, Volume VI, Tractate Sukkah	Neusner
243007	Bavli, Volume XII, Tractate Hagigah	Neusner
243008	Bavli, Volume XXVI, Tractate Horayot	Neusner
243009	Bavli, Volume XXVII, Tractate Shebuot	Neusner
243010	Bavli, Volume XXXIII, Tractate Temurah	Neusner
243011	Bavli, Volume XXXV, Tractates Meilah and Tamid	Neusner
243012	Bavli, Volume VIII, Tractate Rosh Hashanah	Neusner
243013	Bavli, Volume V, Tractate Yoma	Neusner
243014	Bavli, Volume XXXVI, Tractate Niddah	Neusner
243015	Bavli, Volume XX, Tractate Baba Qamma	Neusner
243016	Bavli, Volume XXXI, Tractate Bekhorot	Neusner
243017	Bavli, Volume XXX, Tractate Hullin	Neusner
243018	Bavli, Volume VII, Tractate Besah	Neusner
243019	Bavli, Volume X, Tractate Megillah	Neusner
243020	Bavli, Volume XXVIII, Tractate Zebahim	Neusner
243021	Bavli, Volume XXI, Tractate Baba Mesia	Neusner
243022	Bavli, Volume XXII, Tractate Baba Batra	Neusner
243023	Bavli, Volume XXIX, Tractate Menahot	Neusner
243024	Bavli, Volume I, Tractate Berakhot	Neusner
243025	Bavli, Volume XXV, Tractate Abodah Zarah	Neusner
243026	Bavli, Volume XXIII, Tractate Sanhedrin	Neusner
243027	A Complete Outline, Part IV, The Division of Holy Things A: From Tractate Zabahim through Tractate Hullin	Neusner
243028	Bavli, Volume XIV, Tractate Ketubot	Neusner
243029	Bavli, Volume IV, Tractate Pesahim	Neusner
243030	Bavli, Volume III, Tractate Erubin	Neusner
243031	A Complete Outline, Part III, The Division of Damages A: From Tractate Baba Qamma through Tractate Baba Batra	Neusner
243032	Bavli, Volume II, Tractate Shabbat, Volume A, Chapters One through Twelve	Neusner
243033	Bavli, Volume II, Tractate Shabbat, Volume B, Chapters Thirteen through Twenty-four	Neusner
243034	Bavli, Volume XV, Tractate Nedarim	Neusner
243035	Bavli, Volume XVIII, Tractate Gittin	Neusner
243036	Bavli, Volume XIX, Tractate Qiddushin	Neusner
243037	A Complete Outline, Part IV, The Division of Holy Things B: From Tractate Bekhorot through Tractate Niddah	Neusner
243038	A Complete Outline, Part III, The Division of Damages B: From Tractate Sanhedrin through Tractate Shebuot	Neusner
243039	A Complete Outline, Part I, Tractate Berakhot and the Division of Appointed Times A: From Tractate Berakhot through Tractate Pesahim	Neusner
243040	A Complete Outline, Part I, Tractate Berakhot and the Division of Appointed Times B: From Tractate Yoma through Tractate Hagigah	Neusner
243041	A Complete Outline, Part II, The Division of Women A: From Tractate Yebamot through Tractate Ketubot	Neusner
243042	A Complete Outline, Part II, The Division of Women	Neusner

	B: From Tractate Nedarim through Tractate Qiddushin	
243043	Bavli, Volume XIII, Tractate Yebamot, A. Chapters One through Eight	Neusner
243044	Bavli, XIII, Tractate Yebamot, B. Chapters Nine through Seventeen	Neusner

South Florida-Rochester-Saint Louis Studies on Religion and the Social Order

245001	Faith and Context, Volume 1	Ong
245002	Faith and Context, Volume 2	Ong
245003	Judaism and Civil Religion	Breslauer
245004	The Sociology of Andrew M. Greeley	Greeley
245005	Faith and Context, Volume 3	Ong
245006	The Christ of Michelangelo	Dixon
245007	From Hermeneutics to Ethical Consensus Among Cultures	Bori
245008	Mordecai Kaplan's Thought in a Postmodern Age	Breslauer
245009	No Longer Aliens, No Longer Strangers	Eckardt
245010	Between Tradition and Culture	Ellenson
245011	Religion and the Social Order	Neusner
245012	Christianity and the Stranger	Nichols
245013	The Polish Challenge	Czosnyka
245014	*Gesher Vakesher:* Bridges and Bonds, The Life of Leon Kronish	Green

South Florida International Studies in Formative Christianity and Judaism

242501	The Earliest Christian Mission to 'All Nations'	La Grand
242502	Judaic Approaches to the Gospels	Chilton
252403	The "Essence of Christianity"	Rosa